HUGH JOHNSON'S

GARDENING
COMPANION

HUGH JOHNSON'S

GARDENING
COMPANION

THE PRINCIPLES AND PRACTICE
OF THE GARDENER'S ART

MITCHELL BEAZLEY

First published in 1996 by Mitchell Beazley,
an imprint of Reed International Books Ltd,
Michelin House, 81 Fulham Road, London SW3 6RB
and Auckland, Melbourne, Singapore and Toronto

Publisher: Jane Aspden   **Editor:** Alex Bennion
Art Director: Gaye Allen   **Editorial Assistant:** Kirsty Brackenridge
Executive Editor: Guy Croton   **Production Controller:** Dawn Mitchell
Executive Art Editor: Ruth Hope   **Picture Researcher:** Liz Fowler
Designer: Martin Bristow   **Researcher:** Lin Hawthorne
Indexer: Ann Barrett

ISBN 1 85732 835 3

A CIP catalogue record for this book is available from the British Library

Produced by Mandarin Offset Ltd, Hong Kong
Printed in Singapore

Below: 'The Market Gardener', Pierre Angellis, 1715

CONTENTS

PREFACE   6

INTRODUCTION   9

THE FOUR ELEMENTS   12
And how plants interact with them

PLANTS AND THE GARDENER   44
How plants work, are named, propagated and controlled

WHERE PLANTS COME FROM   76
How plants are judged worthy of the gardener's time, and where
they have been grown

A GARDEN PLACE FOR EVERY PLANT   92
How gardeners have assigned a horticultural niche to each category
of plants, and how they use them

COMPOSING THE PICTURE   200
How to use a discriminating eye to make and maintain a satisfying garden

ROOTS IN HISTORY   234
How modern ideas of gardening have developed in different cultures
over centuries

INDEX   268

ACKNOWLEDGEMENTS   272

PREFACE

It would never occur to most gardeners to write a poem or paint a picture. Most gardens are the only artistic effort their owners ever make. Yet the one art that everyone chooses, or feels in some degree qualified to practise, is paradoxically the most complex of all.

Gardening is complex because it combines aesthetic judgements and practical decisions with science and craftsmanship in a kaleidoscope of variables. A poet is limited to the dictionary, a sculptor starts with a block of stone, but a gardener starts with a plot that is frozen one day and flooded the next, here in sun and there in shadow, teased by wind and tantalized by drought, plagued by insects, toyed with by birds, mined by moles. No two gardens are the same. No two days are the same in one garden. And yet on this flapping canvas an amateur, often without previous experience, and holding the instruction book in one hand, tries to daub his vision of a better world – or if that is flying a bit high, at least to grow vegetables and feed his family.

Because gardening is so universal and has been going on for so long it has accumulated barns-full of folklore, libraries of literature, and a richness of reference that even fiction can scarcely equal. So many people have handled and delighted in so many plants, so many days have been spent in hard work, and perhaps not quite so many in tranquil contemplation, that to approach the subject for the first time is like being a raw recruit in a veteran army embroiled in an old campaign. What, whom, where are they talking about? Where can one start to pick up the thread?

This was the question that led to the first edition of this book in 1979, *The Principles of Gardening*. It seemed to me then, as it does now, that someone has to start at the beginning, without a baggage-train of assumptions, to explain how gardening works to interested readers who may have many inklings but no overall picture.

Having been an amateur gardener now for over 20 years I have many inklings, too. Writing and rewriting this book has made me examine them, going back over ground trodden by so many generations that it no longer bears imprints. At the same time I have tried to comprehend the latest discoveries in the many sciences that have a bearing on gardening, to sum up the current state of knowledge and say what it means to the gardener of today.

From the feeling that there must be many new gardeners who wanted a vantage-point from which they could survey the whole battlefield before deciding where they would stand the best chance of survival, I came to believe that there must be many veterans who would welcome a chance to stand back from their daily preoccupations and see what an outsider has to make of them. That is an author's job: to be an outsider with a passionate interest and concern. His aim is to weigh the options, clarify the objectives, and balance the physical facts against the convention and traditon. It is not easy to remain an outsider from such an enthralling subject for very long.

The Principles of Gardening was a highly illustrated, indeed a very complex book in which, I was sometimes told, the plot risked getting lost in the digressions. Superbly illustrated garden books are commonplace today. This *Gardening Companion* is deliberately much simplified. The words are given the prominence; the pictures and detailed plant description relegated to second place – justifiably, I hope, because comprehensive plant reference books are all around us.

An author's debts are impossible to quantify. Since I first broke gardening ground (in *The International Book of Trees* in 1973) I have enjoyed – as all gardeners do – the unstinting encouragement and advice of every other gardener I have turned to. From my colleagues at *The Garden* and in the R.H.S. to nurserymen, designers and just enthusiasts in many countries I have gleaned far more than a mere book's-worth of lore and learning. And that is not to mention the hundreds of excellent books and thousands of articles that pour from the presses to delight and instruct us all. It has been a fascinating struggle to distil such a ferment of ideas.

ABOVE: *In the author's Essex garden.*

INTRODUCTION

What, if anything, do the infinity of different ideas of a garden, traditional and individual, have in common? They vary so much – in purpose, in size, in style and content – that not even flowers, or indeed plants at all, can be said to be essential. In the last analysis there is only one common factor between all gardens, and that is control of nature, to a greater or lesser extent, by man. Control, that is, for aesthetic reasons. A garden is not a farm.

The essence is control. Without constant watchful care a garden – certainly any conventional garden – rapidly returns to the state of the country round it. The more fertile and productive your garden is, the more precarious its position. Leave the lawn unmown, the beds unweeded only for one summer and it will take a year of hard work, perhaps more, to restore it. Nor is it just a matter of unchecked growth. Even a minimal, super-simple garden, a Japanese courtyard of sand and rocks, has its pattern and emphasis blurred by heavy rain, or simply by fallen leaves.

The rake, the hoe, the shears and the broom lie at the very heart of gardening.

All natural communities of plants have their own inherent stability; stability born of competition. Their inhabitants hold their ground in due relationship with each other by constant warfare. The only plants (and animals) that survive for long are those which have found an ecological niche for themselves; somewhere where their needs and characteristics dovetail with those of their neighbours. Each kind has slightly different requirements, needing, for example, light, moisture and nutrients most at a specific time. Thus the herbs and bulbs of woodland spring up and flower early in the year before the trees grow leaves and block out the light. Every wood, every meadow, every alp, every marsh has a distinct structure of taller and shorter plants. In fertile lowlands, which is where most gardeners garden, a four-tier system is the natural state, with trees above shrubs, shrubs above herbs, and herbs above mosses and other humble earthbound things.

Not so the conventional or traditional garden. Gardeners have learned over centuries to segregate their plants – not into ecological but into horticultural niches. The plants that behave in the same way and like the same soil are thus grown together, with as little competition as possible, protected from diseases, bugs, other plants and each other. When their protector goes on holiday their artificial world is immediately under threat. Instead of the stability of a hard-won Darwinian niche they occupy a pampered place which will be usurped by the quickest, most aggressive, coarsest plants – which are the ones we have come to know as weeds.

The most visible form of plant thuggery is overwhelming neighbours with leaves to rob them of light. Light is essential for growth – although much more

---

OPPOSITE: *Nature has her way in a once-great English garden.*
Was the garden in its heyday more beautiful than this?

so for some plants than others; many are adapted to use low levels of light with great efficiency. Ultimately the plants that dominate are either the ones that can build tallest, such as the trees, or those which can scramble and cling, making up for their lack of a structure by borrowing others'. Some trees are good neighbours, content with the light they need for themselves and not concerned with depriving others. Some, such as the beech, are dog-in-the-manger in the way they build a light-proof canopy so that their shallow roots can have the soil to themselves.

For although it is less obvious, as much competition goes on underground as above. Roots must constantly explore new soil for nutrients, at the same time drawing up water not only from the soil they touch but by capillary action from a considerable area around. The more vigorous a plant the more questing its roots. Its hunt for food is at its height during its main growing season. If that coincides with its neighbour's, both of them suffer. It may on the other hand coexist happily with another plant which needs slightly different nutrients, or needs them at a different time of the year. This is the kind of association that leads to harmony in the garden.

Shoving and elbowing for space is the kind of competition a gardener instinctively controls, if only in the name of orderliness. Competition is severest of all in the seedbed, where like jostles like. Unless the gardener thins the seedlings promptly, giving them elbow-room before they start competing, their growth is irreparably checked.

But it is not only between one plant and another that the gardener feels compelled to arbitrate. He is just as concerned with the internal competition between the different parts of one plant; the shoots, leaves, flowers, fruit. There is never enough food available to a plant to let all its potential buds open. If it grows madly it will flower little.

Most plants are grown in gardens for a particular contribution they have to make. Either the gardener wants the maximum number of flowers, or the maximum size and perfection of a few. Or he wants the most leaves, or the thickest stems, or the most distended and sugar-filled roots to eat.

All the activities of cultivation – fertilizing, pruning, dividing, disbudding, grafting, even mowing – are examples of man directing plants in the way he wants them to perform; keeping them, in fact, under his control.

Besides controlling plants, moreover, the gardener does what he can to keep pests at bay, to combat disease, to manage the soil and even to influence the wind and weather. Gardening in a greenhouse is the extreme example of man taking charge. There nothing is left to nature: light, temperature, soil and water are all his responsibility.

Different fashions of gardening call for different degrees of control. Traditionally the French see a garden as an artefact to be completed, then kept in order. The English, in contrast, see it as something ever-changing, emerging through time, calling for guidance rather than discipline.

On the whole, though, since control means work, which nobody has time for, the more extreme forms of artificial gardening, whether it be the planting of floral clocks or maintaining the even more labour-intensive herbaceous border, have become backwaters of the art. Specialists will always be ready to sit up all night to have a perfect specimen ready to take a prize, but fashion, taking the hint from necessity, has moved towards a relatively relaxed style of gardening in which a little waywardness is considered a virtue. The latest vogue, indeed, is for what at least appear semi-natural plant communities. The ideal modern garden, in some eyes at least, is one so close to nature (but of course with plenty of paved areas) that it becomes a mere view from the window, a framed picture with no job for the gardener at all.

The intelligent way to achieve this is by self-sustaining plant associations borrowed straight from nature. Fashion points more and more in this direction. Modern 'meadow gardens' use grasses and herbaceous plants in a very different way from the old lawn and border. Theoretically they could be made almost to control themselves.

But in fact no such ideal garden exists. For even under your daily surveillance the plants grow, almost always bigger and faster than you expected, or they die, or become tangled and ugly, or are eaten, or fall prey to a fatal fungus. The best the gardener can do is to collaborate as closely as possible with nature.

It is, or ought to be, the gardener's pleasure to be constantly adjusting, correcting, editing . . . editing is the best analogy; editors are forever adding commas, deleting paragraphs, changing phrases – the very stuff of gardening.

Most difficult of all to control, but most essential, is oneself. For a good garden is one with a plan, with variety but consistency, with a firm sense of purpose so that you know where to look and what you are supposed to enjoy. There is a perpetual temptation to anyone who loves plants to add another and another, bending his original intentions until they finally break; adding a colour that destroys a harmony, or a shape that jars, for the sake of growing something new.

ABOVE: *The walled garden at Saling Hall,*
the author's garden in Essex.

THE
FOUR
ELEMENTS

WINE-GROWERS CALL IT 'TERROIR'; THERE IS NO EXACT ENGLISH TERM FOR THE COMBINATION OF PHYSICAL FACTORS THAT INFLU-ENCE THE GROWTH OF AN INDIVIDUAL PLANT. AT ITS MOST RESTRICTIVE THE WORD MEANS SOIL. IN COMMON USE IT MEANS MUCH MORE. 'TERROIR' ENCOMPASSES, ON THE ONE HAND, CLIMATE IN THE BROAD SENSE OF AVERAGE MINIMUM TEMPERATURES, BUT ALSO THE MICROCOSM – THE SMALL DEGREE OF LOCAL SHELTER THAT MAKES A DIFFERENCE, THE SOIL AND ITS PROPER-

TIES, PHYSICAL AND CHEMICAL, THE LATITUDE AND DAYLENGTH. THE ANGLE OF A SLOPE, EVEN THE NATURAL FLORA AND FAUNA, WHETHER VISIBLE OR MICROSCOPIC, MAKE UP THE NATURAL ENVIRONMENT IN WHICH A PLANT GROWS AND A GARDENER GARDENS. ➤

THE WIND AND THE RAIN RAIN NEVER

FALLS WHEN WE WANT IT, BUT IT FALLS IN THE END. AND IF IT DID NOT THERE WOULD BE NO

GARDENS, NO PLANTS – NO LIFE AT ALL.

BELOW: One of the most dramatic stages of the hydrological cycle in its continuous round of evaporation, condensation, precipitation and flow. Clouds break over a Norwegian glacier and water transpired by plants, and evaporated from the sea, begins its downward course.

Water is the life-blood of our planet. In living beings it not only circulates but forms the great bulk of the being – whether a person or a plant – in question. Seventy per cent of your weight, and ninety per cent of your cabbages', is water.

The hydrological cycle, to give the earth's circulation system its formal name, consists of evaporation, condensation, precipitation and flow. Precipitation and flow are powered by gravity; whether they are typhoons or Scotch mists, mountain torrents or field ditches or city sewers, they are simply water sinking back to base level, the sea.

Water on its way down is visible, and frequently spectacular. It is easy to forget that what comes down has to go up. Everything the clouds drop has been evaporated by the rays of the sun.

Plants play one of the leading roles in evaporation, second only to the sea itself. The process is dignified with the name transpiration, but it comes to the same thing:

the act of passively presenting water to the atmosphere to be soaked up and vapourized by the sun's energy.

The plant does it with its roots, drawing water from the ground and filling the open-pored vessels in its leaves with water for the sun to take away. It does it so efficiently that an open water surface like the sea is only marginally more efficient. Of all the rain that falls on a densely planted temperate garden as much as two-thirds is promptly recirculated by the plants. Only one-third drains away into the ground. A big tree may draw three or four hundred gallons a day from the soil and release it into the atmosphere.

Morning dew in summer freshens the garden so much that it is hard to believe it is a mere recycling of the moisture that was already there in the soil. But however heavy the dew there is, alas, no net gain in water to the garden.

Why should it be in the plant's interest to transpire so much? First, because it has no other means of raising water and nutrients from the roots to the leaves. Second, because the whole growth process of photosynthesis depends on the pores being open to receive carbon dioxide from the air. And the pores are only open when all the cells of the plant are tight and distended with water.

Most plants have a way of throttling back when water runs short. Their pores half-close as the cells surrounding them become less distended. In drought, as an emergency measure, they can close altogether, but as they do growth slows down and stops. It needs a water supply to complete the cycle, open the pores, and start the plant transpiring, and the water evaporating, again.

What then of condensation, the second stage in the hydrological cycle? What decides where and when the airborne moisture will form clouds, or the clouds break into raindrops? It is all a question of pressure. The atmosphere is full of pockets and currents of warmer and colder air; usually warmer over the seas in winter and over the land in summer, but endlessly complicated by the facts of geography. Ocean currents, ice-sheets, deserts and lakes and mountain ranges can and do all affect where the rain falls.

Warm air is lighter than cold, just as warm water floats on colder water. But while its temperature is higher, its atmospheric pressure is lower because its molecules are not packed together so tightly. In the spaces between them there is room for water vapour. For this reason warm air can also carry more moisture.

Cold air is denser, thus heavier on the mercury in a barometer, registering higher pressure and therefore tight-packed, without space to hold much water in suspension. Where warm low pressure meets cold high pressure, therefore, it reacts as though it were meeting a mountain.

Air masses at different temperatures don't mix; they displace one another. So the warm damp air is forced to ride up over the cold; the situation known as a 'warm front'. The reverse, cold air advancing on warm and forcing it to rise, is a 'cold front'. In either case, as warm air rises it cools – 7°C (13°F) for every 1,000m (3,333ft) – until it can no longer hold its cargo of moisture. It condenses first into vapour as clouds, then as it cools further into bigger drops, which fall as rain.

Where the rainclouds travel and congregate is determined on a global scale by the prevailing winds, which in turn are caused by the spin of the earth on its polar axis. The hottest air is normally at the equator. As it rises, cooler air from north and south moves in to replace it. But the equator, as it were the rim of the wheel, is moving fastest. The cooler air therefore lags behind the headlong equatorial spin and blows as a wind from the north-east and the south-east – the trade winds of the tropics; the steadiest and most reliable of all the winds.

Meanwhile the hot air of the equator, still spinning at equatorial speed, spreads north and south, gradually cooling and falling. When it reaches the earth again it is still moving faster than the earth's surface. This is the prevailing wind of the temperature latitudes, blowing from the west, against the spin of the globe – the wind that for jets at 10,670m (35,000ft) makes London an hour nearer to New York than New York is to London, and the wind that supplies the west coasts and western mountain slopes in its path with rain and to spare.

ABOVE: *Moisture in the garden as an art form. An enthusiast rises before dawn to brush the dew on the lawn into perfect geometrical patterns with a broom. Morning dew in summer freshens the garden so much that it is hard to believe that it is a mere recycling of the moisture already present in the soil. There is unfortunately no net gain of water to plants however heavy the dew.*

PREVIOUS SPREAD
(LEFT): *Revelling in rain: Scotland's climate has coined its own gardening idiom;* (RIGHT): *The Mediterranean climate is defined by rainless summers.*

ABOVE: *Grape-vines are among the plants often damaged by late frost that strikes after they have made new sappy growth in spring. This is one of the commonest forms of 'tenderness' in what are otherwise 'hardy' plants.*

Between the trade winds and the westerlies, just north and south of the tropics, there is no steady airstream to carry water-laden air from the oceans over the land. These are the 'horse latitudes', flat calm for sailors and arid for farmers. Most of the world's rainless deserts – the Sahara, Arabia, northern Mexico, central Australia, the Kalahari – lie in this windless region. The other great deserts, the Gobi and the western plateau of Nevada and Utah, are deprived of their share of the moisture in the westerlies by mountain ranges. It all falls on the Himalayas and the Sierras, leaving what is known as a 'rain-shadow' to the east.

Such is the macrocosm; remote, perhaps, from a gardener's thoughts, however much it controls his behaviour. The same principles, however, apply to the microcosm. A house, too, has a rain-shadow. Warm air rises and cools as well in a back-yard as on a storm-bound coast.

WHAT IS A HARDY PLANT?

When a gardener says a plant is hardy he means it is adapted, or biologically programmed, to live in the particular climate he has in his garden. If it is killed or badly damaged, either by extreme cold in the dead of winter, by icy winds in spring, or by a sudden sharp frost destroying its unripe tissue in autumn or spring, it is called tender or half-hardy.

To many gardeners the most desirable plants are in the touch-and-go-zone, not because they are in any objective sense more beautiful than more rugged plants, but because each one is an illegitimate addition to his repertoire, holding all the charm of the chancy and forbidden.

Plants in the tropics have nothing to fear from cold. The controlling factor in their lives is water supply; in an equatorial rain-forest they grow non-stop. If there were a drought they would rapidly flag and probably die. Plants that have to compete for light in deep jungle shade have big leaves with a high rate of transpiration and no equipment for reducing it.

At the other extreme the succulents are plants that have adapted to survive the almost permanent drought of the desert, with only the rarest cloud-bursts. They have reduced their leaves to the barest minimum and adapted their stems as reservoirs. The spines of a cactus are in fact its leaves and its swollen stem is a reser-

BELOW: *The west coast of Scotland, washed by the warm Gulf Stream, has a freak climate with little to fear from frost. Inverewe is the most famous of a number of coastal gardens.*

voir for holding water, with a thick or waxy skin that reduces evaporation to a minimum.

Plants that have evolved to inhabit the temperate zones have another problem to face: the seasons. Their survival depends on their being able to grow when it is warm and wet enough, and shut down operations when it is either too cold or too dry.

Shutting-down, or dormancy, can take many forms. For evergreens it is a mere pause; for deciduous trees and shrubs it means dropping their leaves. Both make new buds ready to grow when conditions improve. Herbaceous plants die down to ground level and shelter their buds in the ground; bulbs withdraw to their plump larders in the soil. Annuals disappear altogether, leaving only their seed to come back to life when water and warmth give the signal.

In the warm-temperate regions (the Mediterranean, for example) the deciding factor is normally water supply. Summers are hot but so dry that growth is limited by lack of water. It is winter and spring rain that starts the bulbs sprouting, the seeds germinating, the herbs erupting from the ground and the trees putting on new leaves.

The most noticeable change in the landscape as you reach the zone of Mediterranean influence is that far more, if not most of the woody plants are evergreen, with thick tough-skinned leaves. They are designed to take instant advantage of growing conditions, but with leaves rigid and costive enough to resist the summer-long drought. Plants of the extreme north (Canadian conifers, for example) are evergreen for similar reasons: to have leaves ready to soak up the sun of the summer that comes and goes within ten weeks, but with thick leaves that can virtually stop transpiration entirely when the ground is frozen.

Between the warm-temperate and the downright cold lies the broad belt of well-

ABOVE: *The famous fall colours of New England are caused by the concentration of sugar in the sap of the leaves as growth slows. Sunny days and cold nights destroy the chlorophyll and reveal the formation of other pigments that colour in the sugar-rich sap.*

marked seasons, and generally well-spaced rain, with temperature as its tyrant. Dormancy here is decided by cold. The overwhelming majority of plants are deciduous. Leaves in winter would do more harm than good, asking the roots in the cold ground for moisture they could not supply, while being blasted in the process. Plants here wait for spring warmth, and grow new shoots often continuously all summer long. They ripen their seed gradually towards autumn (trees and shrubs also ripen their new wood) and then shed their vulnerable soft leaves and harden their shoots before winter can harm them.

To temperate-zone plants timing is all. Their whole evolutionary adaptation to life with cold winters is based on their being safely dormant. If they put on new growth too soon in spring late frosts will kill them. Wood which has not reached a safe state of ripeness and turned from green to brown before winter sets in will suffer the same fate.

Millennia of experience have perfected their timing. A plant in its native land is seldom caught out. Random late frosts are the worst risk it runs. The combination of day length and temperature is familiar and peremptory. The instinct of dormancy is so fixed that if you moved the plant to the tropics it would fail to open its buds: no winter means it must still be autumn.

As soon as it is moved to a foreign garden with different conditions its control mechanism receives the wrong data. In many cases the difference is marginal and unimportant, but in others the confusion is fatal. Many plants from harsh climates are tender in milder ones. On their home ground the first warm days are the certain sign of spring; so they start to grow. But in a Gulf Stream climate warm spells happen in winter, to be followed by more frosts, often as late as May.

New shoots, lured by false promise, are cut back in their prime. If this happens regularly the plant may die.

More mysterious altogether is the question of extreme cold. All temperate-zone plants are subjected to freezing from time to time. All will suffer if they are unprepared. But if they are prepared, and dormant, the degree of cold they can tolerate varies enormously. Ice crystals forming in the wood cells of an olive tree tear the delicate structures apart. But a sugar maple can be frozen into a solid block of ice and be unharmed.

The deciding factors, in these cases, are the concentration of sugar and proteins in the cell sap, and the permeability, the rate at which water can penetrate the central membrane, enclosing the cytoplasm that contains the 'works' or nerve centre of each cell.

Pure water freezes at a slightly higher temperature than water with sugar or salt dissolved in it. Therefore when a plant freezes the least concentrated sap freezes first. In a hardy plant the pure water content rapidly migrates out through the walls of the cytoplasm and forms ice between the cells, leaving a highly concentrated solution of sap in the part that matters most. In a tender plant the water cannot do this and the relatively dilute sap freezes in the plant, destroying the cytoplasm by breaking apart its surrounding membrane.

But even a hardy plant must have time to arrange matters. If you put a plant from the garden straight into the freezer there would be no time and it would die. Happily, freezing in nature is normally a gradual process. Autumn weather constitutes a toughening-up programme for plants in itself. The common autumnal phenomenon of sunny days and cold nights is just the right regime. Transpiration (by day) is high while respiration is restricted by the low temperatures. Under these conditions (and no longer using up energy to put on new growth) the plant accumulates more and more carbohydrate in its tissue: the very concentration which will protect the heart of the cell when the real freeze comes.

BELOW: *The direct correlation between altitude and latitude is expressed in the picture of Mt Kilimanjaro. A mountain on the equator which reaches 4,800m (16,000ft) contains on its slopes all the temperature zones from tropical to arctic.*

What happens when it thaws is just as important: a very rapid thaw allows no time for the water to percolate back through the cell walls to where it belongs, and again the delicate membranes will be ruptured and the plant will die. Even plants that are otherwise quite hardy can be damaged by warm sunshine while they are still frozen. For this reason an east wall is a fatal place for plants that incline to tenderness. If the sun strikes them early after a frozen night the thaw will be too fast for them and their cell walls will break.

There are other kinds of tenderness besides susceptibility to cold. High alpine plants can sustain arctic temperatures but succumb to being wet in winter. Bog plants might be described as drought-tender. Each plant, in other words, has a natural regime it will ultimately insist on.

ZONES OF PLANT HARDINESS

The ultimate deciding factor in whether a plant will survive in a given spot (with adequate supplies of light, moisture and nutrients and good drainage) is quite simply the lowest temperature it will have to endure.

In the United States, where a huge land mass almost connected to the North Pole makes severe winters common over a great part of the country, this fact was long ago recognized and embodied in a famous system of plant hardiness zones. These were defined by the Arnold Arboretum of Harvard University, at Boston, Massachusetts, as zones of consistent annual average minimum temperature and have been adapted in a widely-accepted and well-mapped formula for use by American gardeners and nurserymen.

The logic of the North American climate is clear. Cold comes from the central North, much alleviated on the West coast by the prevailing winds off the Pacific Ocean, far less so on the East coast where winter winds are blowing off the cold landmass. In the east it is only the far south that benefits by its latitude.

Europe is almost the mirror image. Temperate winds blow over the north Atlantic, whose water is itself warmed by the north-easterly flow of the Gulf Stream. The main source of cold air is the continental landmass of Eastern Europe, Russia and Scandinavia to the east and north.

With the exception of the Mediterranean, therefore, what counts in Europe is not how far north you are, but how far west – and of course at what altitude. Climate-zones are not so widely referred to by European gardeners, but a map

ZONES OF PLANT HARDINESS
Hardiness zones are numbered from 1 to 10 on an increasing scale of annual average minimum temperatures (below). This list also gives the approximate annual number of 'growing days' when temperature exceeds 6°C (43°F) – the temperature at which grass starts to grow.
Zone 1: Below -46°C (-50°F); 100 days
Zone 2: -46 to -40°C (-50 to -40°F); 150 days
Zone 3: -40 to -34.5°C (-40 to -30°F); 165 days
Zone 4: -34 to -29°C (-30 to -20°F); 195 days
Zone 5: -29 to -23°C (-20 to -10°F); 210 days
Zone 6: -23 to -18°C (-10 to 0°F); 225 days
Zone 7: -18 to -12°C (0 to 10°F); 255 days
Zone 8: -12 to -7°C (10 to 20°F); 270 days
Zone 9: -7 to -1°C (20 to 30°F); 330 days
Zone 10: -1 to 4°C (30 to 40°F); 365 days

BELOW: *The diagram shows the types of vegetation adapted to each altitude/ latitude zone, from equatorial wet jungle up to 600m (2,000ft), or 10° of latitude, to tundra at 3,600m (12,000ft), or 65° of latitude.*

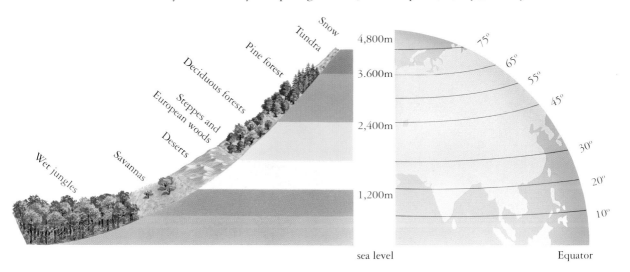

Wet jungles   Savannas   Deserts   Steppes and European woods   Deciduous forests   Pine forest   Tundra   Snow

4,800m   3,600m   2,400m   1,200m   sea level

75°   65°   55°   45°   30°   20°   10°   Equator

compiled on the same basis as that of North America is very revealing. It explains, for example, how the far north-west of Scotland, on the latitude of Southern Greenland, can grow palm trees – and even western Norway is relatively mild in winter.

As an example of how the zone system works, a plant that is described as 'hardy to zone 9' is one that will survive in temperature zone 9 – that is with an annual average minimum temperature of between -7°C (20°F) and -1°C (30°F) – or south of it, but only in exceptional circumstances in the next zone to the north (or east), zone 8, where the temperature regularly drops to -12°C (10°F). In other words it can safely be planted in gardens in Florida and along the Gulf coast, or almost anywhere from Arizona up the west coast to British Columbia; or in Europe anywhere along the Mediterranean coast, in most of Spain and Portugal and in that narrow coastal strip of temperate winters all the way north to Scotland.

Minimum winter temperatures, of course, have nothing to do with unseasonal spring frosts. A plant that has survived a severe freeze while it is dormant may yet be killed by having its new shoots destroyed on a freezing night in spring.

YOUR LOCAL CLIMATE

If the grand movements of temperature, sunshine and rainfall are determined by oceans and landmasses, prevailing winds and pressure zones, the gardener's day-to-day concerns are more local. A range of hills can have the same effect on conditions, though on a smaller scale, as a mountain range, and a lake can exert moderating influences similar to those of an ocean.

Several things can make remarkable differences to the local climate; the altitude, the flatness or slope of the ground, the type of soil, the nearness of the sea or a range of hills, and, perhaps most dramatically of all, buildings. The climate in a city can be so much warmer than in the surrounding country that it brings a different class of plants within range. An olive tree grows and occasionally bears fruit in London, six hundred miles north of its normal limits.

There is a rule of thumb about altitude which is, on its own, easy enough to remember and interpret. For every 125m (400ft) above sea level the temperature drops 1°C (1⅔°F). This is enough to shorten the growing season (defined as days with an average temperature above 6°C (43°F) by several days in hilly country).

More complex and usually more important to the gardener is the slope of the land, its aspect (to north or south) and whether he is at the top or bottom of a hill. It makes a great deal of difference whether the sun's rays strike the ground perpendicularly or at an acute angle – witness the difference between summer and winter, not to mention the equator and the pole. By having ground sloping towards the sun the angle is greatly increased and hence the effective radiation is greater. As wine-growers know, a south-facing slope is much warmer than a north-facing one. It will bring on growth noticeably earlier in spring, and go on ripening fruit later in the autumn.

Early growth, however, can be a snare and a delusion if the same south-facing slope is abruptly terminated by an answering north-facing one on the other side of the valley – or even by what looks like a snugly sheltering wall. For cold air behaves exactly like water. It flows downhill until it meets an obstacle; then spreads outwards and upwards, like water filling a pond. On a frosty night cold air flows off the upper slopes to mass at the bottom, and, according to how cold it is for how long, can make anything from a mere puddle to a whole valley-full of freezing air.

ABOVE: *The Giardino Botanico Hanbury at La Mortola near Menton benefits from a unique microclimate. Here the Alps protect the coast from the north, making frost the remotest chance.*

THE PATH OF THE SUN

The sun in summer rises in the north-east and sets in the north-west, giving some light even to north-facing walls.

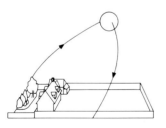

In winter the sun rises in the south-east and sets in the south-west; the north wall is in permanent shade.

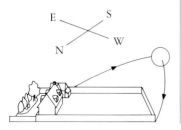

Any garden in a hollow is at risk from frost. The stillness of the sheltered air contributes to the risk as well. The exact mechanism that causes 'radiation frost', the sort that occurs unseasonably on clear still nights, is surprisingly complex.

In the evening and the early part of the night the ground gives off its stored daytime heat to the cool night air. But there comes a moment when the ground cools to a temperature lower than the air immediately above it and starts taking heat back. The result is a thin layer of freezing air just above the soil surface. This air is denser and heavier than the air above it and therefore inclined to flow downhill, like water, to the lowest available point and collect there.

The nature of the soil itself also affects its proneness to frost. Heavy soil heats and cools slowly like the solid block of a night-storage heater. But light sandy soil, or even a finely worked tilth over heavier soil, contains quantities of trapped air and acts as an insulation blanket between the atmosphere and the reservoir of heat in the ground. On cold nights the stored heat in the sub-soil is prevented from rising and frost soon forms at ground level. In the same way any vegetation has enough insulating effect to encourage radiation frost.

ABOVE: *Cold air collects at ground level and flows downhill like water to fill any hollow it can reach, just as if it were a pond. Good 'air drainage' is vital in any area subject to regular frost.*

If a hollow is a frost trap, a hilltop usually suffers from the effects of wind. After sunlight and water supply, wind has more influence on growth than any other factor – not in the visible sense of bending and breaking shoots, but in making demands on the plant's plumbing that it cannot meet. Wind blowing over leaves is no different from wind blowing over washing: the stronger the wind the faster it dries. When the evaporation rate is more than the roots can keep up with, the plant's pores close and its whole life-process slows down.

Often apparently sheltered corners of the garden are quite the reverse. Wind in an open field is damaging enough, but when it reaches solid obstacles like walls it is compressed into gusts and eddies at much higher speeds.

When it hits a house at right angles the effect can be devastating to plants at the foot of the wall. Perhaps half the body of air hitting the wall is forced up over the roof and round the sides, but the other half turns and blows directly downwards, crushing whatever is growing below.

Wind also, of course, affects where rain falls. The gardener's dream is of a steady, gentle, vertical shower on a still day, not falling hard enough to damage plants or compact the soil. In reality, he usually receives squalls of oblique rain on the prevailing wind. Westerly rain leaves a considerable area to the east of the house unwatered, and vice versa. On the other hand, the sunshine and wind on the south and west of walls dries out the soil there faster than anywhere else. It is not safe to assume that wall beds facing the prevailing wind can rely on rainfall.

Among all these imponderables at least one thing is certain: the course of the sun in the sky. It is easy to forget how much it varies from season to season. In winter

ABOVE: *A garden in northern New England battened down for the winter presents an extraordinary sight. The only hope of bringing evergreens through the long months of icy winds is to bundle them up in sacking.*

it rises in the south-east and sets in the south-west, but in summer it rises and sets well to the north. A north wall that sees no sun all winter is well-lit, even baked, on hot summer evenings. This may make it suitable for an autumn-flowering plant, but too hot for something with delicate leaves that asks for perpetual shade.

Even a small house and garden will have a wide range of microclimates: spots where rain never reaches, which heat up quickly in sunshine, where winds funnel to create destructive draughts, where frosts form or water lies stagnant. The growth of the plants themselves creates more areas of shade, shelter or drought. The shadow of the house is usually a dominant factor: its north and east walls, being in shade most of the time, provide the equivalent light conditions to woodland but without the shelter that woods afford. South and west walls enjoy most sunlight, but are also often windy.

A south-west-facing terrace can be a sun trap, which combined with the heat-retaining properties of walls and paving makes it ideal for Mediterranean plants. Plants in tubs or pots on the terrace will need constant watering, but those growing in the joints in the paving have the benefit of a cool root run. Microclimates can be very micro indeed.

A fence or wall facing just east of south gives a good sunny border and an excellent situation for climbers. Clematis planted here has its roots shaded by plants in the border and its top in sunlight: the perfect arrangement. A fence with a north-west exposure is shady in winter but well lit on summer afternoons. A north-facing fence is a good place for cold frames for propagation.

The plantsman's approach to a small garden without any particular variation of terrain, except that provided by the house and fences or walls, would be to maximize the variety of plants that will thrive by matching the soil as far as possible with the microclimatic conditions. If cool and shady areas are to look the part their soil should be made as near as possible an imitation of woodland soil, free draining but with a high organic content.

The sunniest spots will grow the plants of the Mediterranean and South Africa better if they are made as fast-draining as possible with rubble and gravel. A plastic sheet buried round the pond to impede drainage will allow bog-loving plants to grow. This approach sacrifices the unity of one soil type for the interest of diversity of plants. To compose a coherent picture this way is a considerable challenge.

CLIMATE AND THE GARDENER

Gardeners don't give up easily. The challenge is to cheat the elements; to grow plants bigger and better than nature can manage unaided; to have more, earlier and more perfect fruit and flowers. Centuries of trial and error have produced an armoury of devices and techniques for protecting and encouraging plants against frost, heat, drought, wind and flood. Irrigation is an example of climate control; so is drainage.

All the gardener's dodges arise from the same simple law: growth is ultimately controlled by the weakest link in the environmental chain. Whichever essential is in short supply governs the growth-rate, however much of the other ingredients may be available.

The environmental essentials are moisture, light, air and a high enough temperature. Different plants need different amounts of each, but normally there is one that presents the greatest problem for most plants in any given area. In southern California or North Africa the missing ingredient is moisture. In most temperate-zone gardens the controlling factors are low temperature and day length. But the principal threat and bugbear is untimely frost.

There are stoical gardeners who believe in reducing the risks to a minimum: they plant doubtfully hardy plants in sharply drained, infertile soil where they will hardly grow at all. 'Growing them hard' is the English public-school system applied to plants. Every inch has to be fought for. The theory is that by withholding nutrients and moisture, what growth there is will start late and stop early enough for the chance of frost on soft growth to be minimal.

A less drastic precaution is choosing a cool and shady station for an early flowerer, a magnolia for example, hoping to delay its bud-break until warmer weather. Another is in the strategic timing of pruning, which encourages new growth. By leaving it late, new shoots are delayed. Another is simply planting late.

One insurance policy any wise gardener takes out is to choose fruit trees, for example, that flower at slightly different times. If frost or rain prevents the successful pollination of one kind, at least it will not affect them all.

Physical barriers between your plants and the elements can make all the difference. In temperate climates 'the elements' means above all the wind. There are few gardens where growth is not limited at some time by the wind lowering air and ground temperatures. A recent research project in Germany showed that the only possible way of improving conditions for ripening grapes in the country's best vineyards was to plant windbreaks of tall trees, and to align the vine rows so that the prevailing wind of summer blows at right angles to, and not along the length of, the lines.

The most effective windbreak allows some of the wind through, breaking its force rather than trying to stop it dead. Even a slight screen provided by a piece of fine-mesh netting supported on canes to windward of a plant can make the difference between life and death. Walls attempt the impossible, and only succeed in creating worse turbulence. The ideal windbreak is a hedge or shrubby screen with a fairly shaggy texture and a proportion of about two-thirds solid matter to one-third small holes. A beech hedge answers the description. Such a windbreak cuts the wind force to almost nothing for a distance of about twice the height of the hedge in its immediate lee, and it still does some good at a distance of ten times the height. The windbreak should be at right angles to the prevailing wind. But not all gales, of course, come from the same quarter. Only a circular hedge can be effective against all winds.

Walls are used to grow fruit trees and tender climbers for a different reason: they absorb and store the heat of the sun, slowly giving it up again during the night. In the days of cheap fuel, walls for peaches and apricots up to twenty-five feet high were heated from within by furnaces during the flowering season.

Such lavish gestures of climate control are not for today. Very small gardens, indeed, can hardly spare space even for a hedge. Protection must often be on a plant-by-plant basis, even to the extent practised in the northern states of America of wrapping evergreens individually in sacking to keep off the desiccating winter winds. The only hope of bringing evergreens through the long months of icy winds, often in deadly combination with bright sun, while the roots are locked in frozen ground, is to bundle them up in sacking. The plants

BELOW: *Physical protection from snow damage on the north coast of Japan at Kanazawa comes in the form of rigging. Each branch of the precious pines is roped up to a mast placed beside the trunk.*

ABOVE: *The light canopy of netting over a fruit cage is often a sufficient baffle for a slight frost, and serves the double purpose of lowering wind speed as well as keeping off the birds. Fine mesh, however, collects snow and can collapse under its often quite considerable weight.*

are no warmer in their sleeping bags, but the protection prevents them having to transpire when there is no water available. Death would come from drought, not simply from cold.

The Japanese do even better with their highly prized cycads, clothing them in hats and coats of plaited straw. The aerosol age offers a plastic spray to coat evergreen leaves and reduce transpiration. Damage from the weight of snow is another matter. Upright conifers are particularly susceptible. Some gardeners tie the branches up in autumn: again the Japanese do best, sometimes rigging tall pines almost like sailing ships. Others knock the snow off with a pole before it gets heavy enough to break branches.

In very cold areas roses are buried for the winter, and Swedish friends tell me the only way they can keep rhododendrons alive is to turn the sprinklers on and coat them with a layer of ice while the intense cold lasts. Spraying to form an ice layer is increasingly used against spring frost damage, too: a new shoot is safe at freezing point, inside its ice capsule, even when the temperature outside plunges many degrees below. Against less severe frosts it is surprising what slight covering will make a difference: a canopy of bare branches, a wire-netting fruit cage, horticultural 'fleece'; even a sheet of newspaper can save new growth.

Different mulches can have different effects on ground temperature. Dark-coloured ones absorb heat and encourage early growth – which may be a disadvantage. Transparent plastic is effective for warming the ground in spring and allows radiation at night, but black plastic prevents radiation and can cause low temperatures near the ground. A thick mulch on frozen ground can prevent frost heaving and consequent damage to roots.

So far we have talked only of defensive measures: baffles against wind and frost. But we can do better than that. By using glass we can push back the limits of the growing season. Glass, which nowadays includes transparent plastic, traps and intensifies the sun's rays. The so-called 'greenhouse effect' means that more heat comes into a glass structure than goes out. (A note of caution is needed about polythene as a glass-substitute. It does not prevent the loss of heat by radiation.) As long as the plant under glass has enough of the essentials of light, water and air, it can take advantage of the higher temperature to grow sooner and faster.

Glass is used for two basic purposes: either to bring a crop on ahead of its normal time in the open or to protect a permanent plant that would otherwise be killed by winter conditions. Winter conditions include damp as well as cold. Alpines, in particular, fall prey to rain when in their natural home they would be snug under frozen snow. A further use of glass is to provide an in-between stage for greenhouse-raised plants before they are submitted to the full range of natural conditions. Glass-covered frames are often used for 'hardening-off' plants that have been pampered in propagation.

It need not only be the sun's heat that the glass encloses. The old-fashioned way of forcing early crops was to build a deep stack of fresh horse manure, cover it with soil and put a glass-lidded frame on top. The manure fermented, giving off enough heat to produce salads – even pineapples – in mid-winter. The modern equivalent is to bury electric soil-warming cables in the soil under a frame. Compared with other forms of artificial heating this is remarkably economical.

THE LIVING SOIL

Unlike the weather, it can be improved. There are some soils that can even be perfected, so that most plants will show every sign of satisfaction.

The perfect garden soil is a balanced mixture of five constituents: of solids perhaps two-thirds rock particles, of sizes ranging from small stones down to the tiniest specks of clay; one-third animal and vegetable matter, mainly dead and decayed but with a substantial population of living creatures; a considerable quantity of water and a remarkable amount of air. Unfortunately it is a rare occurrence for such a soil to form naturally. To understand why most soils have too much of one constituent and too little of another (at least from the gardener's point of view) we must go back to the ways in which soils are formed in the first instance – not just in prehistory but at this very minute.

When the surface of the earth is bare rock, as it all was originally and still is in such places as mountain-tops and sea cliffs, the weather is constantly chiselling away at the surface. Almost every mood of weather, except perhaps calm air and gentle sunshine, has its abrasive effect. Frost is one of the most powerful agencies for pulverizing rock. Extreme changes of temperature between day and night, causing rapid expansion and contraction, keep breaking pieces off. Heavy rain, strong winds, the pounding of waves and the grinding of glaciers, all reduce rock, sometimes rapidly and sometimes imperceptibly slowly, to mineral fragments. This lifeless stony debris is the beginning of the creation of soil.

Soil is created when mineral detritus is colonized by living organisms. It is the interface between the solid rocky globe and the biosphere; the term for the mere film of life-supporting elements, oxygen above all, that envelops us.

It is normal to distinguish between the top-soil, where the marriage of rocky matrix and biological life has gone furthest, and the sub-soil, where the influence of the biosphere is comparatively slight. Below the sub-soil lies the lifeless mother rock. The top-soil is rarely more than a metre deep – and often only a few centimetres.

So soil starts with geology. Its physical and chemical nature depend in the first place on the type of rock that was worn away. There comes a sharp difference, though, between soils that remain *in situ*, where they were weathered, and those that have been transported by water, as rain and rivers, by glaciers or by winds to be deposited far from their place of origin.

BELOW: *The minute particles of heavy clay soil make it slow-draining and laborious to work but potentially extremely fertile. It warms up slowly in spring but retains its heat well. Clay-soil flowers include hellebores, creeping bugle and* Narcissus pseudonarcissus.

ABOVE: *Chalky soils, common in southern Britain (here on the South Downs) and northern France, tend to be shallow and dry; humus is rapidly decomposed by the lime content. But their natural flora is among the richest.*

'Local' soils tend to be mixtures of particles of all sizes – a healthily heterogeneous mixture of everything from stones to silt. 'Transported' soils tend to be sifted and sorted in the process of moving. The heavier particles are deposited first; the lightest last. If you follow the course of a river from mountain to sea the grading is obvious, from boulders in the upper reaches to finest silt around the delta or on the sea-bed.

Transported soils therefore are inclined to be unbalanced: either all coarse particles or all fine ones, all sand or all clay. The main exception to this rule is the 'boulder clay' often found where Ice Age glaciers did the transporting. Its name tells its own story: clay in one spot and stones in another; here a stratum of sand and there a pocket of gravel.

Soil 'texture', the sizes of the rock-derived particles, and their relative proportions, is relatively easy to describe – and practically impossible to alter. Sandy soils are 'hungry', having an open structure that allows nutrients to be quickly washed away unless humus is constantly being added. They heat up quickly but cool down with equal speed. Sandy heaths have one of the most limited of natural floras, including birch, heather, gorse and pine.

The minute particles of heavy clay soil make it slow-draining but potentially extremely fertile. It warms up slowly in spring and retains heat well. Clay-soil flowers include hellebores, creeping bugle and *Narcissus pseudonarcissus*.

Chalky soils, common in southern Britain and northern France, tend to be shallow and dry; humus is rapidly decomposed by the highest possible lime content. Yet their natural flora is among the richest.

Peaty soils are the precise reverse of chalk soils: occurring in wet areas where lime and nitrogen are washed away. As a result vegetation fails to decompose and builds up an acid layer. The flora is limited to grasses and sedges, and such things as heather and other ericas that tolerate high soil acidity.

Soil 'structure', in contrast to texture, is exactly what a gardener can and should improve. Structure means the way the particles are held together, and what happens between them. It starts in nature with the lichens, which are the only plants that will grow even on unweathered rock. Other plants must wait until the accumulation of organic material has started. In the rocky moraine below a glacier seeds may fall and have air and moisture enough to germinate. But the stones alone give no support or food for their roots and there is nothing porous present to retain water.

Then an animal may die, leaves and other plant debris may accumulate, bacteria and fungi can get to work, and the next seed that germinates can find a foothold in the scanty organic scrapheap. In turn it dies and adds to the organic layer. The mixture of stones, dead plants and animals, living ones, air and water has become soil. The same process continues with generation after generation of plants, each adding to the depth of soil, until big trees can find room for their roots. Steep mountainsides have been colonized and stabilized like this over millions of years of gradually increasing fertility.

The active agents in this process are the bacteria and fungi and their lesser-known colleagues, whose feeding causes decay. Fertile soil has a colossal population of these micro-organisms: the bacteria in an acre of arable land, each one only visible under a microscope, may add up to a total weight of 1,360kg (3,000lb). So fast do they multiply that under ideal conditions one bacterium can become two every twenty minutes. Others such as the actinomycetes, which are said to give the delicious fresh earthy smell to the soil, are just as abundant. Fungi are as active as bacteria in decomposing dead plant material. Without the activity of these creatures there would be no decay, and therefore no recycling of the carbon, the nitrogen and the other elements that plants need to grow.

Earthworms are among the many inhabitants of the soil that are helpful to gardeners, improving its quality by passing it through their bodies and leaving tunnels that are exploited by roots and allow the entry of air. One species of earthworm, *Lumbricus terrestris*, pulls dead leaves down into the ground to eat them in private, a practice that adds valuable humus to the soil. In chalky clay, one of their favourite soils, earthworms may reach a population of 300 per square metre. Their net effect is entirely beneficial.

The chief product of all this industrious digestion, along with nitrogen and carbon dioxide, is the dark brown, crumbly, sweet-smelling decomposed vegetation known colloquially as humus – the chief component and sole object of the gardener's compost heap. Humus is constantly being made by the soil micro-organisms and as constantly being consumed. Its value to the gardener in improving the structure of no matter what soil is discussed on the following pages.

Even here, though, in this essential recycling process, climate plays a decisive part. In areas of heavy rainfall where nutrients (particularly nitrogen and calcium) are washed down – 'leached' – from the top-soil to lower layers few bacteria can survive. In the cold, wet, acid, lime-deprived forests of the north fungi are the chief agents of decay.

But where the land lies permanently waterlogged, as in peat bogs, not even fungi can live. Decay scarcely occurs at all; fertility is minimal and only a few specialized plants such as heather and cotton grass can grow at all.

The vital element that is missing from waterlogged soil is air. Oxygen is essential to all its inhabitants, including the roots of almost all plants. Its presence is the essential difference between the top-soil and the sub-soil. In top-soil, where all the action is and where most of the roots, even of the biggest trees, proliferate, the pores of air can occupy

ABOVE: *An earthworm drags a fallen leaf down into the ground to consume it. In doing so it both aerates the soil and adds valuable humus to its structure.*

BELOW: *Peaty soils are the precise reverse of chalk soils: occurring in wet areas (here the Isle of Skye) where lime and nitrogen are washed away.*

as much as half of the soil volume. Through them flows the soil-water. In them live the bacteria. The ideal soil of the gardener's dream not only all contains the elements in balanced and fertile proportion, but the humus, the clay particles and the sand cohere into distinguishable 'crumbs' which remain separate, leaving ample spaces for the vital air in between.

Exactly why some soils naturally remain 'open' like this remains one of the many mysteries of nature. Which is not to say that you cannot (in most circumstances) eventually achieve the same result by assiduous cultivation, conscientious drainage and copious applications of organic matter.

THE SOIL AS A RESERVOIR

The soil provides three essentials to all plants: a firm foothold, food and water. If one of these three essentials could be called more important than the other two it is water. Transpiration, as we have seen, is the motor of plant life. So the capacity of the soil to store water is a gardener's prime concern.

Soil holds water in two ways: in its organic content of humus and decaying vegetable matter which acts as a sponge, and in a thin film on each of its mineral particles. This film is strongly held together by surface tension.

The big variations between soils, therefore, come with the amount of organic matter involved and the surface area of the mineral particles. This is where sand and clay are poles apart. The comparatively few, relatively big, grains of sand have nothing like the total surface area of the millions of tiny particles of clay. So clay holds far more water than sand, and, since every little particle is equally reluctant to give up its individual film of water, grasps it much more tightly. As far as roots are concerned, then, sand has little water, but what it has is easily tapped. Clay has much more, but is miserly about letting it go.

BELOW: *The chief reason for digging is to open the soil to the air and allow the frost and the sun to break up clods into smaller crumbs, improving drainage and making it easier for roots to penetrate. A secondary reason is to mix in manure or compost, but this can be spread on the surface with almost as much effect.*

When it rains, the open structure of sandy soil lets the water straight in. It percolates easily between the grains and travels down, drawn by gravity, until it reaches the permanently saturated level known as the water-table. As it goes it wets the humus in the soil and leaves a film on each grain. As each tiny cavity empties into the one below, air is drawn into it from above to take the place of the water. At the same time the flood of water passing through dissolves nitrogen and other foodstuffs and carries them with it – the process known as 'leaching'. A sandy soil, then, is an easy and airy place for roots to grow, but in rainy regions tends to be flushed clean of nutrients, so its fertility is low.

A heavy clay soil behaves quite differently. In the first place rain finds it hard to get in. The fine grains of the surface quickly coagulate to become watertight and the rain lies in puddles, only to evaporate again. What water does soak through moves slowly, its progress impeded by the tiny passages between the minute clay particles. Each particle claims its share. Until each layer is damp there is no surplus for gravity to pull lower. Nutrients are locked up in the same way as the water. Clay therefore is hard going for roots and tends to be airless, but holds its 'goodness' well.

The gardener's ideal soil lies about half-way between the two extremes. A 'good loam' is sandy enough to drain well, but has enough clay to hold essential reserves. Whichever way it tends, whether to lightness or heaviness, there is a ready way to improve it: to add more humus.

This is the chief value of the compost heap, manure, straw or any organic matter. It may or may not have food value for plants, but it will certainly improve the texture of the soil. If it is sandy, it will clog the pores and slow down the exaggerated drainage. If it is clayey, it will open the pores and help the water (and the roots) through.

At the same time, the act of digging it in opens the soil to air and water. Undug, humus-starved soil is hard and heavy digging. The more humus the soil has, the easier the spade goes in and the lighter the load on the gardener's back. Both added humus and opening to the weather encourage the formation of soil 'crumbs', the little conglomerations of particles which in turn give the soil a more airy, permeable structure.

But why this preoccupation with drainage? Surely, if water is so essential to plants the more they have the better? Would it not be best of all to have a high water-table that they could drink from as much as they wanted? Gardeners are constantly being told that a plant needs 'moisture-retentive yet well-drained soil'. The phrase is a nursery-catalogue cliché. Why the apparent paradox? It sounds a great waste of effort to water plants and at the same time to take elaborate precautions to drain the water away as quickly as possible.

The reasons are twofold. The first is that roots need air almost as much as they need water. In saturated soil all the pore space, the gaps between the solid particles, is filled with water. Unless they are specially adapted to waterlogged conditions (as some bog plants are), roots kept for long under water will drown. Water passing down through the soil, on the other hand, renews the air in the cavities it vacates, leaving a healthy atmosphere with plenty of oxygen.

The second reason arises from the first. A high water-table restricts roots to soil near the surface, where the air is. Any sort of restriction is a disadvantage. They need as much room as possible to branch and re-branch in search of nutrients. But there is another problem with a root-zone limited to a few inches of the surface. It is inevitably unstable, helplessly subject to the changing weather. As it dries out in a drought, the uppermost roots die and lower ones take over, following the retreating water-table. But when rain returns and the water-table rises, the new roots will be too deep and be drowned.

Roots in a pot are in a more precarious situation than roots in the open ground, since they cannot grow away from stagnant, airless soil. Potting compost should therefore always drain quickly.

The greater the depth of well-drained, well-aerated soil the deeper plants can root and the safer they are in drought and flood. Investigation into the quality of vineyard land in Bordeaux has shown a direct relationship between the depth of drainage and the performance of the vines year after year. In the best stony soil of the Médoc, vines will reach down thirty feet or more. At that level a passing shower

ABOVE: *Where soil lies wet and heavy there may be no alternative to laying drains. Broken clay flower-pots were traditionally the ideal foundation material: covered with turves and soil they allow a deep and free root-run.*

means nothing; the plants grow in ideally constant conditions. To the gardener this means that occasional deep-digging, two spades deep, is a worthwhile operation – provided he puts plenty of compost or manure down in the lower layer.

For precisely the same reasons it is a mistake to water plants little and often. If you merely sprinkle the surface, the roots will be forced to stay up where the water is, in the top few inches. Forget to sprinkle for a few days and there are no reserves of water below, nor any roots to tap them.

The gardener's ideal is a long gentle shower of warm rain (preferably, of course, with fertilizer added). The same principle should apply to watering. A fine spray for a long period does least damage in compacting the surface and soaks in farthest. The golden rule is to water seldom and thoroughly.

To gardeners in Mediterranean-type climates where drought is the natural summer condition, this counsel of perfection is small comfort. The best advice is to limit your planting to plants that nature designed for the climate (and the soil) that you are blessed with. Certainly improve the soil by adding organic matter that will help it to retain moisture. Certainly cover the ground with a mulch against evaporation. But, consider also how shade and shelter from wind can mitigate the demands put on roots by the long, rainless season.

Traditional gardeners were for ever hoeing the surface of the soil between plants to keep a layer of broken 'tilth' an inch or so deep. Although the main reason was to keep down weeds, they also thought that a dust-dry top inch of soil prevented surface evaporation.

Modern theory tends to decry the school of the hoe in favour of covering the surface with a mulch. This is in an attempt to return to the natural state of the forest floor with its fallen leaves, or the meadow with its accumulation of dead herbs and grasses. The mulch may be leaf-mould, compost, lawn-mowings, or even composted sawdust or pulverized tree bark. A 5cm (2in) layer spread over the warmed wet soil in spring has several beneficial effects. Preventing evaporation is the first, suppressing weeds is another (if they do seed in the mulch they are easily pulled up). Gradually adding to the soil-humus by the action of earthworms is a third.

In permanent plantings of trees and shrubs, mulching is undoubtedly beneficial. Heathers are happier for a mulch of peat, leafmould or bark and many alpines for a layer of gravel or stone chips. On the other hand, in parts of the garden where you are constantly planting and replanting, it is impractical to put down a layer you would constantly be disturbing.

Once the mulch has dried out, it works just as effectively preventing rain reaching the soil and preventing evaporation. It takes prolonged rain or irrigation to saturate the mulch before the soil can get even a drop. The great virtue of a gravel mulch is that this does not apply.

Even quite large stones have been used for mulching. Foresters planting eucalyptus to reclaim the rainless fringes of the Sahara have found that planting the trees 60cm (2ft) deeper in the sand than usual is beneficial, if the hole is then filled with stones. Moisture condenses in the 'mulch' at night and waters the trees.

THE CHEMISTRY OF THE SOIL

Before the days of artificial fertilizers there was an ancient principle embodied in all farm lease agreements. The rules of good husbandry decreed that there were certain things the tenant might not take off the farm: the hay and the straw had to be fed to the animals and their manure put back on the land. If they were carted off and sold the land suffered. No one knew that essential potassium went with them. No one knew about potassium at all.

Early in the nineteenth century chemists were able to discover by analysing plants that they consisted of at least eight elements. They could account for the carbon, hydrogen and oxygen as coming from the water and carbon dioxide all around us. But that left nitrogen, phosphorus, potassium, calcium and magnesium, which must, they deduced, come from the soil. Manure, they discovered, also contains these elements. These, therefore, were what the old farming practice had unwittingly been recycling.

Manure, however, contains very little of the essentials in proportion to its bulk: only 13kg (29lb) of these elements together in a tonne (2,200lb). It would be much more efficient to apply the elements direct.

Nitrogen was the first to be a practical proposition. It is easily available either in the form of sulphate of ammonia, a by-product of burning coal to produce gas, or nitrate of soda, which was discovered to exist in vast quantities underground in Chile. Either of these spread on the soil in spring had immediate and wonderful results in promoting lush green growth. Unfortunately they were also leached out of the soil by rain, so they needed to be applied little and often.

The next chemical to be found in a useable form was phosphorus. A young English squire, John Bennet Lawes of Rothamsted in Hertfordshire, became interested in why ground-up bones improved the fertility of some soils but not others. He dissolved some bones in sulphuric acid and found that the answer was simple:

MINERAL NUTRIENTS

POSITIVE EFFECTS	DEFICIENCY EFFECTS
Nitrogen (N) The rate and vigour of growth and colour of leaves. Protein building and photosynthesis.	Growth stunted; small yellow, or possibly bluish leaves. Thin weak stems.
Phosphorus (P) Root growth, ripening of seeds and fruit.	Stunted roots and growth. Small purple leaves and stems. Yield of fruit and seeds poor.
Potassium (Potash) (K) Close links with nitrogen. When nitrogen is increased, so must potash or a deficiency will appear. A fruit-forming fertilizer. Assists photosynthesis and the production of carbohydrate. Protects plants against diseases.	Fruits are poorly coloured, lacking in flavour. Leaves will appear scorched at edges, mottled, spotted or curled. Potatoes will cook badly, turning black and soapy.
Calcium (Ca) Essential for sturdy young plant growth. One of the most important soil foods.	General lack of vigour, growing points die, growth stops. Without calcium, some species are unable to assimilate nitrogen .
Magnesium (Mg) Part of the chlorophyll molecule (which makes leaves green). It is necessary for the formation of amino acids and vitamins. Essential to germination of seed and synthesis of sugar.	Photosynthesis is effected and shows as yellowing of leaves, or purplish/ brown patches between the veins. Leaves may fall prematurely.
Sulphur (S) Necessary for chlorophyll synthesis.	Similar to nitrogen deficiency – leaves become light green.
Iron (Fe) Helps in the formation of chlorophyll.	Chlorosis develops – yellow or very pale upper leaves, thin weak stem.
Copper (Cu) Plays a part in nitrogen metabolism.	Dieback of shoots, terminal leaves develop dead spots and brown areas. Branchless plants, such as cabbage, become chlorotic and leaves failto form.
Zinc (Zn) Legumes require zinc for seed formation. Formation of starch, chloroplast, auxin and internodal elongation.	Malformed leaves, 'mottle leaf' of citrus, 'white bud' of maize. Zinc deficiency leads to iron deficiency – both are thus similar in appearance.

bone 'meal' provided phosphorus (which is essential to good root growth) in acid soils that could dissolve it, but remained insoluble in alkaline soils. His invention of 'superphosphate' made him a fortune and founded the artificial fertilizer industry. As luck would have it, he did not have to dig up the battlefields of Europe (as his detractors claimed) to find enough bones: he was able to use newly discovered natural deposits of calcium phosphate.

Nitrogen is all around us in the air. It should, the chemists thought, be reasonably easy to combine it with the hydrogen in the air to make ammonia. This in turn could easily be made into plant food by oxidation into its sulphate or nitrate. They found that a powerful charge of electricity could do the trick. In fact lightning does it regularly; the rain in a thunderstorm is very dilute nitric acid. By the First World War, German chemists had found a catalyst which made it a simple industrial process, to the consternation of their enemies. Nitrates are a pre-requisite for high explosives and Britain still had to import hers from Chile.

Potassium has long been applied to the soil in the form of fresh ashes from wood fires or bonfires, which contain about ten per cent of potassium carbonate or 'potash'. Its value to plants lies chiefly in speeding the production of sugar in the leaves, and thus speeding the ripening process, the filling-out of beet and potatoes, the sweetening of fruit, the stiffening of grass stalks and the turning of new wood from green to brown. Late summer, therefore, is a good time to apply it.

The need for industrialized production of potassium fertilizers came later, as farmers abandoned their old recycling methods and turned to direct applications. Rock deposits known as kainit, which overlaid deposits of common salt in Germany and Austria, were found to be a valuable mixture of potassium sulphate and magnesium sulphate.

BELOW: *The bonfire (where regulations allow it) is an essential part of garden hygiene. All waste plant material that is too woody to rot readily in the compost, or is full of weed seeds or tenacious roots, or is infected with fungus or virus disease, should be burned routinely. The fresh ashes of the bonfire are a source of potash.*

Of the other major elements magnesium is often in short supply. Its function in plants is in the manufacture of chlorophyll, the essential green pigment. Where magnesium is lacking leaves are parti-coloured, pale or sometimes flushed with purple. An excess of potassium and a shortage of nitrogen is often the indirect cause. A simple remedy is a dose of Epsom salts.

Calcium, on the contrary, was easily come by and indeed had been used for improving heavy clay soils at least since Roman times. Chalk or lime, or marl, which is limey clay, has the property of binding the clay particles together and making them more easily workable. (The word is flocculate, derived from the Latin for wool.) It is only very acid soils that normally lack enough calcium for most plants' chemical needs.

The acidity of their own soil is probably the chemical aspect of it that gardeners are most aware of. To a large extent it controls the range of plants they can grow – indeed the whole style of gardening they can adopt. The measure of soil acidity more or less familiar to most of us is degrees of pH. In as simple terms as possible a pH rating is based on the concentration of hydrogen ions in solution: the higher the concentration the more acid the soil.

A neutral soil has a hydrogen ion concentration of one in ten million (i.e. 1:10,000,000, or ten to the power of minus seven). The figure seven is thus taken as the pH of soil which is neither acid nor alkaline. Most soils are more acid; their pH numbers go from about 7.5 down to about 3.5.

At 7.5 many flowering shrubs do well, but there is reduced availability of phosphate. The Erica family is unhappy; heathers, azaleas, rhododendrons will not grow. Nor will lupins or most lilies.

A pH of 6.5 is the gardener's ideal; optimum for most plants. At this degree of acidity all the mineral nutrients are easily available to their roots. At 6.0 phosphates begin to be bound up in the soil and potassium, calcium, magnesium and trace elements tend to be leached out. Fungi are happy but bacteria are less so.

At a pH of 5.5 nitrates are less available to most plants, and at 5.0 the evidence of problems becomes obvious. Roots tend to be stubby, short and often fanged. Phosphates are largely unavailable.

Extremely acid soil, with a pH of 4.0 or below, is only typical of heath and moorland. Most mineral nutrients become much more soluble and are liable to be washed out, while aluminium appears in harmful quantities. Bacteria and soil-dwelling animals are affected. Many flowering plants fail altogether, although the heaths and rhododendrons flourish – and so in many cases does the exceptionally tolerant common European oak.

Since the early experimental days six other elements have been found to be essential to plants, but they are only needed in minute traces. These 'trace' elements are iron, manganese, boron, copper, zinc and molybdenum. Lack of a trace element *could* be the problem with an ailing plant in your garden, but there are a hundred and one more likely problems to worry about first.

In practice, it is only the first three nutrient elements which need regular topping up, and that only where crops are being taken from the ground that are not returned to it.

The compost heap acts like the gardener's own cow, digesting his waste vegetable matter into a form the soil bacteria will enjoy. But they must be well digested, or rather rotted, or they will rob the soil of the nitrogen the roots are rooting for. Why is this? Because nitrogen is consumed in the process of decomposition. It takes nitrogen to release nitrogen.

ABOVE: *Legumes have nodules on their roots which contain bacteria that can short-cut the normal nitrogen cycle, 'fixing' nitrogen directly from the air without having to convert it first into ammonia, then nitrites, then nitrates. For this reason peas and beans are given first place in the vegetable garden rotation.*

ABOVE: *Such 'natural' or organic fertilizers as ground-up hoof and horn or bones, dried blood, hair or seaweed have been used for centuries. The first man to patent the chemical manufacture of fertilizers was Sir John Bennet Lawes (1814–1900) of Rothamsted in Hertfordshire. His experiments showed that ground bones did little good on alkaline soil unless treated with acid because their calcium phosphate is insoluble in water. He processed first bones then mineral phosphates from Spain and elsewhere into 'Superphosphate'.*

Compost is not only a way of returning to the soil what plants have taken out of it. Well-made compost improves the structure of all soils, lightening clay and giving substance to sand. The essentials of a compost heap are adequate air, moisture and nitrogen (food for the micro-organisms that do the work), and enough bulk of material to build up a high enough temperature to kill weed seeds. This last is vital: no one wants to return to the soil the seeds of all the weeds he has spent endless hours eliminating.

The most practical method for a small garden is to build a double enclosure with air vents in the sides, and preferably ducts for air underneath (which can be made of bricks on edge, or a layer of small branches). Each box should be at least 1m (3ft) square and high. Any animal or vegetable refuse can be put in. Ideally one whole box is filled at once, in 15cm (6in) layers of waste of different textures (e.g. grass mowings alternating with stalky stuff) with a sprinkling of 'activator', or nitrogenous fertilizer, in between. The heap is then thoroughly moistened and covered with a plastic cover or an old carpet.

It should take about a month in warm weather to heat up and cool down again. Another month or more of maturing, while the earthworms mix the compost up, is a good idea. Meanwhile waste can be accumulated in the second box for use the next time.

A well-run compost heap can return to the soil the nutrients removed in growing most ornamental plants. The kitchen garden is another matter. There plants are being force-fed to maximum fatness and ripeness, then taken away bodily and not returned. They can certainly benefit from fertilizers – the choice of the fertilizer depending on whether it is the leaves, the roots or the fruits of the plant that you intend to make a delicacy.

Compost or rotted manure are complete foods for the soil; they feed its structure as well as its chemistry. For those who have to do without them, there are alternatives – at a price: spent mushroom compost, even minced-up refuse from the municipal dump.

Fertilizers, as opposed to composts, act more or less directly on the plant. 'Balanced' garden fertilizers today are carefully designed mixtures of the essentials, with more than this element or that according to their purpose. The big three, N (nitrogen), P (phosphate) and K (potassium), are always included, and their proportions stated, always in the same order. Thus a tomato fertilizer might be N6:P5:K9, heavy on the nitrogen and potash for growth and fruit, while a chrysanthemum fertilizer would have more phosphates for flowers.

'National Growmore', the classic formulation for Britain's wartime vegetable gardeners, is still widely used and has the all-purpose formula 7:7:7 – that is seven parts in a hundred of each of N, P and K.

Gardeners without specialized knowledge do much better to stick to such brands rather than applying the particular fertilizers singly: they are powerful and quick-acting and can do more harm than good if they are overdone.

Some of the compound or balanced fertilizers are entirely mineral, inorganic or 'artificial'; some (the more expensive) are natural or organic; some are a mixture. Of the traditional organic fertilizers, most are the dried and ground-up remains of some form of animal life, from fish meal to dried blood. Seaweed is a more recent addition with valuable properties. But still Squire Lawes' old bonemeal is one of the most popular and generally useful in gardens. A handful scattered in the planting hole is the time-honoured formula. It contains a little nitrogen and a good deal of phosphate which it releases slowly to the great benefit of newly planted roots.

ROOTS, THE SOIL AND THE GARDENER

There is a crucial moment in the relationship of gardener and plant: the moment when he commits its roots to the soil. A gardener is constantly moving plants from one place to another when it is their nature, their very essence, to stay put. He pricks out seedlings from a seed tray when they have the merest thread of root, and he uproots well-grown trees with all he can manage of the ramifications of their roots to lug them to another station.

A large part of his success or failure depends on his care of the roots. However luxuriant the top, if the roots are mutilated it will wither away. If its roots are intact and well planted a flourishing top will follow.

The other vital factor is when he plants. His object must be to give the roots as long as possible to grow before the shoots start to make big demands on them.

Unlike the part of a plant above ground, which follows a precise plan of growth, roots are opportunists with no predisposition to one pattern. What is decisive is where they find the right combination of soil moisture, nutrients, and oxygen in a medium they can penetrate. Also unlike shoots, they grow all the year round if the soil is warm enough – above about 7°C (45°F).

A root bores through the soil by pushing a sort of warhead with an outer layer of expendable cells. The cells just behind the warhead are the ones that multiply to make it grow. As it bores the surface cells are left behind as lubricants to ease its passage through the ground.

But this is a soft and fragile instrument to contend with stones and solid clods. It will always take the easy path if there is one: an old worm-tunnel or the course of a former root that has died and rotted away. What it likes best is 'open' soil, airy and uncompacted, yet rich in humus to conserve water and nutrients.

No one could express it better than the seventeenth-century writer who said, 'Those that plant should make their ground fit [for rose trees] before they plant them, and not bury them in a hole like a dead dog. Let them have good and fresh lodgings suitable to their quality.'

Most plants get their first taste of soil in the potting shed – probably of a nursery. There is no question of it being ordinary soil. The nurseryman talks about his 'medium' or 'compost' (not to be confused with the produce of the compost heap). Ordinary soil would be broken down by the constant watering a pot needs. Potting compost is designed to drain fast and keep its structure. Free drainage, it cannot be said too often, is the most important thing of all. Hence the traditional crock over the hole at the bottom of the pot.

The ideal potting compost was standardized in the 1930s by England's John Innes Institute. It was based on a priceless material known as fibrous loam, made by cutting turves from good pasture and stacking them with strawy manure till the grass rotted, then sieving the result and sterilizing it with steam. Two parts of this with one of peat and one of 'sharp' sand or grit is the perfect light 'medium' for sowing seeds, combining the physical properties of water-retention and drainage in just the right proportions.

BELOW: *The essence of planting is to make complete and intimate contact between roots and soil, distributing the roots evenly and packing loose, well-worked soil among them. The hands are the ideal tool – but they need to be hard-wearing.*

For potting up cuttings and seedlings the mixture is made heavier: seven parts loam to three of peat and two of sand. Fertilizers and chalk are added according to the kind and maturity of plant.

The cost of making ideal loam is so high today that soilless composts are more commonly used; i.e. just peat and sand (1:1 for seeds, 3:1 for potting) or (particularly in the USA) vermiculite or perlite, heat-treated minerals with remarkable powers of absorbing and retaining both water and air. Such composts have no natural nutrient value at all, unlike loam, so whatever the plant needs must be added.

Any plant will grow happily in a pot until its roots have explored the whole volume of soil and extracted its nourishment. But then to keep it growing well, as opposed to becoming 'pot-bound' – a condition only desirable for permanently potted flowering plants – it must be 'potted on' into a bigger pot with more soil for its roots to exploit. Taking it out of its pot to see if its roots have filled it does it no harm. The way to do it is to tap the rim of the pot upside down on the edge of a table. If the roots are growing round and round it is time for a bigger pot.

Most nurseries sell their plants in pots (or 'containers' as they call them) so that the gardener gets them home with no disturbance to the roots. If the timing is right, and the roots have not outgrown the pot and started to spiral, this is the ideal arrangement. A containerized plant can be planted at any time (but preferably in damp weather) between spring and autumn. The essential is to prepare the ground over a much bigger area than the roots will immediately take up – say four times as big – making it as much like potting compost as possible: mixing the original soil with so much organic matter, sand and bonemeal that the roots will not know the difference. A thick layer of mulch over the soil will then keep weeds from taking advantage of the ideal conditions.

With bare-rooted plants the season is the first consideration. The ideal is for the plant to be dormant but for the soil to be warm enough for the roots to grow. In mild-winter areas this means autumn, as soon as the leaves fall. The roots will have most of the winter to expand ready for the big water-demands of spring.

Where the ground is either frozen or waterlogged in winter, though, the roots of a new plant may well be killed. It is better to delay planting until the ground warms up, even at the risk of having to water constantly in spring. Evergreens, which are never fully dormant, present the greatest problem. In mild areas September is probably the best time; the roots may get in as much as four months' growth before the ground becomes really cold. In harsh climates like New England, May is the month generally recommended.

Firm, careful, intimate planting is even more important when the roots are bare. Only by sifting fine soil down among the roots can you achieve the vital close contact. Bare roots can dry out almost instantly if they are exposed to sun or wind. Soak them well in water in advance, then keep them in a plastic bag until the actual moment of planting. Another trick is the old method of 'puddling in': coating the roots with mud by dipping them in a very wet soil-and-water mix before planting them. Planting in mud, of course, would be fatal as the roots would get no air.

The only satisfactory way with plants that have become seriously pot-bound is to treat them as bare-root plants, gently breaking up the soil-ball and pruning off any intractable big roots that still insist on spiralling. If this means unbalancing the plant by leaving more top than root, then the top must be proportionately reduced too by pruning.

The same basic principles apply to transplanting. Dig up as much of the roots as possible and get them as quickly as possible into a spacious hole full of a moist but open and permeable soil. Roots that are badly injured should be cut off above the wound; they will not recover. For this reason such fleshy-rooted plants as magnolias are particularly tricky to transplant at more than a modest size. Thick fleshy roots are brittle with relatively few branches. A large proportion of the root system is bound to be lost. Even fleshy rooted herbaceous plants such as peonies resent moving – whereas any plant with a dense mop of fibrous root can quite easily be unearthed intact. With all plants, stability in their new situation is essential; if the wind can rock them, or if frosts lift them, their roots will have difficulty taking hold. This is one reason why the best size of tree to plant in the long run is the little wispy thing called a 'maiden'.

Maidens need no staking, and start rooting faster than a bigger tree that has been checked by transplanting and lost part of its root structure. Within four years or so a maiden has often overtaken a tree planted as a 'standard' of five times the diameter, and is on the way to becoming a finer specimen. Apparently, the whipping movement of an unstaked little plant in the wind produces hormones that actively promote root growth, whereas a standard tree tied rigidly to a stake almost as tall as itself does not sway and roots only slowly.

The best stake for a standard tree is a relatively short one driven into the ground obliquely at 45° to the tree trunk and tied to it with a felt bandage at no higher than a third of the trunk height. This lets the crown sway and produce the root-stimulating hormone, while keeping the collar where it emerges from the soil unbudgeably firm.

Everything you plant, tree, shrub, or primrose, needs the soil, open, porous and friable though it be, pressed down firmly and authoritatively round its roots and about its neck.

BELOW: *The roots of a magnolia are thick, fleshy and brittle with relatively little branching, making it difficult to dig them up intact. Roots that are damaged should be cut off above the wound.*

SUNLIGHT IS ENERGY THERE ARE TWO PRINCIPAL

WAYS IN WHICH THE SUN'S ENERGY, ITS HEAT AND LIGHT, ARE PUT TO USE TO ACTIVATE WHAT

WOULD OTHERWISE BE A LIFELESS WORLD – AND PLANTS ARE INVOLVED IN BOTH OF THEM.

The first is the evaporation of water. Shortwave radiation (or heat for short) from the sun turns water to vapour. When it condenses and falls the solar energy that raised it is released to erode fields or drive turbines. The second is in the miraculous business of photosynthesis, in which plants feed on the sun's light.

It is a pity there is no pithy old Anglo-Saxon word for a process so central to life. The reconstituted Greek favoured by scientists makes everything sound equally unimportant and unintelligible. What sunlight does to plants is very important indeed, since all our lives depend on it. Directly for vegetarians, indirectly for the rest of us, plants and the sun together provide the world's entire diet. They also provide a large part of its oxygen.

Chlorophyll, the green pigment of plants, is the unique agent for this transaction. Its contribution is to convert the energy contained in light into the energy necessary for chemical change. The chemical change in question is the rearranging of the molecules of water and carbon dioxide to make oxygen and sugar. The sugar is stored energy – which is a way of defining food. Already we are in a tight conceptual corner. How does sugar store energy?

Energy is not in the constituents of sugar but in the force that holds them together. Carbon, hydrogen and oxygen are not sugar until their molecules are combined in the right pattern and proportion – $C_6H_{12}O_6$. But the force that combined them remains locked up until the process is reversed and the elements go their separate ways, or recombine in some other pattern. Then it is released to do other work – to make heat, for example, to build plant tissues or to move muscles.

Given the genius of chlorophyll, then, the three factors needed for photosynthesis are sunlight, water and carbon dioxide. Shortage of any of the three will slow the process down. Most plants grow better in sunlight than in shade.

On the other hand carbon dioxide is rarely in the air in such abundance that plants can take it for granted. Only three parts in a hundred of the normal atmosphere are this essential gas. Some plants can absorb it much more rapidly than others. The internal structure of the leaf is what makes the difference: some are adapted to take in and circulate gases quickly and easily – others are blessed with relatively sluggish diffusion.

The latter gain no benefit from floods of sunlight. Their rate of photosynthesis is governed by their intake of carbon dioxide. For them the shade is as good as the sun – better in fact, since they will not have to transpire so much. These are the shade-loving plants, adapted to life under the trees.

As far as the gardener is concerned the important thing is to give each plant the amount of sunlight or shade it needs. There are no general rules here – it is one of the many cases where a reference book is essential. But the point reference books cannot help with is the local intensity of sunlight. A plant that needs a degree of shade in the south of France or California would be happier in full sun in Scotland. Overmuch sun on plants not accustomed to it can create severe damage; scorching the leaves, and even the bark of trees. The south side of a tree (in the southern hemisphere the north side) has more sun-tolerant bark. In moving

FACING PAGE: *The sun is the ultimate source of all energy on earth. Green plants have the unique capacity to convert solar energy into food by photosynthesis. But they differ widely in the amount of sunlight they need, or can tolerate.*

ABOVE: *Lesser celandine bends to follow the path of the sun in a time-lapse photograph. It demonstrates the phototropism which in green plants is controlled by the blue-violet pigment riboflavin, absorbing violet light.*

mature trees it can be fatal to plant them the wrong way round – although bandaging the trunk can prevent sunstroke.

Conversely a light-demanding plant obliged to live in the shade will distort itself in strange ways to get as much light as it can. The urge to reach the light is known as phototropism. It manifests itself in drawn-out, spindly stems leaning towards wherever the strongest light may be, with leaves often ingeniously rearranged to catch as much of it as possible. The control mechanism in the plant is simple. Cells on the lighter side stay as they are, transferring all their energy to cells on the shady side. These grow faster and bend the plant until the illumination is equal all round. 'Drawn' or etiolated plants, making obvious efforts to reach the light, are common in crowded greenhouses and, indeed, in forests.

For plants not expressly designed for shade another effect of subdued light is to encourage leafage at the expense of flowers. If productivity in the sugar factory is low the tendency is to spend what stored energy there is on building more solar panels. It is when the balance swings the other way and the carbohydrate (or sugar) level is high that flower-buds are formed. Abundant sunshine one year can therefore have a noticeable effect on flower-production the next.

The human eye and the pigments of plants are strangely unanimous about what part of the wide range of electromagnetic radiation constitutes usable (to us, visible) light. It lies between violet and red, or, as radiation is measured, between 390 and 780 thousand millionths of a metre (a unit known as a nanometre). When sunlight passes through a prism it is separated into the familiar coloured bands of the rainbow, each representing a different wavelength of light. Plant pigments absorb and use all the visible spectrum except green, which is reflected. (Which is why plants are green). The different plant pigments, absorbing different wavelengths of light-energy, use them for different purposes.

The pale blue pigment phytochrome, absorbing red light, is responsible for starting both seed germination and flowering. Yellow-orange carotenoids, absorbing blue light, control such plant responses as leaf fall and the ripening of fruit.

Blue-violet riboflavin pigment, absorbing violet light, controls phototropism – the movement of the plant towards light. Chlorophyll absorbs blue and red light. A plant without chlorophyll, such as the leafless, thread-like 'dodder', a parasite on clover and thyme, cannot convert sunlight to energy.

Commercial chrysanthemum growers produce year-round flowering by manipulating the supply of light. The chrysanthemums are misled into 'thinking' the nights are short and flowering is consequently delayed. Growers activate the pigment phytochrome, which controls flowering, by using short periods of red light.

Plants are affected not only by the total amount of light received but by when it comes and for how long. We have gathered into our gardens plants from the low latitudes where days are nearly the same length all the year round (on the Equator all days and all nights last twelve hours) and plants from higher latitudes where a summer day, and a winter night, can be as long as twenty hours.

Since the growing season is the time of year when days are longer than nights, high-latitude plants need long periods of light (and are known as long-day plants). They may flower little, if at all, when grown far south of their natural homes. Plants from the hotter regions similarly need short days. The dahlia, which comes from Mexico, is an example of a short-day plant. It flowers after mid-summer, in the shortening days towards autumn. Long-day plants such as the delphinium tend to flower early and ripen their seed in the heat of the summer, 'knowing' that a northern winter lies ahead.

HOSTILE FORCES

A garden which is a battleground against the less amiable and cooperative forces of nature can scarcely be a source of serenity. The gardener must be a philosopher, accepting that he and his have a place in the cycle of life which nothing, or very little, can alter.

Everything that grows is food for something else. Innumerable hosts of predators, both animal and vegetable, are constantly at work, not only on our precious plants but on each other. The best any gardener can do is to referee the performance with a bias towards his own priorities. Using your wits and common-sense to harness the forces of nature, rather than confronting them, is the secret not only of success but of deep satisfaction.

There are certain precautionary measures all experienced gardeners take that can broadly be called cultural controls. A well-cultivated, well-fed garden is less prone to serious damage or disease than a half-starved one. In plants as in animals, general health and vitality is the first line of defence. The choice of plants can also help. Specialists are always more at risk from disease or specific pests, a wide range of kinds and species is an insurance policy. Some plants are inherently less prone to be eaten: rhododendrons, magnolias, weigelas and day-lilies apparently come into this category. On the whole, the more highly bred a plant is, the more susceptible it will be to disease – another argument in favour of natural species as opposed to garden varieties. More and more modern cultivars, however, have been bred to be disease- and pest-resistant.

Occasional cataclysmic diseases alter the whole face of a country. Dutch elm disease has proved the point over the last thirty years. So has the cypress disease which has devastated parts of Italy. Both are caused by fungi. In such cases there is little to be done. Strict hygiene and rapid surgery may help, but when a whole countryside is at risk philosophical patience is the only realistic response.

Nor can anything be done about the unpredictable haunting menace that can suddenly strike down mature plants. Again, fungi are usually the culprits. In Britain honey fungus is the one that causes most spines to creep. Many old gardens, old woodlands and orchards in which trees have lived and died have it lurking somewhere in their soil, particularly if the soil sometimes lies wet. It lives on dead roots and attacks live ones – usually with fatal results. You get no warning. Suddenly your cherry tree, or peony, or rose, or even daffodil, wilts and is mortally sick. When it is dead you will usually find, just under the bark at soil level, tell-tale black 'bootlaces' – the tentacles of the fiend. In the United States, verticillium wilt is regarded with similar dread, having no special predilections, except perhaps for young plants, and striking down anything from maples to tomatoes.

Coral spot fungus is another menace, though this at least you can see: tiny bright red pustules, at first on dead

BELOW: *The gardener has just as many allies as enemies among the fauna of his garden. The ladybird eating the greenfly is emblematic of the sort of natural balance a gardener should aim for as the ideal. Although reasonable control often means using poisons it is something to be avoided wherever possible.*

ABOVE: *The sweet-smelling fruiting bodies of* Armellaria mellea *are even edible. But honey fungus is one of the scourges most feared by European gardeners. Its black 'bootlace' filaments will probably already be invading the bark of this tree ready to kill it.*

wood, but soon encroaching on to live. Fireblight is another – though this time a bacterium rather than a fungus – specializing in such members of the rose family as hawthorns and pears, hitting them with what looks like a blow-torch attack. Silver leaf disease is another fungus with a taste for the same victims. None of these can be foreseen or guarded against, except by such commonsense general hygiene as burning rubbish, particularly dead twigs. Even protecting wounds and pruning cuts with fungicidal paint or tar seems to make no difference.

There is a more specific group of diseases, again mostly fungoid, that do the rounds of gardens where a particular plant grows. Hollyhock and snapdragon rusts are examples; blackspot on roses is another. The 'wilt' that kills clematis back to ground level is a fourth. Most gardeners are prepared to fight with regular spraying for plants as important as roses, and to be patient and try again with clematis, but there are other things to take the place of snapdragons, and indeed of most plants that have ineradicable problems. The best advice is to destroy them and plant something else.

The key question, of course, is to know if a sick plant is curable or not. If it merely looks ailing and unhappy, without any particular symptoms of blotched leaves or dying-back stems, it is worth looking for commonsense cultural reasons. Drought and water-logging are the first causes to eliminate. Look up the needs of the plant. Should it theoretically be happy where it is? Is it getting too much or too little sun? Is a more vigorous neighbour starving it? Is the soil suitable? If conditions seem to be right and the plant still reproaches you, your own temperament must decide whether to call in expert help or have done with it and make room for something new.

There are diseases – or perhaps conditions is a better word – that are so endemic in gardens that the only answer is to live with them. Powdery mildew is one. It is always ready to feed on plants when the temperature and humidity suit it. It weakens and disfigures the plants but seldom kills them, and can often retire for long periods. On balance it does not matter all that much. The less conspicuous downy mildew is a more serious complaint, crippling and occasionally killing the plant.

At least with fungi we can, if we want, go in to the attack. There are systemic fungicides which, sprayed on the leaves, circulate in the sap and attack the fungus from inside. There are also the traditional sulphur dust and Bordeaux mixture to puff or spray which act on contact.

Virus diseases, often transmitted to plants by aphids and other insects that feed on sap, are a problem the gardener can do little about but burn the infected plants. The symptoms of virus disease are puckered and distorted leaves, or light green or yellow areas, often mottled and known as 'mosaics', or sometimes stunting and malformation of the whole plant.

Viruses are minute living particles, too small to be seen through a light microscope, which depend on a host cell for existence and multiplication. As the host cell divides more viruses are created so that soon the whole plant is infected.

The only way to rid infected but desirable plants of virus disease is to make them grow very fast in a hothouse, then remove the growth tip, or meristem, and induce it to root (in an agar jelly). With luck it will have outstripped the spread of the virus and the new plant will be free of infection.

As to the fauna of the garden that we regard as pests, there are said to be twenty-seven thousand species of insect alone that do damage, beside which you can line up the deer, rabbits, squirrels, slugs, snails and birds. The gardener stands no realistic chance of combatting them. The modern method is to urge them to fight each other.

The whole thrust of gardening today is to try to find natural agencies to fight on the gardener's side. The organic gardening movement began to gather pace in the 1970s. Its first tenet is that nature has a remedy for most ills which will only be hindered by the use of chemicals. The gardener becomes the general in a natural battle, marshalling the relevant predators and parasites to fight his enemies.

Two highly successful examples of such biological control are the tiny wasp *Encarsia formosa* and the mite *Phytoseiulus persimilis* which, introduced into a greenhouse or conservatory in spring, respectively decimate the populations of whitefly and red spider mite. Another is a little 'braconid' wasp that lays its eggs in cabbage white butterflies with fatal results.

Integrated pest management is the catch-phrase for a range of measures including such as these, but also some specialized narrow-spectrum chemicals, and all sorts of physical controls, some natural, some not – from introducing ladybirds to eat aphids and scale insects to grease-banding fruit trees against winter moths, or simply squashing greenfly with finger and thumb.

In a small garden there is no need to tolerate the obviously damaging insects. Caterpillars that chew leaves are easily picked off (though you may be destroying a beautiful butterfly) and – if you are squeamish – it is no great chore to take a puffer of pyrethrum dust with you of an evening to discourage the aphids.

In a bigger garden the simple and natural recourse is to encourage birds. Mischievous they may be, and maddening when they strip your pyracantha of its brilliant harvest just as it starts to glow, but few birds are all bad. Provide plenty of evergreen shrubby cover, nestboxes if necessary, food and water and the birds will repay you by eating up to four times their own weight in insects a day.

Birds will inevitably attack your greens, flower buds, seeds and fruit as well. It is just not possible to keep them bodily off each tempting plant in turn. But there are ruses to distract and discourage them. No bird likes running into an obstacle that it cannot see. A few threads of black cotton stretched between twigs can be as effective as complete netting in protecting, for example, primroses, which sparrows in particular love to peck.

You cannot cotton a whole cherry tree to keep the bullfinches or sparrows from stripping the buds, but try smearing some of the twigs near the buds with fruit-tree grease. Your approach is very much a personal matter. I do not shoot or poison anything except grey squirrels – and slugs. Yes, I put down slug bait where I see they have been nibbling. But even with slugs there is a gentler (if less certain) alternative: a ring of sharp grit around the plant you want to protect. It hurts their feet.

BELOW: *Virus infection often shows as discoloration or distortion of leaves. This cucumber mosaic virus is typical, and is most often spread by aphids which transfer infection from plant to plant on their mouthparts. There is no cure: the plant will need to be dug up and burned.*

PLANTS
AND THE
GARDENER

IF IN THE END THERE IS NOT VERY MUCH WE CAN DO ABOUT THE
CLIMATE OR THE WEATHER, AND ONLY A LIMITED AMOUNT WE CAN
DO ABOUT THE SOIL IN THE GARDEN
(EXCEPT TO CHOOSE PLANTS THAT SUIT
IT), AT LEAST THE PLANTS THEMSELVES
ARE MORE OR LESS UNDER OUR CONTROL.

THE SIZE, THE SHAPE, THE HEALTH
AND THE FRUITFULNESS OF WHAT WE
GROW NEED NOT BE LEFT TO CHANCE AT
ALL. EVEN BEFORE WE BEGAN TO UNDER-
STAND THE MECHANISMS OF PLANTS,
SO MANY GENERATIONS HAD WATCHED
THEM AND EXPERIMENTED WITH THEM THAT A VAST BODY OF
HIGHLY EFFECTIVE INSTRUCTIONS HAD BEEN BUILT UP. ➤

ABOVE: *The bright colours of new bark:*
willow can be pollarded, dogwoods
coppiced to the ground in spring to make a
brilliant display the following winter.

Our great grandfathers, who had scarcely heard of fertilizers and never heard of hormones, raised flowers and ripened fruit as fine as any today.

But today we have the advantage and fascination of knowing to a greater degree not just how, but why plants react to our attentions in the way they do. To understand their miraculous complexities is not just interesting in itself. It allows us to interpret the textbooks and judge for ourselves whether the conventional cultural methods make sense and why. Not surprisingly they usually do. On the other hand they are based on certain assumptions that may or may not apply – at least to you in your garden.

An obvious example is the routine instruction concerning how far apart to plant your vegetables. If a certain amount of light, water and nutrients are available the instructions can be used either to make a few big plants or more smaller ones. Generally horticultural convention is to go for the big ones – in the teeth of gastronomic good sense that says plant them as close together as you like, and pick them before they notice.

Gardeners, particularly new gardeners, are usually ready to accept – indeed clamour to be told – the wisdom of the ancients on precisely how, and particularly when, to plant and sow and prune. The drawback to any such information, couched in exact terms, is that it can only ever be an average estimate over scores of soils and millions of microclimates. Reading and re-reading the textbooks is no substitute for a clear understanding of the principles, and a minute observation of the particulars. If you examine a plant closely, and use your common sense, the plant's health or debility, like the condition of the soil, is written all over it.

The principles we are concerned with here are how plants work and can be controlled and multiplied, but also with the criteria by which we judge them, how they are named, classified and sub-classified, where they come from and how they have been improved in cultivation.

A clear majority of the plants in most gardens are to some extent man-made, or at least man-influenced creations. As soon as man started to cultivate plants he instinctively selected the better ones; the better ones bred together and a whole separate race of 'garden plants' began.

Were it not for the endless variety of new species which have been introduced from distant countries over the last four hundred years the process of selection and crossing among a limited range would presumably have gone so far that true species, or 'wild plants', would be, by now, virtually extinct in gardens; as they are, for example, in great swathes of China.

Happily we have still nowhere near mastered even the species that have been introduced to gardens from all over the world – let alone comprehended the contribution they may have to make in breeding even better plants. What is more there are still thousands more species and varieties to be collected, or in many cases re-collected because they have been lost in gardens for lack of knowledge of how to grow them. There is every reason, therefore, to hope for (and demand) better and more varied plants all the time.

PREVIOUS SPREAD
(LEFT): *The author's garden in spring,*
the busiest time of year for the gardener;
(RIGHT): *There is pleasure in a*
well-kept armoury of tools.

HOW TO LOOK AT A PLANT
IF CONTROL IS
THE ESSENCE OF GARDENING, THE ESSENCE OF PLANTSMANSHIP IS OBSERVATION. AS ONE WHO WAS
HABITUALLY LAZY IN LOOKING UNTIL HE TOOK UP GARDENING I CAN SPEAK WITH FEELING ON THE
PLEASURE OF LEARNING TO OBSERVE.

It is too easy merely to recognize plants, mentally ticking them off as familiar or unfamiliar. Perhaps we look at the unfamiliar just enough to recognize it next time. But we do justice neither to the new nor the old. We seldom settle down quietly to study something – even things we find beautiful and satisfying. Even flowers.

Pick up an old Herbal and taste the freshness of clear observation in new-minted language. 'The bulbous violet riseth out of the ground, with two small leaves flat and crested, of an overworne green colour, between the which riseth up a small and slender stalk of two hands high, at the top of which cometh forth of a skinny hood a small white floure of the bignesse of a violet, compact of six leaves, three bigger and three lesser, tipped at the points with light greene . . .' Gerard had gazed long and lovingly at the snowdrop. He took nothing for granted.

I have found that a good way to get to know flowers is to pick them and keep them close to me for a few days in a vase. The vase on the kitchen table and the one on my desk always contain flowers (or other parts of plants) that I want to be better acquainted with. This approach is particularly good for watching the evolution from bud to flower. I do not think I would have noticed in the garden, for example, that the knapweed's elaborate black-fringed bud holds only a little embryo of its wide, starry thistle: it must grow and spread its ring of fine trumpets outside the bud. Or that the coneflower starts with a ring of insignificant greenish petals not worth the name, that gradually lengthen and brighten until they surround the darkening cone with a corolla of yellow as brilliant as a buttercup. Or that the whole flamenco flower of the oriental poppy is folded complete in the bud like a parachute.

Perhaps the best of all ways of learning observation is to draw. Best not only because you have to look and look again (there are no hiding places for ignorance between pencil and paper) but also because drawing demands a more or less methodical approach: a general sizing up of the whole subject followed by more and more minute inspection down to the finest details.

Without a measure of method you are immediately lost in the infinity of variables. Learning to look at plants means learning to analyse them, however informally. It means first of all taking in the obvious points that distinguish, say, a shrub with permanent wood from a bulb with long, smooth leaves springing straight from the ground. Then the indication of a plant's nature and temperament in where it is growing. Is it luxuriating in damp, leafy soil and shade – then surely it is a woodland plant – or happily cooking on a hot gravel bank? Or perhaps looking miserable and seemingly out of place in its garden situation?

BELOW: *John Gerard (1545–1612) is the most famous of the English herbalists, though more on account of his style than his scholarship. He was an unblushing plagiarist.*

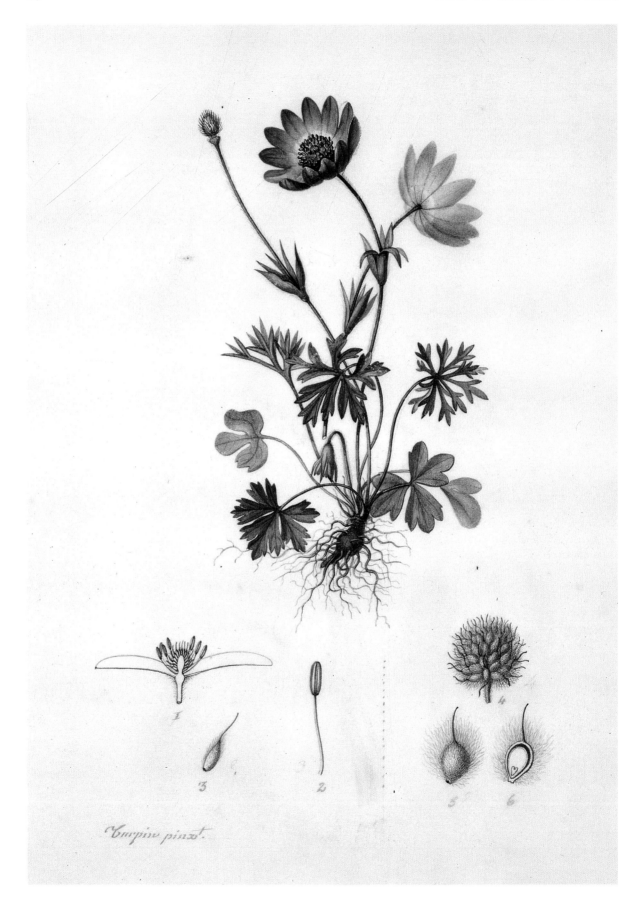

Turpin pinxt.

The nature and design of the flowers is the principal clue to a plant's relationship with other plants. In themselves the flowers may be the main attraction – or scarcely visible. At all events they deserve the closest appraisal of all.

The parts of a flower are set out on page 60. It is often not at all obvious at first which names to give to which parts. But a flower is a functional device, and a methodical examination, picturing how it works – what happens when it is pollinated; where the ovules are and how they will develop into seed – is fascinating, revealing, and fixes that flower in your mind for ever. When you meet its relations, moreover, you will probably recognize them as belonging to the same family.

Yet there are more basic points to consider. The pattern made by the buds, and hence the leaves and side shoots, is one of the most characteristic and consistent features, always falling into one of three categories, and usually the same for all the members of one plant family.

Either the buds are opposite each other in pairs, or staggered (alternate) along the shoots, or they are in whorls of three or more. Out of this pattern and the relative size, strength and stiffness of the shoots or stems arises the plant's general stance or 'habit'. Two plants, for example, may reach the same height, but one of them does it on tiptoe, the other droopingly, with stems long enough to reach twice as high but without the rigidity to support them. The texture of the whole plant, and the way the light strikes it, also largely arise from the more or less intricate pattern of leaves and shoots.

In comparison, the actual shape and colour of the leaves, though nearly always beautiful and interesting in themselves, are so variable that there is much less to be deduced from them. Deviations of leaf colour can apparently be almost at random. It seems to make little difference to some plants whether the basic green is suffused with red, or tinted blue, or variegated with yellow. Leaf shapes often have strong family resemblances. The maples are an obvious case. But if you were given a vine leaf, or the leaf of a Japanese anemone, to mention only two, you might think they were maple leaves. For that matter there is a maple with leaves just like a hornbeam. Chance seems to play a large part in leaf shapes.

Leaf texture has more messages than leaf shape. It is fairly easy to tell which leaves are evergreen, even in summer when all leaves are new. They have a harder feel, often a shiny wax-like upper surface and a more or less hairy, felty or scurfy underside. Among the many hundred rhododendrons the nature of the leaf surface is a main diagnostic feature. Both the hard waxiness and the soft hairiness are adaptations against water loss in whatever season, be it summer or winter.

Hairy leaves are also common among deciduous plants, but mainly in those from hot climates that face drought during their growing season. Most of the popular silver-leaved plants are examples. Not surprisingly, therefore, they want bright sun and sharp drainage in the garden too.

With closer observation and sharper focus less obvious points of detail become equally interesting. There are sometimes little tufts of leaf hairs just in the angle of the veins under the leaf. Some of the adjuncts to the basic stem-leaf-flower pattern can be as arresting as the main design: long, leafy calyces (the protective outer covering of the flower bud) or prominent prickly stipules (protective casing for the leaf bud) can give character to a plant. Even the shoot itself can be round or four angled, smooth or warty or furry, long jointed or short jointed, and almost any colour under the sun.

The need for order in this jungle of distracting detail is as clear as the difficulty of finding any. Botany, or more strictly speaking plant taxonomy, is the science

FAR LEFT: *The anemone opposite comes from what was perhaps the supreme period of flower-painting: early 19th-century France. Redouté is the most famous name of the school. This work by his contemporary Turpin shows that he had his rivals in exquisite portraiture.*

of classifying and naming the plant world. Gardeners usually steer clear of it as far as they are able. It is certainly not essential to them. They have their own ways of grouping plants by their garden uses. Most of this book reviews garden plants horticulturally, not botanically.

Yet it must be said that botany illuminates our understanding of plants in such a way that keen gardeners eventually find themselves using its methods and terminology. It also dictates, inescapably, what plants are called.

Faced with an unknown, unlabelled plant there are three things you can do. You can take it to an expert. You can flick through the pages of a picture book until you find the plant that looks most like it – a highly unreliable method – or you can begin to botanize, just as you would begin to draw, methodically and analytically. If you can get as far as deciding on the genus: it is a tulip, say, or a cypress, botanists have devised an elimination game known as a 'key' which, if it is well done, practically makes the plant analyse itself. Using keys does not come easily at first to most gardeners. Nothing is worse than pursuing a badly-written one (and there are plenty) to no avail. If possible find a botanically-minded friend to help lead you through a few keys. Practice brings proficiency – and proficiency great satisfaction.

THE LANGUAGE OF BOTANY

The jargon of any profession can be provoking to anyone who feels excluded by it. A botanical description is so packed with trade terms of Greek and Latin derivation that most gardeners feel repulsed. Yet the jargon is an essential short-hand to prevent it becoming impossibly long-winded. Good botanists turn to it as little as possible, using everyday speech and imagery wherever they can. As George Bentham, in his introduction to the standard nineteenth-century British flora universally known as 'Bentham and Hooker', said: 'The aptness of a botanical description, like the beauty of a work of imagination, will always vary with the style and genius of the author.'

The only reason for a gardener to learn more than a few common botanical terms is to give him access to the more complete reference books, which he will need if he starts on the seductive path of specialization.

As an example of the genre, this is how Hortus Third, the authoritative American dictionary of cultivated plants, describes the common English primrose:

'To 6 in.; lvs. oblanceolate to obovate, to 10 in. long, tapering to petiole, wrinkled, irregularly toothed; fls yellow, purple or blue, ½ in. across, solitary, on pedicels to 6 in. long, scape lacking. Spring. Europe.'

15cm (6in), in other words, is the overall height; the leaves are up to 25cm (10in) long, tapering to the stalk (peti-ole) end. Oblanceolate and obovate are the extremes of a variable more or less boat-like outline. The pedicels are the flower stalks. They would normally be expected to grow from a central stem or 'scape' – which the primrose apparently does not have.

BELOW: How would you describe a common primrose? Even the greatest botanists cannot agree on the language to use, or the precise construction of the plant.

To confirm Bentham's remark that botany is not an exact science it is interesting to see that Bentham and Hooker's account of the primrose disagrees with this American account. 'If closely examined,' they say, 'the pedicels will, however, be seen really to spring from an umbel, of which the common stalk is so short as to be concealed by the base of the leaves.'

Who are we to believe? Gerard's Herbal is no help. All he says is 'the common whitish yellow field primrose needeth no description'.

I am inclined to put my faith in Bentham and Hooker, if only because Hortus Third claims there is a blue primrose. But what clearer lesson could there be of the need to examine plants closely for yourself?

A DIGRESSION ON NAMES

It is a source of constant inconvenience and irritation to gardeners that they often do not know, and almost certainly cannot pronounce, the names of some of their most cherished plants.

ABOVE: *The Swedish naturalist Linnaeus, or Carl von Linné (1707–78) revolutionized the science of naming and classifying natural objects by his sheer industry and application. No one before him had ever collected such a vast array of specimens – he had twelve thousand plants – and given them accurate descriptions and concise two-word names, embodying their relationships as far as he understood them. Such a work, published as* Species Plantarum *in 1753, immediately and inevitably became the standard reference book. Its system of keying names to dried specimens over the botanist's signature (plants named by Linnaeus are signed 'L') is followed by taxonomists to this day.*

The problem is that most plants have no genuine vernacular common names. There is a safe area of old favourites and what are virtually man-made garden plants: varieties of rose or potato or dahlia or lettuce. The American habit is to concoct a phoney 'common' name for every plant, however uncommon. The result is a mass of banal and unmemorable, not to mention confusing, names of no general validity. But in the end Latin is unavoidable to anyone who has ambitions beyond the most limited and humdrum range. And botanists are not generally given to letting considerations of simplicity or euphony stand between them and proliferating polysyllables. Worse still 'they', the botanists, have been given power over us to change names, apparently at random. Some well-known plants have as many aliases as a Mafioso. To not-very-experienced gardeners names are a serious disincentive to branching out and getting more unusual and interesting plants.

The man who crystallized ideas about how natural objects could be concisely named and arranged in some sort of order of relationships was the great Swedish naturalist Linnaeus. Linnaeus made an immense collection of plants and other objects (his specimen plants still exist at the Linnaean Society in London) and catalogued them with concise descriptions in what immediately became essential reference books.

His greatest single contribution to modern method was almost incidental to his work. He was the first naturalist (in his *Species Plantarum*, published in 1753) to apply a binominal or two-word name systematically to every object in his collection. Like other naturalists before him he gave a concise Latin description as the full name of each plant, but he prefaced each one of his twelve thousand specimens with the name of its genus and species; as it were its surname and given name.

All modern taxonomy revolves around this simple notion. Linnaeus certainly did not invent it. It is already there in such names as, for example, barn owl and brown owl, or for that matter armchair and dining chair. What was new was the discipline of finding a unique binominal for each plant and, as it were, registering it by attaching it to a particular specimen for reference. He added his signature to the description and published it, locked away the specimen, and that was that; the plant was officially, finally, universally named, once and for all.

But why are two words needed to identify a particular plant – and for that matter why are they enough? The answer lies in the radical concept that the species is the basic unit of identity.

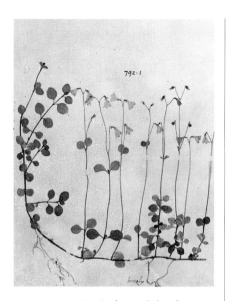

ABOVE: *Each named plant has a type specimen, locked away dried in a herbarium. This is Linnaeus's own specimen of the plant called* Linnaea borealis *– a woodland creeper.*

When we speak of a species we mean a group of similar plants (or animals) that live together in nature, breed together, and produce offspring consistently like themselves. Genetic stability is proof of the integrity of the unit; it says that this is as far as evolution has travelled along this particular path.

When we speak of a genus we mean a group of such species, consistently different in detail, not normally interbreeding, but usually linked in a fairly obvious way. If we are shown a new rose we will know at once that it is a rose, even if we have not seen that particular species before. These two broad categories of similarity have been recognized since ancient times.

A more searching scrutiny of the natural world has also suggested (in the first place to Aristotle) that there are broader groups and deeper relationships to be found. There is no lack of ways of classifying anything. You could make a list of plants with yellow flowers or heart-shaped leaves and have a system of a sort. But it would prove nothing because it would be limited to the characteristic you happened to choose. You could neither deduce nor predict anything from it. Aristotle guessed that there is a natural order of relationships where everything has a place. There was no clue, though, where to start looking for it.

By the late seventeenth century the botanist Pierre Magnol of Montpellier, whose name is remembered in the magnolia, had proposed the word 'family' for a group comprising more than one genus with clear common factors not quite distinct or constant enough to unite them.

Linnaeus took a step further in looking for the elusive 'natural order'. He classified plants by their sexual characteristics: number of stamens, ovaries, and so forth. His instinct was right, yet he admitted his system was artificial and would be superseded when the key came to light.

What natural links he did see he incorporated into a 'fragment of a natural system'. So far as it goes it still holds good. Taxonomists who followed him built on it, until by the middle of the nineteenth century most of the genera of flowering plants had been assigned to families. The families were generally named after their best-known genus with the suffix '-aceae'. The family of the roses and their relations thus became the 'Rosaceae'. For old times' sake some of the earliest families to be recognized and named were left with the names they had first been given – examples are the Compositae, the Umbelliferae and the Cruciferae, whose family names describe the composite, umbrella-like and cross-shaped nature of their respective flowers.

Yet still the key, the link (if any) between genus and genus, between family and family, was unguessed at. It was left to Charles Darwin to supply it: plants are alike because they have common ancestors. Darwin wrote: 'All true classification is genealogical . . . Community of descent is the hidden bond which naturalists have unconsciously been seeking.'

Gardeners' interest in classification, however, far from wanting to chase relationships further and further back into history, lies in precisely the other direction.

For gardeners the species is normally the biggest unit of interest. What concerns them more are the minutiae of variations within species – whether they arise in the wild, in which case they are known as varieties, or in gardens. A gardener's variety – a double-flowered petunia in a bed of single ones, shall we say, or a purple-headed cauliflower – is not a 'variety' but a 'cultivated variety' (for which a botanical conference in Stockholm in 1950 adopted the graceless name of 'cultivar').

To press home the point that a cultivar, however interesting, is a creature of a lower order of importance than a naturally occurring variety, the International

LEFT: *The English bluebell exemplifies the disconcerting way well-known plants can change names repeatedly. As a widespread European native it has long had many local names. In the first wave of classification, English hyacinth was translated into Latin, followed by a brief description. Gerard, in 1597, called it* Hyacinthus anglicus *'for that it is thought to grow more plentifully in England than elsewhere'.*

Linnaeus accepted the old idea that it was a hyacinth, but changed the specific name to non-scriptus *('not before described' or 'unmarked' – a sideways reference to the youth called Hyacinth in Greek mythology).*

With advancing botanical knowledge the genus Scilla, *bluebells included, was separated from hyacinth. Then it was noticed that* Scilla *keep their bulb from year to year while the bluebell renews it, so a new genus,* Endymion, *was created. Finally in 1934 the botanist Chouard rediscovered the name* Hyacinthoides, *coined in 1759 and since abandoned. By the law of priorities this was the correct name.*

The finale (so far) of the bluebell story could be described as a taxonomic cop-out. By applying the strict laws of priority they are now Hyacinthoides non-scripta. *But even botanists sometimes have hearts. Everyone prefers the name* Endymion, *which was the name of the woodland lover of the huntress Diana. The R.H.S. Dictionary Supplement says: 'it is hoped that the better known generic name* Endymion *will be officially conserved'. Rules are made to be broken, even in botany.*

Rules of Nomenclature decree that cultivars must not be given names in Latin, but must have obviously modern 'fancy' names.

Thus, for example, one of the best autumn-colouring maples from Asia Minor, *Acer tataricum*, has a variety with lobed leaves in Russia which is known as *Acer tataricum* var. (for 'variety') *torminaloides*. But a purple form of the Norway maple, selected by some misguided nurseryman in a row of green ones he was growing from seed, has to be called *Acer platanoides* 'Crimson King'. The former is a variety; the latter a cultivar.

The family is divided into genera, genera into species, species into (botanical) varieties and (horticultural) cultivars. The species is locked away in its herbarium with its name, description and the signature of Linnaeus, or whichever later botanist named it, attached. Why then are gardeners constantly being told that the name of a plant they have used all their lives is wrong and must be changed?

It can happen for one of two reasons. One is the application of the law of priority, which says that whoever published the name of a plant first with a correct Latin description was right. In many cases more than one botanist, perhaps in different countries, described plants within a few years of each other. Subsequent research unfortunately often discovers that we have been using a second or third name, which we are sternly – and perhaps not unfairly – told to change to the earlier model. The law must be applied consistently.

The other reason is simply that botanists, no doubt with the best motives and after countless sleepless nights, change their minds – usually about whether a number of species should be 'split' into different genera or 'lumped' in the same. So long as botanists delve deeper and deeper into plant relationships gardeners will have to write new labels and unlearn old names.

But botanists in turn have to accept that to split such a favourite as Chrysanthemum into four different genera, all with unfamiliar names (it happened in 1990) constitutes a high degree of provocation.

HOW PLANTS WORK WHEN IT COMES TO THE WAY THEY

FUNCTION. ALL PLANTS – AT LEAST ALL GREEN PLANTS – ARE ON COMMON GROUND.

Through the agency of the chlorophyll in their leaves they combine water from the ground with carbon dioxide in the air. In doing so they trap and store some of the sun's energy. Using that energy they build more roots, stems and leaves to do more of the same.

After a certain time they reach maturity; the age of reproduction. They go on producing leaves, but now they channel some of their accumulated energy into making sexual organs – their flowers. The function of flowers is to produce fertile seeds. A seed is a small store of energy converted into food, with a set of instructions as to how to become another plant.

In a nutshell, this is plant life. The precise design of the mechanism is decided by the lottery of genetics. Every time a flower is fertilized by pollen from another there is a new combination of genes which could lead to a better plant next time. The management of the routine, however, is entrusted to hormones – tiny particles of protein produced on genetic instructions to travel as chemical messengers through the plant, causing this part to grow or that to stop growing, this to produce a leaf bud, that a flower.

Plants are master chemists: they use sugar made by photosynthesis for instant energy; convert it to starch for storage, or to more complex molecules like cellulose – the basis of all solid tissue in the plant.

Take a daffodil. The sugar made in its long leaves is transferred in sap down to the plant's headquarters, the bulb underground, and distributed, through the diminutive central stem in its heart, into thick fleshy storage organs, the scales of the bulb, which are also the leaves for the following year.

In an oak tree, to take a very different instance, part of the sugar being produced by the leaves may undergo a chemical transformation into lignin, the solid matter that stiffens the cells of wood. Another part might go as starch into an acorn to be the initial energy supply for the next generation – or even into a pollen grain to be cast on the wind as the tree dutifully strives to reproduce its kind.

The principal organs of all plants are relatively few, and all the same. Apart from the flower (itself the most complicated structure) they are the leaves, the stem,

BELOW: *Auxin is the plant hormone principally involved in opening flowers in response to temperature and light. Warmth makes the inner side of the tulip petal grow faster. In crocuses cold reverses the process.*

the buds (which are future leaves or stems in embryo) and the roots, linked together by the vascular system, or plumbing.

The plumbing has two jobs to do. The first is to move water and minerals – raw materials for photosynthesis – up from the roots to the leaves. The second is to redistribute the energy-rich sap – and other finished products – to wherever the plant needs them.

There must therefore be two separate sap-flows in all plants: one up and one down. The mechanism for achieving this is ingenious. It consists of a single layer of cells, from which all increase in the girth of the plant takes place.

This vital one-cell skin, which in woody plants lies beneath the bark, is called the cambium layer (*Cambium* in Latin means exchange). It simultaneously produces one type of cells for the upward stream, another type for the downward one, and more of the same to add to itself.

The cells produced by the cambium on its outer side are known as phloem. Those on the inner side, lying between the central core of the plant, or pith, and the cambium, are called xylem. Xylem forms the upward plumbing to the leaves and aerial parts, the phloem is the return pipe carrying the fuel supply – and a range of other extraordinary products of the plant's chemistry that are stored mainly in the cells of the pith. These include sugar-derived chemicals that are best described as natural disinfectants.

ABOVE: *According to the latest research, the branches of trees should be sawn off to leave the natural 'collar' from which they grow, but no 'stub' outside it. The fungicidal wound paint you see here is unnecessary: the sap contains everything needed to heal the wound.*

Knowledge of these natural disinfectants has radically altered thinking about how plants react to wounding. The understanding that plants produce a range of chemicals that give them the power to heal themselves has recently turned the science of pruning on its head.

For a gardener the most relevant application of this discovery is that a branch should never be cut flush to the trunk, but cut to leave its 'collar' intact. Cambial cells in the collar grow over to seal the wound, and the collar itself is a site of great concentration of natural disinfectants. Wound paint is more harmful than helpful since it interferes with the healing process. The prophet of this new approach is a New Hampshire biologist and plant pathologist called Alex Shigo, in his book *A New Tree Biology*. Shigo is to be read for his passionate involvement with trees, leading to an almost mystical understanding of them. He himself has sliced thousands of trees lengthways with his chainsaw – the only way, he says, of seeing how trees heal their very frequent wounds.

His most important finding is that trees compartmentalize damage by moving chemicals to form protection zones. He has found, for example, that when an

ABOVE: *A branch of a Riesling grape-vine cut through in spring shows the sap rising in the inner xylem wood, surrounded by the cambium layer (too thin to discern) and the outer phloem, beneath the bark, in which the sap descends.*

open wound allows decay into a tree it is only the wood immediately surrounding the wound that suffers; all further growth is sealed against decay by the tree's defence mechanisms.

Our understanding of the control mechanism of plants and the part played by hormones (with such names as auxins, giberellins and kinins) is fairly recent, and still by no means complete. The first growth-controlling hormone to be discovered was named auxin using the Greek word *auxe* for 'increase' – the same root as in, for example, auxiliary.

It has been found that auxin is produced in the growing tips of plants and distributed from there via the sap back through the stems to the root. The concentration of auxin is always highest near the growth point, in the region where cells are dividing and active growth is going on.

Each part of the plant, it seems, has a different optimum auxin level; the level decreasing as it gets further from the growing tip. The main stem needs most; secondary or lateral stems a good deal; the buds less and the roots least of all. A higher level has an inhibiting effect on growth.

If the normal balance is upset by removing the leading shoot, the main growth point and source of auxin, the auxin level in the whole plant is lowered. The lateral stems find the new level to their liking and push on; at the same time the buds are favoured, and some of them will probably open.

This is the reason for the fact, known to gardeners since Adam, that pinching off the growing tips of, for example, a chrysanthemum, stimulates its buds to break and its branches to grow bushy.

In due course the newly-stimulated growth points themselves produce enough auxin to establish their dominance over the rest of the plant. In some plants, with naturally high auxin levels, this 'apical dominance' is obvious. Christmas trees are spire-like for this reason: so much auxin is made by the leader that all the other branches are suppressed to become mere side-shoots in comparison.

Too much light apparently destroys auxins. The control mechanism for phototropism (the bending of plants towards light) depends on there being less auxins on the sunny and more auxins on the shaded side of the growth point, causing the cells to grow faster on that side.

Gravity also affects the distribution of auxins. They sink to the bottom of whatever cell they find themselves in. In the case of roots gravity concentrates the auxins on the lower side, encouraging the upper side to grow, bending the top downwards. In the case of branches there is also more auxin on the lower side, but here it has a positive effect, promoting growth to bend the branch upwards.

Given the basic genetic programme that tells the cells to form the parts of, shall we say, an onion rather than an oak, all the decisions about the order of priorities are taken by hormones reacting to simple physical laws.

CONTROLLING GROWTH

Once having grasped how a plant works and what will be the next step in its routine, the gardener is in a position to anticipate and intercept its growth – to bend it (within reason) to his will.

It is not too difficult for the specialist to know every mood and quirk of his sweet peas or his roses. To carry in your head the timings and inclinations of every plant in a considerable mixed collection is quite another matter. Here, as in so many aspects of gardening, only the gardener's temperament can decide whether he rushes neurotically from reference book to reference book or settles down to use his common sense. As Christopher Lloyd so wisely says in *The Well-Tempered Garden*, 'the right time to do a job is when you have the time to do it properly.'

There are not many plants we grow in gardens that are left entirely to their own devices. Naturalized bulbs and wild flowers are one common case, trees another – but more because they are out of easy reach than because pruning would not improve them. In most cases the gardener keeps sticking his oar in and taking away the plant's initiative. The essence, after all, is control – whether it is mowing lawns, force-feeding vegetables, trimming hedges, disbudding chrysanthemums or pruning fruit trees.

The natural plant has a balanced programme that allows so much growth for roots, so much for shoots, flowers and fruit. It is not so much a question of harmonious government as equal competition between the parts.

The gardener's object, in each case, is to maximize the aspect of the plant that made him choose it. If it is the leaves he is interested in (as with lettuces) he will do his best to prevent it flowering. If (as with a fruit tree) flowers are the object he will discourage strong young leafy shoots and encourage the little spurs of old wood that bear flower buds. Experience shows that if a lettuce is grown fast, without check and with plenty of moisture, flowers will be slow in coming. It also shows that occasional hard pruning in winter encourages long leafy shoots on trees, whereas regular light pruning, especially in summer, provokes an apple tree into forming flower buds. So the lore and skills of gardening were moulded

ABOVE: *Dead-heading roses, or removing the stem that has flowered as far back as the next vigorous breaking bud, is a form of summer pruning.*

BELOW: *In Japan the shaping of plants by pinching out growth tips is applied to many things from chrysanthemums to tall-growing pine trees.*

by generations of trial and error long before anyone understood the physical and chemical principles behind them.

We now know that the principles are the same whether we are dealing with a dahlia or a dogwood. They are summed up in the notion of apical dominance, which decrees the priority of buds from the apex, or main growth point, down to the roots. The role of auxins was discussed earlier. Pruning to control growth can be seen as telling the auxins where to concentrate their energies next. Strangely enough they rush to do man's bidding with extra energy. If pruning does nothing else it reinvigorates a plant.

The simplest example to take is a quick-growing herbaceous plant with a straightforward branching pattern: a chrysanthemum. If the grower's ambition is a flower of great size and splendour, an exhibition specimen, he will pinch off the buds of side shoots that would produce flowers until he is left with a solitary flower bud. The plant will grow absurdly top-heavy, putting all its energies into one great football of petals on top. But it will win a prize.

Another grower with the same plant could have done exactly the opposite. He could have pinched out the centre bud, which would have made the side buds break. As each side shoot lengthened and formed buds, he could have pinched out the apical one again so that no one shoot could take over. The whole plant would have remained densely bushy, eventually to be smothered with hundreds of individual undistinguished flowers. The Burgundian chrysanthemum garden pictured

BELOW: *Apple-trees trained over a frame to form a tunnel are a show-piece of purposeful pruning. Stems bent to the horizontal and beyond are apt to make an abnormal number of flower-buds as a hormone-directed response. A tunnel makes a feature of this profitable fact.*

above is an extreme example – but not by Japanese standards: they apply precisely the same techniques to tall pine trees, and of course tiny bonsai ones.

What complicates the pruning of shrubs, and makes it a stumbling block for so many gardeners, is the time scale. The principle is the same, but the structure of a shrub is made more complicated by its annual accretions of twigs. And unless you know whether it flowers on the new shoots it has just made, or the ones it made the previous year, there is a danger of cutting off the part that was about to bloom. The danger is avoided if you prune immediately after flowering. You can never go seriously wrong because there will always be a year ahead in which to make new flowering growths, which is all any plant needs.

But there are drawbacks to pruning at odd times, particularly pruning spring-flowering shrubs in summer. For one thing it is hard to see the stems for the leaves; for another it usually means trampling over other plants; and above all you are too busy. It would be much tidier if we could do all our pruning in winter. Happily, with most shrubs we can limit ourselves to cutting out only stems that are clearly past their youthful vigour, much twigged and rough-barked, back to the point where vigorous young shoots arise; whether from the base (which is preferable) or part-way up the old stems. This method is foolproof.

One sort of summer pruning that we do regularly is dead-heading, or taking off spent flower heads. The object is not only tidiness. It prevents the plant using its energies in ripening seed, leaving it with more in its current account for the next lot of flower buds. Rhododendrons are dead-headed for the benefit of the next year's display, but with perpetual-flowering roses and many other shrubs (especially those like buddleja whose flowers turn brown and ugly), not to mention annuals and perennials, dead-heading is a good deed that has its immediate reward: the growth of a new flowering shoot within days.

'Pegging down' is another way of provoking more flowers in many plants; shrub roses in particular. If a stem is forcibly held horizontally it will often produce flower buds as if in protest all along its upper side. Another method, practised

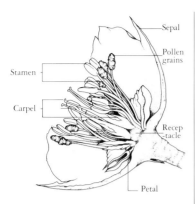

ABOVE and RIGHT: *The parts of all flowers are borne either in whorls (concentric circles) or spirals. The hellebore above and right is an example of a 'perfect' flower – that is one with both sexes – in the usual whorl arrangement.*

The outer whorl or calyx acts as the protecting bud before the flower opens. It consists of sepals, which in this case look to the layman like petals, being much bigger than the next whorl or corolla, which consists of the true petals. The petals of hellebores are small and tubular.

The more usual arrangement is for the sepals to be small and green and the petals large, coloured and often scented. The next whorl is of male parts: the stamens, each consisting of a filament (the stalk) and an anther, which contains four pollen sacs. A hellebore has about sixty stamens. The innermost ring is of female parts or carpels. Each carpel has an ovary at its base, then a stem (the style) ending in a stigma. For fertilization to take place a pollen grain must be deposited on the stigma. Hellebores have thirty or forty carpels. Nectar is produced in nectaries at the base of the ovaries.

particularly with reluctant fruit trees, is bark ringing: taking off a narrow strip of bark to interfere with the sap flow in the phloem and prevent the products of photosynthesis reaching the roots. Even a mere nick in the bark below a bud can increase its share of nutrients enough to galvanize it into action.

THE FUNCTION OF FLOWERS

We now accept without surprise the fact that flowers are the sexual organs of plants, responsible for the awkward task of mating with another individual of the same species, without the facility of strolling over and asking for a dance.

When Linnaeus proposed the idea in the eighteenth century it was considered both improbable and an affront to public decency, if not morals. It still remains a mystery how plants came to evolve a sexual system. For it seems clear that flowers are merely stems with leaves modified to perform their specialized, ambitious and complex functions.

It becomes more strange when you think that most plants can, and do, reproduce their kind vegetatively – that is by means other than seed. Making flowers is a considerable investment of the plant's resources in something which will give it, as an individual, no benefit. The two hundred thousand flowers on a cherry tree draw out something like twenty-five pounds of carbohydrates from the tree's reserves. Fattening up the cherries to tempt birds to eat them will use even more.

Whatever primeval algae first dropped differentiated male and female spores started the exchange of genetic material and the chance of a more efficient plant. Somewhere in the aeons of evolution the basic vegetative parts of plants began to specialize and become male and female organs. The branch of the evolutionary tree that advanced farthest along this path inevitably evolved fastest (as its sexual system grew more efficient) and produced most variations on its theme.

Those variations are, today, our flowering plants, from primitive attempts like the conifers (botanists are loathe to admit that their sexual organs are truly flowers at all since the female seed is naked, without an ovary to contain it) to such relatively primitive flowers as the magnolia (which have all the parts together – the term is 'perfect' – and thus are in theory in danger of fertilizing themselves) to such sophisticated models as the orchids.

One of the biggest steps along the way was the recruitment of insects as part of the team. The most primitive flowers are all wind pollinated. In order to have the slightest chance of landing a pollen grain on an appropriate female organ by means of wind alone vast clouds of pollen are needed. Pollen is largely protein and therefore expensive in terms of energy for the plant to produce. But attract a bee to the flower with a bright colour, a sweet smell and a little nectar, and a mere dab of pollen will be sure of finding its way straight to the mark.

To the gardener flowers can be either a means to an end or an end in themselves: the former when he wants fruit; the latter when it is simply display he is after.

There are many reasons why the fruit is not always forthcoming. It can just be a matter of bad weather or lack of bees. Gardeners deal largely with highly selected, often highly bred, cultivated varieties. In the course of their raising their sexual efficiency often suffers. A fruit-grower, for example, is faced with a baffling array of cultivars whose flowers may or may not be compatible with themselves or others. Unless he plants sorts that are compatible he will have barren trees. Nature plays similar tricks to guard against what amounts to floral incest. Sometimes the pollen ripens at the wrong moment for the ovule; sometimes it simply fails to fertilize it. Occasionally the fertilization takes place but the fruit, as if knowing it was conceived out of wedlock, fails to mature and drops off. Yet there is no general rule about this: many plants regularly self-pollinate and thrive on it. Most garden weeds, indeed, seem to prove it is positively beneficial.

Where the flower is an end in itself, as in most of our garden flowers, its sexual efficiency is of no account, but if anything a drawback. Many flowers stay brilliant and pristine for days or even weeks on end, until they are visited by an insect. But once they are fertilized their colour fades, their petals fall. The plant's energy is transferred from flowering into forming seed.

For this reason the improvement of garden flowers often takes the form of depriving them of fertility. A 'double' flower is usually one whose sexual parts have been transformed by mutation into more petals.

BELOW: *A bee about to pollinate a* Salvia *flower. After landing on the lower petal lip, it climbs up the flower tube in search of nectar. As it goes in, it is touched first by the stigma to pick up pollen it has carried from other flowers, then by the stamens which deposit their pollen to be delivered to another flower.*

Both because it cannot be fertilized and because it has more petals it will last longer and be more ostentatious in display.

The gardener in any case wants to know what conditions encourage flowering. In general they are the ones that make strong growth of leaf and stem impossible. There is a chemical balance in every plant between its store of carbohydrates (sugar and starch) and the supply of nutrients for growth. While nitrogen, in particular, is plentiful, and there is plenty of water to carry it surging through the cells, it will go on making more leaves and shoots. When the supply of nutrients dwindles, often because of a shortage of moisture to dissolve them and make them available, the balance tips and the hormone messengers draw on the carbohydrates to make flowers. In woody plants the great years for flowers often follow dry and sunny years, when the plant was under stress. They are its effort to perpetuate itself: at least to leave seed on earth.

ABOVE: The male catkins of the willow shed their pollen on the wind in early spring before insects emerge. Male plants with their golden pollen are much more ornamental than females.

BELOW: A scientist uses forceps to hand-pollinate the flower of a turnip by brushing the pollen from the anther of one flower (in the forceps) on to the stigma of another; both the parents of the cross are thus precisely identified.

HOW PLANTS ARE IMPROVED

For many hundreds of years men gradually improved the plants they grew by the common sense of planting the seed of the better specimens. They also discovered a very long time ago that you could graft a branch of a better tree on to a less good one. In China the selection of varieties for cultivation was in an advanced state a thousand years ago. The notion of improving on nature's production is not new, but until the last century it could be no more than careful selection of what Nature chanced to provide.

The word hybrid came into use in the eighteenth century to describe such things as mongrel dogs that were obviously the result of crossing two varieties or forms of the same sort of creature. Darwin used it more scientifically in describing the false oxlip as a hybrid between a cowslip and a primrose. But it was not until the work of Gregor Mendel (1822-84) came to light and was seized on and examined at a conference called by the Royal Horticultural Society in 1899 that the science of genetics was born. The ways that characteristics are transmitted from one generation to another, getting mixed up in the process, have since become clear enough to guide breeders in a half-light growing more dawn-like all the time.

The object of breeding is to combine the best points of different plants. Two varieties of one species can be 'crossed'; two species of one genus can be 'hybridized'; very occasionally two species of what are considered different genera can be persuaded to mate – though some botanists take this as *prima facie* evidence that the genera in question are really the same. Hybridization often results in greater vigour, and intergeneric breeding (if that's what it is) even more so. It seems that nature shows its approval of the widest possible genetic mixtures.

Some plants, of course, are much quicker to breed than others. With an annual there is a chance of an improvement every year: hence the great strides in vegetable breeding. Trees in contrast have never been consciously bred for improvement until very recently. It takes years to find out whether the work was worthwhile.

If the microscope were not there to tell us what goes on in the swopping over of sex cells what would we know? Simply that there are certain predictable odds on particular characteristics of parents turning up in their children. The classic Mendelian experiments were made with peas. Mendel showed that when peas of different sizes and colours were crossed (that is bred together under controlled conditions, so that he knew which pollen fertilized which ovule) certain characteristics regularly reappeared in their offspring, suppressing their opposites. A tall pea crossed with a short one gave tall offspring; a red-flowered pea with a white one gave red offspring; a smooth pea with a wrinkled one gave smooth offspring. He coined the term 'dominant' for characteristics that suppressed the alternatives, which he called 'recessive'.

By then letting the offspring fertilize themselves he discovered that a recessive character was not suppressed once and for all, but reappeared in the next generation in a simple mathematical relationship to the dominant character: 1 to 3.

To explain this he supposed that there must be 'genetic factors' (we now call them genes) in the sex cells which have to be paired when mating takes place. When the pairing includes a dominant gene its character will take over. But there is a steady chance of the pairing of the recessive genes. When this happens the recessive character (e.g. a short or white pea) will take over.

The mechanism of the mixing of characteristics was discovered early this century. In its broadest terms, and leaving out the jargon, every living cell has in its nucleus at least some chromosomes – worm-like bodies that carry the genes. Sex cells (sperm and egg) are formed by dividing the genetic material in half so that when fertilization takes place the right amount of (i.e. at least two) chromosomes will be present, half from each parent.

Chance, or various agencies, frequently leads to variations in the mathematics. It is quite common for the first stage of cell division (the pairing off of the chromosomes) to take place but then for the cell to fail to divide: the result is a cell with double the normal number of chromosomes and hence double the size. The whole organism may therefore be bigger and (in the case of a plant) may be considered an improvement.

In practice, if a breeder is, say, trying to improve a cabbage and concentrating on various desirable characteristics, he will cross and recross the plant with its sister seedlings and 'back-cross' it with its parents to try to fix the desirable qualities in it beyond eradication. With certain annuals this process has gone so far that the chance of their 'reverting' is minimal. But in some cases this is not easy, and by far the best results come with the seed of a fresh cross of two slightly different strains, both selected for similar characteristics. The term 'first filial', or F_1, is used for this fresh cross. F_2 seed, from the second generation, is less vigorous and will contain a proportion of throwbacks to undesirable characters.

Improvements come to plants in many ways. Breeding is only one of them. Natural mutations account for great numbers of our better plants. A nurseryman or a keen gardener is always on the look out for seedlings of unusual character, or 'bud sports', when for no discernible reason a plant puts out a branch or a flower different from the rest. If it looks worth having he will cherish it and propagate from it, thus starting a new 'clone'. But seedlings from his clone will usually go straight back to the ancestral norm: it will always have to be propagated by cuttings to keep its special character.

Even with vegetative propagation there is a risk of reversion. The popular variegated *Elaeagnus pungens* 'Maculata' is a case in point; it is always prone to put out unvariegated shoots with more vigour (because of more chlorophyll) than the selected clone. If these are not cut off then the whole plant will eventually revert to green; the entirely green shoots are almost inevitably more vigorous.

MENDELIAN INHERITANCE
If pollen from a climbing rose is dusted on the stigma of a non-climbing rose the plants that grow from the resulting seed will all almost certainly be climbers. The gene for climbing is therefore 'dominant'; that for non-climbing 'recessive'. This first generation of a cross is known as F_1, meaning first filial. If the F_1 generation is self-pollinated the result will be as shown (below), where the gene for climbing is represented as X and that for non-climbing as x. XX or Xx is a climber. Only the one-in-four chance xx is a bush. This experiment in Mendelian genetics was done by the breeder Jack Harkness when he self-pollinated the scarlet climber 'Danse du Feu'. Of 100 seedlings 75 were climbers; 25 bushes. If the recessive character is the desirable one to the breeder it can thus be isolated in the second generation and perpetuated in the third. Two xx bushes crossed cannot produce a climber.

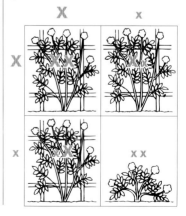

BELOW LEFT: *The progress of a lily
from flower to seed. At the bottom the
ovules are fully formed as the flower
blooms. Next the stamens have shed
pollen; the carpel withers; the ovules are
fertilized and start to swell. At the top
the corolla has withered; the ovules are
seeds, beginning to fill the ovary.*

BELOW CENTRE: *A beanflower is
fertilized; the ovules are already tiny
embryo beans in the ovary at the base of
the carpel. The flower is shed and the
ovary extends to become the pod, the beans
gradually filling the space.*

BELOW RIGHT: *In an apple the ovary
is 'inferior' – i.e. below the base of the
corolla, in a swelling in the flower-stem –
'the receptacle'. As the flower withers it is
the swelling stem that becomes the apple.
The tree lavishes nutrients on the 'fruit' to
make it palatable to birds, and form a
reserve supply of food for the
germinated seed.*

FRUITS AND SEEDS

Flowering plants developed from their non-flowering ancestors because they found
a way of communicating with each other and pooling the results of their most successful (though entirely haphazard) experiments in design.

The physical form this collaboration took was the seed. Far more than being
just a fertilized ovule ready to start a new life, the seed is in itself an elaborate product of evolutionary improvement. For what could be more vulnerable than a minute
plantlet with no resources of its own dropped under the shadow of its parent?
Before it became an effective means of propagation the seed had to learn the trick
of waiting until conditions were favourable before it started to grow, to develop
its own food reserves, to be able to tell which direction was up, and to find a mode
of transport for leaving home.

So although a seed is still undeniably a miniaturized plant it has a number
of extra characteristics plants do not have. It can remain dormant, in some cases
for many years. All seeds have a limited period of viability, ranging from a few
days to many hundred years. The seed can sense when it is right to wake up and
start growing. It has a built-in food bank to power its first stages of growth.
And it has, in many cases if not all, some sort of a means of transport, or at least a
good chance of hitching a lift.

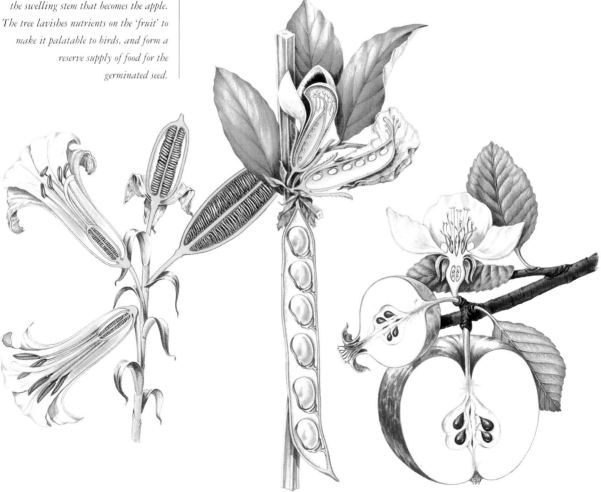

Nearly all seeds have some sort of dispersal mechanisms. Those in berries are attractive and tasty to birds; others (like burrs) have hooks to catch on animals' coats; the poppy has a scattering device which disperses its tiny seeds through a circle of slits when the stem moves in the wind.

Poplar and dandelion seeds have fluff to carry them on the wind; the sweet pea has a spring-like action which ejects its heavy seeds with enough force to carry them yards. The willow-herb has feathery hairs projecting from its seeds to act as a parachute to catch the wind.

Of all these adaptations dormancy was undoubtedly the most important; the one that gave flowering plants a unique advantage over their ancestors. Every time you turn the earth and find you have brought new weed seeds to the surface you can see what a powerful weapon it is.

Every seed has developed a form of dormancy suitable for the conditions it expects to encounter. The chemical computer in a seed coat can calculate whether it is buried at the right depth for germination by taking readings of the fluctuations of temperature, light, moisture, the presence of oxygen and other gases and nitrates in the soil. Perhaps most wonderful of all, this computer can compromise. Seed-coats are sensitive to temperature, moisture, light, oxygen and other gases either separately, or in certain combinations, or in certain sequences, or even in both sequence and combination – rather like the lock of the most sophisticated possible safe.

All this sounds as though it will cause the gardener endless trouble getting conditions exactly right. In practice it does not. Most of the seed that gardeners buy for regular use (vegetables and annuals make up the vast majority) are either not difficult at all, or any necessary treatment to remove inhibition to germination has already been given by the seed merchant.

Certain classes of seed do present special challenges. Many trees are awkward, demanding either that they be sown very fresh (the oak, willow, Japanese maple, walnut are examples) or be subjected to dampness and low temperatures over a long period. The treatment of the latter, known as stratification, consists of mixing the seeds with wet sand or peat and leaving them exposed to the elements through a cold wet winter. Many of the rose family, many conifers, many maples, azaleas and magnolias need stratifying.

The seedlings of alpines would stand little chance if they germinated in the autumn. Alpine seed is programmed to undergo a cold winter and then germinate quickly next spring. Bulb seeds often germinate quickly, but in many cases develop to flowering size only very slowly – which is why most bulbs are propagated by offsets rather than seed.

The majority of seed dries out as it ripens and is stored and sold dry. Before it can start to germinate it must absorb water. A number of seeds have impermeable coats and initially resist any soaking. Examples are some sorts of sweet peas and the pea-tree *Sophora microphylla*. In nature this resistance eventually breaks down, but in cultivation they must be chipped to allow water in. Rubbing them on sandpaper is one method (known as scarifying). Peas and many other plants, with what seems truly remarkable forethought, naturally produce a proportion of seeds much harder than the rest simply to stagger the timing of their imbibition (as the preliminary absorbing is called) and subsequent germination.

The process of germination is illustrated in the right-hand margin. It needs not only moisture but oxygen. A balance of these two factors determines how deeply a seed should be sown. A very rough and ready guide is its own diameter. The soil

GERMINATION

A typical dicot seed such as an acorn consists of two seed leaves or cotyledons, which act as food stores, a plumule or first shoot and a radicle or first root, enclosed in a hard outer coat. Germination starts when the outer coat absorbs enough moisture for the cotyledons to swell and burst it open. First the radicle and then the plumule emerge, bending respectively downwards and upwards. In most dicots the seed leaves emerge on the plumule. In acorns they remain concealed, acting as the energy source until the first true leaves appear.

After three days: The swelling cotyledons force the acorn open and the radicle appears. Gravity attracts it downwards.

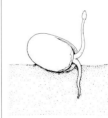

One to two weeks: As the radicle begins to function as a root the plumule emerges, away from the pull of gravity.

Three to four weeks: The radicle produces rootlets and the plumule leaves. The oak is now independent of its food store.

ABOVE: *A false-colour electron micrograph of a cabbage seed just after germination clearly shows the seed (green) in its split seed-coat (orange) and the new root covered with root-hairs.*

should be fine-textured and just moist ('a good tilth') to give close contact all round and yet allow air in. Dust-like seed should be scattered on the surface with at most only the faintest powdering of soil on top. A broad bean on the other hand can be planted one inch deep in winter, when the ground is wet, and two inches deep in summer, when the moisture level is lower (and oxygen has penetrated deeper into the ground). But too-deep sowing is the commonest cause of failure to germinate. All other things being equal, bigger seed is better for the simple reason that it has a bigger food supply.

The normal safe time to sow any seed in the open is in spring, as soon as the soil warms up and dries on the surface. Some will germinate at near freezing point, but most not until the temperature approaches 13°C (55°F). Some slow seed may not germinate till autumn, or until the following spring. If you are experimenting with seed whose habits you do not know, collected perhaps in the wild, it is a mistake to give up hope before two years are up.

The object of sowing seed in a greenhouse or frame is earlier germination, and hence a longer growing season, or earlier crops. In this case, as in any where the seed is sown closely in a restricted space, transplanting is inevitable. The golden rule is the sooner the better. As soon as the seedlings are big enough to take hold of they must be 'pricked out' to a wide enough spacing to give them light and air and prevent their roots from competing with each other. They are lifted gently by one leaf and put in holes made with a pencil in fine soil. In this respect the fatter your fingers the less likely they are to be green.

SHOOTS INTO ROOTS

Plants are not like animals, which must mate or see their kind perish from the earth. As a fail-safe device for procreating, whether they succeed in fertilizing and scattering seed or not, they have evolved, in parallel with their flowers, a marvellous range of ways of renewing themselves from their own tissue.

Bulbs make offsets, strawberries send out runners, daisies form wider and wider clumps, brambles arch over and root their tips, irises multiply rhizomes, trees and shrubs layer their branches to surround the decrepit old parent trunk with vigorous offspring. Each is a natural method of increase which a gardener, adopting it for his own purposes, would call vegetative propagation.

Sometimes it is more convenient to make more plants this way than by sowing seed. Often it is easier or more certain. In many cases it is essential, either because fertile seed is not available or is likely to produce a hybrid. But it is done most often because the plant the gardener wants to reproduce is a garden clone, a cultivated variety which must be kept away from the genetic melting pot if it is to keep its identity. Plants propagated vegetatively are as identical as if they were all part of one great plant – which in a sense they are.

If it is just a few plants the gardener wants, one of the natural or quasi-natural methods of propagation will often best suit his purpose. Most herbaceous plants are easily divided simply by pulling or chopping apart their tangle of roots into separate replantable pieces. Many bulbs can be pulled apart too; most naturally produce 'offsets' – young bulbs beside the old – which can easily be used to increase a clump. A lily bulb is formed of scales (which are abbreviated food-storing leaves) that can be gently pulled apart and will form roots if they are planted in damp sand. Some sub-shrubs such as pinks and carnations are increased by 'pipings'; young stems simply pulled out of their sockets in the node just below and

LEFT: *An impressive example of the propensity of plants to perpetuate themselves from their own tissue. A huge old chestnut tree is producing a forest of young trees by 'layering' its long branches.*

rooted in sandy compost. Even the leaves of many plants (*Streptocarpus*, African violets and some sedums are examples) will form roots if pinned down in damp sand.

With woody plants layering is often easiest, at least if a branch can be bent down to reach the ground. It may take several seasons, but if the branch is pegged down so it cannot move, its bark slightly nicked or scored with a knife, it will eventually take root – when it can be cut off and used as a new plant. Even if no branch will reach the ground 'air-layering' is a possibility. A young branch is wounded and its wound packed in damp moss or peat, tied securely above and below in a wrapping of polythene. Eventually the branch will put out roots into the moss.

This is the domestic, one at a time, scale of operation. For larger, let alone commercial, numbers it is essential to make the most of the parent plant. For woody plants at least this means taking cuttings; short lengths of stem, preferably in growth and with a few leaves on. Such is a plant's will to live that in most cases a cutting given a suitable rooting medium will put out roots – 'strike' is the term gardeners use – and become an independent plant.

A daunting number of variables surrounds the question of which piece of stem to cut and when. Some stems root best as cuttings if they are still green and sappy; others when half-ripe; others not until they are completely mature. Some root best if cut between joints; others at joints – others with a little 'heel' of older wood torn or cut off with them. The younger and more vigorous the stem is (and also the parent plant) the sooner the cutting is likely to root. Flowering stems are less likely to root than non-flowering ones. Soft cuttings work for many herbaceous plants as well as woody ones.

The essential condition for all soft or half-ripe cuttings is that they should be kept in a growing, functioning state during the period while they are rootless. Ideally they should have leaves, but not too many leaves, so that their normal process of photosynthesis continues without making excessive demands for moisture which there are no roots to supply.

Many cuttings will root in water, but roots made like this are brittle and difficult to transfer to soil. The usual rooting medium for soft cuttings is a 2:1 mixture of sharp sand and finely sifted peat, kept permanently moist (but not wet).

One of the best ways of achieving the ideal conditions on a small scale is to put the cuttings round the edge of a clay flower pot within which is a smaller one filled with water. The space between the two, which need not be more than 2.5cm (1in), is filled with a mixture of sand and peat. Water percolates through at a rate that keeps the mixture both damp and airy. Another way is to cover a pot of cuttings

BELOW: *Peas are some of the simplest seeds to sow. All that is needed is a very shallow 'drill', the peas placed in it at pea-size spaces, and about a pea-diameter depth of soil raked over them.*

ABOVE: A greenhouse 'mist unit' produces a constant very fine mist from tiny water-jets to keep green cuttings turgid while they form roots.

BELOW: As long as the cambium layers of scion and rootstock are kept in contact, the many and various forms of grafting are self-explanatory.

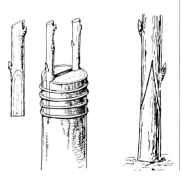

with a polythene bag, prevented from touching them (and thus risking fungus problems) by hoops of stiff wire.

The difficulty is often to find a balance between damp and fresh air. In traditional cold-frames this is done by keeping the frames shut (or shaded if the sun is hot) all the time except for an hour or two in the morning, when they are opened for a change of air. Perhaps the nearest to the perfect rooting conditions yet achieved is in a device called a mist propagator, where the cuttings are placed in an open bed in a greenhouse, with soil-warming cables to provide 'bottom-heat', under fine spray jets which keep up an intermittent drizzle. It works both for quick-rooting soft cuttings and summer or autumn cuttings of such evergreens as rhododendrons – even with conifers which can be notoriously difficult.

The discovery of rooting hormones has made the process much easier and more certain still. Every garden centre now sells little containers of hormone powder which, in very modest quantities (you just dip the base of your cutting in it before potting it up), can stimulate root formation within a mere week or two.

The most important recent development in plant propagation has been the discovery that the extreme growing tips of shoots, consisting of a few actively-dividing cells known as the meristem, are enough material to make a whole new plant. They are cut off with surgical precision and hygiene and made to root in an aseptic nutrient jelly based on agar, which is derived from seaweed. The great advantage of this method is that virus diseases appear not to reach the meristem. Good but infected strains of plants can be 'cleaned' of virus. Another advantage is that so little plant material is needed. Where necessary (as with rare plants or new mutations), if only a few cells are needed for each, one plant can furnish hundreds of identical offspring. For large nurseries, therefore, meristem culture, or micropropagation, though calling for laboratory conditions, can be the logical method.

Grafting a cutting, known in this case as a 'scion', from one plant onto the roots of another may be necessary for a number of reasons. The cutting may refuse to root; its roots may be sickly and weak or prone to a disease or pest (as European vine roots are to phylloxera); extra vigour may be wanted – which is why most roses are grown on briar roots; or the reverse – fruit trees are generally grafted on to dwarfing rootstocks, which limit the ultimate size of the tree. Grafting also saves time; the cutting is immediately given established roots. The roots and top must be of closely related plants to be compatible – of the same family, but not always necessarily of the same genus. Pear is always grafted on quince roots; peach on almond; Japanese cherries and ornamental crab apples on seedling stocks of wild cherry or crab; many weeping tree cultivars onto normal rootstocks of the same species. There are many forms of graft, but one objective: to bring together the cambium layers of scion and rootstock and keep them pressed tightly together until they unite. To the left is one of the many ingenious forms of surgery found efficacious over the centuries. Today, 'budding' is the form of grafting now preferred for many commercial purposes, being most economic of precious scion-wood. It consists of inserting a single bud of the scion plant into a slit in the bark of the root-stock, and then decapitating the natural shoot above it.

THE NURSERY ROUTINE

The business of a commercial nursery is to rationalize the production of hundreds of diverse plants, each of which needs slightly different treatment, particularly in the matter of timing. There are, for example, at least twelve types of cuttings: greenwood, softwood, semi-hardwood, hardwood, basal, heeled, nodal, internodal, stem, leaf, leaf-bud and root. Experience shows that although almost any cutting of some plants will take root, others must be taken from a certain part at a certain stage of development to stand any chance of success. Others will not root at all but must be grafted or budded on to appropriate and compatible roots.

Since most of this development depends entirely on the weather, industrial programming is not easy. Luckily the discovery that cuttings of many plants can be stored for up to two or three months, provided they are kept just above freezing point, has meant that they can be taken at precisely the right moment, even if a log-jam of work makes it impossible to process them straight away. Yet to a nurseryman, as to every gardener, the weather has the final say. If the ground is frozen or water-logged all orders can be held up for weeks on end: it may become impossible to send out plants at the right time for gardeners. Hence an ever-greater reliance on growing more plants – even trees – in containers (usually simply plastic bags) from start to finish.

There is a constant commercial pressure on a large nursery to narrow its range of plants, simplify its routine and give itself the breathing space either to lower its prices, take higher profits or take over less-efficient or smaller competitors and expand their business. A depressing number of well-known older nurseries have yielded to the temptation. Many, if not most, garden centres today are predictable to the point of dreariness, with almost nothing to offer but the plants you see in every front garden.

But the opposite opportunity also exists: to excel by producing new and better plants. The past decade has seen an unprecedented number of small specialized nurseries open their gates, often tentatively at first – to be overwhelmed by the enthusiasm and curiosity of the public. Good nurseries are constantly working on the qualities of their favourite genera. There is always a risk of confusing 'new' with 'better'. Yet more and more nurseries do examine the vast range of old selections,

BELOW: *Meristem culture of* Cymbidium *orchids in its early* (left) *and last stages. A single cell from a growing tip is placed on the nutrient jelly agar, takes root and becomes a whole new plant.*

choose the best and reintroduce them into the country's gardens. The appearance in 1986 of *The Plantfinder*, an annual computerized national catalogue of all plants available in British nurseries, has been the greatest possible stimulus to specialist nurseries. Similar publications have appeared in other countries, and the Royal Horticultural Society has taken responsibility for the original *Plantfinder*.

Yet many keen gardeners still feel that the best way to obtain a highly desirable plant is to make friends with another keen gardener who already has it. The keener the gardener, in fact, the more anxious he is to give away pieces of his best plants – not to do nurseries out of business, but to ensure the survival of something excellent.

WEEDS

WHAT IS A WEED? THE CLASSIC DEFINITION IS 'A PLANT IN THE WRONG PLACE'. BUT HALF THE PLANTS IN HALF OUR GARDENS ARE CONDEMNED BY THIS DEFINITION. THERE IS MUCH MORE TO IT THAN THAT.

Weeds are a race of super-plants, of unfair vigour and tenacity. Either by prolific and fertile seeding, or by delving deep with brittle roots that can regrow from the smallest scrap left in the ground, they hang on to their places in the garden when any well-bred plant would give up. It is their efficiency and aggressiveness that make them so unwelcome. If a weed were a meek little thing, reluctant to grow at all, we should call it a 'difficult subject' and coddle it in a cold frame.

We can only spare garden space for plants of rampant vigour and productiveness if they have something special to offer: brilliant flowers; delicious leaves; perhaps an indifference to wind that makes them valuable as a screen. Weeds are the ones that not only volunteer too readily but are dull and dowdy even at their best.

The objections to such well-adjusted plants are two. They compete with, starve, overshadow or throttle the better things we are trying to grow. And they hide the desired effect, or at least blur its outlines. They spoil the focus of the picture.

Getting rid of weeds, therefore, has its immediate rewards to offer. To me it is the most basic of gardening activities: the essential editing, the blue-pencilling without which the garden as such would cease to exist.

I would go further and say that unless you hand-weed your garden you do not know what is in it. Down in the undergrowth with a hand-fork, sorting out the sheep from the goats, you are faced with the task of identifying every plant. I make it a rule not to pull up anything I cannot name. In fact, I name them as I go: a homely catechism of fat hen, shepherd's purse, groundsel, twitch (with a few expletives deleted), until suddenly there is a little plant which is none of these. Perhaps just a new-born seedling. One gets to know the seed-leaves of the local weeds: but this is different. Is it a holly? A hellebore? Perhaps it is honesty or foxglove. Perhaps something I had never expected to set seed and germinate in my garden.

Whether weeding is a pain or a pleasure depends more than anything on the condition of your soil. To weed in baked, dry ground is utterly frustrating – in fact virtually impossible: the fork won't go in, and the roots won't come out. On very wet ground it is just a muddy mess. Your hands and your tools become clogged, slippery and unusable. The time to weed, therefore, is after, but not immediately after, a good downpour – the interval depending on how quickly your soil drains. Failing rain, weed after a long, steady soak with the sprinkler. Take a small 'border' fork, a hand-fork, a bucket for the spoil, something to kneel on . . . and prepare for a gently pleasurable afternoon.

Paradoxically, the better a weed is growing, the easier it is to extract. Soil in really good heart – open, fertile, well-stocked with humus – yields up its weeds as readily as it nourishes your plants. Furthermore, a well-fed weed is in less of a hurry to flower, set seed, and multiply our troubles. A weed which has germinated in a soft bed of mulch comes up easiest of all: another sound argument for mulching.

The alternative to hand-weeding is to decide that, like Pilate, what I have planted, I have planted – and that anything else is by definition a weed. For the parts of the garden where you are growing crops, be it a row of beans or a bed of petunias, discrimination among odd seedlings is impracticable.

This is where the hoe comes in. All a hoe is, although there are scores of different designs, is a blade that you push or pull just below the surface of the soil to cut off the weeds at their roots. It is only good for one specific job: killing young weed seedlings. So you have to do it often. To hoe deep-rooting permanent weeds, whether with tap-roots like dock or running stolons like ground elder, is worse than futile; it encourages them to sprout and multiply. The only way is to fork them out, laboriously and repeatedly.

With hoeing as with hand-weeding, the better the soil, the easier the job. The ground should be rather drier – though not baked hard, or the hoe will just skim along the surface.

Many gardeners try to minimize the germination of weeds by covering the soil surface with a mulch, either of utilitarian black plastic or woven polypropylene, or in more visible areas with such organic matter as spent hops or mushroom compost – or indeed anything which can be relied on not to be full of weed seeds. A third, theoretically attractive, approach is no cultivation at all, avoiding turning up seeds, so that the soil surface is effectively its own mulch.

The advantage of an organic mulch is that it is gradually incorporated into the earth by earthworms and micro-organisms, improving the soil as it goes. It must then, of course, be topped up with more mulch. But on soil where (as in any typical garden) planting and replanting is a continual process the practicality of keeping such weed-free cover is questionable: each time you disturb it more seeds are likely to germinate.

And then of course there are chemical weedkillers – many in number and brand, but all based on one of three modes of operation. 'Contact' weedkillers kill only the green parts of the plant they touch, which is enough for short-lived weeds but ineffective for perennial, deep-rooted ones. 'Translocated' weedkillers are absorbed into the plant's system by its leaves, reaching through the stem into the roots. Hormone weedkillers work in this way, stimulating the plant into growing so vigorously that it dies. 'Soil-acting' weedkillers are taken into the plant from the soil by roots.

With thorough study, weedkillers can be made an important ally of the over-stretched gardener. But these powerful chemicals should never be casually used. In large gardens they are essential. But in small gardens they are best avoided. They are not only unnecessary and potentially dangerous, but they put a distance between the gardener and his plants. Weeding is not just about weeds: it is about getting to know your garden better.

BELOW LEFT and BELOW: The aesthetic rewards of weeding are immediate. In the classic gardener's phrase, 'you can see where you've been'. On the left, the whole point of a planting in harmonious textures and colours is obscured through spring-time neglect. Grassy weeds in particular can establish themselves unnoticed and gradually blur the definition of the picture. For the gardener the act of concentrating on leaf shapes, to spot any rogue plant before it does any harm, is a good way of training the eyes to appreciate subtleties of form. The more you notice, the more you enjoy. Weeding the bed below was done in the morning (after watering the evening before) using a long-handled border fork and being careful to move the feet as little as possible. Footmarks were then prodded over with the fork.

TOTAL CONTROL

In a greenhouse soil, water, temperature and light are taken, as far as possible, out of nature's hands and decreed by the gardener himself.

The object of the greenhouse (or indeed conservatory) is to increase the range of plants we can grow or to lengthen their useful seasons. It works partly by increasing the average temperature, but principally by keeping out extreme cold. As in the open, given adequate moisture and suitable soil, the ultimate factor that decides what will grow is the minimum temperature. A greenhouse, in other words, is a way of upgrading your local hardiness zone. Most people arrange conditions with a particular kind of plant in mind and heat their greenhouses to just above the minimum that the plant needs to survive.

The word greenhouse originated in the seventeenth century with the building used to protect what were then called 'greens', and we now call evergreens. Keeping frost out was probably all they attempted. But when plant exploration started to bring in more and more desirable and exotic creatures from Central America and South Africa, higher temperatures were needed. Greenhouses became warmer and also lighter (the first had glass only on one side). By the nineteenth century they were hot, light and big enough for tropical palms. The greatest greenhouse ever built was designed by the Duke of Devonshire's gardener, Joseph Paxton, to house the Great Exhibition in London in 1851. It was given, and deserved, the name Crystal Palace.

While fuel and labour remained cheap there was no particular virtue in cooler greenhouses. Many plants were given much warmer conditions than they really needed – more for the comfort of their audience than themselves. There is little question of that today. Only a millionaire could keep a private tropical house – what used to be called a 'stove'. This needs to be kept above 18°C (64°F) for all but a couple of winter months. Today each extra 3°C (5°F) doubles the cost of heating.

The warmest greenhouse climate commonly maintained in cold-winter regions is approximately subtropical, with a minimum temperature of 13°C (55°F). This is enough to keep many flowers in bloom in the winter. At this temperature, in fact, a greenhouse can become a conservatory; an adjunct to domestic life as much as a horticultural device. Even the general-purpose 'cool' greenhouse, going down to 4°C (39°F), still allows the cultivation of such a range of plants that no one could feel deprived, and can serve as a conservatory outside the depths of winter.

It is surprising what can be brought through the winter in a greenhouse heated only to 2°C (36°F) – just enough to stop it actually freezing. The most popular of all greenhouse plants, pelargoniums, fuchsias and chrysanthemums,

BELOW: *No artificial heat is needed in a greenhouse or conservatory primarily intended to ripen grapes. The vine is planted outside the building and its trunk led through a hole at the foot of the wall.*

will survive if they are kept dry enough to be dormant, though of course they will not flower in winter.

Without any heating at all, the function of a greenhouse changes: it becomes a device for keeping wind and rain, snow and ice away from the plants. But it still warms up in winter sunshine much more than the unprotected garden, which means an earlier spring for the plants in its protection, and a considerably earlier start for spring-sown seeds.

The alpine house is perhaps the most rewarding form of unheated greenhouse. It needs the maximum possible ventilation from the sides, day and night. Alpines are completely unaffected by cold: what they dislike is damp. The reward is to have the earliest bulbs in flower in January, undamaged by the weather, and to be able to enjoy them dry-shod.

Not that there is any need to make a final commitment to one regime. The same building will do for all purposes, given the heating capacity. The only structural distinction is that true alpine houses have continuous opening windows along the sides. But you can hardly overdo the ventilation in summer of any greenhouse; both top and sides must be able to open.

The most practical plan in greenhouses longer than about 4m (12ft) is to have a partition wall that will allow you to keep the two parts at different temperatures. The outer or door half could be used as an alpine house, stone cold in winter, while the inner half could be kept frost-free or warmer. The same arrangement lets you adjust the conditions in summer to suit two different kinds of plant; at one end perhaps tomatoes, and begonias at the other.

It is the need for constant adjustment that makes a greenhouse so labour-intensive. Apart from the minimum temperature – which can be taken care of by a thermostat – the supplies of water, air and light are constantly critical. When the sun breaks through clouds, or a breeze gets up, the effects on the plants are exaggerated by their imprisonment behind glass. Excessive heat in summer is one of the main problems: anything over about 30°C (85°F) overloads the transpiration system of any but tropical plants. Orchids tend to be particularly susceptible, demanding an atmosphere at the same time humid and 'buoyant', which means constant changes of air – expensive when it has to be heated. Full-time gardeners can afford to keep an eye on weather conditions and shamble back to the greenhouse to pull down a blind or open a ventilator. But absentee gardeners have no alternative but to rely on automation.

The most invaluable automatic aid is one that opens and shuts the ventilators in the roof according to the ambient temperature. It is simply a cylinder filled with a substance that expands and contracts as it gets hotter or colder, pushing (or not pushing) a piston upwards to open the skylight.

There are also devices for automatically raising and lowering blinds over the roof glass according to the brightness of the light, but these are more complicated and expensive. Most gardeners compromise by painting the outside of the glass with a thin coat of special white paint in late spring and washing it off in autumn. Roller blinds inside the glass are often used, but are much less effective than external (ideally slatted) ones, which intercept the sun's rays before they reach the glass. Once through the glass, short-wave radiation becomes long-wave, which is trapped as a build-up of heat.

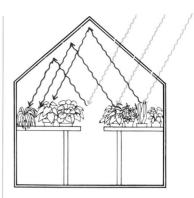

ABOVE: *The so-called 'greenhouse effect' ensures that heat from the sun is trapped inside the greenhouse. Sunlight enters as short-wave radiation which can pass through glass. Once reflected by the plants and soil it becomes long-wave radiation which cannot penetrate the glass to get out. So heat builds up inside.*

BELOW: *An alpine house in early spring with crocuses, irises, anemones and alpine primulas in bloom. An alpine house needs no heating of any kind, but maximum ventilation day and night.*

ABOVE: *Growing conditions for orchids vary widely according to the species, but many demand minimum temperatures above 16°C (61°F) and an atmosphere at the same time both humid and 'buoyant' – which means constant changes of air. The net result is that heating orchid houses is expensive.*

The automation of watering has reached highly sophisticated levels in commercial glasshouses, but to a normal amateur with a mixed collection of plants there is no completely satisfactory substitute for going from pot to pot individually. Furthermore it is his daily opportunity to check the well-being of his plants – even to enjoy their beauty.

The simplest short-cut is 'capillary' watering, that is standing the pots on a shallow tray of sand which can be kept wet automatically from a water tank with a ballcock standing at a slightly higher level. Alternatively, the sand can be watered daily by hand. Water is drawn up into the pots by capillary action (the pots in this case should not have crocks in the bottom for drainage, nor be taller than 15cm (6in)). However, there are two principal snags in the system: all the pots stand on one level, making a tiered display difficult; and the roots soon find their way out of the pots and into the sand, tapping the unlimited water supply and making the plants grow embarrassingly fast.

Despite the snags, this system has the considerable advantage of raising the general atmospheric humidity. The air in most greenhouses is far too dry in hot weather, making the leaves transpire for all they are worth. Houses with concrete or tiled floors are particularly hard to keep humid enough, even if the floor is sprinkled with water twice daily. One way of maintaining a better atmosphere is to have beds or trays of damp sand under the benches (or 'staging') as well as on them.

Perhaps the most important development for economy is the practice of heating the soil instead of the air. It makes it possible to use an unheated greenhouse (or indeed a frame) for propagation that needs heat. An electric cable, in effect a radiator, is simply buried a few inches under the soil or sand. By putting a plastic propagation cover over the soil you can have a greenhouse inside a greenhouse.

If there is a line to be drawn between a greenhouse and a conservatory it is only a matter of purpose. The emphasis in a greenhouse is on the conditions ideal for plants; in a conservatory on conditions pleasant for people. A greenhouse is to some extent a workshop; a place for production and propagation. The high humidity ideal in a greenhouse is inimical to furniture as well as friends. In a conservatory a compromise has to be reached in which decor has a more dominant role and plants are chosen and grouped for more permanent, garden-like effects.

Furthermore a conservatory is normally a room attached to a house, whereas a greenhouse stands free with light from all sides. The aspect of the conservatory wall is therefore a major factor in deciding what can be grown in it – and indeed at what times of day in what seasons it will be most welcoming.

A north-facing conservatory (in the northern hemisphere) only sees direct sunlight on summer mornings and evenings. It can nonetheless be a richly leafy retreat, concentrating on ferns, ivies, bamboos and other foliage plants in winter, and springing into summer life with vines, fuchsias, streptocarpus, prostanthera and many flowers that can either tolerate relatively low light levels, or positively shrink from a baking in full sun.

A south aspect is much more demanding in maintenance. Although it warms rapidly on sunny winter days and is less expensive to heat year-round, any neglect of shading, ventilation or watering can rapidly be fatal. A south-east aspect benefits from a quicker morning warm-up for a winter lunch; south-west from the sun's late rays lingering into dinner-time.

A conservatory should have a hard floor with provision for drainage so that it can be damped down or washed out. Lay a carpet and what you have is a sunroom for house-plants.

The decision as to whether plants should be grown in beds or pots is fundamental. Beds against the wall offer the possibility of big permanent plants, especially climbers; even small trees. Maintenance, especially watering, is much easier: a major fatality, on the other hand, much more serious.

Pots give complete flexibility in arrangement, allowing you to bring forward plants in flower and relegate or conceal anything peaky. Best, in conjunction with a greenhouse, they allow you to run a double shift of plants in and out of their most ornamental seasons.

Watering pots, on the other hand, is a daily duty which not even capillary mats or automated irrigation lines can altogether alleviate. There is a balance to be struck between convenience and appearance. Saucers for water under large pots are a practical proposition. They can easily be checked, may only need replenishing every few days, and meanwhile help to keep the atmosphere moist. There is no such easy answer for a crowd of small pots displayed on staging – except a capillary tray, recalling the aesthetics of the greenhouse.

As for the plants, a counsel of perfection would be to make a decision between a jungle effect and what you might broadly call a Mediterranean look. The lusher the plants you introduce the more humid they need to be to be happy. Mediterranean, Australian and many South African plants suffer drier conditions better and therefore make better living companions.

BELOW: A conservatory must compromise between plants and people. This one faces south-west and needs the shade from the blinds on the roof much of the summer, but in winter is only kept frost-free.

Tall plants and climbers are the essential basic furnishing. An olive tree, perhaps a fig, myrtles, tall oleanders and hibiscus, many Australian wattles of the mimosa persuasion, *Sparmannia africana* and bamboos all make striking big specimens. Citrus trees and camellias are the glittering ornaments of late winter and early spring.

Certain climbers seem almost obligatory in a conservatory. Jasmine, plumbago, bougainvillea, the pink trumpets of *Mandevilla* and the intricacy of passion flowers are in the first rank. A grape-vine in the roof can offer ideal summer shade. . . but this is only to touch on the most routine plants.

More than any part of the garden a conservatory depends for its full effect on constant grooming. In spring and summer an hour a day is not too long to allow to move slowly among the plants, watering and feeding (a weekly liquid feed is mandatory for a permanently pot-bound plant to thrive), picking off damaged leaves and fading flowers, searching for aphids, mites and scale, helping a tendril find a foothold, adjusting and admiring.

The reward should be a plant paradise, immune from the outside world, cossetted, scented and soothing.

WHERE
PLANTS
COME FROM

THERE ARE PLANTS IN OUR GARDENS THAT ARE THE RESULT OF MILLENNIA OF SELECTION AND REFINEMENT – AND OTHERS THAT WERE UNKNOWN UNTIL VERY RECENTLY. BOX AND BAY ARE JUST WHAT THEY WERE IN THE GARDENS OF ANCIENT ROME, BUT THE GREAT MAJORITY OF OUR PLANTS HAVE ONLY BEEN GROWN FOR TWO OR THREE HUNDRED YEARS, AND MANY ONLY WITH-IN THE TWENTIETH CENTURY. IT IS THE NURSERYMAN'S BUSINESS TO BE CONSTANTLY 'IMPROVING' WHAT IS ALREADY GROWN, WHILE THE STOCK OF DESIRABLE UNKNOWNS IS LIMITED TO

THE FEW PARTS OF THE GLOBE THAT ARE HARD TO REACH. TODAY'S NEW PLANTS ARE THEREFORE FAR MORE LIKELY TO BE PRODUCED BY BREEDING THAN BY EXPLORING. ➤

WHAT MAKES A PLANT GARDEN-WORTHY?

THERE IS AN OLD HOLLYWOOD GAG: 'NEW IS EASY. FUNNY IS HARD.' THERE HAS NEVER (OR NOT FOR FOUR HUNDRED YEARS) BEEN A SHORTAGE OF NEW PLANTS TO GROW IN OUR GARDENS.

PREVIOUS SPREAD (LEFT): *Plant-collecting parties like this, crossing a clearing in a* Rhododendron arboreum *forest in east Nepal, have been scouring the mountains for new, better and hardier rhododendrons since the 1820s;* (RIGHT): *The Crown Imperial,* Fritillaria imperialis, *from Les Lilacées of P.-J. Redouté, 1808.*

BELOW: *Perhaps the first criterion of all is that a plant should give pleasure. The spectacular 1m (3ft) saxifrage 'Tumbling Waters' is the pride and joy of its young owner.*

But whether they have been better than the old ones is not always clear. It depends on what the gardener is looking for. There are so many aspects of quality in plants that it is worth pausing to consider what makes a good candidate for our limited space. There is a rough and ready division, of course, between the beautiful and the useful. Any plant that can fairly claim to be both has a head start. But there are many other categories of plant character that have their garden uses. Critical gardeners keep a mental score-card of points for and against plants in order to decide whether they are suffered to remain, enthusiastically propagated, or torn out and consigned to the bonfire.

Most fundamental – except perhaps to a masochistic kind of gardener most often found in an alpine house – is a good constitution: a plant's ability to thrive and wax fat. This does not mean the hooligan temperament of a weed, but the inclination, given an appropriate site, to grow steadily and strongly without fits of the vapours. If shoots regularly die back, or a succession of pests and diseases make it their headquarters, or the plant sits in an apparent coma, it may of course be the gardener's fault. But once he has satisfied himself that he has given it a fair chance it must either thrive or be scrapped. I can think of otherwise unexceptional plants whose chief beauty lies in their rubicund appearance of enjoying life. It is a principal virtue of the tulips (and many other bulbs); the peonies; hostas (at least in spring) some roses; planes; poplars; many pines.

A more specialized form of the same virtue is to be able to thrive where little else can. Plants thus acquire local merit points which do not apply elsewhere. Few trees will stand a full salt-laden sea blast, for example. The sycamore, often regarded as little better than a weed, has won its battle honours as the first line of defence against onshore gales – a lop-sided thing, perhaps, but tough enough to allow something better to grow in its lee.

Similarly there are plants adapted to what can scarcely be called soil; grasses that can bind shifting sand, heathers for dank peat, gorse for dry heathland or the spindle bush for chalk.

In Arctic winters the ability to survive at all makes a plant gardenworthy, whereas in temperate places the sheer perversity of gardeners gives an extra half-point for glamour to plants that are liable to succumb when the occasional hard winter arrives.

Straightforward speed of growth is one of the most obvious qualities a gardener may be looking for. Hedge-plants are generally (but mistakenly) judged on how soon they will reach the required height. The word 'vigour' means both speed and overall willingness to keep growing. But very slow growth is a character equally in demand. Small gardens need scaled-down plants. There is a premium on tiny shrubs and dwarf conifers that take a long time to reach saleable size.

If flowers are the first thing that come to mind as desirable in a garden, there are many ways of judging the quality of a flower. There are those who see true beauty only in the naturally evolved balance and proportions of wild flowers, whether from Sikkim or a local ditch. Others judge a flower on the breeder's success in packing in the maximum number of petals. Others count on the brilliance of its colour. Others put stress on its oddness. A blue rose would be a best-seller regardless of its intrinsic merit. A very few have the depth of knowledge to judge the merits of a flower in the context of its peers, its ancestors, its breeding history and its record in cultivation.

The shape, colour, texture, scent, leaves and habit of a flower are all matters for critical debate. But there are other aspects beside its looks. A plant may gain merit by flowering earlier or later than others and thereby extending the season for that genus or species – or the very same quality may tell against it by making it more liable to damage by late or early frosts.

The length of its flowering season is critical too. Most of the saga of rose-breeding over the last 200 years or so has been concerned with making the term 'perpetual' come true. Such autumn flowers as Michaelmas daisies and chrysanthemums have immensely long periods in bloom. If the poppy flowered at that time of year it could not compete.

ABOVE: *It has taken forty years for this perfect specimen of* Juniperus compressa *to reach the height of the saxifrage opposite. Snail-like slowness can also be a virtue in plants.*

Flowers which having flowered die well or leave beautiful seed heads are worth extra points: those that leave sorry brown rags lose merit. There is extra credit, too, for flowers that dry off on the stem still keeping their perfect form, or that can be picked and dried. Dried delphiniums keep their potent blue.

Scent is a quality not much discussed except in general terms, and little understood. There is a small category of plants grown as much for their scent as for their other qualities. Such herbs as lavender, rosemary and mint; summer jasmine and Dutch honeysuckle; philadelphus; and balsam poplar are examples. With most plants, though (even with roses, which surely have a duty to be fragrant) we put too little stress on scent – which of course attracts insects too. Attraction for butterflies and birds clearly adds merit points.

Flavour was once the chief criterion for fruit and vegetables. Now it is considered secondary to appearance, uniformity and regularity of cropping. The reason for this is because expensive research takes commercial factors into account first.

BELOW: *The sages of horticulture; in the Trial Grounds at the RHS Wisley gardens a committee meets to supervise a plant trial.*

But this is a powerful argument for the planting and study of old varieties by amateurs who want taste, not supermarket shelf-life.

This is only to touch on the inexhaustible list of the contributions plants can make to gardens. Thorny plants make good barriers. Some plants take kindly to clipping and grow dense and snug. Some have flaking or shining bark as a principal feature. Some make dramatic gestures and some take up quaint poses. Some cover the ground as close as a rug and save us having to weed. Some we love for their anthology of associations. Some we must have simply because they are rare.

ABOVE: *John Tradescant the Elder, gardener to King James I of England, was one of the first to travel abroad for new plants: to Russia in 1618 and the Iberian Peninsula in 1621.*

BELOW: *The great French explorer-botanist, Joseph Piton de Tournefort, was a pioneer tourist, seeing all the sights of the Levant. This is the grotto of Antiparos in Greece.*

Few of today's ornamental plants are there at all. The emphasis is on plants useful for food, flavour, medicine, cosmetics or perfumery.

The flowers that were grown compose a list of lovely nursery-rhyme naiveté: 'Roses, red and damask, snapdragons, sweet williams, sops in wine [carnations], sweet briar, pinks, pansies, hollyhocks, cowslips, bachelor's buttons, wall-gillyflower [wall-flowers], columbines, daffadowndillies, lilies, lily of the valley, primroses, marigolds, valerian, love-in-a-mist, lavender, peonies and poppies' are all that are mentioned by Thomas Tusser in his *Five Hundred Pointes of Good Husbandrie*, published in the 1570s.

Botanical curiosity, like all the studies awakened by the Renaissance, was concerned at first simply with interpreting the ancients. Theophrastus or Dioscorides recommended such and such a plant for dysentery or the ague. Which is it? Frequently none of the plants in cultivation matched the description.

Pierre Belon, a Breton physician, was one of the first to go plant hunting abroad when he spent three years, from 1546 to 1548, in the eastern Mediterranean looking for the plants – and not only plants of course but all the wonders – described by the classical writers. He was an observer rather than a collector.

A much more potent influence at that time was the diplomatic bag. Turkish gardening, in the Persian tradition, had long before reached a point of sophistication undreamed of in Europe. The Viennese ambassador to Constantinople in the mid-sixteenth century was the enquiring and diligent Ghiselin de Busbecq, who sent home such Turkish specialities as tulips, hyacinths, anemones and the Crown Imperial, the first hint of the fabulous harvest of bulbs that poured for three centuries, and continues if not to pour, at least to flow, from the eastern Mediterranean and beyond. At various dates now forgotten (but often quoted as 1596, the year of publication of John Gerard's *Catalogus* in which many of them are first listed) a steady stream of plants from the nearer and more accessible Mediterranean was collected into gardens.

One of the first Englishmen to go out and look for them was the royal gardener John Tradescant the Elder, who visited Alicante and Algiers in 1621 and brought home plants cultivated by the Moors; notably an apricot and the Persian lilac.

It was another fifty years, though, before Sir George Wheler visited Greece and Turkey on a methodical plant hunt (he introduced St John's Wort, *Hypericum calycinum*), and not until 1700 that the greatest of French botanists, Joseph Piton de Tournefort, with Claude Aubriet – remembered for the aubrieta

LEFT: *Istanbul was the first entry-point for Asiatic plants into Europe, starting with Turkish bulbs in the 16th century and continuing with poppies, rhododendrons, azaleas, cyclamen . . .*

— as his professional painter, set off on the first major expedition through Greece, round Turkey and as far as Persia. Tournefort's finds included the common *Rhododendron ponticum* and the yellow azalea *R. luteum* on the south shores of the Black Sea, and the oriental poppy on the shores of the Caspian.

With its characteristic summer drought the Mediterranean is essentially a region of spring-flowering, summer-dormant plants. Most bulbs are typical. And the herbaceous plants that flower through our northern summer are over and beginning to die down in the Mediterranean by June. Most of its trees and shrubs are evergreen for the same reason. Many of the plants of the sun-baked rocky garrigues are highly aromatic: our garden herbs.

Even in the twentieth century the Mediterranean, so thoroughly explored for so long, has given us plants never apparently cultivated before. The broom *Genista lydia* was only introduced from northern Greece in 1926, the exquisite *Salvia haematodes* in 1938 and *Geranium dalmaticum* from Dalmatia in 1947.

BELOW LEFT: Rhododendron ponticum *was found by Tournefort in northern Turkey in 1701, but not grown in gardens until over sixty years later.*

BELOW CENTRE: *The common herbaceous peony of cottage gardens was introduced from the eastern Mediterranean, possibly from Crete, before 1548. Claude Aubriet, Tournefort's painter and companion, painted it. The double crimson form, which is now the cottage peony, appeared as a natural mutation in Antwerp shortly after.*

BELOW RIGHT: *The hardy cyclamen is a native of the Mediterranean shores. The more tender* Cyclamen persicum *is the parent of our modern house-plants.*

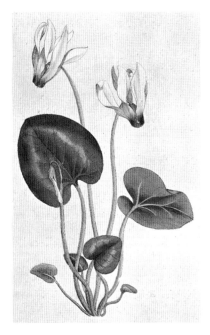

PLANTS FROM THE NEW WORLD

ABOVE: *John Bartram (1699-1777), the first American-born botanist, collected plants for correspondents in England.*

BELOW: *The South American potato was illustrated in the 1633 edition of John Gerard's Herbal.*

RIGHT: *Alexander von Humboldt and Aimé Bonpland explored Central and South America, camping at the foot of Mount Chimborazo.*

This was the year Sir Francis Drake left to sail around the world. The book was a translation of the work of a Spaniard, Dr Monardes.

Spain's new South American empire was tropical and sub-tropical, with Florida as its northern extreme. Its economic plants, which included tobacco, potatoes, tomatoes, marrows and such flowers as marigolds and sunflowers, were the first American plants to reach Europe in the sixteenth century.

Samples of the flora of North America, hardier and therefore potentially of more interest for Europe, came later. It is John Tradescant the Younger who is generally credited with being the first European gardener/botanist to go plant hunting in North America. He travelled to Virginia three times in 1637, 1642 and 1654. He kept no diary, but his catalogue published in 1656 shows that the famous Tradescant collection in London included such new American plants as Virginia creeper, tulip tree, red maple, swamp cypress, false acacia, and such future garden flowers as Michaelmas daisies and rudbeckias.

The equable climate of western Europe has no equivalent in eastern North America; its immense size and southerly latitudes (Boston equates to Rome, and Atlanta to somewhere in the Sahara) makes both winter and summer capable of vicious extremes. Generally, the plants of eastern North America are happiest in the continental climate of central Europe. The Gulf Stream summers of Britain can be altogether too tepid for them, failing to ripen their new growth or their seeds, although a wide range of trees and shrubs from north-eastern North America is successfully cultivated. The number of its species, however, dwarfs that of Europe, almost rivalling that of China, the only other country to have escaped the attrition of the Ice Ages. Whereas European plants in retreat from the ice reached the Mediterranean and were extinguished on its shores, American and Chinese species retreated south in good order, and in due course advanced north again. The

FAR LEFT: *Michaelmas daisies are typical of the North American meadow flowers that have enriched our borders.*

CENTRE LEFT: Fuchsia magellanica *grows in the woods of southern Chile as a tall bush. In northern gardens frost often cuts it to the ground.*

NEAR LEFT: *Dahlias are Mexican, long cultivated by the Aztecs before they were brought to Europe by the Spanish.*

magnolias are an example of a family long extinct in Europe, first discovered in America and later in even greater variety in China.

Missionaries despatched to the colonies by the botanically minded Bishop of London, Henry Compton, kept up the flow of new plants in the latter part of the seventeenth century. North America's first home-grown botanist was John Bartram of Philadelphia, whose employment by a group of plant enthusiasts in England was extremely fruitful. His methodical explorations of Indian country from Florida to the Great Lakes brought more than two hundred new plants into cultivation. Bartram was followed by others, notably John Fraser and André Michaux, who settled in South Carolina to collect plants for the French government, and made the first study of the many American oaks.

Until the mid-eighteenth century, the rich hunting-ground of South America was kept under lock and key by its jealous Spanish masters. The first explorer to begin work on its plants was Alexander von Humboldt, who made a five-year journey (1799-1804) through the little-known continent. Charles Darwin called him 'the greatest traveller who ever lived'.

Chile was destined to be the South American country of most significance for gardeners. Its plants do splendidly in the Gulf Stream climate of North West Europe. The 4,000-mile Pacific slope of the Chilean Andes provides every possible climatic niche for a range of plants very unlike those of the rest of America: indeed, some species are related only to the flora of New Zealand, south-eastern Australia and Tasmania. But glimpses into Chile were rare until it gained independence in 1817.

Most of the important plants were collected by professionals employed by the English nursery firm of Veitch, particularly William Lobb in the 1840s. Fuchsias, abutilons, berberis, escallonia, alstroemeria, eucryphia and tropaeolum are a sample of the more decorative and adaptable Chilean genera. Harold Comber also made an important and successful follow-up visit in the 1920s, finding better and hardier forms of many plants. The flame-tree, *Embothrium* 'Norquinco form', is the most famous.

FLOWERS FROM THE CAPE

Florists that they are, the Dutch who made the Cape their land-fall on the way to the Indies in the seventeenth century must have been fascinated by its strange and brilliant flowers.

Cut off by equatorial Africa and the oceans from contact with other temperate lands, South Africa's plants have evolved in isolation. Although there are floristic

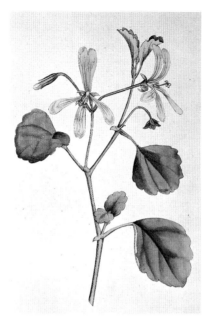

links with distant western Australia and South America, the Cape has scores of
plants that have very few or no close relations elsewhere. Certainly the most famous
is the pelargonium, popularly known as the geranium, but agapanthus, kaffir lilies,
nerines, galtonias and freesias, crocosmias and dieramas and the startling daisies
of gazanias, dimorphothecas, mesembryanthemums and arctotis are all unique to
the Cape. The Cape is the world headquarters of the Ericas, the heathers: 470 out
of 500 species are Cape natives. It is also famous for Proteas.

The coastal part of South Africa has a Mediterranean climate, with long seasonal droughts, and many of its plants retreat into bulbs for the summer. Others,
such as pelargoniums, protect themselves with hairy leaves and aromatic oils.

The early Dutch, oddly enough, did little exploration or systematic exploitation of South Africa's plants. It was not until the botany boom of the eighteenth
century, with Linnaeus conferring celebrity on plants and plant collectors alike,
that the action really started. In 1772 Linnaeus's pupil Carl Peter Thunberg stayed
at the Cape on his way to Japan. At the same time, Sir Joseph Banks at Kew sent
out Francis Masson, who spent three years amassing more than five hundred new
species. 'The famous journey to the Levant made by Monsieur Tournefort . . . at
enormous expense,' wrote Banks, 'did not produce so great an addition of plants
to the Paris gardens as Mr Masson . . . has to those at Kew.'

OPENING UP THE WEST

The plains and mountain ranges west of the Mississippi are a barrier to plants as
well as to people. When Captain George Vancouver sailed up the West Coast in
1792, and twelve years later Captain Meriwether Lewis and Lieutenant William
Clark made the first continental crossing, they entered a whole new botanical realm.

Climatically western North America has more in common with Europe than
the rest of North America: the north perpetually rainy, the central coast tempered
by the famous fogs from the cold Pacific, the south so dry that it corresponds well
enough to North Africa.

In the Ice Ages it was a sea-locked last resort where such species as the redwoods and the monterey pine and cypress survived in isolated coastal groves. Behind

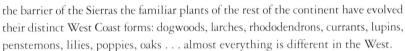

the barrier of the Sierras the familiar plants of the rest of the continent have evolved their distinct West Coast forms: dogwoods, larches, rhododendrons, currants, lupins, penstemons, lilies, poppies, oaks . . . almost everything is different in the West.

Above all it is the world's great repository of conifers. David Douglas, sent from London by the Horticultural Society in 1825 to explore (and to become the most famous of all professional plant hunters) wrote home, 'you will begin to think that I manufacture new pines at my pleasure'. Such trees as the Douglas fir and Sitka spruce have revolutionized the forestry of the northern world as thoroughly as the hardy western cypresses have its gardens: the Lawson cypress in its many forms is quasi-universal today.

Of uniquely western flowering plants the most influential have been the ceanothus, which covers the coastal hills with a blue mist in spring, perhaps the Oregon grape (*Mahonia aquifolium*), the garrya with its winter tassels, the flowering currant, *Ribes sanguineum*, or the ground-covering gaultheria. Certainly a whole host of annuals: California poppies, godetia, clarkia, nemophila, phacelia, limnanthes . . . plants that can take instant advantage of rain at any time of year to begin their brief life-cycles.

ABOVE LEFT: *Many species of ceanothus, the blue-flowered evergreen, cover the coastal hills of California.*
ABOVE CENTRE: *The California poppy was one of the many annuals introduced by David Douglas.*
ABOVE RIGHT: *'Douglas country' in the north-west is dominated by the Douglas fir.*

BELOW LEFT: *Sergeant Gass of the Lewis and Clark expedition kept a graphic diary of events.*
BELOW RIGHT: *The evening primrose (*Oenothera missouriensis*) was found in 1811 by Nuttall and Bradbury while exploring the Missouri.*

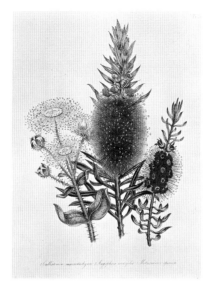

ABOVE LEFT: The 500-odd species of eucalyptus grow in every conceivable situation in Australia but nowhere else.
ABOVE CENTRE: Australian plants, like the bottle-brush, Callistemon, *almost seem to have developed a national character of their own.*
ABOVE RIGHT: The banksias commemorate Sir Joseph Banks. Two-thirds of their family, the Proteas, are in Australia, one-quarter in South Africa and the rest in South America.

BELOW: In 1772, the year after returning from his voyage to Australia, Captain Cook sailed the Resolution *to explore the Pacific.*

BOTANY BAY

Australia's plants began to be added to the catalogue in the closing years of the eighteenth century. It was no less a figure than Sir Joseph Banks himself, a man of fortune who already at the age of twenty-five was an eminent scientist, who sailed with Captain Cook in the *Endeavour* and in 1770 commemorated his excitement by christening his landfall Botany Bay.

The ancient island, so ancient that its very mountain ranges have been eroded away leaving a colossal plain, has developed a flora and fauna after its own fashion. Nowhere else do so few plant genera dominate the landscape. Acacia (or 'wattle'), Eucalyptus and Grevillae make up a vast proportion of the total of trees and shrubs. Eucalyptus is unique on earth in its ecological diversity and dominance: the 500-odd species lord it over dry bush, rain-forest and snowy pass alike.

Australia's flora has close links with South Africa, perhaps surprisingly considering the width of the Indian Ocean. The important Protea family, famous in South Africa for its spectacular flowers, has its headquarters in Australia with grevillea, banksia, hakea and lomatia. But few of these are familiar names to gardeners, and indeed Australian plants have generally been found difficult to cultivate in the temperate north.

The heroes of Australian botany were pioneers of the sort who are temperamentally given to a John the Baptist regime. Most notable of a hardy company were Allan Cunningham, who scoured the bush for fifteen years from 1817, and also visited New Zealand, and James Drummond, who explored south-western Australia for plants from the mid-1830s until his death in 1863.

By then, flourishing botanical gardens, still some of the world's finest, had been established in each of the Australian colonies. Sydney, Melbourne and Adelaide each have a magnificent collection. More recently the hunt had been for hardier forms of the more desirable Australian plants in higher altitudes and in cooler Tasmania, to the south. Blending Australian plants with non-Australian, though, is always a touchy business. Few look at home in foreign gardens.

PLANTS FROM NEW ZEALAND

New Zealand is even more of an enigma than Australia. A very high proportion of its plants are endemic, that is to say known nowhere else. What links it has are evidence of the land-bridge which once joined Antarctica with New Zealand on one side and South America on the other. Before the Ice Ages such genera as Nothofagus, the southern beech, now found in Chile, Argentina and New Zealand, with a remnant population in Tasmania and South-East Australia, must have covered the Antarctic continent.

New Zealand's climate ranges from the subtropical in the north to the alpine and cool-temperate in the spectacular mountains and fiords of the extreme south. It produces few garden plants of brilliant colouring, but a horde of quiet evergreens of subdued design which have made their mark in sophisticated modern gardening, in zones of no very hard or prolonged frost. Hebe and olearia are the biggest groups, and senecio perhaps the best known. Another is pittosporum. Unfortunately the two splendid New Zealand conifers, agathis and dacrydium, like her tree ferns, are tender in most of Britain, but the very striking cordylines or cabbage trees and flax (*Phormium*) are first-class garden plants in zone 8. To alpine gardeners New Zealand is a treasury of plants of subtle beauty, including acaena, celmisia, parahebe and raoulia. Foresters, meanwhile, are often tempted (and frustrated) by the southern beeches, another genus shared by New Zealand and South America – and nowhere else.

Alan Cunningham was the first botanist to visit New Zealand, but the missionary William Colenso, from 1834, was the great explorer of the islands' sometimes disconcertingly different flora.

ABOVE: *On his return from Australia and New Zealand in 1771 the young Sir Joseph Banks was painted by Benjamin West in the robes of a Maori chief.*

FAR LEFT: *New Zealand flax,* Phormium tenax, *has leaves similar to a giant iris which yield one of the finest fibres known.*

LEFT: *Olearias, or daisy bushes, are another New Zealand contribution to mild gardens. This is* O. macrodonta.

ASIA: THE JACKPOT

BEFORE THE ICE AGES THE SAME PLANTS WERE SPREAD IN A GLORIOUS MIXTURE THROUGHOUT THE NORTHERN TEMPERATE WORLD. IT WAS THE ENCROACHING ICE CAP THAT EDITED THEM, ELIMINATING THOUSANDS OF SPECIES FROM NORTH AMERICA AND EVEN MORE FROM EUROPE.

ABOVE: *Sir Joseph Hooker holds court in Nepal in 1849. Collecting looks luxurious; the reality was strenuous.*

BELOW: *A Japanese scroll of the early 19th century portrays the isolated Dutch trading post of Deshima near Nagasaki, with gardeners tending plants destined for Europe.*

As the Ice Cap stayed much farther north over the Asian land mass than over the 'western' side of the globe, China and Japan still have the descendants of almost the complete set, with local variations.

This vast treasure-house of plants remained unknown, apart from a few tantalizing glimpses, to Western gardeners until the last century. Chinese and Japanese gardeners had meanwhile been selecting and breeding the best garden plants for far longer than anyone in the West. At the same time intensive cultivation left no room for wild plants in the populous regions around the ports, so that what the first Western visitors to China and Japan saw was entirely a cultivated flora: their botanizing was done in nurseries.

In 1698 John Cunninghame, a surgeon with the East India Company, was the first into China, where he bought plants and paintings of plants. The camellias he sent home were the first ever seen in Europe. Next, and more significant, were French missionaries, admitted on sufferance by the suspicious Chinese for their scientific skills. Father Pierre d'Incarville arrived in 1740 and stayed fifteen years, sending back to London and Paris all the seed and information he could collect – enough, together with East India Company contacts, to start a craze for chinoiserie in all the decorative arts, including gardening.

Gardeners pestered the captains of merchant ships to bring home all they could for them from China: by this means the China roses reached the West. In 1804 William Kerr, an official plant collector from Kew, was sent out and the stream of plants increased. But China remained obstinately closed to foreign exploration of the interior until after the shameful episode of the Opium War in 1842, when she had no option but to let Europeans in. Thus in 1843 the exploration of inland China was begun by Robert Fortune; a story tense with adventure. Its most far-reaching result was the introduction (by unashamed smuggling) of China's closely-guarded tea-plant to British India.

Japan, not unwilling at first to talk to foreigners, had been quickly disillusioned by Western deceit and closed her doors to all but the Dutch, who were allowed

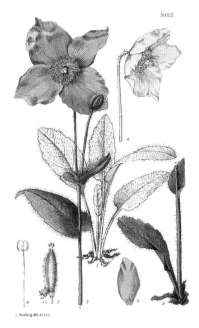

FAR LEFT: *The blue poppy, found by the French missionary J.-M. Delavay in 1886, remained a legend until F. Kingdon-Ward brought home seed from Tibet in 1926.*

LEFT: *Ernest 'Chinese' Wilson explored inland china for the Arnold Arboretum of Boston. His haul was more than 1,000 'new' plants.*

a trading post at Nagasaki. Two doctors with the Dutch Company, Engelbert Kaempfer in 1690 and Carl Thunberg in 1775, were until 1823 the only Western botanists to have seen her plants. As a result many Japanese plants bear their names.

From the 1840s the flow of new plants from Asia to Europe became a spate. The Himalayas turned out to be the centre of rhododendrons, providing hundreds of species from forests of unimagined richness and variety, thick with the primulas, poppies and lilies that were to revolutionize gardening. Inland China had more trees and shrubs to offer than any other corner of the globe. Japan had azaleas, maples, roses, magnolias, lilies and of course flowering cherries – all fastidiously bred in her nurseries into more forms than anyone could ever collect in one place. At first this harvest was gathered in mainly by British and French collectors, later also by Americans.

One of the most famous collectors was E. H. 'Chinese' Wilson, who worked in the early 1900s for Veitch's nursery in London and for the Arnold Arboretum of Boston, USA. Wilson alone introduced at least one thousand new plants to cultivation.

BELOW LEFT: Rhododendron arboreum *was the stimulus to ransack the Himalayas for its relations.*

BELOW RIGHT: *Lady Amherst, wife of the Governor-General of India in the 1830s, introduced* Clematis montana *from Simla, north of Delhi.*

Rhododendron arboreum

Camellia japonica

ABOVE LEFT: *Chrysanthemums, like most plants introduced from Japan, have been cultivated there for centuries and developed into innumerable forms. They were introduced to Japan from China in about AD 800.*

ABOVE CENTRE: *Sargent's cherry, native of northern Japan, is one of the earliest in flower and colours fiery red in early autumn.*

ABOVE RIGHT: *The first Chinese plants known in the West were from gardens, including many forms of* Camellia japonica.

At the same time other parts of western China and Tibet (then a wild and dangerous country racked by civil war and infested with bandits) were being combed for plants by George Forrest, Reginald Farrer (who started the cult of the rock garden), Frank Kingdon-Ward, William Purdom, Frank Meyer and Joseph Rock.

Unfortunately, a large proportion of the great flood of Chinese plants was subsequently lost to cultivation: there was simply too much at once. Nor was the ground completely covered. It remained for the reopening of China in the 1970s to allow a fuller exploration of her endless floral wealth.

PLANT HUNTING CONTINUES

Two World Wars and the Chinese Communist Revolution put an effective end to the introduction of new plants from the most fecund source of all, China – and from most others as well. It was not until the late 1970s that China opened its doors again to tourists. The stimulus of new plant introductions in turn coincided with and stimulated a surge of interest in plants from outside the well-trodden garden round.

If botanical gardens led the way, they were rapidly followed by amateurs with specialist interests and knowledge. Membership of horticultural societies has mushroomed in the last quarter of the twentieth century; both cause and effect of an intensified interest in new, rare, exotic or otherwise different plants to grow. If the majority of these are cultivars spawned in the booming nursery trade, a substantial number are either entirely new, or better forms of already-discovered plants being introduced or reintroduced from the wild.

China's own botanists never ceased exploring. The introduction of *Metasequoia glyptostroboides*, a tree previously known only as a fossil, in the dangerous days of the 1940s is an indication of their activities. Two of the first plant expeditions involving foreigners were the Sino-American exploration of Western Hubei in 1980 and in the following year a Sino-British visit to Yunnan. The latter introduced, among many other plants, new geraniums, new hypericums, a new deutzia and a new pleione.

Since these first sorties hundreds of collectors, many from botanical gardens but many also as free agents in a way that was impossible a generation before, have criss-crossed western China, introducing thousands of new plants to the West.

The best-known is the Englishman Roy Lancaster, who has also written and illustrated detailed and graphic accounts of a plant-hunter's life both in China and Nepal. Since 1979 his introductions have included two valuable new mahonias, *M. gracilipes* and *M. confusa*, two new sorbuses, two cotoneasters, several hypericums, an oak, sedum, epimedium, incarvillea and fargesia.

The Japanese collector Minori Ogisu has concentrated on Sichuan, collecting a new rose, *R. chinensis* var. *spontanea*, new bergenias, hellebores, peonies, alliums and more epimediums. Other Britons include Christopher Brickell and Alan Leslie of the Royal Horticultural Society, Peter Cox, Chris Grey-Wilson and Martyn Rix, (whose introductions include *Corydalis flexuosa* and *Tiarella polyphylla*). American and other collectors have brought home new birches, liquidambars, rhododendrons, limes, hornbeams, stachyurus and pseudopanax – to mention only trees and shrubs.

The Himalayas have never been off-limits in the same way as China. Tony Schilling of the Royal Botanic Gardens, Kew has explored widely in Nepal and Bhutan, deepening our knowledge especially of birches and introducing *Euphorbia schillingii*, *Polygonum tortuosum*, hedychiums and *Cotoneaster cavei*. Other explorer-botanists in the same countries and Kashmir have been Roy Lancaster, Tom Spring-Smith (who collected the superb *Daphne bholua* 'Gurkha'), Keith Rushforth and Chris Chadwell.

Introductions have meanwhile continued from Japan, Korea and Taiwan; also from Australia (especially hardier Eucalyptus) and New Zealand. The Essex nurseryman Graham Hutchins has been the main collector of such New Zealand plants as hebes, sophoras, raoulias and the strangely inert-looking weeping purple-flowered nothospartium.

Mexico remains a fertile source of new species; a land corridor where pines and oaks in particular abound. The Arnold Arboretum in Boston has been especially active south of the border. Mexican introductions in recent years include *Magnolia dealbata*, *Pinus culminicola*, *Hamamelis mexicana*, *Quercus risophylla*, *Mahonia russellii* and many salvias. Texan nurseries are a rich source of unknown or little-known Mexican plants.

The time will come when every species likely to appeal to a gardener will have been gathered in. But plant introductions will not stop even then. Keen observers will continue to find better forms or variants of plants both rare and common – and of course plants will continue to produce mutant forms in the wild. And nurserymen will continue to find a public clamouring for them.

ABOVE: Mahonia gracilipes *from Sichuan is one of the oustanding new introductions from China in the 1980s.*

BELOW: *Roy Lancaster in Sichuan in 1981. The botanist's life in the field has changed in one particular: Ernest Wilson went armed.*

A GARDEN
PLACE FOR EVERY
PLANT

CONSIDERING THE VAST DIFFERENCES BETWEEN THEIR ORIGINS, IT IS REMARKABLE HOW MANY PLANTS HAVE SETTLED DOWN TO A QUIET SUBURBAN LIFE: NORTH AMERICAN WITH SOUTH AFRICAN; CHINESE WITH CHILEAN; PLANTS WHOSE NATURAL HABITATS ARE AS UNALIKE AS THE DRY VELDT AND A WATER-MEADOW ARE FOUND GROWING SIDE BY SIDE IN GARDENS.

TODAY WE CAN LOOK UP ANY PLANT WE ARE EVER LIKELY TO ENCOUNTER AND DISCOVER ITS POTENTIAL SIZE, ITS HABIT OF GROWTH, ITS TASTE IN SOIL AND TEMPERATURE, AND IN MOST CASES ITS CONVENTIONAL OR HABITUAL PLACE, IF ANY, IN GARDENS. YET AS EACH NEW DISCOVERY WAS ADDED TO THE CATALOGUE, ➤

ABOVE: *Borrowing plants from warmer climates is a powerful way of evoking an almost subtropical atmosphere in (in this case) a Devon garden.*

from the first Turkish tulips to the early eastern American trees to the latest alpines from New Zealand, it has been planted by tentative gardeners, not knowing whether they were handling a fragile gem or had a potential menace on their hands, in this soil and that and in various situations of sun and shade. Many plants never survived their first encounter with cultivation. The ones with the best chances were those accompanied by field notes from their discoverers, saying whether they were found clinging to cliffs or buried in forests, at what altitude, with what rainfall, in what depth of what kind of soil.

Until the latter half of the eighteenth century garden designers were extremely conservative about plants, using only those that had been known for centuries. To collect plants was another matter – certainly nothing to do with garden design. The English landskip school (pages 257–8) was particularly austere; curiously enough at the very moment when the passion for new discoveries and the pressure to find garden places for them was rising to a peak.

As we shall see, the austerity of the original designs was usually short-lived; they soon began to accumulate irresistible curiosities. Within the first thirty years of the nineteenth century the sifting of the great stream of novelties was well under way. As new plants came into cultivation they began to be assigned to their places in gardens that were becoming more and more like plant menageries.

Field and meadow plants were accumulated in herbaceous borders; rockeries were built, at first for ferns and then for alpines; bog plants were packed off to pond gardens. The rose garden came into being to accommodate the many new kinds of rose. 'American' gardens were filled with rhododendrons and azaleas, shrubberies with shrubs and arboreta with trees, while patterned bedding was devised as a way of displaying outdoors all the tender plants that could not pass the whole of their lives in the garden.

This section of the book is a review of these conventional horticultural niches, which in due course became the backbone of almost all gardeners' references to plants, supplemented in some cases by the forms they take – bulbs or tubers for example; or their natural habit, as in the case of climbers.

The current trend, however, is to abandon the segregation which the nineteenth century introduced and to treat plants on the basis of common needs, putting all the acid-loving plants together in a damp shady corner, or massing Mediterranean-climate plants in beds of gravel where they can sizzle to their hearts' content. This is certainly the most satisfactory way for gardeners whose concern is concentrating on the plants themselves. It is gaining ground all the time on its ecological merits: more and more plantsman-designers are thinking of habitat first, often with very convincing results.

PREVIOUS SPREAD
(LEFT): *A great garden assembles plants from widely differing countries and climates to form a fantasy of nature;* (RIGHT): *Of all plants, roses have been subjected to the most selective breeding and refinement.*

The alternative, which is perhaps the most ambitious of all ways of gardening, is picture-making in terms of design and texture and colour alone, drawing on the whole plant repertoire and forcing it into patterns – an awe-inspiring undertaking, but the way in which most of the great English gardens of the twentieth century and their imitators were conceived, and have laboriously to be maintained.

TREES IN GARDENS TREES ARE THE MOST PERMANENT

PLANTS IN ANY LANDSCAPE. WHATEVER ELSE YOU MAY DECIDE TO PLANT OR BUILD, TREES WILL

ALWAYS DETERMINE THE OVERALL SCALE AND PROVIDE THE FRAMEWORK.

Their roots, their shelter and their shade dictate the conditions that other plants have to enjoy or endure. Their textures and colours and tracery form the background to your compositions. Their domes and spires create the skyline.

For anyone lucky enough to garden in old woodland there can be no compromise. The trees tell you what sort of garden you have. The way to success is to recognize the character they impose and take advantage of it, stressing the cool beechiness or wild pininess, either by complement or contrast, in everything you plant.

But the more common situation is a jumble of trees of no particular persuasion, some inside the garden, some (just as important) next door or in the street. Some perhaps perfect for their situation, others wildly unsuitable: greedy, messy or just plain ugly.

We tend to accept trees because they are there, and because they take so long (we think) to grow. Yet a tree should have a reason for being there as much as any other plant. Furthermore it should, and can, be the right tree. For the range is almost infinite – in size, shape, colour, texture of leaf, interest of form, speed of growth, time of flowering. If we consider only one of these aspects – usually it is either speed of growth or flowers that is given priority – there may well be a catch in store. The fastest trees nearly always have the greediest, farthest-ranging roots. The most lavish-flowering are frequently as dull as ditchwater once their two- or three-week annual performance is over.

The trick in choosing trees is first to consider what role they have to play, and secondly how many virtues and how few vices we can combine in the plant that is going to loom so large for so long on our horizon.

It applies to existing trees as well as new ones. There is no garden where an ugly and unnecessary tree must stay. Only take time to consider: is it always ugly, and always unnecessary? You must watch it carefully for four seasons before you

ABOVE: *The moisture-loving tupelo of the eastern States,* Nyssa sylvatica, *is one of the finest and most reliable big trees for brilliant autumn colour.*

LEFT: *Lombardy poplars provide perspective and a hint of formality, a silver willow a focus and a deodar cedar a frame in the author's garden at Saling Hall in Essex.*

can answer that. The common alder receives little praise in summer, but in winter its dense clutter of cones and catkins catching the low sun is a major pleasure. Europe's common field maple may be considered boring in spring but ends the year with a lingering glow of gold.

It helps to consider the necessity or otherwise of trees if we enumerate the possible jobs they can do for the gardener. We can codify them as the seven S's of (if you must) silviculture.

Shelter is the first and perhaps the most essential for the sake of the rest of the garden. The power of the wind to reduce the efficiency and performance of plants is something the gardener must always bear in mind. In a small garden hedges or shrubs may be all there is room for in the way of shelter, but a big garden needs a screen of big trees to windward, even at the expense of a view. If the view is so wonderful that it draws all eyes out of the garden it may be better to dispense with the distraction of foreground planting altogether – and hence with the need for trees to shelter it.

In far more cases some kind of compromise is possible, with an oblique glimpse through sheltering trees. But it is a mistake to cut off the lower branches of trees on the windy side so as to be able to see under them: the wind, baffled by their tops, will come through between the trunks faster than ever. If on the contrary the view is spoiled by an eyesore, near or far, a quick-growing tree is the only practicable way to blot it out. The rule to remember here is that the screen near the eye hides more than the screen near the object. A mere bush by the window or on the terrace will be as effective as an oak on the boundary – at least locally, and while your main screen grows.

Seclusion is perhaps the strongest psychological effect trees have to offer. A sense of privacy is not everyone's first thought in planning a garden. Americans seem to get on very well without it in those suburbs where all the houses are set in one big lawn. Yet the need for privacy is a strong feeling in most European countries. To me it is essential not to be seen taking my pleasure among the flowers, or grunting over the potatoes.

Seclusion means more than just privacy. It means the indefinable sense of enclosure and security that a garden should give. Wide skies are stimulating and

RIGHT: *Two avenues of holm oaks severely trained with tight round crowns flank the formal East Garden at the 17th-century Hatfield House in Hertfordshire.*

invoke adventurous feelings; the reverse of the garden spirit of timeless calm. It is an old axiom of gardening that the centre should be kept open – in order that the sides should be seen to be encircling.

The role of trees here is to limit the amount of sky you see by creating the third S, the skyline. It is the strongest line in the whole landscape, yet one which is generally ignored, and very rarely consciously composed. Its dominance is obvious, however, once you become aware of it. The best way to look at the skyline is as the light fades and details blur on a clear evening. The light sky is a definite shape above the dark masses of buildings and trees. Is it a pleasing, interesting shape or monotonous or unbalanced? If there is a pond in the picture the skyline has an added importance, appearing upside down as well. Look at it in the pond. Mirrors always show a fresh aspect of what they reflect.

Shade is a most practical reason for planting, or not planting, trees, according to whether your summers are torrid or temperate. In North America it is probably the single most important factor – witness the fact that the professional amenity tree association is called the Shade Tree Conference.

There are heavy shade trees such as sycamore and horse chestnut and light-dappling ones such as birch, willow or eucalyptus. The choice of public planners is often a late-leafing tree such as the plane, *Robinia* or *Gleditsia*, whose shade develops late and lasts only for the hottest months. Fruit trees, apples in particular, seem to give the ideal shade. An orchard is a lovely place to picnic on a hot day.

An exact calculation of where and when the shade of a particular tree falls can be helpful. The diagrams (on page 20) that map the movement of the sun in the sky show that, for example, a tree to the southwest gives most shade to a house during the hottest hours of summer.

The sense of scale in a garden is influenced by trees more than any other single factor. An exaggerated contrast between tall fore-ground and miniature background trees gives a powerful perspective to the view: the miniatures seem a whole landscape away. The opposite effect is created by a foreground of, for example, orchard trees, with the crowns of trees of middle height behind them, surmounted by distant giants. The distance is telescoped so that all the variants of form and texture seem almost to be in the same plane. The Japanese are specialists in false perspective. By isolating a stunted pine on a rocky outcrop they manage to convey the idea of boundless space in a mere courtyard.

Consciously or not, deliberately or not, the trees give a garden its basic division of volume: its structure. Where they are all deciduous the structure can disintegrate at leaf-fall – the great argument for including a proportion of evergreens in the basic shape-giving planting.

All this is strategy: the use of trees for what they can contribute as the biggest plants in the garden. Most important of all, of course, is the value to the senses of the tree itself, as sculpture to be admired for its own sake.

CHARACTER AND FUNCTION

Trees must be functional: their share of garden space demands it. Their function also dictates whether you choose tall-growing forest trees or orchard-size flowering trees, dense smothering agglomerations of green (or evergreen) or airy balletic structures of much limb and little leaf.

I find it useful to categorize the character of trees under half a dozen general headings. First I divide the deciduous from the evergreen. Then those whose main

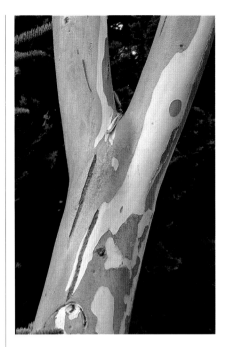

ABOVE: *The hardy snow gum,* Eucalyptus niphophila, *is one of the best of many trees with coloured or peeling bark. The birches have the widest range of colours, from silver to deep pink and near-black.*

season of attraction is spring from those which do their thing in autumn – leaving in a special class of their own those which have two worthwhile performances (or indeed are lovely year in, year out).

In small gardens one annual performance is not enough. However many pink petals some of the cherries and ornamental crabs rain down in spring their leaden leaves for the rest of the year condemn them, unless, like *Prunus sargentii*, they produce an autumn blaze, or like *Malus* 'Golden Hornet' or *M. robusta* they hold heavy crops of glowing fruit far into winter.

The small or medium-sized trees that get on this exclusive list include most of the birches, whose elegant architecture and fascinating bark are as effective in winter as summer; several of the hawthorns, but particularly *Crataegus × lavallei*, which flowers as lavishly as an elder and holds its gleaming leaves as long as its glistening berries; the amelanchiers, for their delicate flowering as the new leaves open and their bonfire orange in October; the medlar, for wide white flowers and a strange medley of autumn colours; many *Sorbus* species, but specially *hupehensis*, pale grey all summer and yellow with white berries in autumn, and 'Joseph Rock', whose leaves turn to everything from purple to orange at the same time as its fruits ripen to canary yellow; flowering dogwoods for all the qualities; the golden acacia, *Robinia pseudoacacia* 'Frisia', for sustained substitute sunshine; the weeping willow for every quality except moderation and some little willows for pretty leaves, brilliant bark, and furry catkins in the dead of winter; a whole catalogue of maples for lovely leaves at all times and unparalleled fieriness before they fall; and magnolias, not just for their wonderful waxen flowers but for the air of aristocracy that never leaves them. It is a crime to stop: pear trees should be on the list; the Italian alder, the quince, the sumach, the catalpa . . .

There are situations where the one thing that counts is speed. Every tree has its characteristic growth curve, given reasonable conditions. Some that start out like hares end as tortoises; others that dawdle for their first years suddenly startle their proprietors by putting on a metre a year.

Wherever eucalyptus will grow they are champions for instant and sustained speed. A cider gum (*Eucalyptus gunnii*) grew 6m (20ft) in two years in my garden (but a small-leaved *E. parvifolia* proved hardier, and looks less shockingly as though it is in the wrong hemisphere). Again for mild climates the two conifer relics of the Monterey peninsula in California, the Monterey cypress and pine, are both alarmingly fast – a Monterey pine, in fact, once grew 6m (20ft) in one year (its fifth) in New Zealand. The nearest equivalent evergreen for cool-temperate climates is the Leyland cypress, which should manage 3m (10ft) in three years. Among hardy deciduous trees it is poplars and willows that hold the records: 25m (70ft) in fifteen years is fair for a black poplar, the same height even faster for a white willow with abundant water. Other potential garden trees with remarkable growth rates, depending on local conditions – I exclude such forest monsters as Douglas fir and Sitka spruce – include the wingnut, *Pterocarya*, the silver maple, *Acer saccharinum*, and the southern beech, *Nothofagus obliqua*. It would be right, however, to label these trees (at least the big poplars and willows) For Emergency Use Only as far as most gardeners are concerned. There comes the moment when they dominate the whole scene and reach their

BELOW: *The Japanese maples have as much to offer in a small garden as any tree: brilliance in autumn but fine structure and intricate texture over a long season.*

roots into every corner of the garden – especially into drains. Dismantling them can be extremely expensive.

The rule should be to plant the faster trees only when essential, and always to plant the tree you really want in the long term at the same time. Although what I call the three-year rule (for three years not much happens) applies to most trees and many shrubs, even oaks, reputedly so laggard, make long enough shoots to give you immense satisfaction when the three years are up. An 'English' oak, *Quercus robur*, can grow 4.5m (15ft) in ten years; an American red oak much more.

The categories continue, to help you in your choice, with the overall shapes of trees, distinguishing those that are cloud-like in maturity (the oak, the sycamore) from those that tower (the elm, the lime); those that fan out with several stems (Japanese maples, magnolias) from those that throw out a few important branches from a single stout trunk (old pines, for example, and cedars); those with regular whorls of branches (poplars, alders, most conifers) from those with many unimportant little branches that stay close to the stem (cypresses, and fastigiate trees such as the Lombardy poplar); weeping trees – there are many besides the willow – from rigid spires such as young spruces and firs.

Some are right for one garden job; some for another. Lightly engineered trees are right for the foreground, framing the view beyond. Solidly billowing ones end the view. Birches, Japanese maples, pines, cypresses and olives are the kinds of tree to plant near the eye; oaks, beeches and yews to keep for the bottom of the garden.

In every department of gardening there is a tug of war between variety and unity. With trees it is most obvious. Let us say you have room for six small trees in your garden. The temptation is to collect the six most startlingly different – one gold, one silver, one purple, one pointed, one with leaves like dinner plates, and one with dazzling autumn colour. I will not suppose you could not compose them to great effect, along with your roses, your rhododendrons, your herbs and your delphiniums. But it would be a restless, unfulfilled effect – a furniture showroom, not a furnished room. Plant it now with six similar, if not identical, trees: six fruit trees, for example, or any six with the same general colour and bearing. The suggestion of an orchard is immediately reassuring. The room is furnished to a purpose, not just to display its wares.

ABOVE: *The magnolias have the most individually opulent flowers of any trees. Magnolia x* soulangeana, *whose flowers appear before the leaves, looks best in relation to buildings; wonderful in a city street.*

PAUSE FOR THOUGHT

Planting a tree, certainly a large tree, is one of the most momentous commitments a gardener can make. It is hard to fully comprehend, as you choose the spot to dig your modest hole, mix a barrow of compost with a handful of bonemeal, spread-eagle the diminutive root system and finally firm around the whippy stem with your heel, that you have put in place something of serious power and permanence.

After a couple of years you note with delight that the annual shoot is over 60cm (2ft) long. After ten you are altering your other planting to allow for the spreading shade. After twenty the tree is a main feature of the garden, and still only one fifth of its potential final size. Some practical considerations are needed,

ABOVE: *The practice of pollarding, or cutting back the head of a tree to the same point repeatedly, can give striking effects – especially with willows. These red-stemmed willows are bursts of brilliant colour all winter, and are cut right back each spring.*

therefore, before you plump for a copper beech or horse chestnut.

The first is a commonsense appraisal of the maximum size of tree your garden can accommodate, remembering that neighbours close by may not appreciate the eventual shade, and perhaps overhanging branches. Any necessary surgery on a big tree is extremely expensive – especially in cramped urban or suburban conditions.

Mortgage lenders and insurance companies also take a thoroughly pessimistic view of trees near houses. Insurance claims arising from soil shrinkage, as tree roots dry out clay soils in dry summers, have resulted in simplistic and sweeping regulations. In Britain it is not recommended to allow any trees of over 8m (25ft) within 10m (33ft) of a building – which means that welcome shade to upper-floor windows becomes impossible.

A more realistic approach would take the soil-type into account. Gravel and sand do not shrink as clay does. Our ancestors chose well-drained gravelly or rocky spots to build whenever they could. Witness the 20m (60ft) Lombardy poplar growing within 4m (13ft) of where I sit in a 300 year old house.

Another practical consideration is the leaf-fall from big deciduous trees. Small-leaved trees (beeches, oaks, *Robinia*, *Sorbus* of the rowan persuasion, and of course conifers) cause far less problem in autumn than such 'messy' big-leaved trees as horse-chestnut and sycamore.

EVERGREENS: WINTER FURNISHING

Of all the things that far-northern gardeners might envy in a garden in a more balmy climate the most valuable are surely the broadleaved evergreen trees, shrubs and even the lowlier plants that look alive all winter.

In a bare winter garden the cheerful shine of a laurel leaf or the benevolent bulk of an old box bush are pleasures as great as any flowers. They stabilize the garden. They furnish its draughty spaces. They reassure us that spring will bring back the leafy enclosures.

In a Mediterranean climate this scarcely calls for comment. It is the normal regime of many plants to hang on to their leaves all winter, and let them go as the new ones come in spring. By being dressed all year they are theoretically in a position to grow whenever the ground has moisture enough. The risk they take is that a hard frost and a nasty wind will sear them instead. Very rarely is the damage more than temporary.

There are conifers with tough little needle-leaves that can take the same gamble in the far north. A covering of snow usually protects them from the worst of the winter. But broad-leaved evergreens are much more vulnerable. Even those whose cells can withstand freezing and thawing are in trouble. Snow can help protect them (though it can also break their branches), but bare to the icy blast, their metabolism in a frigid trance, their leaves become dehydrated. They emerge into spring at best disfigured, at worst dead.

The Ice Age put paid to whatever evergreens there may have been in Britain up to that time, leaving only (as native) the holly (which is odd, since English holly is not all that hardy), the ivy and juniper and yew.

The history of gardening in northern Europe, and the northern United States, since the seventeenth century has been a history of slowly bringing them back to their pre-Ice Age range – at first gingerly, protecting everything 'green', as they were originally called, in greenhouses – then with more confidence; now with a fairly comprehensive knowledge of their tolerance for cold, which is far more than our ancestors believed possible.

The great advance in knowledge has been the realization that wind and sun are as much the enemies as very low temperatures. By providing shelter and shade the northern limits of many evergreens can be pushed back surprisingly far. A few years ago the notoriously windy city of Chicago could hardly boast a single evergreen beyond a few unhappy-looking rhododendrons – the northern species such as *Rhododendron catawbiense* and *R. maximum* which have earned the often-used epithet of 'iron-clad'. Now after trials at the Morton Arboretum the list of evergreens for zone 5 is growing.

The battle-proven kinds include *Euonymus fortunei*, a low shrub with the useful capacity to climb walls, particularly north walls; English ivy; American holly (which unfortunately lacks the lustrous leaves of English holly); Oregon grape, *Mahonia aquifolium*, which does have a good gleaming leaf; *Pieris* (both *P. japonica* and *P. floribunda*, with their respectively drooping and erect creamy flowers in spring); drooping *Leucothoe*, which has something of the stance of a short bamboo; the little-leaf boxwood (very slow and low); even, apparently, a form of the evergreen magnolia of the South. Probably the best all-round garden plant on the list is mountain laurel, *Kalmia latifolia* with its blushing frilly flowers. If *Kalmia* came from the Canary Islands we would heat greenhouses for it.

Life is easier for any evergreen if snow falls early and deep, but those mentioned above have managed without it, given soil to their liking (which is on the whole light and acid), good drainage, shelter from the prevailing winter wind, and preferably the shade of pines. These are the things that should govern their placing in a cold garden.

Even among this limited range there is room for some interesting combinations; of dull leaves with shiny leaves; of upright forms with spreading forms. True, while they are covered with snow it makes little difference whether they have leaves or not, but as soon as it melts they furnish a background to the first flowers of the year.

In milder climates the list of evergreens in general use is a mere nibble at possibilities. Rhododendrons are the mainstay of many winter landscapes, but none are at their best in winter. They seem to fill their space with patient gloom.

Leaving flowers aside and concentrating on what leaves can contribute to the garden in winter, the many variegated hollies and several forms of elaeagnus have glints of gold and silver. Nothing in the garden shines brighter in winter than *Elaeagnus pungens* 'Maculata' – unless it be the

BELOW: *The masterly use of evergreens to provide a formal garden stage for the performance of the seasons. At Johns Hopkins Hospital, Baltimore, sprawling old boxwood hedges emphasize the lake-like level of the lawn, while cypresses lead the eye into intriguing woods. Four stone urns and a pair of flowering dogwoods are superbly dramatized in their evergreen setting.*

ABOVE: *Snow can damage evergreens,
but it can also protect them – and produce
striking abstract effects. The sugar-loaves
here are clipped box pyramids; the
columns, Irish junipers.*

monarch of the female hollies, 'Golden King' (*sic*), which combines scarlet fruit with dashing yellow-edged leaves.

Both the cherry laurel and the Portugal laurel have polished leaves (the first bigger and brighter green). Aucubas lost their good name when their yellow-spotted leaves were flaunted in every Edwardian front garden – but there must be some exciting way of using this most singular plant. Skimmias are excellent for dense and interesting dark shapes, growing eventually as high as a man, garnished, for the fortunate at least, with red marbles. Pyracantha and some of the cotoneasters are rose-relations profuse in their fruiting as well as useful for their winter green.

Another member of the rose family, the photinia (especially *P. serratifolia*) flushes very early in spring with red new growth, much appreciated (and regularly clipped into shape) by the Japanese. For sheer size of leaves that resist cold winters (down to zone 7) nothing can beat the loquat, *Eriobotrya japonica*. In England it can even be in scented flower at Christmas. But then there are evergreen viburnums and berberis, arbutus and escallonia, cistus and brooms – in fact it seems as many evergreen as there are deciduous shrubs.

To these we must now add an increasing range of Australasian evergreens, which are turning out to be tougher than anyone expected. Experiments with eucalyptus show that at least half a dozen forms from colder corners of Australia can be trusted in zone 8. To have big, fast-growing, broadleaved evergreen trees in the cool-temperate north is a revolution: the holm oak, virtually the sole candidate before, is maddeningly leisurely. If you set your heart on an evergreen oak – and have the space – choose the (almost evergreen) Lucombe oak, an eighteenth century cross between the Turkish and cork oaks thats towers in great billowing masses of light-reflecting and very oaky leaves. The specimen at Kew Gardens is the noblest plant in the whole collection.

CONIFERS

As the great forest trees of the northern world, holding all the records as far and away the tallest and oldest vegetables alive – 122m (367ft) and 5,000 years respectively – conifers may not seem cut out for gardens. But they have certain advantages over the equivalent full-scale broadleaves. Neither their branches nor their roots spread so far in maturity. Their leaf-fall is of little consequence, but can normally be left where it lies as an instant mulch, and most of them come into their own in winter.

They are the only big evergreens for very cold gardens. But in any garden they are some of the strongest creators of atmosphere, conveying a sense of changeless calm, gently scenting the air with resin. Few offer any conventional garden beauty, but a great many offer character, and most have some moment of glory, either in bright bold new shoots, surprisingly scarlet flowers, richly detailed cones or scaly, creviced or glowing bark.

As far as gardeners are concerned the big conifers in their early life can be easily classed as either spires or columns. The cypresses, false cypresses, thuyas, incense cedars and all trees with frond-like foliage fall broadly into the column category. Most of the rest, with a few exceptions, start life in Christmas-tree style, developing their strongly characteristic shapes only after thirty years or more.

The spruces and the silver firs go on as unrepentant Christmas trees all their days. Their most eye-catching members , and hence most often recommended for gardens, are the Colorado blue spruce for its icy colour, Brewer's weeping spruce for its mourning veil of near-black and the Korean fir for its heavy crop of purple cones while it is still below eye-level. Less obvious in their appeal, but more elegant and easier to live with, are the neat, tiny-needled Oriental spruce and the narrow tapering spire of *Picea omorika*, the spruce from the dry limestone of Serbia.

Pines are much harder to choose. In due course most pines billow out, forgetting their upright youth and striking fierce poses as they grow older. They vary vastly from the droopy long-leaved white pines to some of those from California with huge bristling brushes of stiff needles, from the intricate curly green-and-blue needlework of the Japanese *Pinus parviflora* 'Glauca' to the heavy bottle-green foliage of the Monterey pine. Finally, common though it is, it is hard to beat the combination of steely blue needles, salmon-orange bark and the wild highland poise of the Scots pine. There is a slow-growing 'golden' form of the Scots pine which would suit any small garden, especially in frosty weather.

Cedars, and often their leaf-losing cousins the larches, grow broadly beamy with age. It takes a hundred years for the cedar of Lebanon to form its famous dark plateaux in the sky, but the icy-blue Atlantic cedar starts demanding elbow-room much sooner and will overwhelm a small garden within twenty years. The deodar, its more relaxed-looking brother from the Himalayas, is potentially no less of a cuckoo in the nest.

A larch, with its look of the high forest near the tree-line, is perhaps too humdrum a choice, but there is one deciduous conifer I cannot overpraise – the swamp cypress. It does not demand a swamp, but in any decent soil will form a narrow tower of fine fresh green all summer turning in autumn to a dark squirrel brown for weeks on end. The much-discussed *Metasequoia*, known only as a fossil until it was found growing in remotest China in the 1940s, grows faster and is similar in many ways, but in colour, texture and floppy habit it is not so good.

The more conventional evergreen relations of these two are the Japanese *Cryptomeria* and the California redwoods, none of them garden trees in the usual sense, however much they dominate nineteenth-century plantations. But the *Cryptomeria* has a slower-growing form, 'Elegantissima', with soft curly foliage which turns a unique reddy-purple in winter; a strange tree which, when it reaches a certain height, falls over and lives recumbent.

The attraction of the cypresses is principally as background material of rich texture and many colours. For a rapid and reliable screen of rather dull matt green the Leyland cypress (× *Cupressocyparis*, a hybrid between *Cupressus* the true cypress and *Chamaecyparis* the false one) has no rival. The biggest Leylands have grown to well over 30m (100ft) in 60 years and kept a perfect flame shape, green from the ground up. Fifty years hence, when all the millions recently planted are full-grown, Britain will be unrecognizable. Ubiquitous as they already are, they are emphatically not the tree for a small garden.

Happily for gardeners the false cypresses have produced more 'sports' than any other tree. These wayward seedlings are our main source of coloured evergreens. There is a roster of a hundred or more of varying colour, size, texture and form – all worth study as garden ornaments. The blue-greys are at their best in summer when their new growth is bright; in winter they can look merely drab

ABOVE: *The hanging near-black shoots of Brewer's spruce from Oregon makes it one of the most dramatic conifers – best in the context of spring-green deciduous trees.*

BELOW: *Dwarf conifers, though rarely as small as the name implies, offer the gardener the chance to collect strange shapes and bright colours in a small space.*

ABOVE: *The quintessence of pine. A superbly trained Japanese black pine in a Kyoto monastery. It is hard to know whether the pine is imitating the eaves or the eaves the pine.*

and cold. The Lawson cypresses 'Columnaris Glauca' and 'Triomf van Boskoop' (the latter much bigger and broader) are two of the best blues. The brightest yellows, much more telling in winter and fairly radiant in summer, are the Lawsons 'Smithii', 'Lane' (syn. 'Lanei'), and 'Stewartii'. *Cupressus macrocarpa* 'Donard Gold' is even better, but can be damaged by cold winters.

The yew is not commonly considered a garden tree, except in its Irish or upright form, common in churchyards and rather gloomy company in a small garden, or as the best of all hedge plants. The juniper is another matter. Where other conifers bring dignity, junipers offer amenity. With as many colours as *Chamaecyparis* and some much more entertaining shapes, sprawling, spreading and gesticulating, juniper is perhaps the most horticultural of all the conifer clans. The only category more horticultural, uniquely horticultural in fact, are the dwarfs.

Conifers are particularly prone to what nurserymen call 'sporting' – producing freak growth, either as ugly ducklings in the seed bed or as witches' brooms – outbreaks of congested or deformed growth on the branches of normal trees.

If these sports can be persuaded to grow and can be propagated (it is not always easy) they provide a whole new range of miniature plants in shapes, textures and colours never seen before.

True dwarf conifers are some of the slowest-growing of all plants and can live happily in a pot for twenty years – but there is no clear dividing line, and many advertised as 'dwarf' are no such thing.

It takes restraint to use pygmy plants effectively in the garden. They must be segregated into a world of their own. They have become part of a whole gardening idiom in conjunction with beds of low heathers. Rock as a background is also suitably neutral in scale: they are gaining ground in many rockeries (often at the expense of more interesting but more temperamental plants).

The identity of dwarf conifers is a study in itself. Many were christened by their captors in a form of pseudo-Latin even worse than the botanical variety – though today the code permits only vernacular names.

It is almost impossible to choose from such a gallery, but the most popular dwarfs include miniature bush spruces, ground-hugging junipers, congested weeping hemlocks, tiny globular thuyas, shrunk cedars, deformed *Cryptomeria* and, above all, endless variations on the already endlessly various false cypresses. *Chamaecyparis* is the big name among dwarfs.

GARDEN HEDGES

IN THE TWIN ROLES OF DIVIDERS OF SPACE AND PROTECTORS OF GARDENS, WALLS HAVE TRADITIONALLY BEEN THE FUNCTIONAL CHOICE, HEDGES THE ORNAMENTAL ONE.

Walls encircled the outer boundaries of great estates, and supported the fruit trees in the kitchen garden. But in the pleasure grounds, as a setting for fine trees and flowers and sculpture, the ideal for centuries has been close-clipped evergreens – box, yew, holly, holm oak or cypress. Today the cost of new walls makes hedges the almost inevitable choice.

We have seen the virtue of hedges as shelter from the wind; how effective they are in speeding the growth of the plants they protect. We will turn later to the merits of dividing the garden space to give variety of scene, making the whole seem bigger than the sum of its parts.

Here we are concerned with hedges as plants – the principles of choosing, establishing and maintaining them. Or not plants, perhaps, so much as crops. It is a good starting point to look on a hedge – at least a formal hedge – as a permanent crop: a row of identical plants planted at unnaturally close spacing to give the effect of one long narrow plant. Like crops, hedges make special demands on the soil. It is easy to forget that even a well-established hedge needs regular feeding to restore what it loses with its annual clipping.

A good hedge starts with a good trench. It is well worth digging a full spade's depth and a metre wide, and putting a generous layer of compost or manure in the bottom, to give the roots easy luxurious feeding while the top is building up a solid structure. At least, as a minimum, loosen the soil with a fork over the same area and spread fertilizer before you plant. Not only do the little plants need to grow fast and keep you happy, but it makes weeding the new hedge infinitely easier if the soil is well cultivated – and weeding is vital in the first years before the roots have colonized the ground and the branches thickened to shade it.

For the same reason – ease of weeding – do not be tempted to plant a double or 'staggered' row of plants, however thick you want the hedge to be. It is far easier to weed a single line, and the final result will be just as impressive.

The new hedge will certainly need watering in its first few summers. But water in winter can be fatal. When young yew hedges die off in patches, which they sometimes do, the reason is often that the roots are drowning. There do not have to be puddles on the surface to drown them. Good drainage below is essential. If the soil is very heavy or the site low-lying it may be necessary to cut drains leading away from the hedge to a ditch or soak-away at a lower level.

The more often you trim the sides of a young hedge, within reason, the better. The idea is to encourage it to sprout and sprout

BELOW: *A hedge does not have to be tall or regular to achieve its effect. Gently-trimmed box, bulky and undulating, has an air of great authority and composure.*

ABOVE: *Formal hedges in hornbeam, holding their brown leaves in winter, are planted to imitate 'crinkle-crankle' snaking walls at Chatsworth in Derbyshire.*

again until it forms a dense thicket of twigs. The bottom should always be left slightly wider than the top to allow as much light as possible to reach it. The top should be left to grow straight up until it reaches the height you want, then trimmed as often as the sides.

The best hedge plants are those most apt to sprout again where they are cut – one of the reasons why yew is unbeatable (the others are its air of ageless permanence, its subtly varied colouring, and its uniquely impressive and venerable, yet slightly wobbly and comical architecture in maturity). Cut an old yew tree back to a bare pole and it will be green-fuzzed all over in the following year. When it comes to the rejuvenation of a dilapidated old hedge this is a vital consideration. Grubbing out a hedge and replanting it is a major operation. Much better to cut it right down to the ground, feed it liberally, and trim the sprouts from the stumps into a new hedge. But certain conifers, notably the cypresses, have no equipment for sprouting from old wood. When a cypress hedge gets bare there is nothing you can do but replant.

The trouble with fast-growing hedges is that they need cutting so often. The ideal, no doubt, would be a hedge that grew like cress up to a preordained height, then only a demure few centimetres a year. It is a decision the hedge planter must make: whether the quick screen or the eventual saving of effort is more important. Among the classic hedge plants, yew, box and holly are relatively slow to start – though yew should grow 30cm (1ft) a year – while beech, hornbeam and other deciduous trees gain height quickly but take longer to thicken into a screen. Once grown, one cut in summer is all these need. Leyland is the best behaved of the cypresses – not only in being extremely hardy but in shooting up 1m (3ft) a year so long as you let it, then slowing down obligingly once you start cutting it. But a fairly light trim is all it will take: once it has got away you cannot make drastic reductions; it will not sprout from its old wood. The fastest (and cheapest) hedges are privet and *Lonicera nitida*, the tiny-leaved bush honeysuckle (but without flowers). But both need trimming aggravatingly often.

Much more in keeping with the spirit of modern gardening is an adaptation of the idea of the old country hedgerow, a mixture of species, usually including hawthorn, dogwood, spindle, dog-rose, blackthorn, often wayfaring trees and even elm and oak. The working country hedge is capable of growing to full tree height but manageable by either regular trimming or occasional 'stooling' back to ground level. A hedge like this suits a wild or woodland garden better than anything formal or evergreen, bearing fruit in autumn, and perhaps sheltering at its foot clusters of snowdrops and primroses in winter.

I have spoken of hedges mainly as barriers rather than objects of beauty in themselves. While there is beauty in a country hedge, in the subtly varying colours of yew and box, or the russet of beech in winter, and satisfaction and amusement in the shapes that can be cut in any solid hedge, there is another class of hedge which is really a way of displaying a favourite plant. Shrub roses, for example, can make a head-high screen. Hybrid-musk-roses such as 'Felicia' or rugosas such as 'Blanc Double de Coubert' work well. Both can be trimmed lightly with shears in summer. A large part of the pleasure, for me, is in the scent: I find the spotty effect of big flowers in a hedge rather irritating.

For low hedges besides paths some of the herbs are ideal. Lavender, rosemary, lavender cotton (*Santolina chamaecyparissus*) and southernwood (*Artemisia abrotanum*) are all well tried – if not as well tried as that ageless component of grand gardens (and friend of slugs) the dwarf box.

SHRUBS: THE BACKBONE THE ESSENCE OF A

TREE IS THAT IT PUTS ITS STRENGTH INTO A SINGLE TRUNK TO REACH AS HIGH AS IT CAN TOWARDS

THE LIGHT. THE TRUNK THICKENS AS THE TREE BUILDS A LARGER HEAD.

There are many shrubs that grow in just the same way, the only real difference being their size. Rhododendrons and azaleas, cotoneasters, cistus and osmanthus are examples of steady builders. But another large class of shrubs is more distinctly 'shrubby'. In contrast to a tree they put up a set of equal stems to carry their leaves and support their flowers. Up to a point the stems thicken, but then they tire and just tick over. The plant's energy goes into putting out new shoots to replace them. The essence of these shrubs is replacement and rejuvenation. A healthy shrub has a canopy which is part old, part new; the new part performing most of the useful work – and being the more attractive.

In garden convention the term flowering shrub is used to distinguish those (mostly deciduous) grown chiefly for their flowers from those (mostly evergreen) that are traditionally used as garden upholstery. A gathering of shrubs constitutes a shrubbery. A shudder goes with the very word. It conjures up a sooty no-man's-land in nineteenth-century villa gardens, the last of which has not even yet been cleared away. Lazy gardeners would throw the lawn-mowings there and small boys learn to smoke.

Its purpose was to fill space once and for all with a substantial mass of vegetation, whether for shelter, to separate one part of the garden from another, to hide something one would rather forget or simply to cover the ground. Each shrub no doubt was bought in response to an enthusiastic catalogue description, usually laying stress on its profusion of flowers. As it took its place in the shrubbery, however, its charm deserted it. It grew lank and spindly and scarcely flowered at all. This, at least, is the account we find in reforming gardening books.

What went wrong? There is nothing inherently wrong with the idea of massing bushes. Nature often does it. The first mistake was lack of control. The notion of permanence, of having 'done' that part of the garden, was fatal. The second was the assorted ingredients. Lilac and laurustinus, rhododendron and elaeagnus, holly and snowberry were all planted together – and close together. A tight group of one plant eventually looks like a single big bush with all its character intact. But a random mixture looks like nothing on earth.

The function of shrubs is as valid – indeed essential – today as ever it was. The winds still whistle, the washing still needs hiding from the parlour window, and, though there may be much less ground to cover, there is far more ugliness to hide.

But the fashion of using them has changed – to treating them as individuals with a precise contribution to make to the garden, not just in flower but if possible all

BELOW: *The variegated dogwood* Cornus alternifolia *'Argentea' is a shrub with a distinctly tiered, wedding-cake habit that can be accentuated by pruning. By contrast the philadelphus on the left relies on its flowers alone; its shape is of no interest.*

ABOVE: Fatsia japonica *is an evergreen shrub of emphatic character, a relation of ivy, instantly evoking a jungle mood, flowering boldly in November.*

BELOW: *Japanese maples are relatively slow-growing (and ask for moist lime-free soil). But they provide shapes, colours and textures as satisfying as any shrubs.*

year round. With little space to spare there is no room for passengers. Lilac, for example, and philadelphus, however lovely in flower and sweet in smell, have to admit to being just a mound of nondescript leaves all summer – and in winter, just a clutter of nondescript twigs.

The shrubs that pay for their space all year long are those with a singularity of deportment. It does not have to be loud, but it must have character.

The sort of character they can contribute is a pronounced and deliberate dome, a violent uprearing of stiff stems, a tiered wedding-cake look or a softly weeping habit. In terms of texture it could be strikingly intricate and fine like parsley, or coarsely detailed like fig-leaves, matt like sea-buckthorn, or glittering like a camellia, or smooth and solid like an aloe. The leaves could be aluminium or brass, verdigris or burgundy.

It would be catastrophic to collect all these eccentrics and make them socialize. There must be a theme running through the garden that embraces the shrubs along with the trees, the herbs, and indeed the landscape. Acid-soil gardens have a wide choice of shrubs, with, at the same time a built-in ecological theme, which is why they are so often harmonious. But the theme could equally be a colour range, or a repetition of shapes. One of the most reliable contributions shrubs can make to the garden is their combination of highly coloured fruit and leaves in autumn.

The ultimate aim must be to integrate the shrubs completely with the other plants, treating them as equal partners with herbaceous plants and bulbs, composing scenes in which all the forms of plant life shelter and complement one another.

One class of shrubs can usefully be segregated from the rest for special mention – the almost instant ones that grow to full size in a mere two or three years or even, sometimes, in one year. With this extreme vigour usually goes great profusion of flowers and often a ready willingness to root from cuttings. *Ribes sanguineum*, many cistus, *Lavatera olbia*, *Abutilon vitifolium*, some buddlejas, some ceanothus and almost all willows come into this category.

These are the best plants of all for giving a look of maturity to a new garden. They can be interspersed with slower-growing permanent shrubs and trees as temporary gap-fillers – though it is worth remembering that their roots are greedy.

Pruning shrubs is very much a matter of personal philosophy. Gardening books often give the impression that it is an essential operation. They come near to threatening that the poor thing's life will be in danger without regular surgery.

The purpose of pruning is discussed on pages 56–60. but it is right to add here that wherever space allows almost all shrubs do best with only the judicious removal of old wood from the base when it loses its vigour. A little snip here and a little snip there may be the gardener's idea of a perfect afternoon, but the shrub in most cases would rather be left alone. If the real reason for pruning is that the shrub is too big for the space allotted to it then it is much better to admit it, dig it up and plant a smaller one.

The next few pages follow the flowering and fruiting seasons with some of the shrubs that give the best value for space. Convention

today segregates the two great groups of roses and rhododendrons from the ruck of shrubs – though they are no less.
I shall follow that convention.

THE EARLY SHRUBS

One gardening writer coined the phrase 'overcoat plants' for
anything that flowered in winter, and would have none of
them. To most of us, though, the few courageous flowers that
choose winter for their annual display are doubly welcome.
We love them first for their own, usually short-lived, beauty,
but even more as tangible evidence that roots are busy in the
ground, sap is moving and cells are forming.

Once you become an overcoat gardener you begin to
notice and enjoy not only the few frost-proof flowers but also
the subtle swellings of buds, whose promise is almost as great
a pleasure as the eventual flower and leaf will be. And shrubs,
by the nature of things, with their buds where we can reach
and see them, are more prone to this kind of enjoyment than most trees or virtually any herbaceous plants.

ABOVE: *The mahonias include some of
the hardiest of evergreens with the noblest
of leaves, profuse with honey-scented
flowers in mid-winter.* M. × media
'*Charity*' *is a fine foil to* Elaeagnus
pungens '*Maculata*'.

We in England hardly know the total clamp-down that grips land-locked
countries in winter. There is always something stirring. Mild spells in December
and January often tempt premature flowers from shrubs that should wait for the
true spring. Happily the return of frost, though it may destroy the flowers, will
do no other harm. It is premature young shoots that are vulnerable.

It is surprising that any shrubs are naturally programmed to flower at what
seems the worst moment. But the approach of the shortest day is the signal for some
of the mahonias to spread their sweet-scented sprays of yellow flowers above their
gleaming jagged evergreen leaves. The witch-hazel *Hamamelis* uncurls its strange
fragrant spiders of yellow and orange. Mezereon, the mauve winter daphne, is a
poignant little plant with its tiny scented flowers on bare, stiff twigs. Even camellias, whose flowers are easily spoiled by frost, start with the sasanquas in November
and keep up a sequence of one or other member of the family in flower all winter.

BELOW: *Where camellias can flourish
without frost spoiling their sumptuous
flowers they are the finest decoration of
late winter and early spring. It is better
to keep daffodil-yellow out of the picture.*

Camellias are by far the most sumptuous of winter flowers. For long after they were
first imported from China it was assumed that
such ostentatious evergreens must be tender
and they were kept under glass. The plants
are in fact hardy at least to zone 8, but frost
damages the flowers. The protection of the
greenhouse is therefore still a good idea in
frosty areas.

There are at least two thousand varieties
of *Camellia japonica*, the common camellia,
besides numerous other species, of which the
most important are the large-flowered but more
tender western Chinese *C. reticulata* and the
Japanese *C. sasanqua. C. saluenensis*, a close relation of *C. reticulata*, was crossed with *C. japonica*
by J.C. Williams in Cornwall in the 1920s to

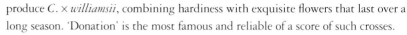

ABOVE: Chaenomeles speciosa, *the
'flowering quince' also commonly known
as* Japonica, *has many virtues as one
of the earliest red or pink flowers of
spring – and no vices.*

BELOW: Daphne retusa *is a shiny
evergreen mound spangled with carnation-
scented pink flowers in April, coinciding
here with* Magnolia stellata 'Rosea'.

produce *C. × williamsii*, combining hardiness with exquisite flowers that last over a long season. 'Donation' is the most famous and reliable of a score of such crosses.

But there is also leisure in winter to enjoy flowers that we would pass by if summer was their season. Many of the earliest flowers are catkins, designed for wind pollination. They have no reason to invest in gaudy pigments for advertising, yet even in monochrome their progress from tight bud to full extension is enthralling to watch. Best of all are some of the shrubby willows (even tree-willows can be kept shrubby by regular cutting back to the base). First they spangle themselves with pearls; then the male catkins miraculously develop a sheath of sparkling gold as the pollen grains emerge.

When all is bleak and bare we are ready to accept the brown catkins of hazel and the grey-green ones of *Garrya elliptica* as worthwhile colours. Indeed the low winter light only intensifies subtle tones of tawny and olive, tan and dusky purple and grey. The waxy cream flowers of wintersweet (*Chimonanthus*) and the strange stiff tassels of *Stachyurus* are in the same minor key that fits the season.

It is surprising, with insects so scarce, that so many of the flowers of the dark days are fragrant. The witch hazels, shrubby winter honeysuckles (*Lonicera × purpusii* is perhaps best) and the modest box-like *Sarcococca*, as well as *Daphne mezereon* and the evergreen *D. odora* all broadcast perfumes of different degrees of sweetness, sharpness and muskiness.

The enjoyment of winter plants depends heavily on their setting. Scattered in the open on a prairie of frosted grass, with nothing but bare twigs as background, they can seem a poor reward for venturing forth. But given a sheltered corner with the solidity of a hedge, a wall, or best of all the deep green of pines behind them, their flowers can seem like jewels.

The Cambridge University Botanic Garden has a small enclosure devoted entirely to winter pleasures. There is a collection of winter-flowering viburnums, pink and white, of great beauty. This garden also demonstrates that flowers are by no means the only rewards of shrubs in winter. The brilliant red and yellow barks of Siberian dogwoods and white willows, the startling white hoops of a bramble, *Rubus biflorus*, the spiralling twigs of the contorted hazel, even the dangerous armament of the bizarre *Colletia armata*, a plant composed entirely of thorns, make a picture full of colour and interest. The floor is largely winter-flowering heather, sheltering winter bulbs. The trees are birches with gleaming trunks and the wonderful cherry *Prunus subhirtella* 'Autumnalis', which flowers repeatedly in every spell of mild weather between November and April.

In spring the authorities shut the gate. There is almost nothing here for summer enjoyment. This is the catch with a garden whose best spaces are devoted to winter pleasures. The ideal is to concentrate your earliest flowers and any plants you love in winter in one sheltered corner near the house, where you will not have far to walk, and perhaps can see from the windows, and is sunlit at noon, not before. Dawn sunshine on frozen buds can be a great destroyer.

Once spring arrives subtlety goes out of the window. The stalwarts of the first great flowering season do not mince their colours. Forsythia is a brave burst of yellow –

unfortunately in most forms the most lurid imaginable. The flowering currant shouts back in hard pink. The flowering quince adds scarlet to the riot. *Berberis darwinii* plunges in with vivid orange. In rhododendron country fierce fights break out. Overhead the cherries and crabs spread a canopy of bronze and blue-pink. Underneath, the bulbs see no more reason to show restraint than the multicoloured pansies and polyanthas of the spring 'bedding'.

This is the season that garden centres sell hardest. The gardener's sap is rising too and he is ready to spend. Cheerfulness is easy in the garden at this time of year: an individual and memorable effect much harder.

For each spring cliché, though, there are less strident and more original alternatives. *Ribes sanguineum*, the harshly 'rosy' flowering currant, has an almost clear red variety, 'Pulborough Scarlet', as well as 'Tydeman's White' – while in April its Californian cousin, *R. sanguineum*, is decked with deep red dangling flowers like an exceptionally elegant fuchsia. *Chaenomeles speciosa*, the ubiquitous 'japonica', has varieties ranging from flame orange to apple-blossom pink. The modest *Daphne mezereon* is quickly followed, in acid soil, by the spectacular, if sparsely-furnished, *D. bholua* from Nepal. 'Gurkha' is the best and hardiest cultivar.

It is not easy to make coherent garden pictures with these early flowers. One answer lies in knitting together the individual splashes of colour with plenty of leaves. A bold green matrix gives the picture cohesion. Most of the leaves must be evergreen if they are to be in place in time for the early flowers. Luckily conifers are at their best in spring, starting their pale new growth in thrilling contrast to the old, dark needles and flowering in their quiet way at the same time.

Such work as shrubs entail for the gardener – remarkably little once the shrubs are well planted and away – is largely concentrated into winter and spring. This is the time for an annual inspection to see whether any old stems are becoming decrepit and need cutting away to encourage new ones, to curb the excesses of shrubs that are bullying their neighbours, and to prune those that flowered in summer and autumn. Warm, damp weather any time between autumn and spring is also the time to cover their roots with a thick mulch of fallen leaves – by far the best way to feed and protect them.

ABOVE: *By late May in England the evergreen* Ceanothus × veitchianus *mingles its deep blue flowers with the pink of* Clematis montana *var.* rubens *and the white of* Choisya ternata – *which can flower all summer long.*

BELOW: *Few shrubs make such striking statements as* Viburnum plicatum *'Mariesii' when its hydrangea-like flowers, their fertile florets surrounded by wide sterile ones, cover the tops of the horizontal branches like snow.*

SPRING INTO SUMMER

The early-flowering shrubs have bulbs as their only rivals. There is little doing among the border plants, hellebores apart, until spring is well under way. But then suddenly the petal count is so high that there is no room in the garden for a fraction of the possible contenders. More wildling species tend to be elbowed aside by selected varieties with bigger or longer-lasting flowers.

ABOVE: *One could collect philadelphus*
for its variety of ravishing scents alone
('Bouquet Blanc', here, has orange-
scented flowers) were it not for the dullness
of the bushes except in June and July.

The tree peonies are perhaps the first shrubs that have the feeling of the fully open spring: broad, fragile flowers with an extravagant number of petals. Unfortunately they tend to flower before it is safe to be so sumptuous, with late frosts a constant threat. But they are worth pampering with careful siting (out of the morning sun) and even a blanket at night.

Paeonia delavayii is the least frost-prone of them, but more appreciated for its splendid doubly-pinnate leaves than for its rather small dark red flowers. The finest flowers are found on such Franco-Japanese classics as the sumptuous yellow and red 'Souvenir de Maxime Cornu' (the group is called *P. × lemoinei*) and in hybrids of *P. suffruticosa* broadly called Moutan peonies. America and Japan have recently seen the breeding of scores of new crosses in colours from yellow to crimson, luscious and brilliant decorations for the garden. This group is broadly known as the Saunders hybrids.

Hard on the heels of the peonies comes the common lilac in its many forms, single- and double-flowered, varying from heavy hanging trusses of white ('Vestale' is as white as a shirt in a commercial) to wine-red ('Souvenir de Louis Spaeth') via creams, purples, pinks and even lilac. 'As with other plants which become the victim of the specialists,' says the catalogue of Hillier's Nurseries severely, 'far too many forms have been selected and named.' Gardeners in the far north are none the less grateful to Miss Preston, who developed some super-hardy hybrids for Canadian conditions in the 1920s. 'Hiawatha', purple red, is the most memorably named of them.

I have already hinted that lilac is a dull, space-consuming plant when its flowers are over. And yet there is no other smell quite so magically spring-like – and the flowers are very fine.

All at once brooms, spiraeas, viburnums and ceanothus are on duty. The last is called wild lilac in California, despite its small leaves and tight soft blue flowering heads. Ceanothus is on the very fast but not very hardy list. The evergreen spring-flowering ones (*Ceanothus × veitchianus* is the commonest) are less hardy than the deciduous summer-to-autumn-flowering group which is led by the first-class 'Gloire de Versailles', whose flowers are pale powder-blue. There are pale pink ones too – but not worth growing.

There is no season without its viburnums, and scarcely a viburnum without merit. Their name does not exactly quicken the heartbeat, perhaps because their flowers are white or pale pink, or perhaps because they are cousins of the vulgar elder, rather than having the blue blood of the ericas or roses.

Viburnum farreri (alias *fragrans*; but several of them are wonderfully fragrant) flowers all winter. So does the evergreen *V. tinus*. In early spring the beautiful deciduous *V. × juddii* and the evergreen *V. × burkwoodi* start up, smelling of carnations; then the guelder rose, *V. opulus* (the variety 'Sterile' is best known as the snowball tree), then *V. plicatum*, which has a form ('Mariesii') in such bold horizontal brushstrokes of white that nobody can resist it. Other viburnums are grown for their splendid leaves (*V. rhytidophyllum*, the 'leatherleaf' and *V. davidii*, low-growing favourite of architects for adding dignity to facile buildings) and yet others (*V. betulifolium*, and *V. opulus* again) for their red berries and yellow and red leaves in autumn.

At this time of year spiraeas are 'only' white, but generous with their flowers, and always graceful – Bridal-wreath (*S. × arguta*) particularly so. The brooms are principally yellow, in all shades from lemon to cream, but include varieties in brown and purple and orange, and mixtures of these. Three genera, *Cytisus*, *Genista* and *Spartium*, are lumped together as brooms, and indeed you could sweep the floor with any of them. They all consist of thin, evergreen twigs-cum-leaves, which bear their bright pea-flowers. The tallest – to 4.5m (15ft) – is the Mount Etna broom, almost a small evergreen tree, flowering in midsummer. One of the lowest and most shapely is *Genista lydia*, a 60cm (2ft) hummock of piercing yellow in spring. The toughest (though not proof against a hard continental winter) is the Spanish broom of summer and autumn. Perhaps the most beautiful is *Genista cinerea*: silky and languid, a cloud of clearest yellow in June.

ABOVE: *The cistuses, ranging in colour through white to pink, crimson and purple, flower in dry sunny conditions in June and July. The white asphodel also comes from the Mediterranean.*

Midsummer also sees the start of the longest-running show in the entire shrub garden: the tireless potentilla, cheerfully flecked from now to November with its little rose-like yellow, cream, white or even reddish flowers. Now the evergreen gummy-leaved *Cistus* produce their fragile papery flowers afresh every day. *C. ladanifer* is white with dark markings and a scent of violets. *C. populifolius* has larger, brighter green leaves than the rest. *C. × corbariensis* is dark-leaved, low-growing and hardy, while for pink flowers 'Silver Pink' is generally first choice.

Meanwhile the air is languorous with philadelphus (or mock-orange, or syringa). All are white- or cream-flowered, and almost all worth growing for their scent alone. The dainty styrax – known in America with characteristic bathos as snowbell – lines its long branches with drooping flowers. A battery of escallonias, deutzias, weigelas, kolkwitzias, daphnes, rubus and one proud buddleja, the weeping *B. alternifolia*, are in action. But then so are the roses. A shrub has to pass rigorous tests to win a place in high season.

BELOW: *No shrubs are more generous with their red autumn fruit than the cotoneasters. This is C. 'Hybridus Pendulus'. The most graceful is C. sternianus.*

LATE SUMMER AND AUTUMN

The second commonest complaint among gardeners, though admittedly following a long way behind the weather, is that there are certain inevitable seasonal 'gaps' when nothing is in flower. To hear some gardeners talk you would think that winter arrived in August.

It is possible to achieve a very dull garden by concentrating on the shrubs of spring and early summer. Most of them pass into a coma after flowering, though many come out of it again with fruit and falling leaves of lovely colours.

But it is not difficult to interweave with your spring-flowering shrubs others that spend the early year forming flower buds to open in the summer holidays. Most things that flower later also flower longer. There is as wide a choice of shrubs as ever, with, curiously enough, a wider range of richer colours. While the earlier season, roses and rhododendrons apart, seems to have been dominated by yellow and white flowers, the later season has a wider and warmer spectrum, leading, it seems with a sort of vegetable logic, to the time of year when green is the exception rather than the rule.

For sheer volume of colour, in gardens or in the wild, autumn stands alone. In summer a metre of rich scarlet in a border delights us. In autumn we can have it by the furlong. Whole trees are the colour of our most vivid flowers. With the turning leaves come the ripening berries. Even the quality of the light, with the sun lower in the sky, intensifies the chromatic climax of the year.

The shrubs that contribute most to the medley of brilliant leaves include the little japanese maples, which can achieve the most piercing scarlet of all, red-orange amelanchiers, yellow hamamelis, scarlet disanthus and several berberis. *Fothergilla major* turns violently orange-red, *Euonymus alatus* equally violent lingerie pink, while cotinus, aronia and many others join in with turning leaves that mysteriously (and unlike flowers) always seem to complement each other.

The list of shrubs that contribute with brilliant glistening fruit is equally long, led perhaps by the cotoneasters, the pyracanthas and hawthorns, the rose hips, countless hollies for red and yellow berries, sea buckthorn, orange against grey, and mahonias, blueberries, some gaultherias and *Viburnum davidii* which provide an intriguing note of blue.

The shrubs that bring most flower-colour to this feast, before the leaves and fruit take over, are the hydrangeas, the hypericums, the fuchsias, the hebes and hibiscus, the buddlejas, the potentillas (still going strong) and in the south the oleanders. There is no shortage here. Remember there are ceanothus still in flower, and I have not touched on the rarer plants: the plumy buckeyes, the tender clethras of ineffable sweetness, the stately eucryphias and hoherias, Japanese bush-clover with its rosy purple panicles, bright blue ceratostigma or violet-blue caryopteris, nor invaded the world of sub-shrubs, where lavender and its associates are going full tilt.

The hydrangeas are the most various and potentially the best garden material of all the summer shrubs; taking over where the viburnums left off – even (though they are apparently not related) to having the same trick of producing two kinds of flowers: one set for marketing and the other for production.

The typical florist's hydrangea that first comes to mind is marketing material only: a mop-head of sterile florets. I find it helpful to think of these by their old-fashioned name, hortensia, which has just the right ring of horticultural pretender about it. Hortensias look well in pots, or in combination with architecture. They are at home at the foot of a shady wall, perhaps the entrance yard of the house, if given enough moisture. For either doing a solo in mid-lawn, or blending with other plants in the light shade of trees (which is what they prefer) there are many other hydrangeas, all better.

The lacecaps have both sorts of flowers. Of these 'Bluewave' is justly the most famous. They also include the smaller *Hydrangea serrata*, which carries to perfection the hydrangea's particular virtue of dying gracefully. In its best form, 'Grayswood', the sterile florets, instead of fading, darken from pink to intense mahogany-crimson. There are lacecaps of all sizes.

The third flower form is the panicle, or branched flower cluster, best known in the tall *H. paniculata* 'Grandiflora' and *H. quercifolia*, which has splendid leaves like an American red oak, even to their autumn colour. Both of these have white flowers.

The coloured hydrangeas are litmus paper for the chemistry of the soil. Where it is acid they are blue; where alkaline, pink. In alkaline soil their supply of aluminium is cut off. Since their blue is altogether a more striking colour, gardeners often try to achieve it even in the wrong soil by adding aluminium sulphate.

Hypericums offer nothing like the same variety. Their virtue is a guaranteed supply of big buttercups on small bushes for months on end. The best known, 'Rose of Sharon', is one of the most-used of all groundcover plants. The best in common cultivation (there are many lovely but rare chinese species) is 'Hidcote', a 1.5m (5ft) bush which flowers so freely for so long that one even begins to tire of its relentless cheerfulness.

Yet in a small garden it is the plants that flower and flower again that must take priority. In this the (so-called) hardy varieties of fuchsias can hardly be beaten. The use of tender fuchsias as bedding is another matter. Of the relatively hardy ones *F. magellanica* is the prototype, arching to 1.8m (6ft) or so, its small red flowers with purple skirts. In a sophisticated garden setting, particularly in shade, its albino version, 'Alba', with paler leaves and just-pink flowers is ravishing. The strongest-growing, for hedges in such privileged climates as Ireland, Brittany and Cornwall, is 'Riccartonii', with fatter, rounder flowers than *F. magellanica* and an altogether more robust air. I have seen it climb the wall of a hotel near Cherbourg to the upper windows. If anything can beat these fuchsias for patiently flowering on and on it is some of the hebes, above all the extraordinary 'Midsummer Beauty', often in flower in southern England at Christmas.

Buddlejas come and go all too quickly, leaving dull brown dead-heads to regret them by. Without their scent and the butterflies it brings they would hardly hold the place they do in gardens. Hibiscus times its single flowering well: after we have expected to see new faces appearing. It is also far hardier than its Mediterranean look suggests.

Not so, alas, the oleander. This is really Monte Carlo material, but so loaded with agreeable associations that anyone with a conservatory should begin to collect the set: pink, white and red, single- or double-flowered.

ABOVE: *The berries of sea buckthorn, orange against its narrow silver-grey leaves, cover female trees up to 3.5m (12ft) high until frosts shrivel them. Birds rarely touch them.*

BELOW: *The culitvated High-bush blueberries are hybrids of* Vaccinium corymbosum. *'Bluetta' is one of the good early varieties. Very acid soil is essential.*

THE FAMILY OF ROSES GENEALOGY MAY SEEM A
LABORIOUS APPROACH TO A DELECTABLE SUBJECT. BUT IF ONE IS TO MAKE ANY SENSE OF THE
BEWILDERING VARIETY OF ROSES TODAY THE PLACE TO START IS WITH THE WILD PLANTS WHOSE SAP.
IN A COCKTAIL OF INEXTRICABLE COMPLEXITY. RUNS IN THEIR VEINS.

ABOVE: *The 'Cabbage' rose,*
R. centifolia, *is the most luxurious*
product of early rose breeding.
P.-J. Redouté painted it for
the Empress Josephine.
BELOW: Rosa gallica *'Officinalis',*
alias the Red Rose of Lancaster, is one of
the oldest known in cultivation. It spreads
freely by sending up suckers. Its petals
keep their rich fragrance even when dried.

There is still no way to fathom in detail the early matings that produced the rich old pink and purple roses of European gardens up to the end of the eighteenth century. From the Persians and Greeks, via the Romans, certain strains of cultivated rose had gone on, scarcely changing. There were no roses that flowered more than once, either in early or late summer, only two yellow or orange middle-eastern species, *Rosa foetida* and *R. hemisphaerica* (known as the Austrian Briar and the Sulphur Rose), and no high climbers. And the 'tea' scent was unknown.

But a mingling of the genes of a dog rose (probably *R. canina*), two distinct strains of climbing musk roses (*R. moschata* and probably *R. phoenicia*) and the deep pink *Rosa gallica* with perfumed petals (which goes back to at least 1200 BC) had produced a range of Damasks, Gallicas and Albas in all the pure tones and shades of clear pink or bluey pink between white and purple. They had heavenly scents – the Damasks in particular inheriting from the musk roses, whose scent is in their stamens, the trick of sending their fragrance far downwind. (They are still the roses grown for attar of roses). Their flower shapes developed over the centuries from single to densely double with charming flat faces of puckered petals.

The Gallicas were mainly low bushes, but musk-rose vigour made the Damasks tall, even rambling, plants. While the Gallicas were thorny with rather dark, dull, roundish leaves, the dog rose in the family was a smooth, pale-foliaged plant, which possibly gave the Albas their greyish leaves and a mere sprinkling of thorns. None flowered at all after mid-July except a few, known as the Autumn Damasks (*R. × damascena* var. *semperflorens*), which produced spasmodic blooms into October.

The high point of breeding with this relatively limited range of genetic possibilities was reached by the Dutch in the seventeenth century, when repeated crossings of Albas and Autumn Damasks gave them the rose of a hundred petals,

R. × centifolia, otherwise known as the Cabbage rose, the Provence rose, or the *Rose des Peintres*. Its heavy head makes it better in a vase (or indeed in a painting) than on a bush. But no flower could be more sumptuous.

The end of the eighteenth century is the turning point in rose history. In the 1780s and 1790s British merchant ships came home with the roses the Chinese grew in gardens – themselves the results of centuries of selection. Chinese roses derived from at least two wild species: the 'giant' rose, *R. gigantea*, a huge climber with big silky creamy-yellow flowers and the wonderful 'tea' scent, and *Rosa chinensis*, a pink or red once-flowering climber that grows in the Ichang Gorge of the Yangtse

River. At some unknown date this had 'sported' to produce a dwarf bush, *R. chinensis* var. *spontanea*, with the priceless attribute of flowering on and on, ceaselessly pushing out new shoots, with every shoot forming flower buds. Crosses between these two are 'Tea-scented Chinas'.

Four of these new introductions to Europe have been dubbed 'the four stud chinas'. Their names have gone down in history like that of the famous Darley Arabian, Byerley Turk and Godolphin Barb, whose blood runs in all race-horses. The roses were Hume's Blush, Parson's Yellow, Old Blush or Parson's Pink, and Slater's Crimson. All the ramifications of rose breeding since 1792 can be traced back to these four: one form of *Rosa chinensis* and three hybrids of the Chinese and the giant rose which brought the gene for recurrent, if not perpetual, flowering into Western rose history.

The man who coined the phrase, and worked out the story, was the great Cambridge geneticist Dr C. C. Hurst. His work in the 1930s, in partnership with his wife Rona, using chromosome counts to reveal forgotten relationships, is the basis of our understanding of rose genealogy. He showed how the new 'remontant' roses were rapidly crossed with the old wherever they were introduced to produce new classes with new characteristics, which were again interbred in an increasingly deliberate and commercial process, leading at length to the Hybrid Teas and Floribundas – or, as they now officially known, Large- and Cluster-flowered bush roses. The only hitch is that the gene for repeat-flowering is, in Mendel's terms, recessive – in other words that two copies of the gene on the chromosome have to be present before this quality becomes apparent.

In the past thirty years breeding has gathered pace to give us ever more precise combinations of desirable characters, in which breeders pick out the genes they need (for perpetual flowering, hardiness, colour, size, shape, foliage and fragrance) to paint new pictures of perfection, culminating – so far – in the group known as the new English roses.

SHRUB ROSES

The early European roses reached the peak of their fortunes in the famous collection of the Empress Josephine at La Malmaison, recorded in the world's most popular flower paintings by Redouté in the first years of the nineteenth century.

From the early 1830s on the 'China' characters of repeat-flowering, of silkier flowers and subtler scent were so highly prized that for a while the old favourites seemed to have been consigned to history. Of the new productions with an admixture of chinese blood the groups known as Hybrid Chinas, Portlands and Bourbons were among those that came and nearly went, leaving only a few treasured survivors out of hundreds in scattered collections.

Of these the pink 'Hermosa' and the vivid crimson-pink 'Fellemberg' are as close to Hybrid Chinas as you will find after a century and a half. The bright red Portland rose is still in existence. It was found by the Duchess of Portland in southern Italy, where China roses may have been naturalized in the

ABOVE: *'Old Blush' retains the character of the first Chinese roses to be grown in the west – may be, indeed, 'Parson's Pink China'. It is a small bush, not very hardy, but flowers continuously, if not profusely, from June well into the autumn.*

BELOW: *The huge collection of old shrub roses at Childerley Hall near Cambridge makes a deep maze lined with soft colours and sweet scents.*

ABOVE: *'Zéphirine Drouhin' is the still-popular champion of the Bourbon roses, brilliant and bountiful, with long almost thornless shoots that can be trained to climb.*

BELOW: *The Hybrid Perpetuals were the reigning class of roses from the middle to almost the end of the 19th century. One of the last to keep its place in the garden is 'Mrs John Laing'.*

warm climate. Bourbons, originally bred on the island now known as Réunion, are represented at their most primitive by the magenta 'Bourbon Queen' (alias 'Reine de l'Ile Bourbon') and at their most successful and sophisticated by the bright cerise-pink, sweet-scented, perpetual and almost thornless 'Zéphirine Drouhin' – both vigorous bushes with a distinct tendency to climb.

As breeding progressed, hopefully towards the ideal combination of brilliance, hardiness and constancy in bloom, the emphasis grew more and more on the qualities of flowers and less and less on those of plants – a reflection of the Victorian mania for exhibition. For most of the second half of the nineteenth century the dominant race in rose gardens were the Hybrid Perpetuals; blends of China, Portland and Bourbon blood which tend to long legs, pointed buds and rich fragrance – though not often as perpetual as their name. The pale pink 'Baronne Prévost' and 'Mrs John Laing' are two of the best Hybrid Perpetuals in cultivation today. Some of the Victorian masterpieces needed a groom and footman in constant attendance to show at their sumptuous best. By the time the Hybrid Teas took over as the supreme roses in the 1900s, rose-garden routine was established as something quite separate from the rest of gardening. The virtues of the rose as a self-sufficient shrub were almost forgotten.

Luckily the old breeds still had a few admirers who kept them going, mostly in France and North America. Their reinstatement began in the Jekyll-inspired return to older, homelier and subtler ways with flowers and continued with such sensitive gardeners as Victoria Sackville-West and Constance Spry. Then, in the 1950s, Graham Stuart Thomas, in his book *The Old Shrub Roses*, made the case for them, catalogued all he could find, and collected and planted them in the National Trust garden at Mottisfont Abbey in Hampshire. He pointed out that if they are shorter in flowering season than modern cultivars, they last as long as most other one-season shrubs – and the hold the rose has over the heart is even stronger in these more tender, muddled and feminine flowers than in their well-organized, often strident, descendants.

Meanwhile new wild species had arrived in the wave of Asiatic introductions to widen the whole concept of the rose and its possibilities, and to re-awaken interest in the lovely, simple, single flower. The Japanese *Rosa multiflora*, which brought profuse cluster-flowering, was first grown and used for breeding in France in the 1860s. The genes of the Austrian Briar, *R. foetida*, were finally harnessed in breeding to bring deep yellow into the mainstream rose palette in 1888. Another eastern Asian species, *R. rugosa*, brought recurrent-flowering combined with extreme hardiness and splendid foliage. Yet another, *R. wichuriana*, was to revolutionize the breeding of rambling roses. The butter-yellow *R. xanthina* var. *hugonis* and the cherry-red *R. moyesii* with its dramatic fruit arrived from China in the 1900s.

Breeders began to turn back to wild roses nearer to home whose genetic potential had never been investigated. Lord Penzance, for example, used the sweet briar or eglantine, *R. rubiginosa*, in the 1890s in combination with various Hybrid Teas to produce the Penzance briars. Wilhelm Kordes in Germany, one of the greatest of all rose-breeders, crossed a Scots briar, *R. pimpinellifolia*, with Hybrid Teas to make the great 'Frühlingsgold' and 'Frühlingsmorgen'.

Thus another category of rose, the 'modern shrub', came into being; strong and healthy, good-looking as garden plants, without the special needs of the florists' roses. Far from detracting from the name of the old roses it enhanced it, for more gardeners began to think of roses as an integral part of the whole garden picture.

What sort of picture then do the shrub roses, old and new, paint in the garden? Despite the grandeur of their Rothschild drawing-room names – 'Assemblage des Beautés' and 'Gloire des Rosomanes' – the general effect of the old pre-China roses, and even of such Bourbons and Hybrid Perpetuals as have proved themselves over a century and more, is rustic and cottagey. This has more to do with the bushes themselves than with the flowers, which can be picked and arranged in high-drawing-room style. But the big, rather coarse-leaved shrubs, drooping under the weight of their blooms, can hardly be made to look formal as modern bedding roses can.

Shrub roses are not only better mixers in the garden, taking part in the general border scene, but they positively need to be mixed, so that other plants can make up for their lack of later flowers and hide their leaves – a strong point of the Albas but of few others. It is impossible to go wrong among their harmonious colours of crimson, purple, violet, mauve and white. All lie safely on the blue side of the spectrum. Their problem is only a tendency to heaviness *en masse*. They need very definite punctuation, both in colour and form. White, grey and blue are the best colours to 'lift' them; hot modern rose colours are wrong. The simple verticals of irises, delphiniums, foxgloves and tall campanulas are perfect company for them.

As for pruning, they need only the same attention as any long-lived shrub: the removal of the oldest worn-out stems from the base. Strong new shoots can be shortened by a third.

The same pruning precepts apply to most roses being grown as shrubs, multifarious as their habits are – varying from the low-growing Burnet or Scots briar, spreading by means of fiercely armed suckers, to the huge round bush that 'Nevada', for example, eventually makes, or the gauntly upright *Rosa moyesii*. Nothing will make a neat bush of this.

Today there is more interest than ever, despite the steady flow of new varieties, in growing such species for their own sake. They offer variety of form, of foliage, of simple flower shapes and colours and plentiful fruit. Gently pruned or not pruned at all they slowly become great features of permanent interest ideally suited to wild or woodland gardening.

A selection almost at random might include *Rosa moyesii*, for fine ferny leaves, brilliant red flowers, scarlet bottle-shaped hips and towering height, ('Geranium' is perhaps the best garden form, more compact than the species) *R. glauca* (formerly *R. rubrifolia* – a much more apposite name for a plant with bloomy plum-coloured leaves) for foliage and orange oval hips, *R. soulieana* for the palest grey-green leaves and masses of creamy-white flowers, *R. virginiana* for a broad suckering bush with deep pink flowers and brilliant autumn colour in parchment, orange and scarlet, and *R. woodsii* var. *fendleri*, which carries more and brighter red hips for longer into winter than any other rose.

ABOVE: *'Gloire de Dijon' is one of the oldest and best climbers, born in 1853 of the Noisette and Tea strains and still vigorous, richly scented and rarely out of flower.*

BELOW: *The chinese* Rosa moyesii *is a huge shrub as remarkable for its bottle-shaped scarlet hips as for its simple blood-red flowers.*

ABOVE: *No other flower can compare in form and texture with the opening individual bud of a perfect Hybrid Tea, such as 'Precious Platinum'.*

BEDDING ROSES

The difference between roses as fully fledged shrubs and roses as well-drilled flower machines is emphasized by borrowing the term 'bedding'. Bedding to a gardener means massed display over a long season: the job of summer annuals, in fact. The Hybrid Teas were developed to provide exactly this, in as many and as dazzling colours as possible. Their productivity is extraordinary: the 'China' urge to go on making new growth, with every shoot ending in a single flower, is developed to the limit.

But they also had another goal; to win prizes for perfect blooms. Prize flowers need long stalks, and have heavy heads; qualities scarcely compatible with giving a good show in the garden. Hybrid Teas thus became schizophrenic plants that need patient nursing and guidance all their lives to perform either of their possible roles well. Moreover, as they became further and further inbred in the search for new colours and shapes, they grew increasingly susceptible to disease.

Those who grow and love them have forgiven them all their faults and are ready to feed, spray and prune them, even to put up with their appearance in winter – like a sinister device for impeding infantry – for the sake of their flowers. And certainly among man-made flowers there is nothing more elegantly sensuous than the bud of a modern rose. As cut flowers, at the just-about-to-open stage, they are supremely graceful and may never be surpassed. The full-blown flower is not nearly so good: there seems strangely little pattern among the many petals that made the sculptural bud.

For bedding purposes – that is to keep consistent colour going in a flower bed as evenly and as long as possible – they have largely been superseded by the Floribundas, or in current terminology cluster-flowered bushes. To create this new class cluster-flowering was bred into Hybrid Teas (the genes came from *Rosa multiflora*, via intermediate stages known as Polypoms and Poulsen roses), combining

RIGHT: *Bedding roses and ramblers in the grand manner in Regent's Park, London. In the foreground is 'Silver Moon'; on the pillars, 'City of York'.*

profuse sprays of flowers with the Hybrid Tea colours and the Hybrid Tea urge to flower and flower again.

Floribundas not only give a more even spread of colour than Hybrid Teas; on the whole they need less cossetting – advantages that have now been bred into more recent Hybrid Teas by combining the two races. Thus there are big-flowered Floribundas (known in America as Grandifloras) and Hybrid Teas with significantly more flowers.

Apart from the elusive true blue, which is thought to be genetically impossible, modern roses cover the colour spectrum. Bright yellow tea roses arrived with the twentieth century. About 1930 a genetic mutation produced a new pigment in roses, pelargonidin, which added a new degree of brilliance: a harsh fluorescence which has been widely used for intensifying reds and oranges. Its ultimate use at present is in 'Super Star', which you almost feel you could pick to use as a torch.

ABOVE: *One of the finest of the floribundas, now officially called 'cluster-flowered' roses, is the pure white 'Iceberg', bred in Germany in 1958 by Kordes. It responds to hot summers by growing strongly and flowering without a pause.*

As to scent – which many hold to be the soul of the rose; the real reason why it has been treasured in history more than any other flower – modern roses have inherited so many distinct scents, from their gallica, musk, damask and tea ancestors, that they are very hard to classify. Many bedding roses (including the early floribundas) are disappointing. Others are as powerfully fragrant as the best old roses. Among the best-scented (but not necessarily tea-scented) Hybrid Teas are 'Fragrant Cloud', 'Shot Silk', 'Silver Lining', 'Prima Ballerina', 'Papa Meilland' and 'Mister Lincoln'. 'Sutter's Gold' is unusual in having the tea scent loud and clear.

Scent was bred into the Floribundas from the 1950s onwards ('Tonnerre' being perhaps the first). The yellow 'Arthur Bell' (1965) and pale pink 'Michelle' (1970) are two with particularly powerful fragrance.

This is where a third group of modern roses, the Hybrid Musks, suggest themselves as the answer. They are largely the creation of an Essex clergyman, the Reverend Joseph Pemberton, in the 1920s and 30s, with parentage derived from Hybrid Teas and the Noisettes, themselves partly *Rosa moschata*. Hybrid Musks are not bedding

BELOW: *The Hybrid Musk race of roses was created 70 years ago by an Essex clergyman. 'Autumn Delight' is one of the best of them; especially in its second, autumnal, flush of flowers.*

roses in the strict sense, but shrubs of such profuse and constant flower that they can serve the same purpose, at least where there is room for a bush 1.8m (6ft) wide. They start flowering late in the season, when the first flush of roses is over, keep going fairly steadily and have a triumphant autumnal show of flowers – all richly scented. 'Buff Beauty', 'Felicia', 'Penelope' 'Autumn Delight' and 'Vanity' are among them.

What happens to bedding roses if they are not given the full bedding treatment, pruned hard back and force-fed to flower to their utmost? It depends on the variety in question. Those that are particularly prone to black-spot, rust or mildew, the three chief enemies, may well succumb. On the other hand, mildew pounces on just that sappy young growth that pruning and feeding provoke. 'Grown hard', with little feeding, particularly of nitrogen, they will be more resistant. There is no law that says that Hybrid Teas must be hacked almost to the ground every winter. Some of them, for example the lovely soft-toned 'Peace', will make tall shrubs and flower well.

ABOVE: *'Mary Rose' is typical of the new English roses, bred to combine the shapes and scents of old roses with the best qualities of modern productions.*

Floribundas can more easily be treated as shrubs – though no doubt at the expense of some of their flowers. In their case, one method is only to dead-head them (cut off their flowered stems down to the next opening bud), which amounts to a light pruning after flowering, and otherwise only to cut away whole stems from the base when they are past their prime. This is also the way to handle the Hybrid Musks.

Disease and insects apart, the principal penance for growing roses is the sucker problem. Almost all commercially grown roses are budded on to a vigorous rootstock of either the dog-rose or the eastern Asian *R. rugosa* or *multiflora*. Sooner or later, usually in reaction to a jab from a probing fork, the rootstock will send up suckers. A noticeably vigorous new shoot, with leaves of a different colour or shape, will almost certainly be a sucker. Trace it back to its source. If it arises below the graft union your suspicions are confirmed. Unless it is promptly removed, all the vigour of the plant will go into it. But cutting it off is worse than useless: it must be torn off below ground where it leaves the root.

NEW ROSE DIRECTIONS

Every year now produces a spate of new roses from breeders in a dozen countries. France remains perhaps the most prolific with such nurseries as Meilland (creator of 'Peace') and Delbard fertile as ever in new ideas, working and reworking the immense genetic resources now stored in modern roses. A recent series from Delbard even mimics the brush-strokes of the Impressionists and takes their names: Monet, Gauguin, Cézanne and Matisse.

BELOW: *The first English rose was 'Constance Spry' (born 1960), a climber of lovely form, vigorous and myrrh-scented, but missing the gene for recurrent flowering – despite which it remains a firm favourite.*

In England David Austin started in the 1950s on an increasingly deliberate campaign to unite the best qualities of the old roses with those of the new. His first successful cross, between a Gallica and a Floribunda called 'Dainty Maid', produced the famously sumptuous and vigorous silky pink 'Constance Spry' – which lacked only the recessive gene for repeat flowering.

Austin used some of the best roses in each class; the perfect white floribunda 'Iceberg' for example, the Gallica 'Tuscany' and the great classic climber 'Gloire de Dijon', a Noisette already 150 years old, to produce such ideal healthy and shapely perpetual-flowering shrubs as 'Mary Rose', 'Heritage', 'Wife of Bath', 'Gertude Jekyll', 'Chianti' and 'Evelyn' – which he called, as a new class, 'English roses' – a name formerly reserved for a certain type of feminine beauty.

All are softly double-flowered, tending to be cupped or flat-faced like most old roses, at their best when open, not as furled buds like most modern roses. All their colours are gentle; whether pink, cream, apricot, peach or lilac, and unmixed: varieties of tone come from light and shade among the petals of the open flowers. All have fragrant petals like old roses: the more petals, the more scent; leaning either in the sweet 'old rose' direction or towards the smoky-sharp tea scent, or blending the two.

The destiny of these English roses is the border, not the bed – to use the increasingly old-fashioned distinction. Their growth-habits vary from stiff to lax, but the object is to avoid the brutalist look that comes from hard pruning for constant flowering. Like Hybrid Musks they tend to be twice-flowering, first from side-shoots on older growth, then later from new basal shoots. Indeed in good conditions they flower almost continually until frost stops them.

CLIMBING AND RAMBLING ROSES

The urge to impose order on a thoroughly heterogeneous lot has led gardeners to classify their longest-stemmed roses, which in nature are given to pouring down cliffs or mounting into trees, as climbers or ramblers according to their conventional garden uses. No rose climbs in the sense that a vine does by deliberately taking a grip on the next handhold in the direction of the light. The rose method is to put up canes, sometimes of amazing length – as much as 9m (30ft) at a time – in hope that support will be forthcoming. Its thorns help it to hang on: the big climbing musk roses have particularly vicious curved thorns behind their leaves.

ABOVE: *The blood of the tall Himalayan musk roses runs in such rampant thorny climbers as 'Wedding Day' – here uncharacteristically under control. Its orange-scented white flowers are mottled pink as they fade.*

But a rose of almost every stature can be found somewhere, in a steady progression from a short shrub to a size to challenge forest trees. Along with differences of size come other important variations: stiffness of stem and a tendency to send up new stems. All three greatly affect garden performance.

To gardeners, climbers are those which tend to produce stiff stems in relatively small numbers (not 'breaking' very often from the base), but capable of reaching, let us say, the eaves of a house. Ramblers usually have more pliable and whippy shoots in large numbers, tending not to grow so long because new ones are regularly coming from ground level to take over – hence, in general, easier to train over arches or pergolas. A third, rather indeterminate class, pillar roses, are short-growing climbers or ramblers, not overtopping about 2.5m (9ft). 'Phyllis Bide' is an excellent but little-known example, sweet-scented, mingling yellow and salmon, often still in flower at Christmas.

BELOW: *Ramblers are the roses to train up pergolas, pillars, or lamp-posts. 'Blush Rambler' is ideal, being almost thornless.*

Just as important as their manner of growing is their manner of flowering. By virtue of sheer size, the tall roses give us more flowers at a time than any other plant. But the ramblers on the whole flower only once, in midsummer or shortly after, while many of the modern climbers either go on flowering, or give us a distinct second season in autumn. It is once again a question of heredity. The ramblers are basically once-flowering musk roses, augmented and improved by hybrids of two eastern Asian members of their group; *Rosa multiflora* (the cluster-flowering rose which lies behind our Floribundas) or *R. luciae*, a sweet-scented, twice-flowering evergreen rose given not to climbing trees but rather to running along the ground.

The musk roses (*R. multiflora* and the shrubby American Prairie rose excepted) are only white or cream, but include the most gigantic members of the genus: roses such as *R. brunonii* and *R. filipes*, whose best-known form, 'Kiftsgate', will occupy a space 12m (40ft) high and wide. Their flowers hang down in trusses of extreme grace; hundreds of strong-scented, five-petalled, yellow-stamened flowers at a time.

R. multiflora brought a purple pigment to a small band of roses via its offspring 'Crimson Rambler'. *R. wichuriana*

ABOVE: *'Ballerina' is the smallest of the
Hybrid Musks; almost a cliché in its
perfect marriage with catmint. 'Patio'
roses are another race altogether, with all
their parts charmingly miniaturized.*

BELOW: *'New Dawn', raised in the
USA in 1930, is near to perfection as
climber or rambler, as good used formally
as lighting up an old yew-tree with its
fragrant falling sprays for months on end.*

has been so important as a parent that a whole class of roses is often referred to by its name. The famous 'Alberic Barbier' might be taken as the type of these: lax and flowing, growing to 6m (20ft), dark green glossy leaved, with a sweet-sharp scent like fine German wine; and apt to produce more creamy flowers, though not effusively, after its early-summer climax. Regular pruning of such vigorous and complex plants is unnecessary, and indeed scarcely possible.

A totally different blood-line produced the climbers. The musk rose is still there as a distant ancestor, but the major influence is Chinese. A complicated series of crosses produced first the Noisettes (in Paris in 1814, the first recurrent-flowering climbers) then the climbing teas, then added old-rose blood – via the Hybrid Perpetuals and Bourbons – to produce Hybrid Teas, and explains why at each stage the genetic potential to produce a climber is present. 'Zéphirine Drouhin', for example, is a Bourbon climber which is still often grown.

Some of the Noisette and tea climbers were as good as any made since, in gentle tones of buff and apricot and cream. 'Gloire de Dijon' and 'Climbing Lady Hillingdon', 'Mme. Alfred Carrière' and 'Alister Stella Gray' are among them. Some missed the gene for recurrence but were so beautiful and so different from their fellows that they have survived anyway. 'Paul's Lemon Pillar' and 'Mme. Gregoire Staechelin' are among these.

The Hybrid Teas, though bred as a race of recurrent-flowering bushes, also have the family tendency to 'sport' into climbers. There are Hybrid Tea climbing sports in most colours. Among pinks, for example, 'Climbing Ophelia'; among flame colours, 'Climbing Mrs Sam McGredy'; among crimsons, 'Climbing Ena Harkness' (and the darkest of all red velvet roses, 'Guinée'); among yellows, 'Casino'. Whites are rare. All can be assumed to be recurrent to some degree – some of them as perpetual-flowering as their sister bushes. For anyone who likes Hybrid Tea flowers but dislikes their bushes, these climbers are the ideal way of growing them.

To this very broad structural and genetic division must be added the filling-in that breeders have inevitably done, though much less in climbers and ramblers than in bushes.

It is generally recognized that the fault with the climbers, Hybrid Teas in particular, is their stiffness. The loveliest thing is the cascade. Enlightened gardeners now want every possible colour in manageable disease-resistant plants that are as recurrent as climbers and as graceful as ramblers.

'Albertine', an early cross between *R. wichuraiana* and a Hybrid Tea, is a wonderful example of the potential. It is not exactly graceful, or recurrent, but it remains a universal favourite. 'New Dawn' is even better, and fully perpetual. Floribundas can also 'sport' into climbers. 'Climbing Iceberg' and 'Climbing Korona' are examples. Another promising development is the new fertile species *R. × kordesii*, produced in Germany by a stroke of genetical good fortune, which combines the hardiness and healthiness of *R. rugosa* with the qualities of *R. wichuriana*. As breeding continues the old distinctions between climbers, ramblers and shrubs are becoming blurred.

RHODOLAND

A FUTURE HISTORIAN LOOKING BACK AT THE GARDENS OF THE LAST HUNDRED YEARS MIGHT WELL CHRISTEN THE PERIOD THE ERICA DYNASTY. THE ERICACEAE IS THE ONE PLANT FAMILY THAT HAS IMPOSED A WHOLE FASHION OF GARDENING.

In fact it has imposed two. The modern heather garden is the latest manifestation of their compelling, uncompromising character. But their greatest and most enduring innovation was the rhododendron woodland – a style that became a rage a hundred years ago and continues to this day.

Like all good dynasties the ericas have a strong family look about them – particularly in the shape of their flowers and their imperious manners. They are not good mixers. They grow best and look best in the company of their own kind. Their kind includes strawberry-trees, mountain-laurel, *Pieris*, *Enkianthus*, sorrel trees, *Gaultheria*, blueberries and bilberries, *Cassiope* and *Clethra* . . . an astonishing diversity of woody plants of every size. Most remarkable of all is the genus *Rhododendron*, which alone has over seven hundred species. There is nothing else we grow in gardens that can compare in richness and range, from creeping alpines to towering trees. All (or nearly all) rhododendrons are flamboyant in flower and at least neat, but often spectacular, in leaf.

Other plants that have diversified so widely have adapted to almost every soil and climate. The ericas, the rhododendrons particularly, have gone the other way and specialized. Somewhere in the history of their evolution (from a branch of the tea family that includes the camellias) they struck up a profitable relationship with mycocorrhizae, or soil-dwelling fungi, which enabled them to exploit very acid soil that is unfertile for most plants. Most of their development has taken place in the cool and rainy mountains of the world, where acid soil follows on the endless leaching of nutrients by the rain; ideal country, with its wet summers and deep snow in winter, for the big evergreen leaves which most of them have. They exist on all the continents except Africa and South America, but proliferate in species upon species,

ABOVE: Rhododendron augustinii *is the bluest of its tribe and one of the best. The Rothschild-bred variety 'Electra' is a glorious sight.*

LEFT: *The Himalayas are the heart of Rhododand. The discovery of the blood-red* Rhododendron arboreum *in the 1820s launched the mania for collecting and breeding the genus.*

as no other plant proliferates anywhere, in the monsoon belt of the eastern Himalayas. The dripping forests and deep gorges between Yunnan and Sikkim, to the north of Burma, where the Irrawaddy, Mekong, Brahmaputra, Salween and countless other rivers rise, was christened by one explorer, quite simply, Rhodoland.

I have borrowed his word for the title of this section because a word is needed to express the whole world of the rhododendron; its fascination, its cultivation, the fanatics who follow it, the garden style they have built round it, and the botanical wrangles it provokes.

SPECIES AND SECTIONS

For a tidy taxonomic mind rhododendrons are one of the great challenges. They demand a system, to group the species into bigger units that have something more in common than just being rhododendrons. Classifying them has provided a life's work for several scholars, notably at the Royal Botanic Garden in Edinburgh.

Although some current reference books still use different systems of classification, in the light of recent Edinburgh research there is apparently at last a consensus which is likely to stick – even if meanwhile it makes old-timers grind their teeth. The old system divided the genus into three principal sections, then the sections into 'series' – of which rhododendrons, as understood by gardeners, made 39.

The new one divides rhododendrons into a logical and hierarchical scheme, whereby the species are mustered on the basis of their botanical affinities. The genus now has eight subgenera, 12 sections and 53 subsections. Four of the subgenera are of immediate interest to gardeners: *Rhododendron*,

BELOW & FACING PAGE: *Twelve of the fifty or so subsections (groups of species) of rhododendrons are represented here. Although lepidote (subgenus* Rhododendron) *species are more numerous in nature they are far outnumbered in gardens by species from the subgenus* Hymenanthes *which are elepidote, and usually more or less minutely hairy. The lepidotes are largely either alpine or tropical. Flower-shapes often vary enormously even within one subsection, from trumpet- to funnel- to bell-shaped, or something in between. The position of the flower is slightly more characteristic. Lepidotes are apt to flower not only from the terminal (end) bud of each shoot but also from several leaf-axils below it, whereas elepidotes are more inclined to flower from the shoot-tip only. There are also differences in the numbers of chromosomes, which makes crossing between the two groups less easy than within them.*

Right: R. arboreum was the tree-species whose introduction from the Himalayas in the 1820s first showed gardeners the brilliance of the genus. Its natural range is so wide that variations proliferate. The best is blood-red.

Above: R. maximum, the 'rosebay', was the first American rhododendron to reach Europe (1736) and was bred into the 'hardy hybrids'. These *R. catawbiense* are the American Ponticas.

Above left: R. augustinii is highly prized for its blue flowers, improved by selection. Its subsection, Triflora, are mainly thin shrubs, including the bluish-white *R. yunnanense.*

Right: R. rex ssp. *fictolacteum* is one of the hardiest of the Falconera subsection – all tall Himalayans including some with the grandest of all leaves. *R. sinogrande* (Grandia subsection) has leaves that reach almost a metre in length.

Left: R. auriculatum from west China is named for the earlike lobes of its leaves. Its importance is its very late flowering, after mid-summer, which is useful to breeders. A famous hybrid is 'Polar Bear'.

Centre left: R. impeditum represents the Lapponica subsection of alpines, forming dense bushes in dry upland areas. The related *R. fastigiatum* and the deep purple *R. russatum* make good rock-garden plants.

Left: The (lepidote) Himalayan *R. cinnabarinum* is a parent of 'Lady Chamberlain' and other famous hybrids. A subspecies is the apricot *R. xanthocodon.*

Left: R. decorum is a Fortunea, together with the tender Himalayan *R. griffithianum*, parent of the famous 'Pink Pearl', and the Chinese *R. calophytum*, a splendid hardy tree.

Above: The beautiful dense-growing *R. degronianum* ssp. *yakushimanum* from southern Japan is the aristocrat of the Pontica subsection, which includes the common European *R. ponticum* and hardy American species. Now much used for breeding.

Above: R. griersonianum with its exquisite flowers was one of Forrest's best discoveries The most used of all rhododendrons for breeding.

Left: R. campanulatum has given its name to a small subsection of two Himalayan species. In Victorian times it was considered outstanding.

Hymenanthes, Tsutsusi and *Pentanthera.* The last two represent the evergreen and deciduous azaleas, which gardeners consider a separate issue.

Members of the subgenus *Rhododendron* are also those known as the lepidotes. Lepidote means scaly. The scaly rhododendrons are the largest group, with some 500 species, and also the widest ranging, with half its members in the tropics of Malaysia and Indonesia (the 'Malesians'), but including also the tough little alpines and the epiphytic kinds that live on trees in warm rain-forests. Although the botanical character of scaliness (chiefly under the leaves) is not obvious without a magnifying glass, that and the way the leaves are rolled in the bud, bottom side out, does seem to link all these species to a common ancestry.

The primary importance of the subgenus *Hymenanthes*, the largest of the 'elepidote' groups, is that it includes the great majority of garden-worthy rhododendrons. Elepidote means 'not scaly'. In practice the leaves of this group are very often hairy, and always rolled top side out in the bud. The hair, or more correctly 'indumentum', is frequently an exquisite feature, especially on the young growth as it emerges

Above: R. campylocarpum was Sir Joseph Hooker's favourite. When he discovered it in east Nepal in 1849 he described it as 'of a sulphur hue and almost spotless . . . of surpassing delicacy and grace'. Yellow rhododendrons on the whole tend to lack vigour. This grows to about 3m (10ft) and flowers in April or early May.

ABOVE: 'Rhododendron × loderi', a
cross made in 1901 between R. fortunei
and R. griffithianum, is generally
considered to be the finest hybrid;
a small tree with richly
scented flowers.

BELOW: 'Pink Pearl' is one of the most
popular of all rhododendrons, raised by
Waterer's nursery in Surrey in the 1890s.
It is a tall bush with great trusses of
deep pink flowers.

in shades of blonde, silver, gold or bronze. They are on the whole bigger plants than the lepidotes; the medium-sized species often grow in mountains around the tree-line, while the tall and spectacularly large-leaved types are found in temperate forests.

Within these groups the species are further allocated to sections and subsections. On the previous pages are set out a dozen of the best-known subsections, covering most of the species that concern the gardener.

Members of the subsection Arborea, for example, are mostly trees or big shrubs with long leathery leaves, hairy below, and many flowers in a dense 'truss' in the white-red-purple colour range. The Lapponica subsection is a complete contrast: dwarf upland shrubs with tiny scaly leaves and short funnel-flowers in many colours.

Falconera shares the characteristic of large leaves with Grandia. They are predominantly stout plants with hairy shoots and bell-shaped flowers in terminal trusses. The leaves of *R. sinogrande* (Grandia) can be almost 1m (3ft) long; one of the most imposing plants of all for wet mild-temperate gardens.

Triflora is a subsection of lightly-branched, thin-leaved shrubs, sometimes deciduous, with speckled flowers in a wide range of colours from yellow to (in one of its most valuable members, *R. augustinii*) very close to blue. Griersoniana is a single-species subsection famous for the beauty of *R. griersonianum* and its value as a parent of hybrids. Its uniqueness lies in the form of its bud and its scarlet and crimson trumpet-flowers, felty at the base.

Thomsonia is a subsection from the eastern Himalayas, medium-sized shrubs or trees with thin leathery leaves and loose terminal trusses of flowers, often bell-shaped. *R. thomsonii* and the related *R. hookeri* are blood-red. *R. cyanocarpum* in the same subsection is a smaller, fragrant, white-to-pink species from Yunnan.

Pontica is a dirty word among foresters. *R. ponticum* is the notoriously invasive mauve-flowered species from Turkey that throttles young tree plantations. The Pontica subsection on the other hand circles the globe north of the Himalayas and includes the lovely *R. yakushimanum*. Clearly gardeners with a disposition to classify and collect have more than enough rhododendrons to keep them happy.

It is not so difficult to grow rhododendrons as it is to choose them, or to site them satisfactorily in the garden. Their needs are simply stated: they must have acid soil, and they prefer damp air. They would rather that the soil was deep, decomposed leaf litter, but they can grow on a mere few inches if necessary as long as it never dries out, or is ever flooded. Being surface rooting they are some of the easiest plants to move, even when fully grown. But they do not like starvation: they need a regular diet of more and more leaves in the form of a mulch over their roots. If the leaves of the forest are supplemented with mature manure so much the better.

The grand manner of rhododendron gardening is to plant them in thinned woodland, where tall oaks, larches and firs filter the sunlight into dappled shade. It was devised by the grandees of the last century in imitation of the Himalayan forests, to provide shelter from wind, frost and excessive sun for plants whose massive features, both flowers and leaves, can easily be blemished by the elements. The myth emerged that they like deep shade, which is far from true. Most will tolerate it, but flower little and become thin and leggy looking for the light. Where they need shade and coolness is at the roots. Once they have equipped themselves with low branches or grown together in a solid phalanx, so that the soil is in permanent shade, their heads can only benefit from sunshine, within reason. Long dry spells are the enemy. Without their ration of mists and rain their noble leaves hang like the ears of a whipped spaniel. They react in the same way to winter cold. Dry, frosty weather is cruel to them; icy winds worse. For all these reasons the best climate, aside from monsoon-lashed mountains, is in the mild, damp, west of Europe and north-west of North America and New Zealand. The more splendid kinds find the east of Europe or America altogether too bracing.

The hardiest kinds, however, are well signposted after more than a century of experience and breeding. Precise codes of relative hardiness have been developed for each country.

HYBRID RHODODENDRONS

The first rhododendrons to be grown in European gardens were the pink-flowering rosebay, *R. maximum*, introduced from eastern North America in 1736, and the mauve *R. ponticum*, which came from Asia Minor in the 1770s. A third, *R. caucasicum*, brought in yellowish flowers in 1803. And a fourth, *R. catawbiense*, came from America in 1809. They were all thoroughly hardy, good-looking evergreens, but on the strength of these alone the rhododendron would never have taken off. Their flowers are at best pleasant, at worst dowdy.

The real launching of Rhodoland took place in the 1820s, when the first of many Himalayan species, sent home as seed from Kashmir, flowered in England. This was a different matter: a tall plant (christened by its botanical godfather *R. arboreum*, the tree rhododendron) with magnificent blood-red flowers. No other known shrub could compare with it.

There was of course a snag. The flowers came in March or April, when they were almost bound to be destroyed by frost – and indeed the whole plant needed protection. It was not by any means a satisfactory garden plant. But it was the cue for nurserymen to embark on a breeding programme that for a century went on at fever pitch, crossing the old hardy sorts with the new Himalayan ones in efforts to combine hardiness with bright, beautiful and, above all, late flowers. Unless the flowers could be delayed until the end of May there was at least an even chance that frost would damage them. It takes little frost to spoil so sumptuous a flower.

The fruits of these labours are known as the hardy hybrids. The nurserymen, above all the Waterer family at Knapp Hill in Surrey and Bagshot in Berkshire, and the firms of Standish and Noble at Ascot and Sunningdale (all on the sandy heaths south of London which are still ideal nursery and horse-racing country) worked in high rivalry and deep secrecy, crossing and recrossing species with hybrids and hybrids with more hybrids. Many of the plants they produced are still among the best of their kind. 'Lady Eleanor Cathcart' (*R. maximum* × *R. arboreum*) and the early-flowering white *R.* 'Nobleanum' (*R. caucasicum* × *R. arboreum*) are examples of well-known plants that were the first generation of breeding.

Of later, more complex crosses of the same blood, a score are still in cultivation. Strangely enough, though by now breeding was in full spate in France, Holland and Belgium as well, nearly all were English raised. Apparently English nurserymen were shortening the generation gap from seedling to flower to as little as four years by grafting seedlings

BELOW: *'Hawk Crest' is one of a series of crosses made by the Rothschilds at Exbury, and perhaps the best of all yellow hybrids.*

ABOVE: *George Forrest was the greatest of all collectors of rhododendrons in the wild. Between 1904 and his death in the field in 1932 he introduced more than 300 new species, mostly from Yunnan and Burma.*

BELOW: *Azalea breeding for bigger and more sumptuous flowers reached its climax in the Knap Hill-Exbury hybrids with such plants as 'Silver Slipper' (here) and 'Strawberry Ice'.*

on to mature roots. By 1870 they had crosses already seven or eight generations removed from the tender *R. arboreum* but still carrying its desirable traits.

In 1851 Joseph Hooker returned from his famous expedition to the Himalayas with forty-three more rhododendrons of great quality but questionable hardiness. The pick of them was *R. griffithianum*. The nurserymen looked hungrily at this lovely flower when it first opened in captivity in 1858. They crossed it with hardy species and hardy hybrids, but its tenderness remained in all its progeny until 1897, when Waterers of Bagshot put on show what still remains one of the most famous and beautiful hardy hybrids – 'Pink Pearl'.

Dutch nurserymen were quick to follow up with their own hybrids, the firm of Endtz using 'Pink Pearl' as a parent to produce the well-known 'Souvenir de Dr S. Endtz', Koster & Sons using other *griffithianum* hybrids to make such famous hardy plants as 'Betty Wormald', and van Nes & Sons taking over the *griffithianum* breeding programme of the Berlin Porcelain factory (including the beautiful but tender 'Queen Wilhelmina') to produce in due course the splendid scarlet 'Britannia'. Evidently they had their eyes on the lucrative British market.

Meanwhile rich amateur breeders were at work on the increasing number of Himalayan introductions, motivated simply by their curiosity and the restless search for new forms of beauty. Cornwall, possessing a mild damp climate, became a centre of cultivation of delicate species. Names such as 'Tremough' and 'Penjerrick' began to appear on beautiful but generally tender crosses. The term 'species hybrid' is often used to distinguish these later, often amateur, productions from the old hardy hybrids of the nursery trade.

To the flow of new kinds from Nepal and Sikkim was added a stream, later to become a spate, from China. The first was *R. fortunei*, discovered by Robert Fortune in 1855 and in due course a famous parent of hybrids. In 1900 Sir Edmund Loder of Leonardslee in Sussex crossed *R. fortunei* with the comely *griffithianum* to produce perhaps the most famous 'grex', or group of hybrids from two species, ever made – *R. × loderi*. This grex (the word literally means flock) has gone on to sire many other hybrids. *R. fortunei* too has been repeatedly used as a parent, particularly in the series of crosses made in this century by Lionel de Rothschild at Exbury in Hampshire.

Three great amateur names dominate twentieth-century rhododendron breeding: de Rothschild at Exbury in Hampshire, J. C. Williams of Caerhays in Cornwall, and Lord Aberconway at Bodnant in North Wales.

The 1900s had seen a virtual invasion of western China by plant collectors. If 'Chinese' Wilson stands at the head of the list for the variety and sheer number of his discoveries, the greatest gatherer of rhododendrons was George Forrest. By the end of the First World War many of their new species were beginning to flower in gardens. J. C. Williams in Cornwall was a subscriber and received seed from both Wilson and Forrest, and was the first to make hybrids of their introductions. Among many fruitful marriages those of Forrest's wonderful red trumpet-flowered *R. griersonianum* from Yunnan are probably the most numerous and important. Wilson's (lepidote) *R. augustinii* was another notable addition, bringing the nearest thing to blue into the range of rhododendron colours in such crosses as Williams's 'Blue Tit' and Aberconway's 'Bluebird'.

Exbury is famous for a vast range of hybrids, both of rhododendrons and azaleas. 'Lady Chamberlain', 'Lady

Rosebery', 'Jalisco' and 'Hawk Crest' are among the best known – each being a grex with several members of differing colour and quality. Bodnant also produced many well-known crosses between the wars; many of them red flowered and of a useful medium size, such as 'F. C. Puddle' and 'Bodnant Yellow'. Slocock's nursery at Woking, Surrey, is another famous breeder. Dietrich Hobbie in West Germany is another, specializing in small and very hardy plants suitable for modern German gardens. The best known are 'Elizabeth Hobbie', 'Baden-Baden' and 'Oldenburg'. In the United States the best-known producers of rhododendrons tough enough for north-eastern winters include David G. Leach, Orlando S. Pride and Gustav A. L. Mehlquist.

In the case of rose-breeders it is often said that novelty is all; that there are no real advances to be made along the lines they are following. Species which might have much to offer are not given a chance. In Rhodoland it is different. There are exciting new developments happening all the time. At the moment perhaps the most important concern the Japanese *R.degronianum* ssp. *yakushimanum* (or yakushimanum for short!) Breeders have their eyes on the unique combination of hardy good temper, delicate pink and white colouring and aristocratic good looks of this incomparable species. Though it is hard to imagine what would constitute an improvement on a plant already so richly endowed. On the contrary, the delicate colouring is usually the first thing to go.

The aesthetics of placing rhododendrons in gardens are less simple than they appear. Small modern gardens cannot imitate the forests of Nepal. The little alpine kinds are at home in rock or peat gardens. But the bigger rhododendrons – above all the wild species – have so much presence that they seem to want to banish all except their own kind from the garden. Roses look wrong with them. The usual cheerful border flowers and annuals look tawdry and out of place. Other shrubs look trivial. Only a select band of flowers, such things as lilies, trilliums, the Asiatic primulas and the Himalayan blue poppy that share the love of acid soil feel right in Rhodoland.

ABOVE: Rhododendron luteum, *formerly called* Azalea mollis, *is as fine a plant as any of its hybrids, with glorious fragrance and autumn colour.*

RHODOLAND: AZALEAS

Linnaeus believed that azaleas and rhododendrons were two different things – based on the fact that (most) azaleas have five stamens, while rhododendrons have ten. As far as botanists are concerned his grave error was corrected in 1870 by Carl Maximowicz of St Petersburg. As far as gardeners are concerned, Linnaeus knew what he was talking about.

Rhododendrons are almost always evergreen: azaleas drop their leaves, or most of them, in winter. The 'evergreen' azaleas shed the few leaves they keep all winter in spring. Azaleas tend to be small, or at least thin branched, and their flower formation, too, is distinct: never in a raceme or spike like many rhododendrons. Above all they are known for smothering themselves in so many flowers that leaves are invisible. They make solid mounds of colour in a wider colour range than anything else except roses. Great beauty is possible with carefully chosen azaleas: loud jangles if they are planted indiscriminately.

Their tastes in soil are the same as rhododendrons': damp leaf-mould is their favourite food. Whereas most of

BELOW: *Gardening has no sight to compare with the startling palette of hybrid azaleas. At Exbury in Hampshire the Rothschild strains are in their element in the shade of thin oak woodland.*

R. luteum (Azalea pontica). Caucasian, European. To 3m (10ft). Flowers May, bright yellow, very fragrant. Lovely autumn colour. Well worth growing.

R. calendulaceum (flame azalea). Allegheny Mts, USA. To 3m (10ft). The May to June flowers are small but brilliant red-orange-yellow. Brings scarlet tones into hybrids.

R. periclymenoides. Widespread in eastern United States. To 2.5m (9ft). The May flowers are in the red-pink-purple range, with a longer 'tube' than the flame azalea.

R. viscosum (swamp azalea). Carolina to Cape Cod. Flowers June and July– sticky, white or pinkish, long tubed, very fragrant. To 2.1m (7ft).

Other eastern American deciduous species: there are fifteen in all.

Ghent hybrids. Originated in Belgium in 1820s. Upright: some to 3m (10ft). Relatively small flowers with the new leaves in late May. Sometimes 'hose-in-hose' or double-flowered (e.g. the yellow 'Narcissiflora'). Good autumn colour and very hardy. 'Rustica Flore Pleno' is a related double-flowered strain.

R. molle (A. sinensis). From eastern China. To 1.8m (6ft). Has fine big yellow flowers in April and May but lacks vigour in cultivation.

R. japonicum (A. mollis). Japanese. To 1.5m (5ft). Flowers in May before the leaves appear. A wide range of colours, mostly red and orange. Scentless.

DECIDUOUS AZALEAS

The story of the deciduous azalea hybrids, which include most of those grown in gardens, is told in this chart. The Ghents are the equivalent of the early hybrid rhododendrons in which European and American blood was first mingled. Bigger, brighter and more showy flowers became possible with the introduction of Japanese and Chinese blood (*R. japonicum* and *R. molle*). The richest genetic mixture (the left-hand line of the chart) has resulted in the finest combinations of qualities, culminating in the Exbury hybrids.

Knap Hill hybrids. First made by Waterer's nursery, Knap Hill, Surrey, in the 1850s but only came to prominence in the 1920s. To 1.5m (5ft). Young leaves often bronze. Fairly fragrant flowers in May stand up well, sometimes with a darker 'flare'. Very hardy. Good autumn colour.

Mollis hybrids. Originated in Belgium in 1860s; developed by Koster in Holland in 1890s. 1–1.5m (4–5ft). Flowers, in early May before the leaves, are sometimes spoiled by frost. Very hardy, likes full sun; brilliant flaming hot colours, but no scent.

R. occidentale. The one azalea of the western United States. To 2.5m (8ft). Lovely white flowers, yellow blotched, in June and July when leaves are fully out. Fragrant.

The Exbury strain. Developed since 1920 at Exbury, Hampshire, by Lionel de Rothschild, by repeated crossings and ruthless elimination. Heights vary from 1.5–3m (5–10ft). Very hardy. Big flowers with strong bright colours, often with darker markings. So inbred that seedlings are all good, but many of the best have been named and won awards, e.g. 'Basilisk', 'Strawberry Ice', 'Silver Slipper', 'Sun Chariot' and 'George Reynolds' (the yellow original of the strain).

Occidentale hybrids. Originated in Holland (Koster, 1895). To 2.1m (7ft). Late May to early June flowering, fragrant with fine, delicate pastel colours, not to be mixed with Mollis hybrids.

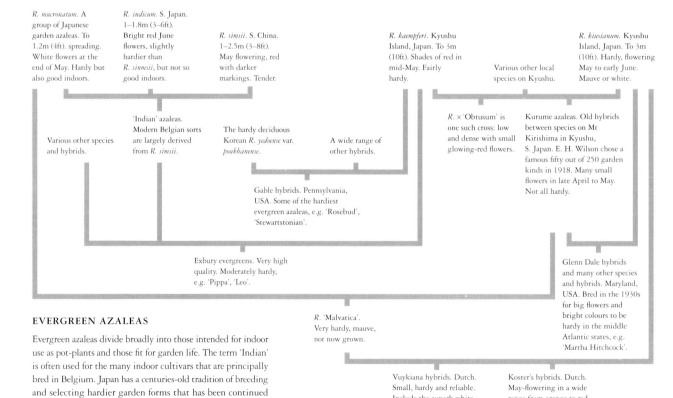

R. mucronatum. A group of Japanese garden azaleas. To 1.2m (4ft). spreading. White flowers at the end of May. Hardy but also good indoors.

R. indicum. S. Japan. 1–1.8m (3–6ft). Bright red June flowers, slightly hardier than *R. simsii*, but not so good indoors.

R. simsii. S. China. 1–2.5m (3–8ft). May flowering, red with darker markings. Tender.

R. kaempferi. Kyushu Island, Japan. To 3m (10ft). Shades of red in mid-May. Fairly hardy.

Various other local species on Kyushu.

R. kiusianum. Kyushu Island, Japan. To 3m (10ft). Hardy, flowering May to early June. Mauve or white.

'Indian' azaleas. Modern Belgian sorts are largely derived from *R. simsii*.

Various other species and hybrids.

The hardy deciduous Korean *R. yedoense* var. *poukhanense*.

A wide range of other hybrids.

R. × 'Obtusum' is one such cross: low and dense with small glowing-red flowers.

Kurume azaleas. Old hybrids between species on Mt Kirishima in Kyushu, S. Japan. E. H. Wilson chose a famous fifty out of 250 garden kinds in 1918. Many small flowers in late April to May. Not all hardy.

Gable hybrids. Pennsylvania, USA. Some of the hardiest evergreen azaleas, e.g. 'Rosebud', 'Stewartstonian'.

Exbury evergreens. Very high quality. Moderately hardy, e.g. 'Pippa', 'Leo'.

Glenn Dale hybrids and many other species and hybrids. Maryland, USA. Bred in the 1930s for big flowers and bright colours to be hardy in the middle Atlantic states, e.g. 'Martha Hitchcock'.

EVERGREEN AZALEAS

Evergreen azaleas divide broadly into those intended for indoor use as pot-plants and those fit for garden life. The term 'Indian' is often used for the many indoor cultivars that are principally bred in Belgium. Japan has a centuries-old tradition of breeding and selecting hardier garden forms that has been continued in Holland and the United States. Many points of parentage remain obscure, but the basic blood lines emerge fairly clearly.

R. 'Malvatica'. Very hardy, mauve, not now grown.

Vuykiana hybrids. Dutch. Small, hardy and reliable. Include the superb white 'Palestrina' and 'Vuyk's Scarlet'.

Koster's hybrids. Dutch. May-flowering in a wide range from orange to red-purple. Leaves colour in autumn, e.g. 'Anny'.

the bigger rhododendrons are happiest in modified or tree-filtered sunlight, most azaleas are creatures of open scrubland where the sun reaches them all day. A baking does them no harm.

For practical purposes there are two main groups of azaleas, the deciduous and the evergreen – or nearly so – roughly conforming to a botanical division into two 'sub-genera'. Under the new Edinburgh regime the two kinds are subsections: the deciduous species are *Pentanthera* (meaning five anthers); the evergreen species are *Tsutsusi* – which at least has an aptly Japanese ring.

Each of the two groups is now a tangle of hybrids so numerous that they are referred to by historical – rather than botanical – names. Ghent, Knap Hill, Kurume, Exbury are the places where the crosses were originally made. Mollis, the name of the other main deciduous batch, is one of those fossilized blunders that pepper the pages of gardening literature. *Azalea mollis* was at the time the name of the Japanese parent of the group. The same plant is now called *Rhododendron japonicum*. To make matters worse the old *Azalea sinensis*, the Chinese parent, is now called *Rhododendron molle*. Hence, you may well suppose, the retreat into hybrids with names that stick, even if they are in Japanese.

The family trees opposite are the only clear way of telling this complex story and explaining how diverse qualities of hardiness, habit, size and brightness of flower and time of flowering have been combined over the last hundred years into such reliable garden plants.

In general the colours of the deciduous azaleas are better in the hotter part of the spectrum, the flame colours; while the evergreens, where they are hardy (generally not below zone 8), have pinks, mauves, lilacs and blue-purples to offer.

But flowers are not all. The deciduous azaleas often form distinct tiers as they grow older, making bushes with considerable character, especially when hoary with lichens. In autumn few things in the garden turn more glorious or more various colours. Among the evergreens are plants that mound up prettily or spread massively. The Japanese habitually shear them all over to encourage dense bushiness. The Western method is to pinch out the growing tips.

I must not give the impression that it is only hybrid azaleas that are worth growing. Few if any of the hybrids have the range of qualities of the common yellow European wildling *R. luteum* (alias *Azalea pontica* – or *A. mollis*), the great-grandfather of them all. For flower, for leaf colour in autumn, for stature and for an intoxicating sweetness of breath it is still superlative.

One azalea seems to have been unofficially christened 'Royal' for its combination of qualities. The rosy pink *R. schlippenbachii* is exquisite, from its early unfolding of purply red leaves to its sumptuous autumn colour. It lacks scent, but otherwise its only fault is that springtime eagerness that dogs gardeners in Britain and much of France. April warmth woos it from the bud, only for May frost to cry 'got you' and bite its head off.

Deciduous azaleas fall more readily into place in a mixed planting than others of their family. They have so many of the qualities of a first-class shrub that they can blend into any woodland scene, even into a mixed border. They appreciate a good leafmould mulch but do not demand moisture and acidity. I grow *R. luteum* in a bed with *Ceanothus thyrsiflorus repens*; a good blue-yellow combination.

The principal mistake that gardeners make is to mix their colours, the whole range from blue-pink to orange, in a sprawling mass in the middle of a lawn. Even the Edinburgh Botanic Garden does this. What is it about azaleas (rhodos too) that seems to make even good gardeners colour-blind?

ABOVE: *'Palestrina' is one of the loveliest white azaleas, a hybrid of* R. *'Malvaticum' and* R. kaempferi. *When it flowers in May its leaves are a fresh brilliant green.*

BELOW: *The deciduous azaleas give an autumn display of colour almost as bright as their flowering.* R. luteum *is as gorgeous as any.*

CLIMBING PLANTS
THE GREAT ADVANTAGE OF CLIMBING PLANTS IS THAT THEY ADD THE VERTICAL DIMENSION OF THE GARDEN TO THE SPACE YOU CAN COVER WITH LEAVES AND FLOWERS.

The smaller the garden the more important this is. A little urban backyard has more wall than floor. Climbers take very little ground space, yet can clothe any wall with beauty, or at least with soothing greenery.

Not that it is a climber's nature to grow on walls. A climber is a plant that decided (in an evolutionary way) to concentrate on length rather than strength, to throw all its energies into gaining height with the aid of other plants rather than becoming a responsible self-supporting citizen of the woods.

The majority of climbers are woodland creatures that rely on bushes and trees to help them as they grow upwards to the sun. They are light-demanding plants. That is why they climb. But their roots are accustomed to the cool, shaded soil beneath the trees. A wall provides no all-round shelter, but brusque draughts; no deep damp humus at its foot, but rubble and dust. On south-facing walls the whole plant is grilled all summer long. Walls are definitely not their element.

Climbers have varied and ingenious ways of hanging on. Plants such as ivy and Virginia creeper use the adhesive method: ivy has aerial roots, the Virginia creeper and Boston ivy small sucker pads. Tree trunks are their natural home, but at least walls provide a solid vertical surface.

Then there is a class of climbers that hardly deserves the term at all. They simply put out long lax shoots directly upwards and hope to find something to support them. Climbing roses are the commonest example. You might count their curved thorns as crampons, but unless they encounter a branch overhead they will eventually flop to the ground. Another shoot will rise, fail, fall on top of the first, until the rose is a huge tangled mound. A wall gives them no help at all. A sturdy old tree is their essential prop.

The most ingenious kind of climber uses something that seems remarkably like muscular reaction to grab hold of a twig or branch on the way up. The grape vine is a good example. It is a tendril-climbing plant. The tendrils are like long leaf stalks without leaves, which can weave about like the limbs of an octopus until they touch something that feels promising as a hand-hold. Then the cells on one side of the tip grow with amazing speed while those on the other side stay as they were, and the tip quickly forms a curl. Many clematis use the same muscular-seeming reaction, but having no specialized tendrils, curl the long stalks of their leaves round any likely support.

The commonest of all climbing techniques is the serpentine spiral or twining motion adopted by honeysuckle, bindweed, wisteria, summer jasmine and a score of other well-known plants. Again it is faster growth of one side of the stem than the other that causes the curling motion. Some

BELOW: *The ornamental ivies can create rich effects.* Hedera colchica *is the Caucasian Persian Ivy. The variety 'Dentata Variegata' has deep yellow or white margins to its long lush leaves.*

twine clockwise, some anticlockwise. Whether like bath-water they change their minds at the equator I have not discovered.

In each category of climbers there are both permanent woody plants and herbaceous ones that start again each year. The woody ones can eventually strangle their hosts. Once honeysuckle has wound its wiry loops round a twig it is only a matter of time before the twig, trying to grow thicker, throttles itself. I have seen wisteria in the forests of Japan with a main trunk 3.75m (12ft) in girth. The tree it originally climbed had long since died and decayed and the monster was held up by half an acre of tentacles proliferating in the forest canopy above. It was a salutary reminder that the size of a climber must be matched to the size of its host plant if the poor climbing-frame is to survive.

This Japanese forest contained wild wisteria and tall paulownia trees, in bloom simultaneously with flowers of the same pale lilac tint – not an arrangement any economically minded gardener would allow. The sensible thing is to grow an early-flowering climber over a late-flowering bush or tree, or *vice versa*, giving a double performance. I do it with the lightweight *Clematis macropetala* over a browny-red form of the smoke bush, *Cotinus coggygria*. First comes the clematis with its violet-blue flowers, just as the young brown leaves of the bush appear. Then, when the bush produces its purple puffs of 'smoke' in summer, the clematis has silky, silvery seed heads.

Alternatively, a climber that flowers at the same time as its host, but in a different colour, can be a remarkable sight. The white *Clematis montana* over a scarlet hawthorn works perfectly. Or there is the contrast of leaf colour to play with. One day I hope to see the white wisteria I have planted under the outskirts of a copper beech hanging its snowy tassels all over the tree's purple dome.

Climbers on walls need support suitable to their mode of gripping, which could of course be an established tall shrub or tree, a ceanothus or a magnolia perhaps, planted against the wall. But this takes time. To do the job quickly, for climbers without directly adhesive habits, there is nothing for it but to provide a system of wires or trellis. The essential here is that it stands out well away from the wall – 10cm (4in) is not too much – and that its supporting nails or screws are strong enough to hold what could eventually be a very heavy weight. There is of course no need to limit yourself to one climber per pitch. Mingling climbers is perfectly fair game. A rose can take a clematis, or a wisteria a passion flower, as passenger.

Think hard before mixing these non-adhesive climbers with the self-adhering kind, ivy or Virginia creeper or the climbing hydrangea, *H. petiolaris*. The one with the sucker-pads will win. Having its own holdfasts and a permanent structure, on the other hand, an adhesive climber can be clipped right back to the wall. I have even seen ivy clipped into formal pilasters on a classsical facade. But add a rose or clematis and the tangle becomes total.

Whether on walls or under trees climbers need generous planting, with due regard for the normal poverty of the soil in such places. It is a good plan never to plant closer than

ABOVE: Tropaeolum speciosum *is a delicate-looking herbaceous climber which loves damp woodland soil.*

BELOW: *The true Virginia Creeper.* Parthenocissus quinquefolia. *is un-rivalled for autumn colours.*

ABOVE: Clematis montana *var.* rubens *is partnered here with 'Early Dutch' honeysuckle in a glorious uncontrollable tangle.*
BELOW: *The deep velvety red of* Clematis *'Niobe' mingles with the brilliant mauve of 'Comtesse de Bouchaud'.*

45cm (18in) from the foot of a wall, and then to dig deeper and make a richer soil mixture than for other plants. My technique for planting under trees and among shrubs is to excavate well, then to bury a large cardboard box (the dozen-bottle size), fill it with compost and plant in that. By the time the box has rotted away, the climber's roots are strong enough to compete with anything.

CLIMBERS FOR FOUR SEASONS

A south-facing wall is the gardener's equivalent of prime time on television. A tantalizing choice must be made between the plants that demand the wall's shelter and warmth to grow at all and those that show their gratitude by producing twice as many flower buds from their well-ripened wood. On the whole climbers are likely to come into the second category. Remembering their native woods, they will grow satisfactorily (in appropriate hardiness zones) with any aspect. The south-facing wall should therefore be saved for plants that will repay VIP treatment with outstanding quantity and quality of flowers.

The two real florists' climbers are roses and clematis. If you are looking for the longest, brightest, finest show of flowers, and you can provide for them, you need look no further. Climbing roses are discussed on pages 123–4; clematis fill even more of the year with flowers – starting in the very depths of winter.

The first to go, even in January, is *Clematis cirrhosa* var. *balearica*, a lacy leaved evergreen, miniature in detail but potentially massive in spread. Its scented flowers like little creamy hellebores hang down from high on sheltered walls and trees. The Chinese *C. armandii*, white or pink with thick, hard, evergreen leaves, comes in early spring. It has a reputation for tenderness which seems to arise more from the fragility of its new shoots, and the damage the wind can do to its evergreen leaves, than from the results of frost. Full spring brings *C. alpina* and *C. macropetala*, blue-purple lanterns on lightweight scramblers.

Clematis montana from the Himalayas flowers in late spring in rampant sheets of white or strong mauve-pink (*C. montana* var. *rubens*). Then early or late in summer – in some cases both – come the large-flowered cultivars, single or double, from white and pale pink to blue and royal purple. 'Lasurstern' is one of the best blues, 'Marie Boisselot' a splendid white (best in shade), 'Ville de Lyon' a clear wine red, and 'Jackmanii' the most prolific purple. Blue is perhaps the most valuable of all, since no roses are this colour. Varieties with a darker bar on each sepal, which need rich feeding, are typified by the pinky-mauve and carmine 'Nelly Moser'.

Another group with abundant small white, red or purple flowers, *C. viticella*, has a long summer season. Then later summer brings the 'lemon-peel' clematis, *C. orientalis*, with silky seed heads, and the heavenly-scented *C. flammula*, with a mist of tiny white flowers.

Clematis like, but do not necessarily demand, alkaline soil. The question of pruning them is the one that taxes most gardeners. Spring-flowering kinds flower on lateral growths from old branches; late-flowering kinds from the current year's growth. Prune them at the wrong moment and you can lose a year's flowers.

The simple answer is to prune them all in the winter, but to prune them to different degrees. Early flowerers should only have old tangled wood cut out from time to time (not always an easy task) but a strong framework always left in place. An old plant high in a tree is almost impossible to prune at all – but it will still flower. Late flowerers can be cut down to a convenient height a metre or so from the ground – and given a good feed at the same time. Cool, well-fed roots are the essential.

Once you become climber minded, not just walls but every potential support in the garden – every tree, every shrub – becomes a volunteer to be climbed on. There are flowering climbers for every moment of the unfrozen year, and ivy in endless variety to close the winter gap.

From time to time violent debate breaks out as to whether ivy is harmful to trees and buildings. The best authorities agree it does no harm to tree trunks or walls, despite its vigour. Trouble begins if it reaches out along branches and steals light in the canopy of a tree, which is very rare, and of course when it reaches, and starts to grow among, roof tiles.

At least a hundred cultivars of ivy have been given names. They vary in leaf shape and colour, often variegated yellow or white, very much in vigour and to some extent in hardiness. All, however, do the same strange thing when they are about to flower: they cease to be climbers and become shrubs, sending out stiff branches from the top of tree or wall. Cuttings taken from these will root and grow – but only as bushes.

Common green ivy, especially the big-leaved variety known as Irish (the one commonly sold as groundcover in the USA), is too powerful to be allowed among garden shrubs and trees of value. But many smaller cultivars are ideal. 'Goldheart' has small almost triangular leaves with radiantly cheerful yellow centres. 'Glacier' describes itself. Then there are curly-leaved, arrow-leaved, parsley-leaved . . .

The flowering season for climbers starts (and finishes) with clematis. Winter jasmine – a climber by convention only,

ABOVE: *Sweet peas can be grown casually or in the spirit of competition, but the secret is always plenty of food and water, sunshine and steady picking.*

BELOW: *Wisteria on a house wall needs strict management to flower well within bounds.*

ABOVE: *Leaves alone are enough in their spring freshness. Hostas provide form and variety (*H. fortunei *the broad bluish leaves) and euphorbias brilliant bracts in yellow-green or (in* E. griffithii) *brick red.*

BELOW: *The bearded irises flower with azaleas in May. They ask only to be divided and replanted when their woody rhizomes become thick and congested.*

On the whole early flowers, flowering in the longest days of the year as midsummer approaches, tend to have a shorter season than those that flower in the shortening days of the summer. Partly it is a question of simple size: late-flowering plants have all summer to put on more bulk and make more flower buds.

Large areas occupied by these early plants may easily be flowerless, untidy or even empty altogether in high summer, unless later plants are interspersed with them. Dicentras and Virginia cowslips, for example, disappear by midsummer. No harm can come by planting a late flower, such as a Japanese anemone, hard alongside in the same plot. Lupins and oriental poppies need a sequel to cover their shabby leaves after flowering: *Acanthus* or *Artemisia lactiflora* would blot out any sign of them. Bulbs require the same approach. The notion of following bulbs with hostas has occurred to thousands of gardeners. Annuals can also be started off in the kitchen garden, brought out ready to flower and planted in the spaces between the early perennials.

Hostas have a unique place in the garden now for the simple beauty of their leaves, sprouting salad-fresh, unfurling as they go. Later in summer or autumn come lily-like, usually fairly modest, flowers. There is a vast and bewildering range of names to choose from; Japanese gardeners have been selecting them for colour and size (including miniatures) for centuries.

Hosta sieboldiana is the boldest, with blue-grey leaves as much as 30cm (1ft) wide that turn a vivid buff in autumn. The variegated forms are almost as various as hollies, yellow or creamy-white with green either in the centre or as a rim round the leaves, which in *H. crispul*a and *H. undulata* have elegantly wavy margins. Among the best are *H. fortunei* var. *albopicta* (yellow leaves with green rims) 'Thomas Hogg' (green leaves with cream rims) and *H. plantaginea* var. *japonica* for both bright green leaves and intensely sweet-smelling flowers over a long summer season, a favourite in pots in Mediterranean courtyards.

There are other early plants whose leaves are worth as much as their flowers and do them credit all summer. The evergreen bergenia, London pride, epimedium, heuchera, the deciduous Solomon's seal, lily of the valley and brunnera are all good-looking without flowers.

Low-growing wood anemones are almost as valuable early in the year as the tall Japanese anemones are in late summer. They light up woodland, or any shady spot, with their delicate white, pink, or lavender-blue faces up-turned from clumps of pale, fretted leaves. The florists' bright red and blue creations look frankly like artificial, even plastic, flowers beside them.

Aquilegias, the columbines, are up early, keeping the irises company with their graceful greyish ferny leaves. They hybridize eagerly: the wild *A. vulgaris* will dominate and muddy the clear colours of the many carefully selected better kinds. Their Latin and English names, meaning 'eagle' and 'dove', both refer to the flower's bird-like shape.

From winter into spring there is one family that cannot be overdone: the hellebores. Alone among border plants they stand up to the weather and announce the spring with incredibly long-lasting flowers of incomparable texture and quality, quiet coloured but forming with their deeply sculpted evergreen leaves some of the most satisfying plants you can grow.

Hellebores, the Christmas and Lenten roses, are the infallible sign of a keen, even a highbrow, gardener. They are a confusing race, but it scarcely matters as all are worth growing. They like shade, even a north-facing wall, and appreciate shelter. Under deciduous shrubs is an ideal place to grow them, although one species, the Corsican hellebore, builds itself up almost to low shrub stature. They like fairly damp soil (though they tolerate drought), and have no objection to lime.

Four species are well-known – and many lovely crosses between them. The Christmas rose, *H. niger*, has broad leaves and white or faintly pink flowers rising from ground level, often open by Christmas. The stinking hellebore, *H. foetidus*, has a striking combination of narrow, black-green leaves and pale green flowers with purple margins in late winter. The biggest is the Corsican hellebore, *H. lividus*, with stiff, toothed, white-marbled green leaves and pale green flowers that last for months. Last comes the Lenten rose, *H. orientalis*, with less important leaves and flowers in any colour from white to maroon, often beautifully speckled within.

As the hellebores mature, primroses usher in the spring. The 500 species of the primrose genus embrace alpines, meadow-flowers and bog-plants, all spring flowers of almost childish charm – the very opposite of the sophisticated silk-and-satin irises. A tendency to 'mealiness', or a coating of leaves, stems and buds with 'farina', adds to their crisp, laundered look. All like leafy soil with humus, though some like it drained; some not. Most, despite the air of mystique that surrounds the genus and probably prevents many gardeners from trying, are easy to grow.

All primulas are perennials – though a few are very short-lived. Most grow rapidly from seed. The common English primrose often begins to flower in winter. Garden forms of the primrose crossed with cowslips are called polyanthus – in colours relentlessly called 'jewel-like'. They need dividing regularly, or alternatively growing as biennials.

Auriculas, from the European Alps, have been highly bred into exquisite show-flowers in endless colour combinations. They have thick evergreen leaves, often densely covered with 'meal', or farina, giving them a thoroughly starched appearance. They flower early in spring. Some need alpine-house treatment; all like good drainage. The alpine aristocrat *P. marginata* belongs in the same 'section'.

The Himalayas are the real primula family home. Himalayan kinds include the winter-flowering *P. malacoides*, *P. obconica* and the hybrid *P. × kewensis*, lovely graceful flowers which need a frost-free greenhouse and are usually grown as annuals. The 'drumstick' primula, *P. denticulata*, comes from Kashmir. It needs wet ground and actually prefers cold winters. From Sikkim comes the yellow *P. florindae*, the latest to flower; an easy hardy perennial for moist or wet ground.

Most rarefied looking, but not at all difficult in damp soil, are the 'candelabra' section, with flowers arranged in whorls around the stem. It includes the crimson *P. pulverulenta* ('Bartley Strain' is a pink version), the orange *P. aurantiaca*, magenta *P. beesiana* and *P. japonica* in various colours.

BELOW: Helleborus orientalis *flowers in the first three months of the year, until spring crocuses come to match its intricate and varied rosy and purple spots and colours.*

ABOVE: *Primulas have been bred into many hundreds of varieties. The Barnhaven strains are among the more showy, though many gardeners prefer more natural-looking species.*

Oriental poppies are briefly splendid in early summer, in colours from pure poppy red to pink, and a dramatic white with jet-black markings. They like dry soil and sun. Their pale, hairy, deep-cleft leaves are excellent up to flowering time, then rapidly degenerate and need hiding. This is their drawback; they are sprawling, top-heavy plants; in a tidy garden they need support. Like most poppies they can also be prolific self-seeders.

Garden lupins have been bred from the blue wildflower of the American West into a whole spectrum of colours, popularized by Russell's nursery at York. Russell lupins can be bought as seed (mixed colours) or plants of a named variety. Unless they are dead-headed their seed comes up in unwanted places, usually in unclear pink. Dead-headed, on the other hand, they will often flower again.

The peonies are the earliest border plants to produce such sumptuous flowers in such resounding colours. The old double red form from the Mediterranean is a cottage-garden tradition, though scores of varieties have been bred in all colours except blue, and shapes ranging from simple to outrageously frilly. They are based mainly on forms developed in Chinese gardens from *Paeonia lactiflora*.

All peonies are slow-moving but apparently immortal, encouraged by feeding but reliable even under neglect, given deep soil and sunshine. Their season is short, but their leaves are good-looking, red when they open and often red again in autumn. One species of great beauty is *P. mlokosewitschii*, with single-yellow flowers among flushed grey-green leaves. The equally gorgeous 'tree' peonies appear at the same time.

Early summer brings the climax of the long season of the irises. Few genera are so consistent in their style of flowers over so many species (there are 300) yet so diverse in their way of life. Roots vary from rhizomes to bulbs or tubers, and habitats from dust to mud. The flower of the bearded, or German, iris epitomizes the design: three petals upright (the 'standards') and three drooping (the 'falls'). The 'beard', appearing in this group only, is a soft, hairy patch on the upper surface of each fall.

Bearded irises like well drained soil in full sun. Endless cultivars have been produced in all colours except red, and many combinations, in a range of sizes from April-flowering dwarfs to 1.2m (4ft) that flower in June. The unbearded Pacific Coast hybrids are of medium size, in many subtle and exquisite colours, and enjoy the same conditions. Slightly damper soil suits cultivars of *I. sibirica*, with much smaller, butterfly-size flowers and tall grassy leaves. Close-to the veining of their falls is wonderfully intricate. These are elegant and very easy plants.

Similar soil suits the bulbous irises of early summer: the Dutch, Spanish and English kinds, which flower in that order. Bulbous irises have slender leaves and stems and fair-sized 'flags'. Any soil and any degree of shade down to the densest satisfies the evergreen *I. foetidissima*, or Gladdon, which is grown not for its small, unshowy flowers but its fat pods of brilliant autumn berries.

The miniature winter-flowering bulbs *I. histrioides* and *I. reticulata* need sharp drainage: alpine conditions. The tuberous *I. bucharica* of spring simply needs a snug spot. Mid-winter iris, *I. unguicularis* (alias *stylosa*), likes it very dry; the base of a sunny wall. The flowers emerge from deep in dull foliage but their delicate mauve colour and sweet scent are ravishing indoors.

Really damp soil, and even shallow water, suits the common European yellow flag, *I. pseudacorus*, and the Japanese *Iris ensata* (better known by its old name, *kaempferi*). With centuries of Japanese breeding behind them the many varieties of *I. ensata* have the most regal flowers of the genus.

THE MID-SEASON BORDER

Although it is arbitrary to divide the continuous succession of flowering into periods, there is no question that the mid-summer season represented here (or strictly, in Britain, the season starting at the end of June) is the climax of the year for perennial border flowers.

While the true spring flowers are over, many families that had a few outriders in spring now arrive in force; genera such as the hardy geraniums and daylilies, and above all the daisy family. Even the latest-flowering plants have filled their allotted spaces, at least with leaves if not yet with flowers. There is no natural break between now and the waning year.

Whereas among spring flowers there are many that tolerate or even prefer some shade, all the emphasis now is on sunshine. Compared with the generally low, even ground-covering, spring flowers, the mid-summer field is tall (and may well need support). These are mainly meadow and prairie flowers – a good number of them from the prairies of North America.

For solo performances, as a garden feature in a corner or by a door, divorced from others of their kind, some of the most architecturally interesting, reliable and longest-lasting in flower are *Acanthus*, *Aruncus*, *Crambe* (which is capable of looking after itself in long grass) and *Macleaya*. *Eryngium*, *Astilbe* and *Achillea* have beautiful seed-heads to decorate the border later, or they can be dried for winter decoration indoors.

A really ambitious traditional border, based on the premise that everything in it should be flowering at once, would inevitably be based on this period. Every colour is available in almost every shape; which makes the task of choice and organization not easier but very much more difficult. There are all the annuals to consider; and such late bulbs as some of the alliums. At the same time the roses have reached their first peak, adding to the opportunities for rich but controlled, or riotously muddled, combinations.

There is a danger of overdoing the daisy motif from now onwards. There are so many of them, leading on to later Michaelmas daisies, cornflowers, chrysanthemums and dahlias, that they need to be consciously kept away from each other by alternating them with different flower forms, substantial leaves or perhaps grasses.

Delphiniums are inescapably the stars of the show; nothing else either early or late challenges their true-blue steeples for everything we desire in garden decoration. Their cultivation demands attention, from good feeding to protection from slugs, not to mention high-level support. The choice of colours in the garden hybrids is almost complete – although to choose white, cream or even red seems perverse in a genus whose unique glory is its range of blues, from the palest to the most sumptuously suffused with purple.

The tall campanulas are their rivals, though they never quite achieve the same brilliance or air of dominating the scene. It is easy to recognize the bell-flowers, but not so easy to remember which is which.

BELOW: *The components of a mid-season border should include flowers of such horizontal form as achilleas, verticals such as salvias and delphiniums, and soft hummocks of geraniums or alstroemerias.*

ABOVE: *The hardy geraniums or cranes-bills are easy, self-reliant and excellent for covering ground. Colours range from pink to such strong violet-blue as this* G. × magnificum, *flowering in early summer.*

BELOW: *The strong verticals of the midsummer border, delphiniums and even foxgloves, are used to airy, aspiring effect in a Cambridgeshire garden.*

The violet-blue *Campanula lactiflora*, especially 'Prichard's Variety', is among the best of the tall ones, growing to 1.2–1.5m (4–5ft), along with the liberally self-sowing *C. latifolia*, *C. pyramidalis*, the Chimney bell-flower, statuesque in pots, and the smaller, more delicate *C. persicifolia*. *C. carpatica* is one of the best of the small ones: a 30cm- (1ft)-high hummock spangled with up-turned bell-flowers in white or blue.

All the campanulas share a clean-cut freshness in their simple flowers, and always hover on the grey and purple side of blue. But their colours, their shapes and their timing fit them perfectly to accompany old roses, and they need little special care, beyond well-drained soil. They are not specially demanding of sunny spots. A note of caution, though: they include a few, such as *C. rapunculoides*, which are pretty, but ineradicable weeds.

If one can say that any plant is essential, at least to the scent of the summer border, it is phlox in one of the many varieties and crosses derived from *P. panicu-lata* (or *P. paniculata* itself). *Phlox* has the quality of looking at home anywhere from a cottage garden to the most formal border (it prefers moist ground), of bringing soft colours in the white to purple range (there are also wine-red ones), but above all for wafting its far-carrying, uniquely sweet scent all round the garden.

The other almost-universal and immensely wide range of species and varieties are the day-lilies, the *Hemerocallis* genus. Their breeding possibilities have led nurserymen, particularly in America, to elaborate endlessly on species which could well be considered perfect in themselves: healthy mounds of strap-leaves over-topped by elegantly poised little 'lilies'.

Most charming, early, very fragrant (but slightly wandering) is the pale clear yellow *Hemerocallis lilio-asphodelus* (alias *H. flava*). Although each flower lasts only a day (hence their name) the supply seems endless. At the other end of the season *H. citrin*a is like a taller, evening-flowering version.

In mid-summer the soft-orange, double-flowered *H.* 'Kwanso Flore Pleno' is one of those plants so reliable, self-sufficient and long-flowering that one can too easily take it for granted. Certainly the many more recent cultivars based on *H. fulva* var. *rosea* (a pink mutation) are more striking and offer every colour from scarlet to lavender, as well as stripes and contrasting centres. The day-lily breeder's goal is also a flower with thick, curving-back petals, which may lack the grace of the species but lasts better under the summer sun. Few genera offer a wider choice for the border with such reliable performance over a long period.

In complete contrast are the soft hummocky cranesbills or hardy geraniums. Their mounds of fingered or lobed, densely ground-smothering leaves, sometimes red in autumn, would justify growing them even without their flowers.

The cranesbills cannot be fitted tidily into a single season. *Geranium sanguineum*, the bloody cranesbill, is out in May, while *Geranium wallichianum* 'Buxton's Variety' lingers into autumn. They are often underrated because their individual flowers are modest by border standards, but the flowers have long seasons. The brightest summer cranesbills are the early violet-blue *G.* × *magnificum*, and the mid-season *G. psilostemon*, 1.5m (4ft) tall with magenta-crimson flowers and splendid leaves. One of the most useful is the early 'Johnson's Blue' for its colour and dense lobed leaves; another the wide mat-forming and utterly weed-proof *G. macrorrhizum*, especially the pale pink 'Ingerwersen's Variety'. *Geranium sylvaticum* is tall, graceful, an airy wildling with a lovely white-flowered form, *albiflorum*.

The salvias are an even wider family of hardy and not-so-hardy perennials merging into sub-shrubs (the kitchen sage included) and species so tall that in a conservatory they become permanent decorations in the roof.

There are a score of handsome herbaceous salvias, all lovers of sunshine. All are hairy, aromatic plants with spikes of hooded dead-nettle flowers. The best known border plant among them is *Salvia superba*, with sheaves of violet-purple 1m (3ft) spikes. The most beautiful are perhaps the sapphire-blue *S. patens*, which needs winter protection in cold areas, and the tall Cambridge-blue *S. uliginosa*, with waving willowy stems.

Bigger species include the bright silver *S. argentea* and the pale lavender *S. haematodes*. The most dramatic perhaps are *S. cardinalis*, a flower as red as you will find, a water-lover, and the oddly named Vatican sage, which could hardly be more different: a huge hairy and smelly-leaved biennial with quietly lovely lavender and buff hooded flowers. The scarlet bedding salvia is *S. splendens*, a half-hardy perennial grown as an annual.

The daisy family, the Compositae, is the largest of all families of flowering plants, with more than 13,000 species in up to 900 genera. Most of this vast array are herbaceous plants. Inevitably the garden risks being overwhelmed with these cheerful and easy flowers; particularly the border in mid- to late summer when many of them bloom at once. The family includes plenty of less obvious daisies: thistles, for example, and such varied border flowers as yarrow (*Achillea*) and golden rod (*Solidago*). Hundreds of them are annuals or biennials.

There are at least eight well-known genera of border daisies beside the chrysanths, Michaelmas daisies and dahlias of the late summer. In approximate order of flowering, they start with *Anthemis tinctoria*, the ox-eye chamomile, a good border plant from June to August, its leaves fresh and finely cut, its flowers ranging from pale to deep yellow. It will flop without support. The slightly earlier silver-leafed, white-flowered *A. punctata* subsp. *cupaniana* is another good plant, forming a dense carpet.

Erigeron (Fleabanes) have been bred in all colours from pink to purple, with single or double flowers. The effect is like early Michaelmas daisies flowering from June to August. *Coreopsis* (Tickseed) has some of the prettiest leaves, and at only 60cm (2ft) needs no support. 'Goldfink' is only 30cm (1ft) high (June–September).

Gaillardia (Blanket flowers) are the most brazenly painted, in circles of red, yellow and brown. At 1m (3ft) they need support for their long season from June to October. *Heliopsis* are brassy and loud in July and August; grow 1.2m (4ft) tall and need props. *Helianthus* (the annual sunflower is one) are tall, spreading, greedy, but bright from July to September. *Inula* includes some huge plants, best of all the 1.8m (6ft) *I. magnifica*, coarse, broad-leaved, heroically vivid and loud with its deep-yellow daisies 15cm (6in) wide. *Helenium* (Sneezeweed) is last to go – August to October – with suitably autumnal colours including velvety brown.

With the big genus of *Dianthus* we hover between perennials and annuals and biennials. There is no clear-cut line, but none of them can be called permanent. Frequent propagation is necessary – but happily easy; from cuttings with

ABOVE: *The day-lilies,* Hemerocallis, *have been bred and rebred to form an enormous collection. Each trumpet flower only lasts one day, but the supply can last eight weeks or more.*

BELOW: Phlox paniculata *is essential for its far-flung fragrance in mid to late summer. 'Prince George' is one of a great many named varieties. They like moist humus-rich soil.*

ABOVE: *The lilac-blue* Campanula persicifolia. *growing to 1m (3ft) but delicate in structure. is one of the longest in flower in summer. Its basal rosettes are evergreen.*

some, seed with others. There are countless named cultivars, breaking down into eight or nine essential kinds. They are rock rather than meadow plants by nature; all like dryish limy soil and full sun. Most have more or less narrow grey or grey-ish leaves; the perennial pinks mounding up into low ever-grey shrublets.

Old-fashioned, Garden or Cottage pinks; growing to about 30cm (1ft) and summer-flowering only, are the most perennial of this magically fragrant family, lasting for up to five years. They can be single- or double-flowered, classified by colour-pattern into Selfs, Bi-colours, Laced and Fancies. Modern or Allwoodii pinks are Old-fashioned pinks crossed with perpetual carnation, flowering in summer and autumn. They are generally faster-growing but shorter-lived.

'Loveliness' is the best pink for shade or damp soil. Its colour-range is wide and it flowers for months, but it is best treated as a biennial, like Sweet Williams, whose small but prolific flowers often have concentric rings of different colours.

Border carnations are the tallest of the confusing family; descendants of the Elizabethan Clove Gilliflower, smelling of cloves. They grow to 60cm (2ft) and need support – also frequent propagation. Indian pinks, often dwarf, single or dou-ble, usually in mixed colours, are grown as annuals.

THE LATE BORDER

Somewhere about the middle of August the mood of the garden imperceptibly changes. The sun is lower in the sky; the morning wakes with dew on spiders' webs; trees and shrubs are a heavy green with few flowers; the first leaves fall. Even the scent in the air changes from sweet to sharp.

The shift, one might suppose, would be into a minor key as the year wanes. But the richest and most splendid passage of tone and harmony is still to come. The tints of turning leaves add to the colours of flowers. As flowers fade, curious intricacies of seed-containers and bright gems of fruit appear. Strong full-grown plants, uncorsetted, billow and lean at perilous angles and in voluptuous curves.

There are still pinks and blues as clear as in the spring among the flowers, but the mood of the season is best expressed in rich and subtle tones of violet and crimson, cream and bronze. Chrysanthemums and Michaelmas daisies are vital ingredients: a garden cannot be said to be truly autumnal without them.

BELOW: *The purple-spiked sage.* Salvia × superba 'Superba'. *is one of the fundamentals of a summer border: a strong vertical among less tidy plants and excellent with the horizontal yellow plates of achilleas.*

There is still a distinct preference for full sunshine among the latest plants to flower. Leaves and overall habit and structure become more and more important as the climax of flowering passes. Plants that are mere border-fodder, with pretty faces to hold up in serried ranks like a school photograph, are not enough. With late-flowerers it is important, too, that the burgeoning clump looks interest-ing before it flowers. Some of the popular classics of the season (Michaelmas daisies, red hot pokers, cheerful yellow rud-beckias or cone-flowers for example) need help from interesting neighbours, whether in flower or not, in the build-ing-up period before they start to bloom.

For sword-leaves and upright or arching flowers with the smoothness of bulbs, crocosmias and red hot pokers fol-low the departing agapanthus. South African plants and bulbs have their big season in late summer. Galtonias, the white cape hyacinths, are followed by the sugar-pink ner-ines and the pink or scarlet *Schizostylis.*

Conscientious picking-off of dead flower heads keeps the season going for most border plants as well as for roses and annuals. Dahlias in particular seems to have endless reserves of flowers that only frost can stop.

As the border-plant season ends there comes the question of what to cut down and clear away, and what to leave to outface the winter in its withered brown state. Soft, leafy plants make their own decision and collapse with the frosts. Others that have made almost woody stems stand with still-recognizable flowers or dried seed pods until gales or snow cut them down – sometimes until spring.

The tidy-minded often like to clear the ground of such vestiges, prick it over with a fork and stare virtuously at the flat bare earth all winter. But there is more inter-est in a garden with a raised brown fist of flowering thistle here or truncheon of polygonum there. Any plants that turn deep reddy-brown and crisp are worth keeping. Some Michaelmas daisies do. In winter sunshine it is remarkable what value warm patches of brown assume. The succulent sedums, especially 'Autumn Joy', with its slow transition from sea-green to mahogany, provide an anchoring dome-like mass.

The flowers still known to most laymen as chrysanthemums (though now botanized as *Dendranthema × grandiflorum*) are the most indispensable of the later daisies. Formerly the name chrysanthemum covered what are now a dozen or so genera that appear in marvellous variety all summer long, coming to a climax in autumn with brown, red and yellow flowers that epitomize the season. The mop-headed late-summer ('early-flowering') kinds were originally developed in China and Japan, where they are still enormously popular – indeed, the Imperial flower. These are exhibitors' flowers, coaxed and pampered to improbable size and per-fection. Like dahlias they have their own exhibition jargon. The Chinese favour them 'incurved'; the Japanese 'reflexed'.

For general garden use, having the same autumnal flavour and sharp evoca-tive smell, derivatives of the hardy Korean 'chrysanthemum' with flowers in sprays are prettier and less trouble. The colour range only lacks anything approaching blue – which can be supplied by Michaelmas daisies.

Botanists also recognize as a *Dendranthema* the very similar former *Chrysan-themum rubellum* (of which the pink 'Clara Curtis' is best-known). But such famous old relations as the white Shasta Daisy and the shrubby marguerite are distributed to other genera. The Shasta daisy is now seen as a hybrid, *Leucanthemum × super-bum*; the marguerite or Paris daisy, tender in frost but hardy in Mediterranean climates (and its native Canary Islands) is *Argyranthemum frutescens*.

The variety of dahlias, such as it is, is almost entirely man-made. They all come from two or three variable Mexican species (possibly already hybridized in Aztec gardens) imported to Europe early in the nineteenth century. From the begin-ning a never-ending succession of variation of colour, shape, size and petal arrangements were produced. The botanist soon shrugged his shoulders at what to him was a load of haberdashery. The classification in use today has been devel-oped by florists. Culturally they divide simply into bedding dahlias, small slightly

ABOVE: *A late summer border at the RHS gardens at Wisley leans heavily on dendranthemums (formerly chrysanthemums), with* Aster ericoides, *a small-flowered Michaelmas daisy and the white Japanese anemone 'Whirlwind'.*

BELOW: *No flower of late summer and autumn excels the vine-leaved Japanese anemone,* A. × hybrida, *whether pink or white, in grace, hardiness and endless flowering.*

ABOVE: *In the long catalogue of summer daisies the inulas are worth consideration. This* I. royleana *is a fine plant for cool soils. Its bigger brother, yellow* I. magnifica, *also appreciates moisture.*

variable plants raised from seed each year, and border dahlias, larger plants sold as tubers and by precise name. On the show bench it is a different matter: The Royal Horticultural Society recognizes ten groups; the Dahlia Society thirty sub-groups.

Dahlias are gratifyingly easy to propagate, either by dividing the tubers with a piece of stem attached to each, or by short cuttings from the new growth in spring. The joy of the dahlia is the ease with which it makes a big plant laden with flowers in any colour except blue. All it asks is deep-dug soil with a high organic content to keep the roots moist. Competitive growers double-dig in autumn, lacing the bottom spit with mature manure. The disadvantage is that the sausage-like tubers will rot, left in cold wet ground. But it is easy to lift them and keep them in a dry frost-proof place in winter. Staking is the other problem; such lush plants need firm support, which is hard to hide.

Compared with such exotics the Michaelmas daisies are a relatively simple clan. The original Michaelmas daisy is the violet-blue *Aster novi-belgii* from the eastern States; tough, greedy-rooting and apt to seed, but now available in every shade of pink, white, red and purple blue. The tall blue 'Climax' is perhaps the best of its scores of derivatives.

Its chief garden rival is *Aster novae-angliae* (from New England), taller, more mauve in nature, whose best varieties are pink. Several Aster species are also worth growing; notably the airy white *A. tradescantii*, the vivid bluish *A. spectabilis*, and *A. divaricatus*, with little white flowers weighing down distinctively dark wiry stems. The most rewarding of all, though, is the Euro-Asian hybrid *A. × frikartii* 'Mönch'. It produces clear lavender-blue flowers indefatigably from summer to late autumn. It is hard to imagine a late border without it.

As exclamation marks in the brimming late-summer garden the red hot pokers or torch lilies from South Africa are worth warm corners and well-drained soil. The 'original' red hot poker is *Kniphofia uvaria*, tall and orange-red. Now most are hybrids, available in heights from 60–150cm (2–5ft) and colours from cream to flame. The hotter shades are beautiful with the lavender and mauve Michaelmas daisies. Perhaps the coolest and most elegant is the cream 'Maid of Orleans'. One lesser known but very hardy species, *Kniphofia caulescens*, has an almost aloe-like rosette of grey-green leaves and flowers in subtle green, pink and plum.

RIGHT: *The formal garden at Anglesey Abbey near Cambridge is one of the grandest examples of bedding with dahlias. In the foreground is the red-leaved 'Bishop of Llandaff'.*

THE ANNUAL CHOICE IT IS NOT SURPRISING

THAT WHAT MANY GARDENERS, PARTICULARLY LESS SOPHISTICATED ONES, MEAN BY 'FLOWERS'

ARE ANNUALS. FOR ANNUALS ARE AT THE SAME TIME A CROP AND A CELEBRATION.

They are the most eager of all plants to put their energies into display – which means in most cases brilliant flowers. They have only one season in which to grow, flower and set seed. Given good conditions they do it with an abandon that gives more colour for a longer period than any other plants.

The good conditions are a prerequisite, and meanness in providing them is probably the commonest reason why gardeners who have tried annuals have been disappointed and given them up. If they are to be worth stooping over they must be sturdy, hearty plants. And there is no second chance – no 'giving them a good feed next winter'. They must grow strong roots and a bushy top from the start. They want just the same treatment as vegetables – total indulgence. Their will to live and urge to reproduce is such that if you can get round to picking off the fading flowers before any seed is set, more and more flowers will follow.

But that is as much as, and really more than, you can say about growing annuals in general. They vary in their tastes less than most plants, but still enough to need careful study.

Certain definitions are essential. The three terms hardy, half-hardy and biennial each trigger off a sequence of operations which are simple in themselves but confusing until you know which is which. Biennials of course are not annuals at all but plants that need a second year to reach flowering age. But since they entail yearly sowing and transplanting they slot naturally into the sequence.

It must be remembered that these are gardeners', not God's terms, based on the most successful management of the plant – which is why there are perennials which are conventionally treated as annuals for top performance, and 'annuals' which will go on for years in hot, sheltered or particularly dry places. A giant sage which dies every winter in good soil in my garden has sown its seed high in a wall, where it shows every sign of becoming not just a perennial, but a shrub. A wallflower in a bed is usually grown as a biennial, whereas self-sown: in a wall it can live for years and years . . . but back to the rules.

What gardeners call hardy annuals germinate at low temperatures and suffer spring frosts gladly. They are therefore sown, usually where they are to flower, as early in the year as the soil is fit for them; perhaps in March. 'Fit' means loose and friable – neither frozen nor dusty nor muddy. A number of annuals could well be placed in a separate 'very hardy' class. These do best of all if they are sown in autumn, as nature intended, to germinate and spend the winter as small plants. The spring and summer forget-me-nots, love-in-a-mist, poppies, the baby-blue nemophila and above all

BELOW: *It would be difficult to produce such a sustained show of cheerful colour as this with anything but annuals.*

the weather-proof pansy are all the better for this early start – which in a sense reclassifies them as biennials.

Biennials are sown in summer in order to have half a growing year to establish themselves before winter. From the garden management point of view this normally means sowing them in the vegetable plot, where they can be thinned and pampered along with the salads, then moving them as substantial plants in autumn, winter or spring, according to the climate and the state of the soil, to what the text-books charmingly call their 'flowering stations'. Most biennials (typified by the wallflower) flower in spring. Foxgloves and Canterbury bells are about the last to perform – and by August the next generation of foxgloves has already started its little rosettes around its parents.

Half-hardy annuals behave like hardy annuals, with the all-important difference that they must be kept indoors until after the last frosts. They must be sown early to be ready to flower in summer. But they need a temperature of 10–15 °C (50–60 °F) to make them germinate (some higher; some lower; *vide* the seed packet), and once they have germinated they have to be housed, in their growing bulk, in good light and reasonable warmth. Like all seedlings they must be thinned, pricked out, if necessary potted on and generally kept on the go: it is fatal to try to slow them down by letting them become crowded. Thus the space problem grows ever more acute as spring goes on. Cold frames will do to keep the last frosts off them, but by that time frame space for 'hardening-off' is at a premium. For all these reasons most gardeners buy their half-hardy annuals ready-grown at planting-out time in boxes or flats from commercial nurseries – which greatly limits their choice and by no means guarantees that they will get the best varieties.

If you are ready to go to the trouble of raising half-hardy annuals, intensive study of seed catalogues is worth your while.

There is not the slightest reason to segregate annuals into a separate bedding department of the garden, as tradition would have us do. Where segregation comes naturally, as in window boxes, hanging baskets, vases and tubs, annuals are ideal. But they can also add their special vitality to every sort of planting: traditional border, shrub bed, modern mixture of the two, kitchen garden (in the French style, both for general *agrément* and for picking) – anywhere they can be offered a good start in well-prepared soil. This is the only inhibition anyone should have about mixing annuals with perennials as generous, long-flowering components of the summer garden.

To make handsome plants of annuals, the thinnest sowing, the most conscientious thinning, appropriate pinching-out to make them branch, and where necessary support with brush-wood or canes, are all essential.

The principles being established, these are what I consider to be the essential annuals – a personal choice:

Sweet peas, for fresh and varied colours, for their ability to sprawl among tall plants, but above all for their scent.

Nicotiana for its evening scent; *N. sylvestris* for its magnificent leaves.

Pansies for their imperviousness to weather and their glowing colours.

Wallflowers for their warm colours in cold weather and their unmatched smell.

Cosmos for their wide innocent daisies of pink, purple or gleaming white among asparagus-ferny leaves.

Cleome for its stature, structure and unique spreading spider flowers, pink or white.

Petunias for their long performance and resistance to drought.

BELOW: *Cornflowers, California poppies and convolvulus with nasturtiums, whose leaves are just visible, to follow them: a good example of grouping annuals with similar tastes and harmonious colours. All these will put up with dry conditions.*

Opium poppies for their soft grey leaves and their silken ruffled flowers in
    sumptuous colours.

Nasturtium for gay orange/yellow/scarlet flowers and fresh juicy leaves –
    both on difficult dry banks and in salads.

Sunflowers for childish entertainment.

Salpiglossis or *schizanthus* for soft chintz colours, especially in pots.

Dimorphotheca for the sharp-edged reflecting brightness of their daisies.

Stocks, 'Brompton' in spring, '10 weeks' in summer, for their sweet night
    scents.

Primulas for their drumsticks in spring in the conservatory and later at the
    water's brink.

Coreopsis for their unpretentious yellow cheerfulness all summer long.

ABOVE: *The evening-scented* Nicotiana sylvestris *is the noblest of the tobacco plants, standing up to 1.5m (5ft) with great lush leaves.*

BEDDING WITH TENDER PLANTS

What goes around, comes around. Summer bedding with tender plants in patterned displays of uninhibited colour was the pride of the Victorians. It was the embodiment of the Industrial Revolution come to horticulture. It bespoke acres of glass, tons of coal, and squads of house-proud gardeners. It was almost forced on gardens, one feels, by the pressure of the greenhouse boilers. Here was all this exotic stuff: what were they going to do with it? At great Victorian mansions it was not unknown to change all the flowerbeds between weekends, like the bed-linen. And now it shows signs of coming round again.

Much of the bedding was done with annuals raised from seed sown in heat in late winter. But another major source of bright, strong and exotic plants was the tender perennials imported from South Africa and Central and South America. The stock plants, kept in greenhouses, supplied thousands of cuttings or seeds to be grown on in pots and bedded out when the risk of frost had passed. Of all these plants by far the most successful and popular were the South African geraniums.

Geraniums have had a unique role as *the* bedding plants since the Victorians discovered their qualities. They are highly coloured in endless variety, perfectly adapted to mass production and as near indestructible as can be. Strictly speaking they are all really pelargoniums. In popular use the name pelargonium is applied only to the showier of them with the biggest flowers: the Regals. It is one of the rare cases in horticulture where democracy has successfully routed botany.

The South African origin explains one of their great virtues – ability to survive drought. None of them can withstand freezing, but because their metabolism can slow down to almost total dormancy when dry they are as easy to overwinter as if they had tubers like begonias or dahlias.

But an even greater virtue is that cuttings root with effortless ease any time from spring to early autumn. They need slightly different treatment from most other cuttings

BELOW: *The art of carpet-bedding can still inspire much admiration when it is done with such geometrical precision as in this successful example in the Parc Tête d'Or at Lyons in France.*

ABOVE: *Fuchsias can be bedded out as soon as frosts are passed to flower without pause until autumn. If they vary in stature more than character they demand little except water in dry weather.*

– but what it amounts to is simply less water at every stage, including airy rather than close conditions. There are six simple categories of geranium to be aware of. Within these their variety is prodigious.

First are the zonal geraniums, so-called because their leaves have a darker central zone, sometimes distinct, sometimes faint. These are the kind most used in bedding, with red or pink, often veined or marbled flowers all summer. Their flowers may be single or double but are individually relatively small.

Coloured-leaf geraniums have been bred with emphasis on shades of gold or brown or 'silver' in the leaf and have more modest flowers. They are used similarly for bedding.

Miniature geraniums are just that: no more than 20cm (8in) tall, very varied and good for windowsills – if anything. Ivy-leaved geraniums are another matter; infinitely brilliant in flower, with trailing stems and shiny little leaves like miniature ivy. These are the dazzling geraniums of hanging baskets and window boxes all over Europe. 'L'Elégante' and 'Roi des Balcons' are two of the best.

Scented-leaved geraniums, though not showy in flower, are some of the most interesting to collect, especially in a conservatory, for their enormously varied leaves that range in shape from round to lacy, in texture from corduroy to velvet, and in scent encompass lemon, rose, pine, peppermint, apple and spices.

But Regal, Fancy and Show pelargoniums have by far the most luscious flowers. Too luscious, indeed, to stand up to the hurly-burly of a bed. They are usually displayed in the protection of a greenhouse, where they come into flower earlier and go on longer than the mere 'geraniums'.

If geraniums have a rival in sheer complaisance in cultivation it is fuchsias. Fuchsias have most of the advantages that make geraniums such popular bedding plants. They are fast-growing, colourful (at least at close quarters), have a very long flowering season that lasts well into autumn and are extremely easy to propagate by cuttings. Two geranium qualities they lack are drought resistance and infinite variety. Many feel they make up for them in the elegance of their dangling flowers and their sometimes startling colour combinations in the range purple-red-pink-white.

They are principally natives of Central and South America, where in the extreme south *F. magellanica* is the hardiest species. Most cultivated kinds (there are hundreds) are hybrids of this with *F. fulgens* from Mexico. *F. magellanica* with its small red or pale pink ('Alba') flowers is hardy enough to make hedges in the maritime climate of North West France, Ireland and South West England.

The traditional third member of this summer party of exotics is the begonias. There are three broad classes of begonias, all of which have similar uses to fuchsias and geraniums and are managed in greenhouses in much the same way. Like fuchsias they need plentiful food and water when in flower. But begonias are classified in cultivation by the nature of their roots.

The grandest are the tuberous-rooted begonias, weighed down with lush show flowers, lusher even than Regal pelargoniums. Most are cultivars of the Tuberhybrida group in brilliant colours and with exciting crystalline petals. Rhizomatous-rooted begonias are chiefly grown for their striking, usually ear-shaped leaves marked with various, not always pleasing, colours. Among fibrous-rooted begonias are the low-growing bedding plant *B. semperflorens* with small red, pink or white waxy flowers, still crystalline; one of the most reliable, if not inspiring, of bedding plants. Today there is a fourth plant for summer to challenge the begonia for ease of propagation and (almost) variety of colour, if not form. The new Marguerites are the *Argyranthemum frutescens* and its cultivars of the Canary Isles, Madeira and South Africa. To older gardeners they are *Chrysanthemum frutescens*.

In the past few years breeders have seized on this simple bushy daisy with white, yellow or (in one species) pink flowers and bred it into a range from pink powder-puffs to red stars. Many gardeners will think they fail, though, to beat the charm of the pure white 'Paris daisy' with its finely-fretted pale grey leaves.

Bedding had (and has) its own conventions, its own vocabulary and its own seasons. 'Spring bedding' consists of such weatherproof annuals or biennials as wallflowers and double daisies, pansies, forget-me-nots and polyanthus, usually accompanied by either tulips or hyacinths.

Extremely ambitious gardeners may then install a fresh late spring bedding before the risk of frost is over and the tender plants can be put out for summer. Sweet Williams, Brompton stocks, Canterbury bells, nemesias and tall salpiglossis are the quiet before the riot.

'Summer bedding' starts with a laborious cultivation and rich manuring of the beds. The standard plant mixture is of annuals and tender perennials. Geraniums, fuchsias, tuberous and other begonias and ageratums are mixed with red-leaved coleus and beet and the silver of *Senecio cineraria*, with calceolarias and celosias, heliotropes and *Salvia splendens* and gaillardias, using blue lobelia and golden feverfew as the low edging, all laid out with elaborate geometry.

'Carpet bedding' is defined as forming carpet-like patterns with dwarf coloured-foliage plants, which, the RHS Dictionary notes, need 'constant attention with regard to pinching and keeping them within their allotted space'. *Alternanthera*, *Calocephalus* (syn. *Leucophyta*), *Sagina* and *Echeveria* are perhaps the arch-carpet-bedders. Where a taller plant is used to stand up among the dwarfs it is known in the trade as a 'dot' plant.

Subtropical bedding demands greater resources. Botanical gardens and the major parks departments are alone in using it today. It is largely a matterof moving out into the open plants that would normally live under glass all year and rather gingerly plunging them, pots and all, in the most sheltered bed for the hottest months. Big-leaved plants such as agaves, palms, bananas, cordylines, yuccas, ficus, grevilleas, *Eucalyptus globulus* and tree ferns get pride of place, along with such fast-growing annuals of tropical appearance as castor-oil plants and herbaceous solanums, and the tender perennial cannas.

Bedding is a state of mind. It demands an extrovert, 'Go for it' approach which some gardeners find natural; others vulgar or quaint. What is certain is that this painting-by-numbers approach is enjoying a strong revival, encouraged by plant breeders as they work on the components to make them perform to order. Above all the old bedding game today applies to pots, hanging baskets, urns, vases, tubs and every sort of container. A noble vase overflowing with a mixture of plants that would look wildly exotic in the garden around is the richest eye-catcher of all.

ABOVE: *Pelargoniums are undemanding bedding plants, preferring dry conditions for summer-long flowering. For baskets, window-boxes and balconies the trailing ivy-leaved* P. peltatum *is best. This needs food and water.*

BELOW: *Tulips, wallflowers and violas (also pansies and polyanthus) are the basic ingredients of most spring bedding. The tulip here is 'Pax', wallflower 'Scarlet Bedder' and* Viola *'Princess Cream'.*

BULBS AND OTHER PACKAGES

BULBS WERE SURELY INVENTED BY A DUTCH INDUSTRIAL DESIGNER – THE FUNCTIONAL LINES.

THE BUILT-IN PACKAGING, THE SHEER CONVENIENCE OF A PLANT THAT CAN BE HANDLED

SO EASILY DURING SUCH A LONG DORMANT PERIOD . . .

ABOVE: *Snowdrops can be in flower before mid-winter and continue into spring. There are several double varieties (this is* Galanthus *'Double Charmer'). They are showy but lack the simple grace of the single flower.*

They all point to a backroom genius in the garden-centre business.

The tidiness of the whole idea is appealing. Out of this capsule, on a signal received from the atmospheric temperature and moisture, come the roots to drink, the leaves to feed, the stem and flower to mate. They build up a replacement module, make their attempt at reproducing their kind. Then they fall away, their jobs done, to be recycled in the soil. The refuelled, or rather rebuilt, bulb lies low, as safe as a plant can be, oblivious of lack of water, waiting for the right sequence of cold and wet to set it going again. Meanwhile it can be poured down chutes into boxes, displayed on counters, put up to auction: the perfect packaged flower.

These eminently satisfactory arrangements evolved with a different object in view. The bulb routine is an efficient way of life in countries with brief rains, usually in spring, and long dry summers. The Mediterranean, the Near East and such countries with similar climates as South Africa are the homes of most bulbs. Our crocuses come typically from shallow soils in Greece and the islands; tulips from parched hills and plains in the steppes of central Asia; daffodils from Spain, Portugal and North Africa. True there are Pyrenean daffodils accustomed to wet summers – and lilies tend to break the rules by growing in damp but porous woodland soil – but with all the exceptions taken into account there is remarkable homogeneity in the broad group that the layman calls bulbs.

Nearly all, for a start, are monocots like the grasses, with long smooth leaves with parallel veins. They tend to flower on 'scapes' or stems that rise straight from the ground independent of the leaves – also smooth, with an inclination to be brittle and sappy. With one possible exception they never exceed about 2.5m (8ft) in height, nor grow woody, nor show any tendency to climb. Most of them belong to only three families, which in turn must have a common grandparent.

RIGHT: *The Lake District daffodils of Wordsworth's poem were probably the Lent lily,* Narcissus pseudonarcissus, *here growing wild on the shores of Lake Windermere.*

Of the three main families the Liliaceae has the widest range. It includes lilies, hyacinths, tulips, fritillaries, alliums (the onion tribe), scillas, grape-hyacinths, trilliums, colchicums and erythroniums, the 'dog's tooth violets'. The Amaryllidaceae, besides of course the amaryllis, includes narcissi, snowdrops, nerines and sternbergias. The Iridaceae, besides irises, contains crocuses, gladioli, crocosmias and freesias.

Not all the members of these families have evolved as bulbs. Among irises the truly bulbous are in a minority. The notion of food-storage is there, however, in all these flowers in one form or another. And the bulb, though the word is convenient for the broad category, is strictly speaking only one particular design of storage organ. The others should be called by their proper names of corms, tubers, tuberous roots and rhizomes.

ABOVE: *Autumn sunshine dramatizes the nakedness of the leafless colchicum in September. This is* C. autumnale 'Alba'. *The broad leaves that follow the flower easily distinguish colchicums from the true autumn crocus,* Crocus speciosus.

All share not only the storage habit but the habit of bypassing the sexual process and making new plants by some form of division; either by forming new buds which soon become independent bulbs, or building new corms on top of, or new tubers besides, the old. They are like herbaceous plants in this: they renew themselves centrifugally whether they have any luck sexually or not. Unlike herbaceous plants which stay in one piece, bulb 'offsets' detach themselves and live independently, making them ideal units for commerce.

As far as bulb catalogues go it is not the botany but the package that counts. They include flowers with the same convenient habit which are quite unrelated: notably cyclamen, which are a kind of primrose, and anemones and aconites which are cousins of the buttercup.

The international bulb industry has had its base in Holland for four hundred years. The volume of the bulb trade today is remarkable. In 1994 there were nearly 8,000 hectares of tulips in Holland, over 3,000 of lilies, 1,750 of gladiolus, 1,320 of daffodils, 750 of irises, 500 of crocus and many more of dahlias and the smaller or more specialized bulbs. The USA, the biggest export customer, spent 115 million US dollars on Dutch bulbs, although growing most of her own lilies and much else besides.

There are many ways of using bulbs in the garden. The same flowers can give quite different effects used formally as bedding and casually as incidents. But whether they are dressed by the right, tucked away among shrubs, naturalized in grass or woodland, given a sun-baked cranny or rockery, or even treasured in pots and sheltered in frames, certain principles of cultivation apply.

BELOW: *The hyacinth has a true bulb, consisting of overlapping swollen leaf bases or scales on a basal plate surrounding the embryo flower, the whole thing wrapped in a coat of expended scales.*

All bulbs need good drainage. Even those that like perpetual drizzle must not lie in saturated soil while they are dormant. With few exceptions bulbs like

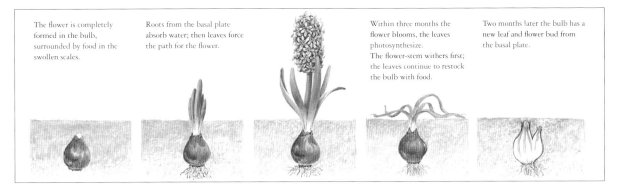

The flower is completely formed in the bulb, surrounded by food in the swollen scales.

Roots from the basal plate absorb water; then leaves force the path for the flower.

Within three months the flower blooms, the leaves photosynthesize. The flower-stem withers first; the leaves continue to restock the bulb with food.

Two months later the bulb has a new leaf and flower bud from the basal plate.

Bulbs

Lily

Daffodil

Corms

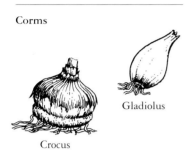

Gladiolus

Crocus

Tubers

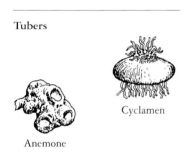

Cyclamen

Anemone

Tuberous Roots

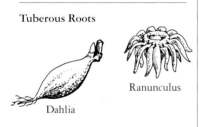

Ranunculus

Dahlia

Rhizomes

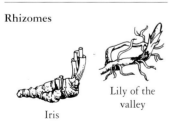

Lily of the
valley

Iris

ABOVE: *The principle of the bulb is food storage in an underground organ. Such organs can be buds, swollen stems, leaves or roots.*

to be planted as deep as the bulb is tall. If they need to go deeper they pull themselves down by their roots. All bulbs demand to have their leaves left intact while they feed, flag and finally wither. If you cut them off during the period after flowering, next year's bulb is deprived of its rations. After flowering is the time to feed and water established clumps if you have any reason to think they need it.

In formal bedding-out schemes, particularly of tulips, this is the time they are lifted and moved to a quiet sunny corner to ripen off. Once the leaves have withered the bulbs are dried and stored, to be replanted in autumn.

The best time to shunt any bulbs round your garden is not during the commercial break while they are dry and dormant, but when they have just flowered and are in full leaf. Then you can clearly see and get hold of them without stabbing them with your fork, and you can remember which is which. The sooner they are moved the quicker they will become re-established.

BULBS FOR SPRING

Bulbs and the spring are almost synonymous in most gardeners' minds. No sooner has the snow gone, leaving grubby heaps in corners and the grass pale, blotched and ill-looking, than from the chilly soaking ground green dagger-points begin to poke. Within two days the snowdrop has freed its upright white antenna from the protecting leaves. For a few more days it lengthens it stalk. Then, at a moment I have never caught, its capsule opens and the bell nods down. If you must start spring somewhere it is surely here.

There is a texture to the flowers of spring bulbs which is easy to recognize but hard to describe. E. A. Bowles came very close when he described them as 'crystalline': there is a sense of seeing through a transparent skin into faceted layers inside. The freshness and tenderness of the effect, and the clarity it gives to its colours, is unique to the season – except, says Bowles, for the sumptuous glittering petals of tuberous begonias in summer and, one might add, nerines in autumn. I find the magic also in the thick petals of some camellias; this extra dimension of reflecting light both coloured and clear – like, indeed, a diamond.

It is rash to look too closely at a snowdrop. Its pixie purity and the subtle variations between the score or so of different kinds can become an obsession. *Galanthus nivalis* is the common native of Europe as far east as Ukraine. Its double forms are also common, and perhaps more vigorous. For those who want everything bigger *G.* 'Atkinsii', *G. plicatus* and *G. elwesii* have more imposing flowers on taller scapes. The two last have broader leaves of a grey cast.

Snowdrops have three short 'petals' alternating with three long, variously notched and blotched or striped inside with green. Their cousins the snowflakes, *Leucojum*, have six 'petals' of the same length. *L. vernum* is the early spring one, rising on a tall deep green scape, generally in damp ground. Its later flowering sister, *L. aestivum*, is as tall as 60cm (2ft) with bright green leaves in May.

The first bulbs to show themselves may not be the snowdrops, but crocuses or the tiny irises, blue *histrioides* or yellow *danfordiae*, flowering no more than 7.5cm (3in) above the soil. You might expect to find a certain disproportion in the size of the flowers. In practice the little bulbs which are all flower and no plant have the same kind of charming illogicality as the tiny alpines that wear flowers several sizes too big. But like the alpines they need to be either in the palm of your hand or in unusually large sheets on the ground to be really effective. A dozen or a score of crocuses in a bed 9m (30ft) away is of little value. It is better either to plant extravagantly or to grow them in a pot, a frame or a raised bed by a path, where you will stop and take in the details.

The Dutch, of course, have an answer for this, breeding great fat strong-coloured crocuses almost like young tulips. But those who have only seen Dutch crocuses have missed the fairy delicacy of the genus – not to mention its variety, or the fact that it furnishes flowers all winter and well into spring and again in the autumn. An ice-bound winter delays the performance, but the earliest crocus species flower in a warm December to be followed by a succession up to March.

The Greek *Crocus laevigatus* and the Italian *C. imperati*, two of the earliest, are the kind that beg for close-up inspection; they blend so many subtle colours and patterns in their petals, their outsides veined or feathered with dusky mauve. *C. flavus*, a clear yellow, appears at the same time, and only a little later *C. chrysanthus* offers almost every colour from ivory to gold to deep lilac, all with flushes or feathers of deeper colours. In practice, for scenic effect, the important differences between these species are the overall colour and the time of flowering.

In reasonable conditions (which includes relative freedom from mice) these early crocuses will spread and spread. The mauve-to-purple *C. tommasinianus* ('Tommies' to their friends) are the most prolific of all. The finest living memorial to the extravagant Miss Willmott, whose Essex garden in Edwardian days kept a hundred men busy, is a whole roadside field of perhaps ten acres which has been colonized by her crocuses since she departed: an incredible sight in February. What the crocuses do not provide is true blue: all their blues are more or less washed with purple or lavender. The early daffodils cry out for a strong blue to set off their yellow – happy and gleaming as it is. Luckily one of the earliest and easiest little bulbs to naturalize is the Siberian Squill, *Scilla siberica*. *S. siberica* 'Spring Beauty' is the perfect brilliant blue to pull the daffodils up with a jerk: a plant only 20cm (8in) high with diminutive flowers, but with the impact of a gem lying in the grass. Bluebells, in contrast, need to be seen *en masse* for their variable purply blue to make an impact.

There is a fairly strong blue among the variable anemones, too. But even the bluest, the Greek *Anemone blanda* 'Ingrami' syn. 'Atrocaerulea' (literally 'dark blue'), looks washy besides 'Spring Beauty'. (They flower at the same time). The grape hyacinth will provide a low background of a rather light blue for the later daffodil season, at the same time as their big brothers, the bedding hyacinths. But these last belong to a different school. Hyacinths and daffodils, even the grossest and stiffest of daffodils, were not meant for one another.

Perhaps the greatest joy of spring bulbs is that they are an extra dimension you can add to any part of the garden. Because they come and go before the garden fills up, they, with hellebores and early woodland flowers, are a scene in themselves which you can develop over the years. The only place not to put bulbs is in beds where you are constantly digging and planting. Plant them in places which will be undisturbed for years. By far the best value are the bulbs that naturalize. As clumps grow thick you can divide them after flowering, lifting them gently with a fork, holding them by their leaves and pulling them apart to separate them; then replanting them at wider spacing.

ABOVE: *The snake's head fritillary, F. meleagris, is a native of damp meadows in Europe; here at Magdalen College, Oxford.*

BELOW: *Tulips are the showiest and most predictable of all bulbs for formal display. Such a tour de force, however, is labour-intensive. Every bulb will need to be lifted after flowering and moved to a resting plot.*

BULBS: THE GREAT THREE

Three bulbs dominate the garden in turn from early spring to late summer. Even such familiar friends as crocuses and such seasonal spectacles as Crown Imperials must be classed as minor themes and embellishments beside them. The narcissi, tulips, and more recently lilies have been bred in truly infinite variety.

Over the centuries other bulbs have come in for intensive breeding. Thousands of varieties of hyacinths, ranunculus and anemones have been raised with great excitement, only to be lost again. For none of these were garden flowers.

The tulips were the first of the big three to attract breeders because of the range of their colours, and because they are subject to viruses that make the colours 'break' in bizarre patterns. Tulip fever, when fortunes were made and lost on single bulbs, raged in Holland from 1643 to 1647.

'Daffadowndillies' were popular in Elizabethan times, but the fact that yellow was their only colour moderated enthusiasm for breeding. Modern narcissi only began in the last century.

Lilies were regarded as difficult and cussed plants (as most of them still are) right up to the last thirty years or so, when intensive hybridization, mainly in Oregon, has produced reasonably easy cultivars of what can be the most spectacular of all bulbs.

Now all three are elaborately categorized for judging purposes by the size and shape of flower, or the historical backgrounds of the strain. The limitation of this system is that it treats most of the natural wild species as second-class citizens.

The hoop-petticoat daffodil, all trumpet and practically no petals, is a species with no 'improved' forms; it belongs in Div. 10. It naturalizes well in damp spots, flowering in late March and early April.

'Golden Harvest' is one of the commonest yellow daffodils, grown by the field-full for market in March. Technically it is Division 1.

'Edward Buxton' is one of the best large-cup and 'Carlton' is a good short-cup narcissus, flowering respectively in March and April (and belonging separately to Div. 2 and 3).

Double daffodils, with the simple trumpet replaced by a scramble of 'petaloids', have not been fashionable since the seventeenth century. 'Texas' (March-flowering) typifies this group (Div. 4.)

DAFFODILS

Narcissi, and daffodils, which are narcissi with trumpets as long as their 'petals', are among the hardiest and easiest to grow of all the bulbs. Starting with about sixty species, mainly from the Mediterranean, over eight thou sand named varieties have been produced. They are officially classified into twelve divisions by the proportion of their flowers, and sub-divisions by colour combinations. For most gardeners this is academic. A dozen kinds is ample to furnish the garden from earliest spring to May with distinct forms. Temperature largely decides flowering time. The first flowers are out in January in warm areas, March in cold ones. Times of flowering given here for comparison apply to the south of England.

Narcissi with the blood of the little Portuguese species, *N. triandrus*, have drooping flowers in clusters, their petals usually swept back. 'Thalia' is one of the best (Div. 5.)

The early dwarf species *N. cylamineus* has a long trumpet and petals swept right back like a cyclamen's. It naturalizes well in damp soil. 'February Gold' is one of the best of its garden hybrids (Div. 6.)

The jonquils with their long rush-like
leaves have the richest scent of all
but flower rather late and need a warm
corner. They are lovely in bowls indoors.
'Trevithian' is one of the best garden
forms (Div. 7).

LILIES

Lilies demand a high price for their undoubted glamour.
They are among the wayward plants that demand both
plentiful moisture and rapid drainage. Unlike other bulbs
they have no protective 'tunic' and never entirely stop
growing. The fleshy scales of their bulbs are therefore always
vulnerable; above all to drying out if they are dug up and
stored. They should always be kept moist. Never buy des-
iccated lily bulbs. Virus and botrytis are the other problems
lily growers must face. They are not plants for casual disposal round the garden for summer colour. They ask for
woodland soil and semi-shade. Lilies have been hybridized
partly for bigger and brighter flowers but also to make
them easier to grow. The selection here is of some of the
best of the more elementary kinds.

The Bellingham hybrids are big
West Coast Americans, of the reflexed
Turk's cap persuasion and hot colours,
demanding lime-free soil and semi-shade
but responding with rude vigour, growing
to 2.1m (7ft) or more and making
big clumps.

'Paper white' (now known as *N.
papyraceus*), flowering in mid-winter and
therefore usually grown indoors, is cluster
flowered and sweet scented. It is included
with the Tazettas in Div. 8.

The Madonna lily, *Lilium candidum*, has
been in gardens for 3,000 years and is
still unsurpassed for scent and simple
beauty, flowering at mid-summer. It is
almost alone in preferring dry, limy soil
and full sun on its shallow roots.

'Marhan' is an improved version of
the European martagon or Turk's cap lily,
made by crossing it with a similar species
from Korea, *L. hansonii*. It combines the
scent of the Korean with the tolerance of
the martagon – and hybrid vigour.

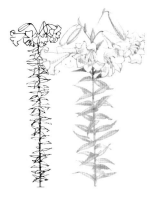

'Green Emerald' is an example of the
Oregon trumpet-flowered lilies, July- or
August-flowering, for semi-shade. Their
names are hypnotic: 'Black Magic', 'Black
Dragon', 'Golden Clarion', 'Golden
Splendour'. Olympic hybrids are similar.

The Pheasant's Eye or poet's narcissus,
N. poeticus, flat faced with a red or red-
rimmed cup, is one of the latest to flower.
The Poeticus narcissi belong in Div. 9.

'Enchantment' is perhaps the most
famous of all the hybrids from the
Oregon Bulb Farms. It carries up to
sixteen flowers, 15cm (6in) across, on
each stem in July and tolerates hot
weather and most soils, or a pot.

Lilium regale was one of E. H. Wilson's
most valuable Chinese finds: deeply
fragrant, easy to grow, increasing quickly
by seed and offsets. Like many lilies
it is top-heavy and profits from a
supporting shrub.

The Oriental hybrids include the most
artificial-looking of all lilies, with wide-
open, banded and spotted, heavily scented
flowers. They like full sun. 'Imperial
Crimson' flowers in late summer.

TULIPS

The broadest division of tulips is between the garden varieties, the result of breeding begun in the sixteenth century, and the 'botanical' or species tulips, which are more recent imports from the East, generally shorter-stemmed, often smaller and in some cases much earlier-flowering. The former are conventionally treated as bedding plants, planting them in late autumn and lifting them after flowering in spring. The latter are grown with more or less success as permanencies in sunny dry soil; the smallest in rock gardens. There are fifteen official classes of tulips, based partly on when they flower, partly on shape and partly on ancestry. Those illustrated here represent the six most distinct bedding categories and the three species hybrid groups which are first-class garden plants, arranged in their approximate order of flowering. The true species have divisions of their own.

One of the earliest and easiest of tulips is the charming little wildling *T. turkestanica*, which carries as many as seven star-like flowers on each slender 73cm (9in) stem in February.

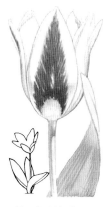

The water-lily tulip, *T. kaufmanniana*, is a variable species with wide leaves and narrow petals, flowering in March. It has produced excellent hybrids, many with the mottled leaves of the scarlet *T. greigii*.

'Madame Lefeber' is a selected form of the biggest-flowering species, *T. fosteriana* from Samarkand. It flowers in early April. Crossed with (Single Late) Darwins, it has produced the earlier and finer Darwin hybrids.

Single early and double early are the first categories to flower, about mid-April (though they grow well in pots for forcing in February). 'Peach Blossom' is a typical double.

The 'mid-season' (mid-to-late April) tulips are principally the Darwin hybrids and the 'Triumphs'. 'Athleet' is very striking.

Lily-flowered tulips are distinguished by their pointed petals, curling over as they open, that make them the most elegant of their race. They flower in late April. One of the finest tulips of all is 'White Triumphator'.

Parrot tulips (above is 'Red Parrot') have their petals twisted and dishevelled and bordered with a jagged fringe. They are mostly sports of Sinlge late tulips and like them flower late, in May.

The ultimate in stately formal tulips are the 'Single Lates', up to 75cm (30in) high, waiting for good weather in May. Their flowers are square-bottomed and their petals blunt. Above is 'La Tulipe Noire'.

'Broken' tulips, made from 'breeder' tulips by injecting them with virus-infected sap, were the passion of early Dutch florists. 'Absalon' is a Rembrandt, the stripes and feathers are typical.

BULBS FOR SUMMER AND AUTUMN

Later bulbs forgo the psychological advantage of answering our anticipation of spring. They have to compete for our interest with many things that might be growing on the same spot.

Lilies, the aristocrats of summer bulbs, have nothing to fear. They can command attention in any company. Lilies apart, though, there is a general midsummer pause, as though few bulbs were willing to risk comparisons they might lose. The big gladioli parade themselves in their paint and powder. They leave me, I fear, completely unmoved. Otherwise only the onions, more politely known as the alliums, have the cheerful self-assurance to keep going.

There are characters among the onions that should be more widely known. The flower shape is an interesting one for a start: a star-burst of bells on stalks. In some species stiff stalks form a drumstick shape; in others they droop gently. The colours are seldom brilliant, but out of about 450 there are a dozen species that earn their modern keep. Sun is all they ask.

The red-purple *Allium carinatum* ssp. *pulchellum* is an easy, even invasive plant, flowering in July and August, seeding freely as most alliums do. The colour-range extends from the pearly-white *A. neapolitanum* in spring to the little yellow wildflower of midsummer, *A. moly*, the bluebell-blue August *A. cyaneum*, and the joker of the race, *A. christophii*, whose violet flower heads rise like balloons 45cm (18in) above the border in July. The Californian *A. unifolium* is the most exuberantly coloured.

The bulb world reawakens towards the end of summer with performances that cannot be ignored from South African bulbs, and also with the start of the long-running cyclamen and crocus, alike in having a season that pivots round the winter rather than the summer.

The true autumn crocuses are easily confused with other flowers of remarkably similar construction, until you get down to the details. Autumn crocuses look very like spring ones, though rather taller and less robust. They tend to be knocked flat by autumn gusts. Colchicums, which are usually called 'autumn crocuses' as well, are lily- rather than iris-relations, showing it by having six stamens instead of three, and stressing their differentness by having not modest grassy leaves like real crocuses, but wide floppy ones that follow like retribution after the flower is past. Instead of the vertical streaking that marks the crocuses, their superficially similar goblets are often patterned more or less distinctly with a pink chequerboard or tesselated effect. In some rare and tricky species it is clearly drawn. In common ones, *Colchicum autumnale* and *C. speciosum* and their forms and hybrids, it can usually be faintly traced. Moreover they are pale pink, which no crocus is, whence their vulgar name of 'naked ladies'.

It is just as well that cyclamen are timed to go off at intervals: some such basic clue is needed in telling them apart. The dozen-odd species vary more in their tenderness or tractability than their looks. The whole plant is so captivating, from its clear-pink little long-eared flowers, like a spaniel in a wind-tunnel, to its deep green shield-, heart-, or kidney-shaped, often notched or scalloped leaves, that I will uncritically plant as many as I can lay my hands on, of the kinds that are reputed hardy. They are Mediterranean flowers, sold in bunches in markets in Italy, Greece and the South of France. It is remarkable, therefore, that at least two are very much in evidence right through an average British winter. *Cyclamen hederifolium*, which flowers in late summer, decorates the winter ground with its leaves alone. *C. coum*

ABOVE: *The globular flower- and seed-heads of the alliums make unique features in a border. This is* A. christophii – *a generous sower of its own seed.*

flowers in early spring, sometimes as early as December, combining flowers and foliage in a picture of grace that leaves me speechless. The bun-shaped brown tuber that produces this vision is almost comical. The ivy-leaved cyclamen of autumn is so absurd as to root from the upper side of this moribund-looking lump, leading many gardeners to plant it upside down. (It can survive even this if planted shallowly enough.) But given a dry, rather shady place and a soft bed of old leaves, (even the needle-fall of a giant old cedar), ground too starved for even grass to grow, the tubers will grow to loaf-size, seedlings will spread, and a great tribe of marvellously varied plants will spring up. They would be worth collecting for their leaves alone: no two seem to be alike. The florist's cyclamen, an inflated version of the tender *C. persicum*, entirely lacks the sense of humour of its country cousin.

Most of the South African bulbs are tender or risky in zone 7. In zone 8 they ask for the sun-baked foot of a south wall where they will receive a Veldt-type baking. They then need a late-summer soaking to start them off.

The rule applies to the pink-trumpeted *Amaryllis belladonna*, which flowers without leaves, to *Crinum × powellii*, which sprays its pink to white lily-flowers allium-fashion in a long succession above a bushy leaf-clump, and to the nerines. The true amaryllis is a smaller and hardier plant than the huge trombone of a flower grown under the name in pots – which is really a *Hippeastrum*. *Amaryllis* will grow in a warm wall-border in Britain. The leafless stem rises 60cm (2ft) and carries four pink trumpets, redolent of the Riviera.

Nerines are the ones to choose if hot spots are rare in your garden. *Nerine × bowdenii* is the hardiest, and worth making efforts for. Its flowers are like spun-sugar spiders with unique qualities of catching and holding the light. As cut flowers they have unusual stamina – up to a two-week life in water. If your treatment satisfies them, they will multiply to form dense clumps and last for ever. The only quality they lack is scent. The even lovelier *N. sarniensis*, known as the Guernsey lily (apparently because bulbs from a ship-wreck were found on a Guernsey beach) is best grown under glass for the summer baking its bulbs need. Pure white as well as lighter and darker forms can be had.

Best tempered of the South African bulbs is the Cape or summer hyacinth, *Galtonia candicans*, which asks no more than a fairly sheltered spot, not too dry, to raise its 1m (3ft) steeples of white or greeny-white bells. Tucked in among border flowers that are beginning to hint at autumn, their waxy whiteness is like a theme from the first half of the symphony gently repeated by the woodwind in the second.

ALPINES AND ROCKERIES THE NOTION

OF GROWING MOUNTAIN PLANTS IN GARDENS GOES BACK PERHAPS 150 YEARS, TO THE TIME

WHEN THE ALPS WERE SUDDENLY DISCOVERED TO BE BEAUTIFUL AS WELL AS FORBIDDING.

Romantic gardeners of the early nineteenth century were more interested in the rocks and caverns of the Alps than the flowers. They had climbed no higher than the lower cataracts, still overhung with larch and fir. Mosses and ferns were their idea of alpine plants. The gardeners enjoyed the gloom, and made more or less convincing imitations of it when they went home.

ABOVE: *The flowers that follow the snow: the mountain betony of Kashmir,* Pedicularis pectinata, *is untypical of alpines in exposing so much sail-area to the freezing winds.*

Then tourists climbed higher. Above the tree-line they found another world, where low bushes of rhododendrons and juniper and willow were exposed to bright sun and high winds, where the snow lay thick and late and revealed a host of hidden plants when it melted; all rushing into flower at once. The higher they climbed the shorter the plants became, hugging the ground closer and closer, all their parts foreshortened to avoid the gales and find what little warmth and shelter there is in the ground.

All foreshortened, that is, except the flowers, which seemed to get bigger and brighter the higher they climbed. On the high alps little cushion-like plants were often totally hidden with a mantle of intensely coloured flowers.

The conditions that produce these brilliant midgets are simple enough to understand. Their whole growing season is packed into a scorching three-month summer. Winter means snow cover, under which roots can lengthen and buds form. Snow can lie for years in some deep glens, only melting in an exceptional drought. But as soon as the snow goes, everything needed for growth is there in abundance: moisture from the melting snow, warmth from the sun high in the cloudless sky, and light of an intensity we never see in the lowlands.

Flowers take priority because the season is so short. They must have time to ripen seed before winter comes again. At high altitudes annuals are almost unknown: there is no time for the necessary procedure of germination, growth, flowering and setting seed in one year.

But why the short joints; the stunted growth? Because, it seems, the periods when cells can divide and tissues grow are only those between bright day, when the plant is under too much stress of transpiration, and the alpine night, which is too cold: only, in other words, the brief twilight. Any vigorous upward growth, moreover, would probably soon be wrenched away in a storm.

If the alpine climate is fairly uniform, given that there are slopes facing every point of the compass, the terrain is not. There is first of all the basic rock: granite in the Alps, the Himalayas, the California Sierras; limestone in the Dolomites, the Pyrenees. There is every degree of slope, from soil-less precipice and overhang to flat, stagnant marshland even high among the peaks. Below cliffs there is scree: the deep accumulation of rock debris, a dry habitat in summer where plants

BELOW: *The traditional garden rockery bears little relation to alpine conditions. It functions as a home at eye-level for any mat-forming or low-growing plant.*

RIGHT: *Alpine pinks are common in the mountain ranges of Europe and make easy rock garden plants, often seeding themselves and sometimes hybridizing. They flower in early summer.*

willows with sparkling catkins to go with early bulbs. Such small winter flowers as cyclamen, snowdrops, crocuses and irises rarely look better than cradled in a rocky cranny, where they set the scale of the self-sufficient scene.

HIGHBROW ALPINES

The alpine and rock garden plant catalogue is immense. I am purposely only dipping into the extreme ends of it: everyman's alpines and those one might call highbrow, part of whose appeal, at least, is that they are very difficult to grow. Only a fanatic will waste time on a dull plant just because it seems intent on dying. The challenge is that if you can find the formula the results are sensational.

The miraculous beauty of some of these plants can only be seen either by climbing the right mountain at just the right moment, or by visiting a show where the crack alpine gardeners are competing. It is not just the plants that are worth seeing but the way they are presented, in hand-made pots that are almost heirlooms, the pot in proportion to the plant, the surface dressed with stones that set off, in colour and size and texture, the character of the 'subject'. Even the labels are considered part of the exquisite still life: the favourite being a narrow ribbon of dull lead with the name embossed, curling round the rim of the pot.

BELOW: Saxifraga oppositifolia *is distributed in nature from North America to the Himalayas; an early-flowering alpine for cool conditions.*

But they are hard to grow, and the reason may be obvious or it may be a mystery. There are alpines such as moss campion that grow perfectly well in gardens, but never flower as they do in the mountains. Nobody really knows why. One of the commonest hazards is rot in the damp of an un-alpine winter; a risk chiefly for plants whose leaf formation traps water in their crowns. Rosette plants such as lewisias and ramondas are examples. When they are grown outside they are commonly planted on edge in a crevice where rain cannot settle in them. Under glass, watered from below and with a deep mulch of stone chippings to keep their 'collars' dry, they are safe.

Another problem is a decided taste in soil which the grower can only meet under the controlled conditions of a pot: and it may take him years to discover exactly what that taste is. It can range from peat and sand – with plenty of sand – for alpines from the woods, to almost pure ground-up tufa rock; a way of administering lime and drainage together in the maximum possible dose.

A further problem is the imperative that desert plants, bulbs in particular, have their period of total drought at the right time of year. Yet another is simply that some plants flower too early to be a practical proposition outdoors. Many bulbs are grown in pots simply to be better enjoyed, tranquil and unmuddied. Early-flowering saxifrages are another example of impetuosity. Some of the most desirable androsaces, which might be described as something between a saxifrage and a primula, come into the same bracket.

Pots are essential for moving alpines about and taking them to shows, but they add greatly to the labour of growing them. If there is a key to success with alpines it is drainage: indeed water supply both coming and going. In nature their roots occupy large volumes of stony ground with water flowing through it. It is the flow that matters: the water is always fresh and full of oxygen. The way to achieve the same effect in a pot is to mix plenty of sharp little stones with the soil – be it peaty or limy – and to make the pot fit the roots as tightly as possible. The roots should occupy all the soil all the time to prevent it stagnating. It follows that if the plant is to grow it must be repotted into a slightly bigger pot at least once a year. Keeping the pots plunged up to their rims in damp sand or peat is essential for even temperature and humidity. It all adds up to a considerable operation.

An easier way to provide the right conditions is to build up deep beds in your alpine house or frame and fill them with suitably stony soil – acid in one bed, alkaline in another, according to what you are going to grow. Alpines planted directly into this will root as they do in nature, avoiding the trap of stagnant soil and constantly pushing on to fresh feeding-grounds.

ABOVE: *The lewisias, from the western United States, have some of the most sumptuous flowers of any alpines. The evergreen* L. tweedyi *needs rich but dry, lime-free soil and shelter.*

THE PEAT GARDEN

Surely the human race can be divided into the moist and the airy. There are those who love cool, damp air and the scenery and plants that go with it, and those who must have wide open spaces and daily sunshine. There are those who dream of the highlands of Scotland and those whose hearts are in the isles of Greece. Scotland itself would not be such a cradle of gardeners and botanists if the swirl of mist and the patter of rain did not excite deep horticultural emotions.

The manner of gardening that epitomizes the joy of the rainy heath and the dripping copse was one of the last to come into being. It was the invention of Scottish gardeners in the 1950s, rapidly brought to perfection at the Royal Botanic Garden, Edinburgh; its lore and learning set down in a book by Alfred Evans in 1974. The book is *The Peat Garden and its Plants*.

The word peat always brings a faraway look into a keen plantsman's eyes. No doubt racehorse trainers feel the same about oats and rally drivers about octanes. Peat looks, feels and is the stuff that plant roots like best to burrow in. Not that it has great food value: it has very little. Its virtue lies in its texture and its ability to absorb and retain vast volumes of moisture.

BELOW: *Peat is the accumulated vegetation of boggy ground like this on the Isle of Skye, which never entirely decays for lack of oxygen. The structure of the dead plants (largely sphagnum moss) remains, providing a perfect root-run.*

ABOVE: *All the meconopsis, including the Himalayan blue poppy and, here, its close relation* M. grandis, *love damp, peaty conditions and rain.*

BELOW: *Jack Drake's famous nursery at Aviemore near Inverness epitomizes the Scottish speciality of the peat garden.*

The problem, as every eco-conscious gardener now knows, is that in some countries, and notably the British Isles, peat is a finite resource; a commodity whose extraction threatens delicate and precious habitats. Any substitute must also be lime-free, water-retentive, have high air-filled porosity and be slow to decompose . . . a tall order. Various alternatives are now used; the most satisfactory at present being coir, the fibrous matter from coconut shells. But leaf-mould (from acid soils), composted bark, chopped bracken, or a mixture of these will serve.

The peat garden was conceived as a way of cultivating and cosseting small plants that need damp acid soil and the moist atmosphere immediately above it. Such plants are found almost everywhere in the world's rainy highlands; in the Himalayas, Japan, the Rockies, Scotland, the Alps. Many of them are alpines in the strict sense, but not rock plants: their only interest in a rock would be to hide in its shade. The peat garden is therefore complementary to the rock garden. The same sort of devoted plantsmen revel in both. But from the practical point of view it has marked advantages. It is far quicker, cheaper and easier to build a peat garden. And the range of plants that can be satisfied by slightly modifying its conditions (adding, for example, more stones for drainage, or lime) is enormously wide. It can be adapted to give almost any small plant short of a confirmed rock-dweller the time of its life.

A peat garden is a bed of acid soil richly and deeply laced with peat or its alternatives, in a proportion of about half and half, sloping preferably to the north, well-supplied with rain or other soft water but also adequately drained, with rubble below if necessary. The softness of the water is crucial; water from a chalk spring would be useless.

The plant families that provide most candidates for this special treatment are the ericas, the primulas and the lily family. Among ericas the dwarf rhododendrons are the obvious first choice; there are hundreds of them. Then there are such creepers as *Arctostaphylos*, the 'bear grape', gaultherias (which include the pretty 'partridge berry' and the over-vigorous *Gaultheria shallon*), and vacciniums (including cranberry, bilberry and blueberry). There are some lovely little shrubs; cassiopes with reptilian scales; elegantly tiered *Enkianthus*, shedding its leaves in scarlet and gold; *Kalmiopsis,* the baby brother of the calico bush; *Leucothoe,* faintly resembling a bamboo; pernettyas, which keep their purple or white berries all winter . . . it is a long list. The heath and heather part of the erica family would love it here, too, but heathers with their vigour would soon take over at the expense of more precious things.

The primula list is almost as long. This is the ideal place for such rare and otherwise difficult species as *Primula vialii*, with a sharp spike of violet flowers, or *P. whitei* with a gentle nest of icy-blue ones.

Most lilies love peat beds. So do their relations the trilliums, fritillarias, erythroniums, and above all, from the plantsman's point of view, the rare high-Himalayan *Nomocharis*. Gentians luxuriate in peat. So does the Himalayan blue poppy and its relations. The list, in fact, is far too long to investigate here.

PLANTS FOR THE WATERSIDE

THERE ARE GARDENERS FOR WHOM BIG-LEAVED PLANTS GROWING STRONGLY IN WET GROUND ARE

RANK WEEDS IN A DITCH; OTHERS WHO FEEL THAT THIS IS WHERE THE PLANT WORLD REACHES ITS

MOST LUXURIANT AND FULFILLED.

It is certainly where temperate gardens come nearest to the tropical jungle.

Plants that live in water or at the water's brink, in permanently wet ground, must be physiologically adapted to airless soil. Where the soil is always saturated there is no drainage; hence no air being drawn down into the pores of the soil; hence very little and seldom enough oxygen for the roots. The roots need a peculiar structure or chemistry to acquire oxygen. Swamp cypresses put up woody knees above the water as they grow old, apparently simply in order to breathe. Other plants have long air ducts from the surface into the mud-delving roots. True bog-plants, in other words, form a distinct class separate from the much more numerous ones that need the air in a 'moist, well-drained soil'.

The easy and obvious way of using wet-ground plants is in conjunction with a pool or stream. Where there is abundant water, above all flowing water, the gardener can take his pick of all such plants; making a true bog here, a damp bed of open, porous soil there. Many bog plants will happily grow in shallow water, and most artificial ponds are built with shelves to accommodate them in the exact depth of water they seem to prefer. On the other hand the surface of the water itself is the prime aesthetic attraction of a pond. It is a pity to mask it with too many plants – certainly plants that do not need to be in water. To keep a patch of ground really wet it is a simple matter to excavate a shallow basin, line its bottom and sides (not quite to the top) with plastic sheeting, refill it with fertile soil and then let the hose or the overflow from the pond run in.

Remember, though, that you cannot hoe in mud, and forking is extremely unpleasant and difficult. Under these circumstances some weeds, once installed, are there for good. The ground elder in my bog garden is a particularly fine example. It is worth going to great pains to begin without weeds; more to the point be well advised on what is and is not a weed in wet ground. A number of plants sold as suitable for water-gardens are uncontrollable: the yellow musk, *Mimulus guttatus*, for example (though other *Mimulus* species see reason); buttercups, certain rushes and reeds . . .

The best way to achieve a moist, well-drained bed depends on the water-table. If it is very high it may be necessary to raise the level of the soil; if the drainage is good it may be necessary to bury a plastic sheet, but this time to cut drainage holes in it and fill it with grittier soil; even with some half-bricks in the bottom. Where water is in short supply the out-and-out bog garden is easy enough, but the moist bed, needing a constant flow, may not be possible.

The great advantage water-plants have over all others is that moisture stress is unknown to them; the sun cannot ask them for more water than they can supply. They are always free to transpire to their hearts' content. Hence their tendency to make lush growth and often to have big, sometimes prodigious, leaves. Waterside plants in fact have the tendency to produce nothing but leaves unless they receive plenty of sunlight.

ABOVE: *The huge creamy-white spathes of* Lysichiton camschatcensis *emerge from the mud in early spring.*
BELOW: Gunnera manicata *spreads its great rhubarb leaves above candelabra primulas in the water garden at Saling.*

ABOVE: *Degrees of wetness from the pond and its banks up to drier ground allow for the predilections of a wide range of plants.*

BELOW: *Golden club,* Orontium aquaticum, *is one of the most striking plants for water up to 45cm (18in) deep. It flowers in spring. Behind is the variegated yellow flag iris.*

By far the biggest leaf of any plant we can grow in Britain belongs to the Brazilian *Gunnera manicata*, like a rhubarb with a 3m (10ft) wingspan, which luxuriates in boggy ground. Among other plants whose impressive foliage is the main reason for growing them are two members of the rhubarb family (the gunnera only looks like rhubarb), *Rheum alexandrae* and *Rheum palmatum* 'Rubrum', whose unfurling in episcopal tones in spring is one of the events of my boggy calendar.

The rodgersias are a clan of several species with big leaves of strong character; the best known of them suggesting a horse chestnut. *Darmera* (formerly *Peltiphyllum*) *peltata* is an eccentric and valuable member of the saxifrage family. It puts up tall stems topped with pink flowers from bare ground, then follows them with 30cm- (1ft)-wide leaves on stalks as much as 1m (3ft) long in marshy ground.

Hostas grow to great size and substance in rich, damp ground (and so do slugs). Even better is the *Lysichiton*, or skunk cabbage, which follows its foot-high buttercup-yellow or white spathes emerging from the mud in early spring with simple great paddle-leaves of enormous size.

Long thin leaves are even more numerous among water-plants than long wide ones. There are all the rushes and reeds, for a start. The great reed mace (commonly known as bullrush) is scarcely a plant for gardens, but its 1m (3ft) cousin *Typha laxmannii* is almost essential to a boggy scene. Sedges, galingale and several tall grasses have emphatic character to contribute – bamboo even more so; making the best of all backgrounds and windbreaks for a bog-garden. As leaves for leaves' sake, two of the finest ferns, the royal and the shuttlecock-shaped ostrich fern (*Matteuccia*), need boggy ground to be seen at their best.

Perhaps the most important single genus of wet-ground flowers is the primulas, from *Primula denticulata* in early spring to *P. florindae* in summer, with a long succession of graceful candelabras in endless changing colours between. Next must come the water-irises – but only in June and July. The Japanese *Iris ensata* is the most impressive, with its wide, flat flowers. *I. laevigata*, on the other hand, is hardier and has a lovely form with vividly white-variegated leaves, which look superb rising from shallow water and greatly lengthen its ornamental season.

For the spring the yellow kingcups are essential. In early summer trollius, the globe-flowers, take up a similar theme. Later in the summer come the musks, brilliant in yellow, scarlet and orange; and the astilbes in colours from mahogany to candy-floss. Day-lilies love the brink of a pond.

Once we are out of the mire and into the drainage area we can simply start adding border flowers that like moist conditions. There is no hard and fast dividing line, any more than there is between plants that were designed to grow in bogs and those that will stand knee-deep in water.

PLANTS FOR THE WATER

There is a mystery and calm about water-lilies which reaches everybody. That such marvellously modelled flowers should emerge from the bosom of the lake is always a source of wonder. Far out among the water-weeds the crowding of rich green plates, each with a triangular notch, tells you where to look. Then one morning in midsummer a perfect chalice of white, or yellow, or throbbing red suddenly lies open on the surface. More and more follow, in incredible numbers. The leaves rise up, jostling and shoving as though the hidden plants were erupting. It is rather as though the most splendid and prolific of peonies was anchored to the bottom and could only produce its leaves and flowers in one plane.

The marvel of it all is that water-lilies are exceedingly easy to grow. If they look at their most romantic far out across the mere, they are a most intimate joy nestling among their perfect gleaming leaves in a wooden tub by the garden door. There is no need to have a lake or even pond to grow them; there are water-lilies for every depth of water.

India and the Middle East are the richest source of species, though there are water-lilies native to almost every country. They include the sacred lotus of Egypt, *Nymphaea lotus*, and perhaps the most beautiful of all water-plants, the lotus of the Far East, *Nelumbo nucifera*, in whose flower Buddha sits. This lotus raises its pale sea-green leaves and fragrant white flowers, pink tinged, high above the water. Alas it cannot be counted among the hardy kinds.

Most of the coloured water-lilies we grow today are hybrids, arising from the work of the great French breeder of the nineteenth century M. Marliac, who crossed some of the more richly coloured but less hardy species with the hardy European *Nymphaea alba* and others. Of common kinds it usually can be said the warmer the water (within reason) the better they will thrive.

To plant water-lilies in a natural pond is a simple matter. In late spring take a piece of an established plant, complete with roots and at least one shoot, and tie it up in a sack with a load of good soil – old manure and chopped turf for preference – the shoot emerging. Weigh the sack down with stones and drop it into water of the appropriate depth. By the time the sack has rotted the roots will have taken hold of the bed. In a concrete or plastic pond or a tub the plant will have to grow in a plastic or wire container, full of compost and lined with turves, and weighed down with stones. Beware, however, of waterfowl which eat the emerging shoots.

Of the score of full-size cultivars available the classics are the red 'James Brydon' and 'Escarboucle', the yellow 'Sunrise' and the magnificent gold-centred white 'Gladstoniana'. These are for water from 60cm (2ft) to even 1.8m (6ft) deep and would completely fill a small pool. M. Marliac's 'Layerdeckeri' strain are more suitable for small pools, but are all in shades of pink, purple and crimson. Another Marliac hybrid, 'Chromatella', provides a first-class yellow of moderate size. At tub-on-patio level there are also miniatures that need a bare 30cm (1ft) of water; hybrids and cultivars of *N. tetragona* such as 'Alba', 'Hyperion' and 'Rubis'.

Nothing rivals the display of the water-lilies, but there are plenty of other fascinating or quietly charming plants for open water – all of them good for the healthy balance of the pond. Some need to root on the bottom, others float free and take all their sustenance from the water. The water hyacinth, *Eichornia crassipes*, is a Mexican cattle-fodder plant which will either live afloat or take root. It needs warm shallow water and full sun to flower in cultivation and can be killed by frost.

Water soldier (*Stratiotes aloides*) is a curiously spiky rosette with a habit of resting on the bottom, then floating to the surface to flower. The water violet or featherfoil, *Hottonia palustris*, should really be called water primrose, since it belongs to that family and flowers like a miniature candelabra primula in early summer. It floats free; just throw rooted pieces in the pond. Water hawthorn or Cape pondweed, *Aponogeton distachyos*, is in flower almost all year, and sweetly scented, too. It roots in the bottom of water up to 60cm (2ft) deep.

Several plants live most of their lives completely submerged, but are none the less valuable for the oxygen they produce. Water moss (*Fontinalis antipyretica*), water starwort (*Callitriche platycarpa, verna* and other species) and hornwort (*Ceratophyllum demersum*) are three with very pretty foliage which are easy to keep in control – the first consideration when choosing water plants.

ABOVE: *The water hyacinth,* Eichornia crassipes, *is a Mexican cattle-fodder plant that will either live afloat or take root. It needs warm water and full sun. Frost kills it.*

BELOW: *Water-lilies need full sun. They look best as distinct 'rafts' with water separating them. They should never cover the whole surface.*

FOR THEIR LEAVES ALONE ORNAMENTAL

GRASSES ARE AN UNAPPRECIATED BY-WAY OF GARDENING. CONSIDERING THE IMPACT THEY CAN

MAKE AMONG MORE CONVENTIONAL GARDEN PLANTS.

ABOVE: *The plumy tufts of the annual squirreltail barley.* Hordeum jubatum.

BELOW: *The golden bamboo is the most beautiful form of* Phyllostachys bambusoides, *the Japanese timber bamboo. In the south of France, it grows to 9m (30ft), but suffers from hard winters.*

Hardly anyone can name the lovely things that wave their feathery flowers in a summer meadow. Only the avant garde would consider moving them wholesale into the garden: to most people the waving meadow effect is the very antithesis of gardening. It is easy to forget that an isolated clump of what is by nature a plant to be seen *en masse* can be immensely striking.

The simplicity of the drawing, the reiterated line of the narrow leaves rising parallel, then bending, criss-crossing and swaying, can make impact enough in a scene of broad leaves, fingery leaves and general jumble. But most garden grasses have been selected for eye-catching colours as well, many for very graceful and beautiful plumy flowers, and some for magnificence of stature.

There are grasses that grow 3m (10ft) in a season, then die off leaving a great straw-coloured fountain to the mercy of the winter weather. And of course there are dwarfs that stop at 5cm. There are grasses that will grow in liquid mud, though most prefer sunny steppe-like soil. There are also grasses such as couch that are a major menace, sending brittle running roots with uncanny speed to invade their neighbours – roots that snap at the first sign of an avenging gardener, every little white scrap ready to explode into an incredible yardage.

The first principle of gardening with grasses is to avoid any that spread by runners underground. They include, alas, the very decorative white-striped gardeners' garters (one of the few that has a well-known common name).

The other aggressive way grasses can break their allotted bounds is by seeding. Several of the prettiest are annuals – the delicate pearl grass, *Briza maxima*, with hanging heads like a cross between an oat and a Chinese lantern is one; Bowles's golden grass, slight, stooping and wonderfully yellow, is another. Bowles's seedlings, being bright yellow, are easy to identify, but most grass seedlings, annual or perennial, are more or less interchangeable to the lay eye – so it is better to treat them all as enemies unless you know them to be friends.

Grasses look best as individuals or small clumps, used as a punctuation mark in a stretch of other plants. The place for a full stop is at the end of a sentence – say the corner of a bed or where a path turns out of sight. But grasses are equally good as the less emphatic commas and semi-colons of the garden; to form a gentle interruption in a stretch of low planting, or to provide neutral colouring and soft texture in contrast to plants of strong colour or hard etching.

The bigger grasses can stand on their own as singular features rising from a lawn, or even from the gravel of a drive. Such blatantly artificial isolation, where you can see the whole plant from top to toe, shows off their extreme elegance perfectly. Pampas grass grown like this is a cliché, but the 3m (10ft) *Miscanthus sacchariflorus*, given plenty of moisture, would be a splendid landmark.

The association of tall grasses and water is always successful. The waterside, of course, has its own range of grass-like plants – the rushes, reeds and sedges. Pictorially they all work well by contrasting their vertical or drooping lines with the smooth horizontal of the pond. The sedges (including the graceful *Carex pendula* and the brilliant golden *Carex morrowii* 'Variegata') and the *Cyperus* (umbrella sedges or galingale, like the Egyptian papyrus) are the only ones normally planted, but several others would relish the conditions.

Bamboos are grasses that aspire to be trees by forming permanent woody stems. Some of them actually achieve their ambition, reaching 18–21m (60–70ft), and that with such thin stems that they need the shelter of thick woodland. The common hardy (to zone 7) bamboos do well to reach 3.5m (12 ft), but form such dense evergreen clumps and screens that nothing can match them. They provide the atmosphere of the jungle, complete with sound-effects.

Many of them have the failing (given good conditions) of running roots. Indeed only *Sinarundinaria*, *Thamnocalamus* and the Chilean climbing bamboo, *Chusque couleou*, always remain reliably in clumps. Rather than exclude such splendid plants for that reason, it is worth forming concrete barriers that they cannot pass; 45cm (18in) is as deep as they need to go. Or simply mow around them. A mower will destroy new shoots coming up out of bounds.

The biggest bamboo hardy in north-west Europe is *Phyllostachys bambusoides*, the timber bamboo of Japan. There the 12m (40ft) canes grow to their full height within a few months. The grove is thinned by removing new shoots for food and mature stems for building. Timber bamboo is remarkably winter-hardy, but only grows to its full height in a damp climate with hot summers. (Here 4.5m (15ft) would be impressive). Such a universal provider is not surprisingly regarded as sacred.

Unfortunately, bamboos are a botanist's paradise. The faintest difference of stem colouring provides an excuse for a new name. Perhaps as a result, few nurseries grow them. Metake (*Pseudosasa japonica*), unfortunately a spreader, is the only true common one, although the similar *Fargesia* (syn. *Sinarundinaria) nitida* can be trusted to stay in a clump. The shorter, broad-leafed *Sasa palmata* makes an admirable contrast, but this one is rampant.

FERNS AND MOSSES

Most gardens get by very happily without an intentional fern, or any moss to speak of. If they are there at all, they come uninvited – and indeed they are not things you can buy in every garden centre. Yet there are few plants that carry such a cargo of atmosphere. Ferns are the embodiment of green thoughts in a green shade, and if a leafy shadow could take root, moss would surely be the result. There are gardens where any such thing would be irrelevant and ridiculous; where all is sunlight and airy exposure. But there are others, and probably parts of most, where a poor, sour shade could be given a luxurious leafy cloak by planting ferns and encouraging moss to carpet the ground.

Moreover, despite their appearance of being the inhabitants of dripping caves, there are ferns, and even mosses, that are tolerant of perpetually dry ground. Since the combination of drought and shade is the ultimate in gardening problems it is odd that we are not greeted by ferns in every dim backyard.

Ferns and mosses are cousins of a sort. They both belong to the flowerless part of the plant kingdom that has an in-between stage in its reproductive process. Ferns produce spores by the million, usually on the undersides of their leaves, where they form rusty patches. The spores drop off, take root, and perform the sexual functions for the fern, as it were by proxy, but never grow into ferns themselves. Instead they produce the 'seed' from which the next generation of ferns grows. Mosses have the same habit of alternating sexual and vegetative generations, only with them it is the sexual generation which is the taller and showier (if that's the word) plant.

BELOW: *The palm-like tree ferns of Australasia are the most spectacular of their race, but only hardy in such mild damp climates as the south-west of Ireland, where they have become naturalized.*

ABOVE: *Ground-covering moss is one of the glories of the gardens of Kyoto with their warm wet summers. But there are mosses which can give the same effect in a cool dry climate.*

Most ferns are quite easily propagated by sowing the spores very thinly on moist peat under a pane of glass. The plants that will appear look very like the sexual generation of mosses – almost like small green toadstools. In turn they will produce the tiny fern plants. They need careful weaning in damp conditions before they are hardened off ready for planting out. On the other hand the majority of ferns can quite easily be divided like any herbaceous plant, so long as the pieces are planted in damp soil with peat, leaf-mould or compost.

The easiest way to establish moss is to procure scraps, of whatever kind is common in your neighbourhood. (This is not a licence to plunder; you need permission). The north-facing slopes of roofs are often a fruitful place to look if you want moss for a dry site. Pin the moss down with hair-grips on bare moist ground where you want it to grow. A light scattering of peat or sawdust among the pieces is a good idea. Happily moss is encouraged rather than killed by contact weedkillers, which will keep down any competition. An occasional watering with a normal dilution of a paraquat-type weedkiller will prevent it being overtaken by more vigorous plants. The fact that the north side of roofs and tree trunks is the place to find it shows that many mosses dislike direct sunlight. Yet nothing can be drier than a roof in summer.

The Japanese are the artists in this genre. For them moss holds the place that grass does in English gardens, but then most of Japan has a steamy summer, which is just what moss likes best. As for ferns, the Japanese manage to pack so much emphasis into one plant, placed just so at the foot of a stone lantern or by a stepping stone in a brook, that you feel the last word has been said on the subject.

Ferns were a passion of Victorian gardeners. North-facing greenhouses were tricked out with a few flints and a trickle of water and designated ferneries. Every idiosyncratic fern (many are given to sporting odd forms) was treasured and given a long Latin name. A century later there are signs of the passion returning. Specialist fern nursereies are thriving as the unique textural qualities of ferns for mass planting, as well as for sumptuous specimens, win converts.

There are ferns that will survive almost total neglect. The male fern, *Dryopteris filix-mas*, is the toughest and suitable for the driest, most hopeless corners. It has a very pretty golden-green brother, *D. pseudomas*, which is scarcely less tough, and looks rather more special. Even tougher, of course, but not to be admitted to your garden, is the ineradicable bracken of sandy heaths.

BELOW: *There are ferns for all soils from dusty to boggy. The royal fern,* Osmunda regalis, *grows well here on the margin of a stream and its bright green foliage invades the water itself.*

At the opposite extreme are such delicacies as the maidenhair, its fronds forming perfect arcs on fine black stems (this must have shade); and such intricacies as the cut-and-cut-again-leaved version of the soft shield fern, *Polystichum setiferum* 'Plumoso-multi-lobum'. In complete contrast to this laciest of ferns is the one with a totally uncut strap of a leaf – the common hart's tongue.

There are ferns that like bogs, too: the royal fern and the shuttlecock fern only grow to their full dignity in wet ground. A water garden is their perfect setting. As for the Australasian tree ferns, the palm-like monarchs of their race, only those who garden in such truly 'soft' conditions and high rainfall as southwest Ireland can enjoy them out of doors.

SUB-SHRUBS

The botanical term is suffruticose. At one point in the seventeenth century frutex threatened to become the English for a shrub; suffrutex for a sub-shrub. We had a lucky escape.

What is or is not suffruticose depends to an extent on the climate. There are many plants that fail to ripen the tips of their new growth in places where the summer is too short or too cool. Hardy fuchsias, for example, are completely fruticose in Ireland; substantially herbaceous in most of England. Pragmatic gardeners therefore use the term sub-shrub for anything that is shrubby by inclination but low, sprawling and soft-wooded, or just simply dwarf in stature.

The biggest single class of plants embraced by this definition must surely be the heathers. Then there are the woody herbs. Then there is an army of popular and useful plants ideal for small gardens and unclassifiable in any other way, particularly the grey-leaved little bushes. Such little shrubs offer a look of well-furnished stability; the same advantage, or disadvantage, depending on your tastes, as a garden of heathers: nothing much happens. It looks well-organized and tasteful, but the changing seasons are not exactly stressed. Little disturbs its well-bred calm.

Grey-leaved plants are generally adapted to drought and heat: a question mark always hangs over their hardiness in northern gardens. The cotton lavender, *Santolina chamaecyparissus* (*incana*), is one of the hardiest. Clipped occasionally it makes a pale and solid mound of great 'design' value. The artemisias, the family of sagebrush and absinthe, have the finest of all feathery grey fronds in *Artemisia arborescens*, but this is not guaranteed against hard frosts. The pale green southernwood is the toughest of them.

The New Zealand genus *Brachyglottis* provides some of the most popular grey-leaved plants: the sprawling offspring of *B. laxifolia* and *B. greyi* known as Dunedin hybrids. *B. monroi* is a neater form with smaller crinkly leaves. Far more silvery and outspoken, but also more tender, is *Senecio cineraria*, with broad deeply lobed leaves: this is used as tender bedding in cold gardens. Those who do not approve of bright yellow daisies often clip the flower buds off senecios and santolinas in early summer to keep the plants compact.

One of the most varied and intriguing contributors in this field is the New Zealand genus of hebes, which old hands know as shrubby veronicas. At one extreme they offer little bushes like dwarf cypresses (the 'whipcords': notably the green-brown *Hebe armstrongii*). At the other they put up tall spikes of lavender-blue flowers (*H. hulkeana*). Then there is *H. rakaiensis*, like box, *H. pinguifolia* 'Pagei', a frosty little groundcover, and *H. macrantha*, with wide white flowers almost like a campanula.

ABOVE: *Midsummer brilliance is provided by the helianthemums or rock roses, in ideal contrast to the sobriety of box. Valerian grows in the background.*

BELOW: *Jerusalem sage is the best-known of several solidly useful phlomis. Its sub-shrubby nature makes it sprawl; it has no wood strong enough to stand straight.*

If you are looking for a dark green dome of great authority, with flowers like scented apple blossom and red berries, *Daphne tangutica* (Refusa group) would be your answer. If you want an evergreen hummock of silver-silky leaves and flowers all summer with pink buds opening pure white, *Convolvulus cneorum* is a bindweed as lovely as a bride: it loves to sprawl on a sunny terrace. If what you want is sheets of pink or yellow or orange flowers in midsummer, plant the helianthemums. If an indefatigable classic is what you are after, you cannot improve on lavender.

HEATHS AND HEATHER

There are no half-measures with heathers. Even more than the heavies of their family, the rhododendrons, they impose their personality on any garden where they get a foothold. In theory a little patch of heather sounds a reasonable way to vary the planting. In practice it is all or nothing: you must either embrace the ambience of the heaths and adjust your garden to it, or shun it altogether. Heathers and roses, heathers and delphiniums, heathers and annuals all look equally grotesque together. It is only in the rock-and-peat mode that heathers can sometimes be used as a sub-dominant theme. But you are still playing with fire.

I am speaking of aesthetic, not physical aggression. Heathers are the basic groundcover of rainy, peaty mountains, where their scale matters no more than the length of the grass in a panorama of pasture-land. But bring heathers into the garden and their demure precision of small leaf, small flower, low mound – without the endearing disproportion of alpines, top-heavy with flowers – seems like a rebuke to plants of stature, be they coarse or elegant. One little heather looks absurd, so you plant a group. The group gang together into a mass of even flower and texture, spreading inexorably (but too slowly to be exciting). You are recommended to have a patchwork of different colours and to relieve their monotonous flatness with little conifers. Eventually, after eight or nine years, you have a mature heather garden.

BELOW: *The winter-flowering* Erica × darleyensis *is massed to great effect in the Valley Gardens in Windsor Great Park.*

Yet look at the picture below. If you are beginning to suspect that heathers are not my favourite plants, let me freely admit that it is hard to imagine a more inviting winter garden scene. It is limited to one strain of heather, the hardy *Erica × darleyensis*, whose colours are all in the range of pink/purple or white. There could hardly be a more coherent and convincing planting. This is in the Valley Gardens at Windsor and is one of the most inviting parts of that great garden to explore on a winter's day.

What is always advertised as the strong point of the heathers is that they have representatives in flower in almost every month of the year. They also have forms with leaves in strikingly different colours, which do not need to be in flower to show up distinctly as colour in the patchwork. Some of them also keep their old flowers, withered and tobacco-brown, in such numbers that this colour becomes another element in the heathscape. Although the winter-, summer- and autumn-flowering kinds vary enough close-to to be worth looking at, the net effect en masse is simply of the

same plants performing a light-show of colours at a snail's pace. I cannot under-stand a gardener who would celebrate summer with such a denial of all its qualities.

The vast majority of heathers are natives of South Africa and (I nearly said luckily) tender in northern Europe. All the dwarf or low-growing hardy kinds com-mon in gardens come from Europe's own moorlands. They belong to three genera: *Calluna*, which has only one species, ling or true heather, the springy substance of the Scottish highlands; *Erica*, with a dozen European species; and *Daboecia* with two, one from the Azores and one from the Atlantic coast from Ireland to Portugal.

Yet out of this mere score of species have sprung hundreds of cultivars; enough to provide almost any flower-colour in the range from red to white, against any leaf-colour in the range of green, gold, grey or bronze, at almost any time of year.

A rapid catechism of the heathers from winter to winter begins with the hybrid *Erica × darleyensis*, up to 60cm (2ft) or so in height, generally pink in flower, capable of flowering from November to May and tolerant of limy soil. It has a gold-leaved variant and a well-known white form from Germany: 'Silberschmelze'. Hard on its heels comes the shorter, equally hardy and lime-tolerant *Erica carnea* (alias *E. herbacea*) from the Alps and Appenines. Rosy red is its 'normal' colour, but as usual there are forms with gold leaves (e.g. 'Foxhollow'), pink forms, 'ruby' forms and the popular 'Springwood White'. Its flowering season is over in March.

About this time come two taller but less hardy heaths from the Mediterranean *E. erigena* and the 'tree' heath, *E. arborea*, growing respectively to 1.8m (6ft) and 3.5m (12ft). Both smell deliciously of honey; *arborea* with white flowers, *erigena* generally pink or red, but also with a white variant. Zone 8 is about their limit of hardiness: the tree heath is sometimes killed by frost at Kew. Where they can be grown, though, they greatly relieve the insipid mass of the lower heathers.

The first heather of summer is *Daboecia cantabrica*, the Irish bell heather; the rock and peat of Connemara is its home. This is a straggly 60cm (2ft), pink or white in flower from June to autumn. The white form and its hybrid 'William Buchanan' are said to be the best. Also in June the common bell heather of many open peaty moors, *E. cinerea*, comes into flower. At least a hundred clones exist in cultivation, putting up with far warmer and richer soil than they were designed for. Two taller, more straggly heaths, *E. ciliaris* from Dorset and *E. tetralix*, the cross-leaved heath, follow it. These are less tolerant, demanding damp, acid soil. A much better and more reli-able plant is the upstanding – to 2.5m (8ft) – lime-tolerant *E. terminalis* from Italy, which is rarely seen in gardens.

Then, well past midsummer, comes the Highland ling, in almost every colour, and sizes from 7.5cm (3in) to 1m (3ft). At the same time, lasting well into autumn, the Cornish heath, *E. vagans*, flowers in a style of its own, with jostling spires of pink or white reaching up eventually to 1m (3ft).

Heather gardens are not as effortless as they look, for two reasons. First, the ground between the plants must be endlessly weeded until they join up. At the recommended planting distance – 45cm (18in) for most kinds – this is usu-ally a matter of three or four years. Second, the soil is usually too fat for them: they tend to grow too fast and become gaunt and bare. Neat regularity is only achieved by pruning and shearing: of the spring-flowering kinds after they have flow-ered; of the autumn-flowering kinds in spring.

GRASS & OTHER GROUNDCOVER

FEW WOULD ARGUE WITH THE PROPOSITION THAT A GARDEN NEEDS A VISIBLE FLOOR. THE GROUND LEVEL NEEDS TO BE FIRMLY ESTABLISHED SOMEWHERE. PREFERABLY CENTRALLY, BY AN OPEN SPACE FREE. OR RELATIVELY FREE. FROM THE JOSTLE OF PLANTS.

ABOVE: *It is sometimes a hard decision whether or not to mow the daisies that turn a mere lawn into a tapestry of delicate colour.*

As the landscape-philosopher Humphry Repton said, 'A plain space near the eye gives it a kind of liberty it loves.'

Paving is ideal for small yards and patios. But on a larger scale something green and soft is most natural and more soothing. Grass is the automatic answer wherever it will grow.

The art of the grassy lawn was developed in England. Some say it was invented by the huge flocks of sheep that cropped, manured and compacted with their hard little hooves the naturally grassy areas round country houses. It was perfected in Tudor times, when a bowling green scythed to a flawless finish was a status symbol. The word *boulingrin* for a plot of grass passed into French – though never quite the attitude of mind that went with it.

The air in England is apparently full of grass seed. You have only to leave ground bare to see the process start. The climate favours it – damp summers with cloudy skies and moderate winters are ideal. I have made a perfectly acceptable lawn by doing nothing – sowing no seed, laying no turf – simply mowing the naturally occurring plants on a patch of bare ground every other week for a summer. By the end of the first season the grass had the upper hand. By the end of the second year I could use the word lawn. Grasses are among the few plants that survive and thrive with having their heads cut off at frequent intervals.

Not everyone is so lucky. Though grass of some kind will grow almost anywhere in temperate climes, the good lawn grasses resent extremes of climate. Few grasses will tolerate long periods of hot sunshine. In the sub-tropics the only resort

RIGHT: *The grasses of the temperate world will not survive in the tropics. The Brazilian artist/plantsman Roberto Burle Marx used Bermuda grass for this romantic landscape near Rio de Janeiro.*

may be the Bermuda grasses, which unfortunately have dormant periods in winter, when
they turn a dreary brown. They can be sown
with annual cool-climate grasses to hide them
in winter or even (according to the Sunset
Western Garden Book) dyed green. Several non-
grass-plants such as *Ophiopogon*, or lily-turf.
are used as substitutes in the tropics.

A good lawn will flourish only where
the soil is deep and well drained. When we
mow and collect the trimmings we remove
nutrients which the roots must replace; if the
root-run is shallow, constant feeding becomes
necessary. The ideal conditions for a lawn are
5cm (2in) of sand over 30cm (1ft) of good rich
soil and then a fast-draining sub-soil – an

unlikely combination in nature. The sand prevents the surface compacting or water-
logging; the rich soil invites the roots to run deep; and the drainage makes sure
they do not drown.

Given that very few gardeners are likely to prepare such perfect conditions
lawn-seed is normally sold in judiciously balanced mixtures of the more or less
aristocratic and demanding kinds – the fine-leaved creeping fescues that call for
the daintiest treatment; the tougher meadow-grasses (*Poa* species), more tolerant
of damp and shade, the vigorous longer-stalked bents and sometimes the not easily discouraged brawny perennial rye-grass. The precise prescription varies by
merchant, by region (with allowances made for local climate) and of course by the
intended use of the lawn. A football pitch needs very different grasses from a polite
suburban sward.

There are lawn fetishists to whom anything but the finer grasses are anath-
ema. Perhaps they should open their eyes to the virtues of clover, which stays green
when drought browns the grass, and moreover is self-feeding with its nitrogen-
fixing roots, and even – in appropriate sunless places – moss. Moss takes advantage
of neglected, starved grass – especially on very acid soil. The broad-leaved weeds
such as plantain and dandelion break the even surface of green and spoil the effect.
Daisies on the other hand are beautiful in themselves, and are usually sufficiently
discouraged by mowing.

A 'perfect' lawn is the garden's greatest consumer of energy, in the form of
fertilizers and weedkillers and in the Saturday-morning roar of a million mowers
getting cracking. And that is only the start of it. A lawn needs regular raking to
pull out the 'thatch' of accumulated dead grass, spiking to aerate the soil and rolling
to compact it again.

The energy spent on maintaining lawns in the United States would revolu-
tionise the agriculture of a goodish part of the Third World. The argument for
compromise between lawn and meadow is a powerful one. Yet compromise is not
easy to put into effect.

In a small garden orderly trimness is likely to be the object of having a lawn
at all. Even in a large garden it turns out to be less laborious to mow short regularly than long occasionally – which lets you in for the sweaty business of haymaking.
If you mow often enough you need not even collect the cut grass – a saving of both
time and fertilizers.

ABOVE: *To a lawn fanatic, mowing is
a pleasure in itself: the noise of the engine,
the smell of exhaust and oil and the
warm green cuttings. For the richest
green and most pronounced stripes
2cm (¾in) is the best length.*

THE HERB GARDEN

Whether we would really enjoy either the process or the results today is immaterial to our instinctive approval of such a natural, wholesome, surely happy and fulfilling business.

We should imagine seventeenth-century tastes as rather more robust than ours, lest we mislead ourselves. I once visited a house in Kent where rosemary and rushes were still strewn on the stone flags in the great hall, Tudor fashion. The combination of crushed rosemary underfoot and smoke from the apple logs piled in the grate gave me a vivid flash-back to the days of our ancestors in doublet and hose. How pallid and genteel our ideas of scent and flavour have become.

How limited in scope, too. The herbals of the seventeenth century were based on the broad faith that everything in the garden had a use, whether for medicine, cookery, preserving, cosmetics, or often quasi-magically to raise or lower the spirits of the depressed or overexcited. The recipes read today as though the symptoms were filled in after the cures were concocted. It may have been so, although most modern drugs are derived from plants. In any case the garden repertoire was uninhibited, as were the recipes. Dozens of plants that we consider 'flowers' rather than 'herbs' were pressed into service. As a result the herb garden in its original form was a much prettier place than it is today. Today it wears an air of restraint, of containing only rather dowdy plants whose merits are all in their juices. We have either forgotten the uses of the more flamboyant ones, or promoted them into the flower garden regardless.

Yet the same air of restraint gives the herb garden a unity. The prevailing colours are green and grey and brown with a few quiet purple, pink, yellow and soft blue flowers. A separate bed (or better still enclosure) with herbs alone is a restful change from the brighter colours of the rest of the garden. Not all herbs are in scale together — angelica and fennel for example tower like trees over the *maquis* of the lesser herbs — but all are at least harmonious.

One of the best plans is to grow herbs in a chequerboard pattern, alternating little beds with paving slabs, which provides somewhere to stand while you pick them. The soil in the beds can be varied to suit the plants, and beds for invasive herbs such as mint and balm can be lined with cement down to a depth where even mint roots give up. Wherever I have seen such a cabinet of herbs it has been almost too much of a conservation piece: so much lore and legend attaches to each

BELOW: *The delicate colours of herbs make them particularly suited to formal treatment. Lavender, box, bay and rue, framed by a grape-vine, make a completely satisfying picture.*

plant. But since it does provoke discussion it is a good idea to put a large label in each bed. The names, in the mother tongue, not Latin, have a runic quality which makes you look twice at even the dullest little clump of leaves.

The term herb is by no means restricted to perennial plants. Many are annuals. An important minority are the aromatic shrubs and sub-shrubs of Mediterranean hillsides, the plants that grew wild where the first European gardens were made.

The shrubby herbs are all good garden plants whether you use them in the kitchen or not. Bay is one of the handsomest and hardiest of evergreen trees. Thyme in its many varieties is ideal cover for a dry bank or low stone wall. The two culinary thymes are the common and the lemon-scented (which has a pretty golden form). Corsica also has one called *herba-barona*, which reputedly has a caraway flavour. Lavender, though an eccentric ingredient in cooking, carries a potent charge of old-garden association. Rosemary is one of the best companions for old roses, and looks good in any border. The form known as 'Miss Jessop's Upright' makes a superlative marker or point of emphasis, given the shelter of a wall.

Sage, with its zinc-grey leaves, may seem a dull plant, but I have seen it used to great effect in broad sweeps on a stony hill, and its colour-forms in purple and greeny-gold are excellent. Rue, vile smelling though it is, has exquisitely fretted leaves and is marvellously easy to grow: so much so that the blue-leaved 'Jackman's Blue' has become a cliché with lime-green lady's mantle in old-English gardens. Hard drainage is the rule for all the shrubby herbs. Aim to remind them of their home in Provence.

The annual herbs need more sympathetic soil. They vary from the essential parsley, which needs moisture and appreciates shade, to basil, which insists on the warmest spot. The majority vote with the basil, so it makes more sense to keep your herb bed in the sun and grow your parsley in the shade by the kitchen door. Coriander, dill (the top herb in Scandinavia), sweet marjoram and summer savory are all annuals that enjoy a warm place with fairly rich, moist soil. The one valuable herb that would prefer to be with the parsley is the rather similar but subtler chervil, the secret of *omelettes fines herbes*.

Alone among the herbaceous herbs mint likes moisture. There is even a lovely mint that lives in water: treading on it wading in a stream is a moment to remember. It seems that only the British and Arabs cook with mint, but it would be a pity to leave it out of a herb garden, invasive as it is. There are two culinary kinds: spearmint (with pointed leaves) and apple mint, whose leaves are round, soft-hairy and have a better flavour. Apple mint also has a white-variegated and a grey form: both attractive enough to plant for decoration alone.

The other herbs will all be happy with a well-drained garden soil, needing little feeding but more or less frequent dividing and replanting. This is particularly true of the two indispensables, chives and (sadly tender) tarragon. No doubt alecost, lovage, lemon balm and sweet cicely would appreciate it too. Alas all they tend to get is a leaf torn off, tasted and briefly discussed from time to time.

ABOVE: *Herbs have been associated with the strap-work patterns of knot gardens since the Middle Ages. This intricate parterre in box is at Barnsley House, Gloucestershire.*

BELOW: *Herbs informally planted, and admitting such cheerful edible annuals as nasturtiums, make a coherent theme for a little dry garden with stepping stones.*

THE KITCHEN GARDEN

A kitchen garden has the satisfaction of inevitability. There is only one way to set about it. A boat must have a sharp end; vegetables must be grown in rows – or at least regular patches. Their ground must be measured, marked out and made ready. It must be kept fertile and clean. If all this is well done it is more expressive of the harmony of man and nature than anything else a gardener can do. Here we are not just looking for pleasure (which is perhaps why we find it); we are looking for a measurable return for labour. The word efficiency creeps in. Comparison with the price of vegetables in the shops is unavoidable.

The object of growing crops (as opposed to just growing plants) is to produce the maximum quantity of a quality that will satisfy us in as small a space and in as short a time as possible. It is common sense not to grow anything that is being raised commercially at much lower cost. There are vegetables that flood the market at certain times of year. It is useless to have your own glut at the same time as everyone else. Far better to grow something different – perhaps even rape – for maturity at that time, or (as far as you can) advance or delay your crop so as not to coincide with the glut.

THE PRINCIPLES

Although the whole principle of growing vegetables is to pump them full of nutrients so that they grow as fast as possible, to be as juicy and tender as possible, it may sometimes be better to reduce the apparent efficiency of your turnover. For example, you can grow a crop in relatively unfertile conditions, which will make it hardy enough to stay in the ground over the winter. Spring is the leanest time of year for supplies, and leeks, sprouts and cabbages that have survived the winter are marvellously welcome before the first early crops can be forced along.

In general, however, the object is to give vegetables a short life and a pampered one. A perfect kitchen garden needs warmth, sunlight, shelter from the wind, soil in good general 'heart' (easily worked and well-drained), additions of fertilizers when they can do most good, an ample supply of water and weeds kept well at bay. In an exposed place shelter from the wind might be the overriding factor. Nothing discourages tender young leaves so much as a howling draught. In a hot and sandy place the most important thing will be the amount of moisture-retaining humus you can manage to incorporate into the soil. In a sad bog drainage must come first . . . and so on.

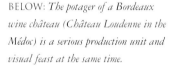

BELOW: *The potager of a Bordeaux wine château (Château Loudenne in the Médoc) is a serious production unit and visual feast at the same time.*

Certain points of layout apply very generally. Shelter from the north and east, by walls if possible, means a quick warm-up in spring. A south-facing slope raises the soil temperature, but there must be an escape route for cold air on frosty nights at the lowest point or a frost-pocket will result. A wind-baffling fence or hedge on the side of the prevailing wind is very desirable, but not if it also shades the ground for a significant part of the day. Plant-rows running north-south receive most sunlight. Hard paths are essential when the ground is wet.

Paths also provide a welcome permanent framework and pattern. The custom (at least in substantial kitchen gardens) is to divide the space into three parts for a rotational cycle (to avoid growing the same crops in the same soil twice running) and keep a fourth part for such permanent fixtures as rhubarb, asparagus or soft fruit, or as an additional step in the rotation of potatoes. If you want both the plan will need five parts.

The rotation system classes almost all vegetables as 1) pea or onion family, 2) cabbage, or *Brassica*, family and 3) a root crop. The three classes like their soil rich and well-mucked in that descending order. Ideally therefore you plan to dig and manure the ground; grow peas, beans, onions and leeks in it first; the next year cabbages and their relations; and in the third year carrots, parsnips and the like. In the latter two years you use fertilizers. Then you start again. Meanwhile, irrespective of rotation, you dart in and out with quick 'catch' crops of whatever you think you can get away with: the elementary and instant radish; lettuce; carrots; spinach; endive. . . .

Instruction manuals and seed packets are generally very clear on such matters as spacing: how far apart the plants should eventually be. Closer together they will shelter one another but also compete. As in all garden questions the decision is finally the gardener's one. Would you rather have four small cabbages or two big ones?

THE ROUTINE

The human race has been eating for a long time but only recording its menus for a short one. The early history of most of our food plants is lost. Many of them are developments of wild plants of the Mediterranean and the Near and Middle East.

Plants of these areas tend to have large food storage organs (roots, rhizomes or seeds) evolved to keep through a long dry season and grow like fury when it rains.

The process of selection over thousands of years has obscured the wild origins of some vegetables completely: the onion, for example, has no obvious wild ancestor. But the majority advanced surprisingly little until the dawn of science. The first illustrations we have of vegetables, from the sixteenth century, show how primitive they were. The seventeenth century brought new introductions: the potato, maize, the tomato, beans and the marrow from the New World, but conservative gardeners did very little with them.

Not until the end of the eighteenth century did methodical selection and breeding begin. Early in the nineteenth century M. de Vilmorin experimented with wild carrots, selecting seedlings with fleshy roots from the majority (which had merely fibrous ones). By sowing their seed, selecting again and repeating the process three times he produced within four generations from the wild plant a vegetable very like that which had taken thousands of years to develop. From that time on, with the principles of selection and breeding increasingly being understood, vegetables constantly improved and diversified almost beyond recognition.

High tide came some time in the first quarter of this century, when an astonishing range of vegetables for every sort of taste and local conditions was available. Now the tide has turned and is on the ebb. Most modern 'improvements' are nothing of the kind as far as gardeners are concerned. The expensive business of breeding new vegetables is undertaken only for commercial growing, where taste is a minor consideration beside uniformity, looks and cropping and storing qualities. Worse still, in Europe EU regulations have outlawed all the old varieties not on a short list agreed among commercial interests, declaring them to be broadly synonymous with varieties that are on the list, whether they taste the same or not. A stiff fine is imposed on anyone who should transgress these regulations, aimed at a stultifying uniformity – and bound, moreover, to have serious genetic consequences as the breeding potential of the outlawed varieties is lost. Happily Britain's Henry Doubleday Research Institute is leading a fight back against such irresponsible bureaucracy.

For an amateur the criteria (economy apart) for deciding to grow a vegetable must be either that it is a better variety, or that he can grow it better than the commercially available kinds. Growing it better includes having the chance to pick and eat it at exactly the right moment.

THE LEGUMES

Peas and beans are members of the legume family, which includes wisteria, laburnum, the acacia (or locust) . . . all plants that have nitrogen-fixing bacteria in their roots and thus leave the soil better off (as far as nitrogen goes) than they found it.

The legumes come first in the pecking-order of rotation after the big dig, and the manuring that goes with it, partly because the nitrogen they add is ideal for the leaves of the brassicas, partly because they have deep roots, but mainly because they appreciate the moisture-holding properties of the manure. Some gardeners have buried soaking newspapers and rags (while their peas were looking the other way) and found that it served the same purpose. Potash is the other thing that is hard to overdo, at least in its harmless form of fresh wood-ash. Like all vegetables except potatoes they prefer the soil alkaline rather than acid. Being big seeds they are easily sown in their permanent places, but since mice enjoy them peas are often dipped in paraffin before sowing.

Broad beans are the ancient European kind, easy, fond of heavy soil, hardy enough to sow in autumn in many places for a spring crop. They need support against wind and should be grown in double rows to ensure pollination. Their only real problem is blackfly, which concentrate on the growing tip. Pinch this off (it is good to eat) as soon as the first pods have started to form near the bottom of the plant.

Runner beans and French or string beans are both imports from South America; the former, like the tomato, originally as an ornamental climber. Both are too tender for winter planting. The French bean is put in light (but fertile) warm soil in spring; the runner bean not planted out until frosts are over, but then given a veritable underground compost heap of its own; really rich damp ground to delve in. Although every British gardener builds a bamboo tent or wigwam to let the plant run up as high as possible no harm is done by pinching it out to make it form a bush – or indeed letting it climb an apple tree.

LEFT: *Runner beans were first introduced into gardens as an ornamental climber. At Helmingham Hall in Suffolk they are trained as a tunnel. Picking them is a pleasure.*

ABOVE: *Onions (which particularly resent competition from weeds) are usually given the second turn in the crop rotation after the legumes. Their leaves are bent over to give their skins full exposure to the sun before harvesting.*

The French eat 'their' bean, the haricot, in various states of freshness or dryness: as *haricots verts* in its crisp prime, as *haricots sec* dried and yellow, and as flageolets in between. They are awkward plants to handle and harvest, needing a certain amount of support (even the dwarf varieties) and being brittle – and also camouflaging their fruit among their stems and leaves. For this reason the purple-podded variety is a boon. It takes half the time of stooping and fumbling to harvest the crop when you can see it clearly.

Peas were amongst the first vegetables to be systematically improved, with the object of breeding some of the hardiness of the round-seeded kind into the much sweeter wrinkly, or 'marrow-fat', peas. The earliest ones, sown in autumn, are still round and scarcely worth growing in rivalry to commercial frozen peas. It is a questionable use of space and effort to grow even the best spring-sown ones today. The (also spring-sown) tender French petits pois and mangetout or sugar peas, which you eat pod and all, are more worth the amateur's time and trouble – especially in small batches sown at intervals to lengthen their season.

Onions and leeks are conventionally given a place in the legume plot to take advantage of recent manuring. Most amateurs today however grow their onions not from seed but from 'sets' – small seedling bulbs started in a nursery. All the gardener does is fatten them, which demands nothing more than a general fertilizer. Shallots are the same, except that they multiply offsets instead of growing fat. Nor do leeks need extravagant manuring – they are transferred in summer (in much the same state of maturity as onion sets) from a seed-bed to their final spacing. There is no hardier or more valuable winter vegetable.

THE CABBAGE FAMILY

Brassica may seem a somewhat esoteric way of referring to the cabbage and its relations, but there is a good reason for bracketing them all together: they are all the same genus. Remarkably enough kale, cabbage, red cabbage, savoys, spring greens, cauliflowers, calabrese, Brussels sprouts, broccoli and kohlrabi are simply selections of the wild *Brassica oleracea* of the sea-cliffs of Europe – a crinkly reddish-leaved plant with pale-yellow summer flowers. Chinese cabbage and bok choy are their East Asian counterparts (and require appropriate pampering in consequence).

In the kitchen garden brassicas share both tastes and pests, being united in thriving only in thoroughly fertile ground with a steady water supply. There are serious pests and diseases that move in on undernourished brassicas – the worst by far being club-root. Brassicas of whatever kind should therefore be moved on to a fresh plot every year; the plot that had its three-yearly deep digging and manuring a year ago and has meanwhile grown peas and beans, acquiring extra nitrogen in the process. Keeping the soil decidedly limey discourages club-root.

The brassica routine therefore goes: autumn digging and liming with 250g (9oz) of ground chalk to each square metre; leave the ground to settle over winter (they like it packed-down and firm); sow seeds thinly in a separate seed-bed with plenty of general fertilizer, transplant the seedlings with a root-ball of soil in good time before they start crowding; plant them firmly so they do not rock in the wind. It was once considered a prudent practice to bury a mothball under each plant to distract pests that home in on the brassica smell.

Kale is the hardiest of the brassicas, essential in the far north as winter greens but in the south generally consigned to the cattle. Brussels sprouts are an old Belgian development of a sprouting kale ('Cottager's kale') which are almost equally hardy, but need constant selection or re-crossing to prevent them becoming kale-like again. F1 hybrid seeds for sprouts are therefore common in catalogues. Since Brussels sprouts are tall and top heavy and need to stand all winter, firm soil is essential and staking a good idea.

Cabbages have been developed to mature in each season. Football-like winter cabbages and Savoys (which differ only in their alligator-hide leaves) are sown in spring. 'Spring greens' are sown in late summer, transplanted in autumn and remain as little plants all winter. The trick is to give them a sheltered place and feed them with a handful of general fertilizer when the ground starts to warm up so that they grow their loose heads rapidly. Red cabbages are also planted in late summer, but take a whole year to mature.

The other versions of *Brassica oleracea* have been developed for their flower-heads rather than their leaves. The glamorous member of the party is the cauliflower, which was originally developed for a Mediterranean climate. None is more greedy for fertilizer or sulks more if conditions are not ideal. There are winter cauliflowers now of considerable hardiness as well as the traditional summer ones, and new Australian ones that mature in autumn. Summer cauliflowers are sown under glass in autumn and kept in a frame until spring. Autumn and winter ones are spring-sown in a seed bed like winter cabbages.

In cold areas broccoli is a much surer and easier plant to grow. It is sown in spring for picking over a long period, sprout by sprout, the following late winter and early spring. Calabrese might be called summer broccoli; a short plant like a cauliflower sown in spring to be ready for picking in late summer.

LEFT: *Whatever form brassicas take they are generally six months or so in the ground – thus lending themselves particularly well to decorative arrangement with other plants – here an espaliered apple.*

ABOVE: *The tomato vine is worth training up a strong (and perhaps decorative) support to carry the weight of the fruit and display its colour.*

Kohlrabi is the odd one out, linking these brassicas with their first-cousins the turnips and swedes. It is a cabbage with very little leaf and a stem swollen into an ugly ball above ground. It is scarcely epicurean, but a summer standby for dry gardens and meagre soil.

THE SALAD BED

Salads are intended to be eaten uncooked, so they should be grown fast in rich moist ground to give no chance for fibres to form. Of all salad plants lettuce is the most important and versatile; with planning and cloches or a cold frame lettuces can be grown almost all year round.

There are scores of varieties, but four principal and recognizable types: the soft round cabbage-hearted or 'butterhead'; the crisp round cabbage-hearted; the loose lettuce with no heart and the Cos – crisp with narrower upright leaves. All grow best in the freshly manured legume department, but are often sown almost anywhere for a quick catch crop. They like lime.

The secret, as with all salad crops, is to sow little and often, and to thin the rows almost continuously, using even the smallest thinnings for salads as you go. Since some are transplanted, others sown in their rows, and the cloche/frame routine varies from variety to variety and month to month, the seed-packet is the place to learn this information.

Without growing under glass there is a gap in the lettuce season in winter; a gap that the many versions of chicory were designed to fill. The Italians, with their penchant for bitter flavours (think of Campari) are the champion chicory-growers. In northern Europe the commonest form is the Belgium witloof, commercially forced and blanched and very expensive to buy. But the beautiful red Verona kind or the green 'Pain de Sucre' can easily be grown in the same manner as lettuce, sown in early summer, and stand moderate winters without protection. Any chicory can be made sweeter by forcing. For mid-winter use transplant it in autumn into boxes of rich soil in a warm dark place, or for spring eating cover it with straw and soil in the garden.

Endive is loose- and curly-leaved chicory. The shaggiest and most tangled is a June-sown, late summer crop. The less curly Batavian endive is more like a bitter Cos lettuce, sown in late summer to crop in winter. Again, its bitterness can be reduced by blanching.

Other good winter salads include dandelion (sown in spring for late autumn) and corn salad, lamb's lettuce or mache, sown in August in rich soil and harvested leaf by leaf all winter. Cloches keep it in good condition and free of splashing mud.

Of the many possible summer additions to the salad bowl, to be sown as catch crops, some of the most worthwhile are the savoury-flavoured Italian rocket (*Eruca*), American cress (for a damp place in shade) and the succulent-leaved Golden Purslane (Pourpier doré) – and of course spring onions and radishes. Sow from March onwards.

Compared with these rapid crops of almost weed-like ease celery and bulb (or Florence) fennel are major operations calling for a luxurious moist and peaty bed. Spinach looks for similar conditions. Courgettes and marrows (overgrown courgettes) are like runner beans, asking for a compost heap of their own and constant cropping. The outdoor or 'ridge' cucumber, a prickly fruit like a gherkin, asks for the same, while the real cucumber needs the warmth and humidity of a frame. Pollination makes cucumbers bitter, so buy female only varieties.

The cultivation of tomatoes, aubergines and peppers in a greenhouse is not difficult, but they do demand daily attention. If they can be given a warm enough place outside they are less demanding. Moreover the best salad tomatoes of thick flesh and Provencal flavour ('Marmande' is one) are unhappy under glass. In Britain everything depends on the summer – as it does with sweet corn. In a hot season sweet corn can be one of the most exciting, satisfying and beautiful vegetables to grow. Sow it in spring under glass in peat pots – to avoid transplanting damage – and plant it out in a block (not a row) in the sunniest corner of the bean department in June. Rush the cobs to the boiling water as soon as they are plump. In no vegetable is freshness more important.

EDIBLE ROOTS

The root vegetables take third place in the succession of crops, after the brassicas have had the best of the fertility. They have no simple organisation or allegiance. In general they like a lighter soil than the greenery (not that you can change your soil from one year to another). They do not like fresh manure; it makes their roots divide. Nor for obvious reasons do they like stony ground. They are sown where they are to grow and not transplanted. A general fertilizer is all they need, except of course for ample water. Nothing but tough old roots can come from droughty starved conditions.

Two of the rootcrops, turnips and swedes, are brassicas and need the brassica routine for good health. Turnips in fact break the rules and benefit from rich ground and quick growth. Sow them at intervals in spring for tender summer roots, harvesting them very small. Turnips grown for their palatable cabbage-like tops and coarse roots are sown in autumn. Swedes are like bigger, sweet-flavoured turnips sown in spring to be ready from autumn onwards.

LEFT: *Potatoes like ground freshly manured, or manured the previous year. They are planted as sprouted tubers (or parts of tubers) in early spring, their early shoots protected from frost by earthing them up (or a covering of straw), then lifted, according to variety, from as early as June to as late as October.*

The most generally useful group of roots are the beets – all developments of the same European seaside perennial, *Beta vulgaris*. Sugar beet, mangolds, beetroot, spinach-beet and Swiss chard (or seakale beet) are botanically from the same stable. Of these the first two are purely agricultural; good beetroots can easily be bought, but spinach beet and Swiss chard are first-class roots to grow, paradoxically, for their delectable leaves.

While real spinach is a temperamental plant given to running to seed unless the soil is rich and the summer damp enough, and in winter needs protection, spinach beet keeps up a perpetual supply of only slightly less tasty leaves with no histrionics. If it is sown in spring it will be bearing well by late summer. Summer sowings crop well in winter. Keep picking the outer leaves to encourage more. Swiss chard is almost as good-tempered though not quite so hardy. Spring sowings are superb in summer, with crisp and juicy white-ribbed leaves. The similar ruby chard has brilliant red leaf-stems. Summer sowings need covering in winter with cloches to be ready for spring cropping.

In summer carrots are almost a salad crop. A succession of small sowings from spring to midsummer keeps a supply of crisp little roots perfect to eat raw. 'Maincrop' carrots are sown in summer and lifted for storage in late autumn: useful for stews but a root without romance. All carrots prefer light sandy soil and need protection from the carrot fly, which is attracted by the smell, particularly during the essential operation of thinning the rows. 'Pelleted' seeds, which are big enough to sow singly and thus save thinning, are one way round the difficulty. For heavier soils there are short stumpy carrots which taste just as good.

Parsnips are an old English native, related to parsley and celery (an umbellifer, in fact) and like parsley slow and uncertain in germination, but very hardy and very sweet. Quick-germinating radish seed is usually sown with the parsnips in March to mark the rows. The long deep roots are ready about October.

Salsify is another one-of-a-kind root, a member of the daisy family, which is grown in much the same way as parsnips, but also sometimes left until the following spring when its new shoots and leaves are good to eat in a time of general vegetable dearth.

Celeriac is a godsend for soils too dry or gardeners too lazy to grow the time-consuming celery. It is a sun-loving, surface-dwelling root of evil appearance but excellent celery flavour, either raw or cooked. It needs a long growing season, which means early sowing in a greenhouse or frame, planting out in early June, and moderate feeding and watering until it is as big as a croquet ball in late autumn. Then like all roots it can be lifted and stored in sand out of the reach of frost.

PERENNIAL VEGETABLES

Meanwhile, apart from all this digging and sowing, there are four valuable perennial vegetables that are looking for a permanent home – not necessarily in the kitchen garden since all, in their season, are beautiful plants.

BELOW: *Globe artichokes and the taller cardoons (seen here) are the handsomest of the perennial vegetables, worthy of a place as ornamental plants in their own right.*

Asparagus is the most luxurious, demanding most space and most care, besides taking four or five years to come into full bearing. Yet its commercial price makes it worth growing if the space is there. It requires light or sandy well-drained ground and a copious top-dressing of manure or fertilizer in late winter. Even the odd couple of asparagus plants are worth tucking away somewhere, perhaps in the flower garden. They will provide two or three intimate suppers in summer and glorious golden ferns in autumn.

Globe artichokes, with their jagged grey leaves, are also quite handsome enough for a border and need minimum upkeep. Replanting offsets from the base every four or five years is enough. A straw mulch in winter protects them and gives them a good start in spring. Cardoons are a rather taller version of the same plant grown for their edible leaf stalks, cropped in the autumn.

Seakale has some of the most beautiful leaves of any perennial, in scallops and volutes of palest grey. Forcing it indoors (traditionally in a cellar) in winter for its succulent shoots is an epicurean pastime.

Rhubarb sounds more worthy but is scarcely less decorative, and deserves a well-manured corner of any garden. Early summer is the normal cropping time for the sanguine stalks (the leaves are inedible), although they, too, are often forced with a box full of straw to be ready a month or so earlier.

SOFT FRUITS

Among vegetables anything short of apple-pie order is immediately obvious. You cannot just let a kitchen garden drift. Because fruit trees and bushes form a permanent part of the garden picture it is easy to pass lightly over them as scenery, forgetting that they have a purpose and should have a routine as clear-cut as a row of cauliflowers.

There is nothing morally wrong about the relaxed attitude that considers it a bonus if a fruit tree actually produces any edible fruit. In a small garden, though, space must work, and if the black currants are not bending and the gooseberry bushes groaning under the weight of their crops it might be better to yank them out and plant roses instead.

LEFT: *Pots are used for rooting the runners of strawberries in summer to move them to new ground. They can also be used as a decorative and clean way to grow a few for eating. This is the early variety 'Gorella'.*

Pruning is the essence of producing a good crop. Unfortunately it is not a thing
one can get right by instinct, since the different bushes bear their fruit on wood
of different ages. It sounds complicated, and it is.

All soft fruits have one thing in common – the need for well-manured, deep-
dug, well-drained but amply watered ground, slightly acid in reaction. Sun is
important, but it is not their first need: better the right soil in a degree of shade.
They also need conscientious weeding, since their roots are shallow and weeds can
give them serious competition. Very light hoeing, herbicides or – perhaps best –
a deep mulch are recommended rather than forking over, which damages the roots.

At some stage they all need protection from birds: the bush fruits in winter
when their buds have formed and again in summer for their fruit; the cane fruits
just in summer. Congregating them all into a fruit cage therefore makes sense.
Ideally the cage should have permanent sides but a removable netting top, which
can be taken off before snow and also during flowering to allow access for polli-
nating insects.

With good cultivation and hygiene (not leaving old leaves, rotted fruit, prun-
ings and other rubbish lying about) and plenty of potash (which all fruit needs for
ripening its wood), disease should not be a problem. Chemicals should only be
used with reluctance and infinite precaution. When eventually a virus or other bad
disease strikes – it will usually catch up with raspberries after eight years or so –
burn the plants and replant with new healthy ones in a different place.

The formal division of soft fruit into those that grow on bushes and those
that grow on canes is a good start for understanding their pruning. Bush fruit
includes gooseberries and black, red and white currants, each of which have their
own idiosyncrasies. Black currants are the easiest to understand: they are sturdy,
vigorous, long-lived bushes that fruit on their newly ripened one-year-old stems.
The principle is therefore to feed them well and prune them hard, cutting off up
to a third of the old wood down to the base each year after it has fruited. 1.8m (6ft)
apart is not too far to space them.

Red currants (and white, which are simply a variety of red) bear their fruit, in contrast, mainly on spurs on their old wood, which makes them very suitable for training as cordons. Pruning them consists of shortening all the main shoots by half the length of last year's growth and the later (or side) shoots to two buds from their base; in other words keeping a main frame of mature wood with short spurs coming off it at intervals. Only when a main branch grows old and feeble is it cut off at the base and a new one trained to replace it.

The gooseberry routine is more like red currants than black. They also fruit on spurs on old wood, but in addition on one-year-old stems. The object with a gooseberry bush is to build up a permanent framework of strong branches to last several years. The laterals are kept short, ideally in a summer pruning session that encourages new fruit buds. With a well-organized bush (it can also be grown as a cordon) you are less likely to lacerate yourself on the prickles.

CANE FRUITS

Raspberries and blackberries, and loganberries, which are a cross between the two (the work of a Scots exile in California), never make anything worthy of the name of bush. Their nature is to keep pushing up long thin canes from the ground to fruit either in their first or second year.

These cane fruits, to be manageable and productive, must be trained on horizontal wires or against a fence. Each needs slightly different treatment, though the principle for all is the same: constant renewal and tying up.

Raspberries are planted only 45cm (18in) apart in rows 1.5–1.8m (5–6ft) apart. They are cut down to near the ground and given a summer to push up new canes, which are tied in to two or three wires, up to about 1.8m (6ft). In their second summer these canes fruit and are then immediately cut off at ground level. A clutch of new replacement canes are meanwhile shooting up in their place. The best six or eight of these are tied up, the rest cut off. Suckers also appear from the

LEFT: *It is not easy to persuade raspberries into such an orderly pattern as other soft fruit. New canes are continually arising from the base and need tying in to a trellis (or uprooting if they step out of line).*

ABOVE: *Fig trees are disorderly by nature. The gardener's main contribution is to simplify their branch structure and to restrict their roots to encourage fruit.*

BELOW: *Cordoned apple trees forming hedges take the place of the spreading domes of old orchards today.*

roots in the fairway between the rows. These are cut off or, better, pulled out. The exceptions to this routine are autumn-fruiting varieties, which are cut to the ground entirely each February and are up and in fruit by September.

Blackberries and loganberries (and also boysenberries) have a slightly more complex routine. They need horizontal wires closer together so that their year-old canes can be tied in at oblique angles to bear fruit while their new canes shoot straight up. The new canes need tying to the top wire while the old ones fruit. The old ones are then cut off and the new ones tied at the same oblique angles as their predecessors were. 2.5–3m (8–10ft) between plants is the conventional spacing for them.

Strawberries, though undeniably soft fruit, are usually grown as part of the vegetable routine and moved every three years or so to newly dug ground. They propagate themselves by sending out runners that root along their length at the tip. If runners which have made good roots are replanted in August in the new bed they will start to crop the next year, but it is better to pick off the flowers and any new runners and be patient. The following year will be the bumper crop. As soon as the fruit starts to form (but not before) put down a mulch of straw or polythene sheet to keep it off the ground, and cover it with bird-netting. When the orgy is over clear up the straw and weeds and cut off all the leaves, and feed the plants with sulphate of potash. 'Perpetual' strawberries never have enough fruit at once to make a real feast.

FRUIT TREES

Hardly any part of the garden has changed more in this century than what used to be the orchard. The traditional evocative picture of spreading standard apple trees is no longer a domestic one and may soon not be seen in commercial orchards either. The revolution of this century has been the almost universal adoption of dwarfing rootstocks, and with it the chance of squeezing more fruit of more varieties into less space – and also making its management, pruning and picking much easier and more economical.

Lovely though the mossy gnarled old apple tree may be, it is a symbol of the past. Where there is room it may well be grown for that very reason. Modern gardeners with little room to spare might do better to be nostalgic about the old standards of craftsmanship that produced fruit trees in perfect fans, cordons, umbrellas and even chandeliers.

The term 'top fruit' applies to apples, pears, plums, cherries, peaches and nectarines: everything that used to be or can be grown on a tree with a trunk. Size-controlling or 'dwarfing' rootstocks were classified (at first only for apples) at the British national fruit research station at East Malling in Kent. Any variety of apple can be grafted on to them and never exceed a predetermined size. They are known by their Malling (or M) numbers: M 27 produces a tree never more than 2.5m (8ft) high; M 9 (the commonest) gives a tree up to 3m (10ft); M 20, M 7 and MM 106 (it was no logician who gave them their numbers) give progressively bigger trees. Quince roots were found to be compatible with pears and made smaller trees than ungrafted pears. Less progress has been made in finding effective dwarfing roots for plums and peaches. Acid (Morello) cherries are always grafted and a manageable size. Sweet ones long defeated the root experts and remained vigorous trees. But new developments have restricted these too.

In deciding what top fruit to grow the gardener should first look at his local conditions. The size, form and number of trees will depend on the space, but in small gardens a large variety of very small trees, ideally cordons, is undoubtedly the best policy. The introduction of 'Ballerina' trees, upright, single stems, offers a new dimension to orchards altogether. Apples in general are least trouble, with no special soil requirements beyond good drainage, generally flowering late enough to escape frost and find enough bees for pollination. But in some districts they are so plagued with bugs that the struggle may not seem worthwhile. Four hundred assorted pests and diseases are said to attack apples in the North Eastern United States.

Pears flower earlier than apples. Late frost is more often a problem. They are generally self-sterile and need another pear tree within 30m (100ft). For good crops they also need more nitrogen than do apples. But the chief problem with pears is catching the fruit in its brief moment of perfect ripeness, between greenness and sogginess. 'Comice' and 'Williams' (American 'Bartlett'), though not the easiest to grow, are the most popular because they keep a good texture longest.

Plums, their inferior form, damsons, and their celestial form, gages, also flower early, are often self-sterile, are demanding of space, light, moisture and nitrogen and cannot readily be restricted. Winter pruning brings the risk of disease. Birds, moreover, often entirely strip the buds. The only plum worth growing in a small garden is the best – the gages, green or yellow, which prefer drier soil and more summer warmth than the others. The 'Victoria' plum has the advantages of being self-fertile and also flowering in midseason, when it can pollinate many others.

Since any trained and restricted fruit takes time and trouble it is logical to choose the most expensive and exotic your conditions will allow. A south-facing wall is an invitation to plant a peach, or better still a nectarine, to train as a fan. Apart from the almost unavoidable peach leaf curl disease, which means regular spraying with fungicide, a peach is no more difficult to manage than a pear. Success with all fruit lies entirely in appropriate pruning, some moderate feeding, and where necessary spraying. It is a test of your mettle as a gardener to be told that apples are today being 'pruned' with a hedge-trimmer with no loss of crop or quality. If your sensitive soul shrinks from the idea of broken twigs and rough ends instead of a precise bud-count you are one of the elect.

ABOVE: *In a French pear orchard each fruit is protected by a paper bag as it grows to ensure unblemished perfection.*

BELOW: *Apricots break into growth and flower very early, making them an uncertain crop in areas with an unpredictable spring. Wall protection is essential.*

COMPOSING
THE
PICTURE

AS EVERY PHOTOGRAPHER KNOWS, A GARDEN WITHOUT A STRONG
ELEMENT OF ARCHITECTURE, UNDERLYING AND OCCASIONALLY
EMERGING FROM THE JUMBLE OF PLANT PATTERNS, IS ALMOST
IMPOSSIBLE TO CAPTURE AS A MEMO-
RABLE PHOTOGRAPH. THE EYE AND THE
MIND BOTH NEED THE REASSURANCE
OF A FIRM LINE SOMEWHERE IN THE
PICTURE BEFORE THEY CAN BEGIN TO
ENJOY THE RICH DIVERSITY OF DETAILS.
IN CLASSICAL EUROPEAN GARDENS THE
LINE WAS PROVIDED BY VISTAS, STAIR-
CASES, SCULPTURE, BALUSTRADES. IN JAPAN IT IS NATURAL
UNSCULPTED ROCKS, REGARDED AS THE UNCHANGING FEMALE
PRINCIPLE IN CONTRAST TO PLANT GROWTH, THE FICKLE MALE. ➤

ABOVE: *Gardens whose layout and character are firmly imposed before planting begins have great advantages. In this 17th-century English garden Proportion, Unity and Utility are almost assured.*

PREVIOUS SPREAD
(LEFT): *Purposeful, simple and bold infra-structure in the gardens of the Villa Noailles near Grasse;*
(RIGHT): *The power of the human form to catch the eye, in Sir Frederick Gibberd's garden at Harlow in Essex.*

The rock-like element of conscious and finished design is something that is missing from most gardens. Many gardeners will probably say they are happy enough without it; that their pleasure is in growing plants. Yet the best gardens are undoubtedly those with the most coherent and clearly stated theme, or mood, or plan – none of which come by accident.

They were, in fact, designed, either on paper or in someone's head. And in most cases the design was built solidly into the site in the form of walls, paths, hedges and steps, pools and bridges, as the groundwork before the subtler, more transitory furnishing with plants was developed.

Design with plants is the ultimate art of the gardener, but design of the spaces between plants is just as important.

Professional garden designers sometimes shock plant-loving amateurs by specifying with great exactness how high each wall shall be, how wide each bed, and choosing their bricks and paving with extreme care (and at great expense) – then leaving only vague directions about the plants to clothe their engineering. There are, strange to say, effective designers whose plant repertoire is brutally limited and banal. They are effective because they work to a well-thought-out brief. They decide what garden picture they want to achieve, survey what resources are at their disposal, and then apply a series of well-tried principles of design which in the abstract may have an air of unreality, but in practice make all the difference between satisfaction and an uneasy feeling that somehow all is not as it should be.

Humphry Repton, who wrote in the days when abstracts were current coin – and still gives every subsequent writer the feeling that it has all been thought, said and summed up for good – spoke of Unity, Utility and Proportion.

By Unity he meant a consistent theme without jarring incidents. By Utility he intended fitness and likeliness for its purpose: avoidance of the far-fetched. And when he said Proportion he meant keeping the elements in reasonable relative scale – not planting an oak in a rockery.

Unity is the ideal that is very rarely reached – at least by amateur gardeners. There are too many temptations to wander into irrelevant and distracting by-ways. Every magazine article that makes you form a mental picture of another 'feature' in your garden is the voice of the devil. Unfortunately it is new features that give most gardeners most fun.

Utility means something much more earthy to us than it did to Repton. Very often it means fitting a quart into a pint pot. We are forced by constraints of space to concentrate on the utilitarian parts, at the expense of growing all the plants we would like, or indeed of a coherent and pleasing design. The more utilitarian our gardens are, however, the greater the need for fit and suitable materials and a logical, workable plan.

The ideal is a garden that fits the habits of the household and at the same time makes the most of its site; that works as outdoor living space and yet uses the relevant resources of nature to make it beautiful, refreshing and inspiring. The first part is rarely achieved by amateurs: the second not often by professionals.

ASPIRATIONS AND RESOURCES

THE HAPPY GARDENER IS ONE WHO HAS FOUND A BALANCE BETWEEN WHAT HE WOULD IDEALLY

LIKE AND WHAT HE CAN AFFORD BOTH IN TIME AND MONEY.

Not perhaps perfect equilibrium: as one of Browning's characters says: 'A man's reach should exceed his grasp, or what's a heaven for?'

Victorian gardening books used to begin with a chapter called Choosing a Site, which recommended a gentle south slope on medium loam with a gravel sub-soil, not to mention shelter from the prevailing winds. It is a very rare modern householder who picks and chooses among soils and subsoils. Today most gardens of any size have had previous owners.

For that reason, a keen gardener is likely to choose an old property that will give him more scope – and hope that its builder read Chapter One. An old garden will also give him some sort of start with mature plants. His approach, therefore, will be quite different from that of somebody moving on to virgin ground. Both gardeners will in the end impose their will on the place. But a new garden needs building, while what an old garden needs is watching.

It is as well to credit your predecessor with having had some reasons for arranging the garden as he did. His thinking may not be obvious at first. But the reasons may well emerge as the seasons change. Who knows what bulbs may be lurking? A weed is a weed and must be pulled, but everything else should be left where it is for a year and duly noted while you formulate your plan.

There are two crucial elements in your calculations, both entirely human and both much more important than mere horticulture. The first is what the garden will be used for, by whom, and when. The second is how much time you, or any-one else, are ready or can afford to devote to it.

From the first question comes a list of the elements you would ideally like. Is the garden to be primarily a playground, an outdoor dining-room, or a picture from the windows of the house? Do you want flowers for arranging? Do you yearn to be cradled in nature's bosom? Is the garden there to fill the freezer, or to let you

LEFT: *A garden planted entirely with low-growing shrubs may not be to everybody's taste, but it carries conviction and a sense of purpose, using difficult ground to memorable effect.*

South or South-west

Bit of jungle for children, to be converted one day into woodland

Tools, compost, bonfire

Vegetables, fruit and flowers for cutting

Main view and prettiest part of garden, with green centre for a feeling of space

Herb bed, or perhaps conservatory-greenhouse

Eating-out area – handy for kitchen and living rooms

Special collection of favourite plants, perhaps miniatures, to be enjoyed at close range, or place to hide swimming-pool behind a screen

Clothes-line, fuel store and other unromantic necessities

Kitchen

Living rooms

Garage, maybe workshops

Approach and parking space

ABOVE: *Before even considering the layout, the style or the individual plants, a personal stock-taking session will provide a brief to work from. It is helpful to imagine that you are your own client. Above is an example of a possible way of assembling the ideas and considerations which will eventually need turning into practical reality. Doodling like this is a good way of trying out different combinations of elements without commitment. Potential inconveniences soon become apparent. The outlook in various directions, the state of neighbouring gardens, the prevailing wind and other notes can be added round the edges to see how they impinge on the developing plan. Such questions as changes in levels, soil, drainage and frost pockets can also be marked.*

lie by a swimming pool? Will you be there every day, or only in the evenings, or only on alternate weekends?

A professional designer would ask a client all these things as a matter of course. Amateurs often forget that they are their own clients and press on with plans that have little to do with the way they live, drawing inspiration from their neighbours' gardens or a local garden centre without questioning its relevance to themselves and their lives.

The upkeep question is harder to answer. Perhaps you are keen to start with, but will be side-tracked to fritter away your life playing golf or ten-pin bowls. Perhaps gardening will grow on you and become a passion: when the children leave home you will want acres to devour. Perhaps help will come. Perhaps it won't.

The essential is to be aware of how long gardening operations take. It is not at all easy to generalize – digging, for example, takes much longer on heavier soil; grass-cutting (one of the major time-takers) takes more time in a wet season – but it has to be faced. Weeding can be a perpetual task, but it can be organized out of existence with mulches and weedkillers. Given (say) five gardening hours a week, would you rather spend them on repetitive chores such as mowing, or hard physical work such as growing vegetables (which, from digging to cropping, provides the most exercise in the garden) or gentle handicrafts requiring more mental than physical effort, such as raising cuttings or tending alpines?

It is a good idea to look round the garden and list the areas which seem to take care of themselves. There are some parts of my garden where I need only go once a year, if that, to tidy up fallen twigs and perhaps dig up elder or sycamore seedlings. They were not necessarily planned as 'labour-saving': they have simply achieved a balance which is more or less self-perpetuating. Areas of heavy shade under trees, for example, may not be thrilling in themselves, but they have a stability that releases your efforts for other parts of the garden – and by contrast they make the sunlit spaces brighter.

The rule is to match your available time to the aspects of gardening you most enjoy, and organize the rest to take care of itself as far as possible. But labour saving can go too far. It is a pity to go out on a fine spring morning with high horticultural anticipation to find that there is nothing whatever to do. I strongly suspect that this is what so often sends householders round to the garden centre looking for kicks. They see some shrub they haven't got, cheerfully in bloom, and hurry home with it. The garden eventually becomes a magpie's nest of ill-assorted plants bought on impulse, with neither unity nor harmony, plan nor purpose. We return to the idea of a plan. The conventional wisdom of gardening books tells us to make a decision about the lay-out, commit it to paper, and then follow it as circumstances allow.

It is a counsel of perfection that few people follow. In the United States it is common practice to have the place 'landscaped' once and for all, but in Europe most gardens emerge over time. Rather than committing themselves on graph paper their owners carry their ideas in their heads, modifying and moulding them as they go along. There is sound sense in this. Creation is much more fun than maintenance. It is a pity to have all your fun at once and have nothing left to look forward to.

Where a plan is probably most helpful is as a survey of the property: its possibilities and drawbacks. A working document like this can record your experience of conditions of wind and weather, sunshine and shade, soil and drainage. By observation of which corners catch most of the sun and least of the wind, where the frost lies longest, where the ground dries out fastest (or lies wettest), you can make an ecological map which will suggest what should go where. There is social ecology too, of course: exposure to the road or the scrutiny of neighbours, nearness to the kitchen for an eating-out place. Views, good and bad, beyond the garden can also be marked.

A ground-plan is also extremely useful for calculating the quantities and details of the garden hardware: its paving, fences and the rest, and precise disposition of plants. It is the method always used by designers.

But when it comes to visualizing alterations, a paper plan is not necessarily the best idea. To those not used to dealing with them, designs on paper have a spurious authority. Once you have drawn a possible place for the path or the line of a border, the matter seems settled. It is probably wiser for amateurs to plan on the ground, using canes and string or flower pots or plastic cups weighted with stones as markers to help them visualize what they propose. Once the concept is agreed, sketches and photographs are invaluable aids. I find that as a non-artist the effort of drawing in itself (especially in perspective) teaches me a great deal about the scene. You cannot draw without observing closely: it is the secret of surveying the garden, as it is of knowing its plants.

Photography has another advantage: it is ruthlessly candid. While your eye can gloss over patches of muddle, a photograph reports them faithfully. It should be in black and white, which brings home the essentials without flattery.

A combination of camera and sketch is best of all. You can draw with a wax crayon on a glossy photograph, or use a tracing-paper overlay and draw on that. Be decided about how far into the future you are projecting; the immediate effect after the alterations or the scene five years hence.

As to priorities, there are two logical starting points (this is for the practical layout of the garden, not its planting). They are the working area of tool-shed, compost heap and frames, the centre of horticultural activities, which cannot logically be thrust away into the farthest corner but needs a secluded spot reasonably near the house, and what the French call the *coin de repos*, the place where you will take your ease.

BELOW: *A London garden planned with total success as a miniature fantasy country garden; its limits screened and its depth exaggerated by intelligent use of perspective.*

ABOVE: *The cottage garden style depends for success on a harmonious muddle of favourite flowers that ignore the surroundings. It can be as convincing in a street as in the depths of the country.*

BELOW: *The formal style is instantly evoked by alignment and repetition; shown here with lavender and young pleached lime trees.*

THE SEARCH FOR A STYLE

Successful gardens, gardens that we remember and return to when we can, have a strong sense of place, a powerful identity that unites their various parts. They may agree with the landscape round about, sharing its views, its land-form and its trees, or they may have to shun it, shutting out a city or a desert behind a wall and starting afresh to make a fantasy world. To be convincing, though, gardens must be coherent. They must settle on a theme and follow it all the way. They must not be waylaid by irrelevancies or seduced by decorations. They may change key for a passage; certainly they must vary their rhythm. But as music respects the dominant, so they must return to their basic style.

Style can mean many things. In garden design it inevitably has undertones of history. It is impossible to be unaware of the centuries of gardening that lie behind us and still shape all horticultural conventions.

Yet there is no precedent for the way we live; for our affluence curiously coupled with scarcity of space and time; for our reliance on society in general without being able to rely on other individuals; for our access to boundless knowledge without the time or the mental training to make use of it. Nothing like us has happened before in history. We cannot garden like our ancestors, and if we could it would be a mere pastiche. We have to find a true style for ourselves in our present condition. And this is where we run into trouble. There are too many pre-packed ideas on offer in books, magazines and catalogues. The resulting muddle is all too obvious wherever we look – including, I hasten to add, in my own garden.

It seems perhaps easier, certainly safer, to take our ideas from books and magazines than directly from our own observations, our experience of nature, or even from other people's gardens. But observation is where style starts. The finest essay on style of modern times is in Russell Page's *The Education of a Gardener*. He describes how as a designer he learnt to look for a starting point. He walked not just round the garden but round its neighbourhood, again and again, noting consciously (and subconsciously) elements that make up its character: the native plants, plants that flourish in other gardens, building materials, building details, the lie and rhythm of the land. The very breadth of the sky and the way the clouds pass may be hints.

Then he selected. From a notebook cluttered with details he distilled what seemed the essence of the place. This of course is where his genius lay: it would be foolish to pretend that everyone can diagnose what is essential with such deft economy. But there is a plodding method.

Inevitably the scale is the first consideration. It is useless to think in terms of wide skies in a hemmed-in yard. By the same token fussy planting in an open landscape will be wrong. One tall tree can dominate the sense of scale in a garden, making other trees look puny. But add a seat, some steps – something on a human scale, and the small trees are given their dignity, the tall one its grandeur.

Climate comes next. The garden should be appropriate for the prevailing weather. In England this is easy: there

are relatively few days in any season when it is not reasonably pleasant to be outdoors. Shade is rarely considered
necessary. Shelter from the wind is the characteristic need
which has given England its tradition of high walls and
splendid hedges. In Scandinavia a sun-trap is the most important thing: the garden should look south and have no trees
overhead more solid than birches. In Spain, shade is all that
matters. Californians have many times had reason to reproach
themselves for having attempted eastern-type gardening in
a rainless land. Two years of drought suddenly make endemic western plants fashionable again.

Then the underlying geology makes itself felt in the
shapes of the landscape; fluid or flat or craggy. Traditional
building materials – stone of a certain colour, brick or tim-
ber – agree with the geology; there were neither means nor reason to build with
anything else. Today concrete is common currency, yet even concrete can be handled and finished in a way sympathetic to local traditions. For not only colours and
textures but scale and proportions were dictated by the local resources.

The soil expresses itself in the dominant local plants. The trees give the country its characteristic outline and texture. This is the broadest hint of all. In cities
and suburbs, however, where all the trees are deliberately planted, there is more
likely to be confusion. To add to the medley with yet another nurseryman's job lot
of one green tree, one gold and one purple is certainly in keeping. But this is not
what we mean when we say style.

In many modern gardens the social environment is a more important factor
than the underlying ecology. The sort of street, the size of plot, the styles of buildings around are overwhelmingly relevant.

Whatever the eye and the mind perceive as the indicators of the sense of place
can form the basis of a style – so long as it genuinely arises from the place itself
and what people have done to it in the past; not out of generalized reminiscence.
Only pastiche can come of that.

This is where courage is needed. For having selected, you must stress. You
must carry the theme to its logical conclusion, eschewing rival ideas which can only
detract from the effect. Self-discipline is essential to produce a recognizable style.

A limitation of any kind makes the decision
easier. A very acid or chalky soil planted simply with the plants that like it best already
begins to have a coherent style. The best-
conceived small gardens are often those of specialists, having the unity of single-mindedness
– boring though a whole garden of irises or
saxifrages may be to more frivolous minds.

A well-kept kitchen garden or orchard
is always enjoyable, because a forthright work-
manlike honesty is forced on it. The utilitarian
style need not be tedious at all – even if it is
hard to make it original. Far better to have a
row of nut-trees and a row of artichokes than
a blue spruce and a sickly palm forlorn in a
patch of unloved lawn.

ABOVE: *The woodland style here is
conjured up by profuse planting of shrubs
to give an effect of heightened naturalness.*

BELOW: *The abstract style of modern
design can be bold and simple enough
even to set beside the visual dominance
of the sea.*

THE HARD CHOICE

There is a fundamental rightness about using the raw materials of the neighbourhood: stone in places where it lies near the surface and shapes the contours of the land; brick in the clay-bottomed valleys; timber in forest country. Materials cannot be a cliché; only the way they are used.

Since hard surfaces of various kinds are essential, for the drives, the paths to the house doors, the terrace and the main garden paths, and since they loom large in anybody's first impression of the garden, they are worth as much creative thought as the plants round them.

As they will also cost more money than any other essential part of the garden – far more than any plants – they should repay in interest and pleasure, in long life and low upkeep, whatever you spend on them.

Bare, hard, plant-free surfaces have three important functions. The practical one is to provide dry going and prevent summer dust and winter mud from finding its way indoors. The aesthetic ones are to furnish the transition between house and garden, fusing them into one unit; and to stand out in contrast to all the billowing, gesticulating growing things around them, acting as the frame to the picture. To be functional they must be well-laid, and above all well-drained. Whatever the surface, whether gravel or wood or stone, the paving process should start with the excavation of 15cm (6in) of soil. If it is good top-soil it is well worth having for other parts of the garden – indeed it would be a crime to bury it under paving.

Into this hole goes 10cm (4in) or so of rubble, small stones or clinker, or anything hard and permanent that can be made stable by ramming or rolling without packing down solid. For slabs or bricks, a smooth surface of raked sand or fine ashes is needed on top of this.

A path made like this has the added advantage of providing drainage for the garden on either side. If the ground is particularly wet it would be worth excavating a bit deeper and laying land drains in the rubble at the bottom of the hole – thus killing two birds with one load of stone. The drains would need a slight slope and a ditch or soakaway at the end. The paving needs a camber or gentle tilt too, to prevent puddles.

Given that the choice of surface is influenced by the local geology, there are still opportunities for the imagination in combinations of textures and patterns of laying. The European masters of paving are the Italians, with their marbles of the musical names – Piastraccia, Arabescato, Travertine, Rosso levanto, Carrara, Portoro machia – and their tiles of subtle colours. By using bands and panels of different colours, or perhaps the same material cut to different shapes, they give a terrace or patio the richness of a carpet.

BELOW: It makes both visual and practical sense to give the garden of a brick-built townhouse a hard floor of the same material. A circular design attracts the eye to the centre.

The detail of Japanese garden paving is full of lessons in the vivid handling of simple stone. Stepping-stone paths are used to extraordinary effect, somehow suggesting tentative, even perhaps illicit, traffic. In one famous piece of paving in Kyoto a stepping-stone path accompanies a severe march of rectangular slabs in an interwoven counterpoint, like the flutterings of a geisha round a man of martial calm. In other places a tide of moss seems to be ebbing from a beach of perfect hand-picked pebbles.

This may be the poetry of paving, but the prose has no need to be dull. Gravel is the cheapest material both to buy and to lay. Alone and unembellished it has no interest or charm, but give it an edging of 60cm (2ft) of brickwork or stone, or perhaps buried baulks of timber, and the contrast immediately gives it the value it lacked.

There are a dozen different ways of arranging bricks (though they always look better on edge) and they can be banded with stone or concrete or bricks laid a different way. As a general rule two materials or textures are enough – more risks becoming a muddle.

With rectangular stone or concrete the interest lies in the pattern of joints as well as the colour and texture. They can be regular or all in line, or busily interlocking – and again there can be panels of another material. Concrete with a smooth cement finish is deadly dull, but with the aggregate exposed by brushing before it sets, and with wide joints (perhaps planks on edge) to stop it crazing as it expands, it can have as much personality as stone.

ABOVE: A wooden board-walk recalling a jetty is completely appropriate to this reed-lined pathway in Lake Forest, Illinois.

BELOW: It is an axiom of design that a detour or even slight curve in a path must be justified by an obstruction. This walk among tall grasses at the woodland edge needs only a lantern to motivate its course.

PATHS AND STEPS

No single element in the design of a garden is as important as where you put your paths. Once paths are made they dictate, not just to the feet but to the mind, the route to follow, the points from which the planting will be seen, indeed the whole shape of the garden. They are the dynamic element in its structure – the track the eyes move on. Even a path you choose not to follow leads your imagination the way it goes.

Someone once made an analogy between a garden and a golf course. In each case there should be tees from which you survey the scene and drive off, bunkers and rough to waylay you, and greens to arrive at and putt (or potter) on.

Paths are therefore worth thought, observation and experiment. They can emerge naturally from use or they can be imposed according to a plan, but any plan must start by considering who goes where. The first object of a path is an unobstructed dry-shod passage. The groundwork paths of any garden must link the doors of the house to the places people go from them – the front gate, the garage, the greenhouse and the rest.

On the other hand, a garden simply criss-crossed with the petrified footsteps of people going about their daily business would be at the same time humdrum and chaotic.

ABOVE: *A steep site demanding long flights of steps is more typical of Italy than England. These steps with high risers are not so much an invitation to climb – they look hard work – as a suggestion of another garden world in the sunlight above, or in reverse as a descent to mossy and ferny depths.*

The planner's mind must see, if it can, a certain pattern in the necessary routes that can be either regularized or romanticized, according to his intentions for the garden as a whole.

If it is to be based on a rectangular grid with straight lines like the classical gardens of the past, any curving path will look out of place and uncertain. The dictates of geometry make it almost inevitable, too, that a right-angled corner of a lawn or a bed will lie across somebody's urgent path somewhere. A short-cut will soon make itself visible. Better to pave the short-cut, perhaps with stepping stones, and compromise the symmetry of the plan than to have a tell-tale bare patch in the lawn or a hole in the border.

The French view of the English style of curving paths is summed up in what was supposed to be a devastating remark: *'On n'a qu'à enivrer son jardinier et à suivre ses pas'* (All you need to do is to get your gardener drunk and follow his footsteps).

The curve, the dominant shape in most modern gardens, is far harder to make coherent and convincing; yet it is infinitely more adaptable, and to modern minds more sympathetic. You may still not achieve your bee-line to the garage, but in the spirit of compromise you will not mind turning a gentle corner round a sweet-scented bush.

How many paths should a garden have? In general the answer must be as few as possible – if only to make them look authoritative. Too many look, and make the looker feel, indecisive. Their business is to conduct you to all the best places, and it is just as well if they let you know when you have arrived by bringing you to a landmark; a seat or summer house or a view. Paths should live up to their promises.

It is even more important to be decisive about changing levels. A slight slope is a marvellous opportunity to make the dynamics of the garden work in another dimension. It should be seized and made obvious, at least with a flight of steps, even when the fall is scarcely enough to justify them. From the top you survey the scene below you; from the bottom you are aware of heights above. 'Sunk gardens' used to be made to introduce the vertical dynamic in level gardens. They have a value as a psychological incident which is in danger of being forgotten.

With levels as with paths the well-worn division into formal and informal rears its head. Formal, straight-line gardens demand levelling, at least on one axis, with walls supporting the artificial horizontals. Informal gardens are all the better for slopes and undulations – not to mention precipices and ravines – so long as they are easily negotiable by steps.

A formal garden on a steep site demands levelling into terraces to be workable. The actual angle of slope that makes terracing essential is about 30 degrees. Even at a lesser angle you can get the uncomfortable feeling that everything is sliding downhill unless at least a broad level path crosses the slope to 'hold' it.

Perhaps the chief reason formality is out of fashion is the cost of the essential groundwork. To 'cut and fill' – the technical term for taking earth from one part of the slope and adding it to another – on any scale is a major operation. What complicates it is the fact that topsoil is topsoil and subsoil is subsoil, in which nothing will grow. If you simply barrow the topsoil from the hump to the hollow you will have double the depth in one place and none in another. To do it properly means taking off all the topsoil first, then cutting and filling the subsoil, then spreading the topsoil evenly again.

It is also essential, or at least highly desirable, to build a wall to support the upper level. A steep earth bank is one of the hardest spots in the garden to plant and maintain. Grass grows badly and is almost impossible to cut. Shrubs are difficult to establish. A 'dry' (or unmortared) stone wall is a wonderful planting opportunity, but a heavy expense – even if you live in natural stone country. A brick wall is very formal, as well as expensive.

For steps as for paths simplicity and generosity are the secrets of success. Garden steps are not like stairs indoors, trying to climb as fast as possible in as little space as they can manage. The risers should be slight – 12cm (5in) is ample – and the treads broad – not less than 30cm (1ft), but more if possible. They should be wide, gradual and substantial in every way. If the height calls for more than a dozen steps it is handsome to have a pause, a landing, perhaps a change of direction. One detail that is always worthwhile if possible is to give each tread a 'nose' – a very slight overhang. The object is to cast a shadow and emphasize the orderly parallels of the treads. The eye looks for such hints of architectural stability in a garden and is strangely satisfied by them.

WALLS AND FENCES

Walls have in the past been so basic to gardens that when in the twentieth century they became expensive luxuries beyond most gardeners' reach it had a devastating effect on design and techniques. All the books that make casual reference to the protection afforded by south-facing walls have taken on an increasingly poignant tone as the cost of simple bricks and mortar has moved inexorably from the unwelcome to the unreachable.

The only walls in most gardens today are the walls of the house and perhaps of the garage. A lucky few still have old garden walls. For the rest the realistic choice is between hedges or barriers of plants, and the range of fences and screens which are the miserable modern substitute for bonded brickwork or morticed stone.

The virtues of walls are not just nostalgic imaginings. They are the appropriate symbol and the actual provider of the shelter and privacy which are proper to a garden. Aesthetically there can be no question that the air of permanence about a wall is a basic garden need. It cannot be met by a fence, which at best tends to look provisional; at worst rickety and improvised. For the look of permanence a hedge is the best substitute. But a hedge takes years to mature. It also deprives the gardener of the great horticultural virtues of a wall: its foot and its surface as the place to nurture plants that need protection, and the warmth that brick or stonework stores long after the sun has gone down.

It is all the more essential then to make the best use of what walls we have, not wasting them on plants that would be equally happy in open ground. Fruit-trees, such climbers as roses that can excel themselves in the extra

BELOW: *The solidity of a wall gives the strongest sense of enclosure and protection, especially when an opening allows the eye to penetrate to another enclosure beyond.*

ABOVE: *Fences and gates allow endless scope for imaginative and inexpensive detail, whether of shape or colour.*

warmth, shrubs of doubtful hardiness and bulbs that need a summer baking all clamour for a south- or west-facing wall. Even north- and east-facing walls have a degree of protection to offer and suit many woodland climbing plants. The one important proviso to bear in mind is that walls exposed to strong prevailing winds develop powerful up, down and side draughts. Climbers, clingers and wall-trees are good for baffling the wind and protecting soft plants below; but they must themselves have sturdy anchorage in the form of well-fixed wires or trellis.

If high boundary walls are at an absurd premium, at least low edging walls still remain a possibility as scaled-down shelter for smaller plants and bulbs. In country where stone is available, dry-stone walls up to 1–1.2m (3–4ft) are not unduly expensive or difficult to construct. Built with thorough and efficient drainage but packed with good soil they can combine the growing conditions of a rock garden and the lee of a sheltering wall.

There will be places, though, in every modern garden where there is no alternative to a fence. No room (and perhaps no time) for a hedge or a group of shrubs; perhaps a desire to grow climbers or fruit trees. It is worth remembering that solid fences are inevitably more expensive, needing more timber, and almost always uglier than see-through ones. Is it really essential to provide a total barrier? Or will a half-open one have virtually the same effect at a distance? It does not take a fortress wall to define a boundary. The job can be done with a mere visual hint: a row of posts will do it, if a boundary is all you need. If the boundary must be a barrier without a chink then close-boarding may be the unavoidable answer.

With all garden construction boldness, honesty and simplicity are essential virtues. With most they are also expensive. Fences are no exception. Flimsy matchboard is both ugly and a waste of money: you need the thickest timber you can afford, supported by the strongest uprights.

If you must save somewhere, save on the infilling, but invest in posts that will see you out. By exaggerating the proportions of the posts you will help to give the essential character of permanence and fitness to the whole fence.

In practice no fence stands for ever: however well-cured the timber, the panels or planks will begin to deteriorate and need renewing after five or ten years, depending on the quality of the wood and the dampness of the climate and exposure

RIGHT: *A wooden trellis fence adds intricacy and vibrancy to a paved terrace which could have been severe without it.*

of the site. One way of preserving and also giving character to a fence which is certainly worth considering – especially in a town garden – is painting it. An imaginative, not a lurid, colour on the fence might be the starting point for colour schemes within the garden.

Nobody has studied fencing with such care and inventiveness as the Japanese. Although permanence is not a quality they particularly respect – even their houses are essentially temporary constructions – they give their fences character and authority by using bold details. They add a deep cap or cornice, or contrasting panels of bamboo and bark, or hold them together with elaborate knots.

This sort of inventiveness and courage is the only answer for gardeners who can no longer afford the first-class materials that were once used as a matter of course in laying out the ground-work of a garden.

ABOVE: *The sense of looking through something, here an airy iron pergola, but also a massive giant thistle, adds depth and hints of mystery.*

SCREENS AND FRAMES

It is a fundamental of good garden design to provide both a sense of direction and a motive for movement: to lure the visitor from one scene to another, so that however delightful he finds the spot where he is, something compels him to explore farther. The sense of curiosity should always be awake. Leaving a door ajar, either literally or metaphorically, is the simplest way of arousing it. Thus the gate, the archway, the frame, the transparent screen, the division that does not divide have an important part to play in gardens.

The power of suggestion is strong. It is enough to place two pillars or plant two cypresses athwart a path for the mind to accept that a new space starts. In the same way a barrier needs no strength to stop the mind. No more than a feather-weight hurdle is needed to provide a sense of the limits to an area. The Japanese close a path to traffic simply by laying in the way a small stone tied up with rope. It is enough. The eye is adept at picking up pointers provided by anything placed in rows, and the feet can be compelled by simple repetition, whether of fence posts, an avenue, a pleached walk or any planting at regular spaces.

BELOW: *The ancient technique of pleaching – in effect of growing a hedge on legs – combines the suggestive effects of screening and framing.*

Even light alone can be an effective form of invitation. A pool of light, like a clearing in a forest, draws the feet irresistibly.

One of the most remarkable examples of the power of suggestion is the art of treillage: making bogus architecture with flimsy trelliswork. The power of making light batons suggest massive masonry reached perfection in eighteenth-century France. It is still absurdly easy to trick the eye with false perspectives made of trellis on a flat background. Alcoves and arcades imitated in trellis laid flat on a wall are effective in pushing out the oppressive limits of small town gardens.

This is not to impute virtue to flimsiness or lack of genuine solidity. A look of

ABOVE: *Improvised sculpture can be compelling. A dead elm tree has provided the material and the inspiration for an abstract sculpture shaped with a chainsaw.*

scene (though they are much safer indoors). In such cases the garden, or part of it, should be made round the statue.

Unfortunately mass-produced copies of a few favourites (which for some reason are never the best) have become commonplace. In the same sense in which original works of art are alive and add their peculiar vibrations to the scene, familiar copies are dead. As Sylvia Crowe says in *Garden Design*: 'It cannot be the genius of the place if it has already been seen in the same role elsewhere.'

It is possible to find a new way of using an old statue to make a fresh point. But luckily the problem is being solved by a new generation of sculptors who have found new ways of creating the essential tension. Where these are abstracts, they have an obvious relationship with the natural rocks which the Chinese and the Japanese have admired for so long.

In very small gardens abstract sculpture or *objets trouvés* have particular value. Where a figure would dominate a small yard, and give the feeling of an alien presence, a beautifully shaped stone, or an enigmatic form of metal, perhaps reflecting the light (an idea totally foreign to classical sculpture) has the opposite effect: liberating the imagination and hence enlarging the apparent space.

Detached pieces of architectural detail can have the same effect. Such things as columns or pieces of architrave out of context and out of scale often have great presence – a useful trick for little city yards. By being surprisingly, almost shockingly, big in a small space they will distract attention from the confining walls and contradictorily make the area seem larger than it is.

If a seat is given a permanent place in a garden it should fill a double role: as an object to be enjoyed for itself, and as the viewpoint from which a well-composed picture is revealed.

Its first role is sculptural. It can be airy and elegant or solid and monumental, but it should be apt for its setting, have an air of permanence, be reasonably comfortable and, preferably, original. (There are as many clichés in seats as in statues).

Its second role is to put the visitor in the place of the gardener, the designer, or whoever contrived the garden. The way a seat faces is itself an invitation. 'Look at it this way', it says. Its view need not be the longest, but it should relate to something palpable, whether it be a broad perspective or a suggestive glimpse, a pool of restful shade or even the scent of a honeysuckle.

RIGHT: *An airy iron seat across a path plays the role of sculpture first, of resting place and vantage point second.*

LIVING WATERS THE GREATEST ASSET ANY GARDEN CAN

HAVE – GREATER THAN A METRE OR TWO OF NATURAL POTTING COMPOST OR A VIEW OF MONT

BLANC – IS ITS OWN NATURAL WATER.

Water wakes up a garden. It is the one element which is biddable to paint pictures and evoke moods at will. The first gardens were water gardens. In desert countries, indeed, gardens are simply celebrations of places where water is plentiful and it is possible to grow trees to create shade and escape the relentless heat. But water is scarcely less valuable in climates of perpetual mist for the liveliness or drama a foaming cascade or a mossy weir can bring to the scene.

The range of water's moods is one of the gardener's greatest opportunities. By merely lying in a placid pond it paints a patch of sky on the ground, throwing the light up again and reflecting the clouds, the blue, the colours of the flowers or the green shade of trees. Then the wind stirs and the ripples race, or dance, and another naiad takes charge.

In movement its moods range from the clockwork monotony of a drip to the varied cadences of a cascade or the proud plumes of a fountain. Any manifestation of water, however small, gives a garden life. It need be no more than the little tinkling dribble that runs into a hollow stone at the gate of every Japanese garden – a perfect symbol for the refreshment of the spirit that waits inside.

An unexpected sidelight on the value of fountains and cascades emerged in research into why the hot dry winds of southern Europe, blowing from North Africa, have an irritating and depressing effect, sometimes even driving people to suicide – as indeed they do. They are charged, it appears, with positive ions, which seem temporarily to alter the chemistry of the brain. The same research suggests that the air around breaking water, on the seashore, under waterfalls and around fountains, is charged with negative ions, which may have the opposite effect: of soothing and giving a sense of well-being.

The Japanese are the masters of garden water. In most of their classical gardens, tucked under the wooded mountain slopes of Kyoto, running water is plentiful. Where there is none, garden designers feel it is so essential that they make believe it is there, making waterfalls of stone and dry stream-beds of sand.

So sensitive are the Japanese to the behaviour of water and its messages to the senses that not even a shower of rain is wasted. The guttering is arranged so that rain becomes an entertainment. As you sit quietly on the matting watching the drops glistening on the pine needles, or weighing down the tall bamboos in graceful arcs of green, the sound of water, splashing, pattering, gurgling and running, rises to a climax with the shower.

Rather than pushing it hastily away into a hole the gardener is playing games with it.

BELOW: At Ninfa near Rome a crystal river is the inspiration and the heart of Italy's most romantic garden, planted in the ruins of a medieval walled city.

ABOVE: *A stream is totally formalized at Buscot Park in Berkshire, dropping in slow degrees through a narrowing glade to a lake in utmost urbanity.*

The water from one bamboo gutter glides into the open top of a vertical cane, to splash out below on to a casually placed rock and form a tiny lake, suggested by a dip in the gravel with mossy sides. Another gutter is of bronze hoops down which the water leaps and glistens into a brimming stone basin. Water from a third is made to shoot into a bronze hopper with a ringing sound.

The Japanese live on rainy islands, yet instead of turning their backs on rain as commonplace they revel in it as a sensuous experience. This is the secret of using water, as it is of using plants.

The best example in Europe of the exploitation of every aspect of wateriness is the fourteenth-century Moorish garden of the Generalife, built on a hill above Granada in the spring-lined route of the snow-water from the Sierra Nevada down to the plain. The limitless water pressure is ingeniously controlled so that while the flow in one place is headlong, in another it ambles along or bubbles with gentle persistence. The famous staircase with liquid handrails is often mentioned: you trail your fingers in a miniature cascade on each side of the stairs. The most postcarded hydraulics of all are the arching jets over the narrow canal in the Patio de la Riadh. But there are scores of other tricks. In one courtyard a natural-looking cave in the hill, curtained with creepers, hides a spring in its mossy roof, constantly dripping water on to ferny rocks. In another a deep stone tank of curious form catches five arcs of crystal water. Before a cloister of creamy stone, honeycomb-roofed, the nipple of a marble font pours out a quiet insistent stream.

Most telling of all, when you have passed through court after court to the brow of the hill, where the ground appears to plunge directly from an alabaster look-out hundreds of feet to the town below, your eye falls, not to the valley floor, but to the little box-hedged garden within speaking distance beneath your feet. From the centre of the garden rises a single sparkling jet to intercept your view of the outside world of dust.

The spouts and mossy shelves of the Villa d'Este, the preposterous hydraulics of Versailles, the calm lakes of Capability Brown are all great set-pieces of garden waterworks. But the possible moods are endless. It used to be thought very funny to squirt visitors with sudden jets – particularly up ladies' skirts. Water could be droll. It can equally be dignified: nothing adds to the dignity of a building so much as its reflection in a looking-glass of water at its feet.

The only mistake which is often and easily made is to confuse the artfully natural with the frankly artificial. All garden waterworks can be divided into the formal, which includes all pools of regular shape, all fountains and any water in a situation where it clearly could not arrive by itself, and the informal, which can only look right if the mind can accept that it flowed there of its own accord.

PONDS AND STREAMS

'Plant the hills and flood the hollows' is perhaps the best-known maxim ever uttered by a landscape gardener. The likeliest fault with naturalistic gardening is that it will look unnatural. A pond will look unnatural anywhere but at the lowest point.

It will also look unnatural if there is an abrupt drought by the brink. A formal lily pond can stand in crisp turf and look correctly neat. But if we are to pretend that the water is there of its own accord then the surroundings, or part of them, must look wet as well. This is the principal difficulty in making a naturalistic or informal pond look real without a stream to feed it.

A perfect pond is easy to imagine. Beneath a crystal surface where shoals of golden orfe are basking your eye reaches the depths where coloured carp smoothly manoeuvre. Gleaming pads support rosy cups of water-lilies, while dapper wildfowl preen and shake spray from their harlequin coats.

Why do we never see a pond like this? Because the waterplants that alone keep the water clear are caviar (or at least asparagus) to both ducks and fish. Wildfowl, moreover, foul the water and raise its nitrogen level, while carp stir up the bottom.The water in a pool or pond is just as full of activity and varied in its population and components as any soil sample. It is not just a simple see-through medium but a living system, composed of water, gases, mineral nutrients (solid and dissolved), plants and animals.

But unlike soil, water rapidly becomes foul if something is missing from the system. A proper economy, a balance of producers and consumers, is essential for any pool or pond to stay clear and smell sweet.

The producers are plants, playing the same role as on land: photosynthesizing and in so doing consuming carbon dioxide and producing oxygen. In most water various kinds of algae, microscopic floating plants, are the most important producers. But in a densely planted or shaded pool bigger plants may have the upper hand.

The consumers are fish, newts, tadpoles, insects, snails and a whole host of greater and lesser fry that eat living plants and each other, consume oxygen and breathe out carbon dioxide.

Below both in the ecosystem come scavengers: animals that eat dead particles, both of plants and animals; and decomposers: microscopic bacteria and fungi that break down dead and waste matter into simpler substances.

The significance of this to a pond-proprietor is that all these orders of life are essential for a 'balanced' system to operate successfully. Small fish can find a place in it; large ones, unfortunately, not.

To garden by a constant stream is a happy state few gardeners achieve. I labour on with pumps and pipes (which, incidentally, are the greatest fun) while studying the successes of my riparian friends. It seems to me the finest effects are always made by damming the stream to obstruct its flow and widen it into pools. The pools provide deeper water (with possibilities for fish) and a constant margin, which makes planting much easier, while the abrupt changes in level at the dams, or weirs, or cascades provide movement, drama and soothing sound.

Again the best effects are made by people who do not overdo the planting – either in the water or on the bank. Two thirds of the water surface at least should be clear of plants to form a simple mirror. And a good proportion of the brink should be clear, too, particularly on the near, or viewing, side. It is too easy to let the rushes, the reeds or the irises get a hold and hide the margin, and a good part of the water.

BELOW: *A stream – natural or artificial – falling over rocks provides the plantsman-gardener with a chance to use marginal plants in an almost alpine idiom. But such a carefree effect takes study and intense maintenance.*

ABOVE: *The serene stepped fish-ponds at Olivers in Essex are naturalistic, but they flank a ride through woodland formal enough to be French.*

There are of course natural ponds without streams, but these present the same problem as unnatural ponds. Above all when the banks dry out in summer. To garden satisfactorily round any pond, in fact, you must be able to keep it brimming full and, at least now and then, slightly overflowing. If you have no stream and no spring then you must have recourse to a hosepipe.

Happily small pumps give us a means of making a big splash with a meagre supply of water by recirculating it. The natural affinity of rock to water, coupled with modern pumps, has given rise to a new style of gardening, one might say the most positive and creative contribution of this century to small gardens in places without natural advantages. For given rock rising sheer from the water, the idiom is immediately rockery or alpine rather than water-meadow or bog. Copious supplies of water are not needed to keep margins wet, except here and there for a patch of primulas. Admitting the unlikeliness of an outcrop of rock and a spring in a small back garden, by borrowing a little of the imagination of the Japanese one can accept a good garden in this style as a miniature landscape with its own laws; naturalistic, but at one remove from the strictly natural.

Since water is in short supply, the first requirement is to make the pond watertight. The old formula used to be puddled clay; that is heavy clay rammed and trampled down in a 30cm- (1ft)-thick layer that no water would ever pass. But there is no mechanical method of clay-puddling. Today's materials are either concrete or plastic or butyl rubber sheeting. Concrete is the surest and most permanent, the least obtrusive, the most adaptable and subject to the finest adjustments. It is also the most expensive and time-taking to lay. 10cm (4in) is the minimum safe thickness, and more is needed if the ground is subject to any kind of movement. Cracks are very difficult to repair.

Sheeting of any kind is simple to put down (on a smooth stoneless bed of sand so that no stones can puncture it). But it remains subject to puncture, and it presents you with a problem round the edge: what do you do with the necessary rim just above the water-line? It is not easy to arrange marginal paving and plants so that no sheeting is visible anywhere – and even a glimpse has a sharply disillusioning effect.

Whatever the lining material it is wise to have no right-angled corners. Curves are easier to clean. With concrete it is prudent to have sides that shelve gradually so that ice can expand upwards and not force the walls out. With all ponds it is useful to have a sump – a distinct low point in the bottom – to make pumping out easier. Indeed a small pond could usefully have a plug leading to a drain or soak-away. 60cm (2ft) is plenty deep enough.

The shape of a pond under construction looks decisive and immutable. In practice it is not so important. So long as there is a good water-holding shell the shape of the water surface can be altered at will by building low walls inside it. The little wiggly-edged ready-made plastic pools sold by garden centres are as unnecessary as they are repulsive. A simple rectangle can be turned into a 'natural' shape by walls retaining soil inside the pond. On the principle that too many marginal plants spoil the view of the water, however, it is best to start with roughly the final shape, then adapt it with plants either in the water or overhanging it from the banks. The plants for these places are discussed on pages 171–3.

More important than the shape is the level. All ponds look best brimming full. To have concrete (or worse plastic) bank showing above the water-line on one side mars all. If the pond is to have an outflow to a stream, a cascade or another pond the height of this weir is your determining factor. The weir should be wide and shallow, not narrow and deep, to hold back as much water as possible. If the levels of the rest of the bank are carefully adjusted with a spirit level and the final height of the spillway is left till last it should be possible to have the pond filled to the brim and just running over at the weir.

If possible a water garden that strives to look natural, even on its own terms, should be screened or set apart from the rest of the garden. If it has rocks, they can provide a spring show of alpines. Summer will bring on the waterside plants and floating water-lilies. At all seasons there can be fine leaves of every imaginable shape, size and hue and in winter the glowing stems of dogwood and willow. But brilliantly coloured bedding plants, above all roses, should be kept out of sight. Both the pond and the bedding would look banal and absurd in juxtaposition. Even in falsifying – perhaps most of all in falsifying – it is vital to preserve integrity.

POOLS AND FOUNTAINS

A formal pool is quite a different proposition. Here you are not borrowing or re-creating the picturesque passage of the hydrological cycle. You are frankly decorating with water. The emphasis is not on its natural life but on its capacity to reflect, to glitter, splash or cool.

There will be no question of making the pool fit in with the landscape: its purpose is to stand out. An improbable site is all to the good. One of the simplest ways of emphasizing a pool is to raise the water level above the ground: to make it a walled tank. The reflections, being nearer the eye and at an unexpected angle, make more impact than if they are lying tamely at your feet. The famous tank garden at Hidcote in Gloucestershire carries this principle to an extreme. Almost the whole of a circular yew-hedged enclosure is taken up with a waist-high stone tank, brimming full. Walking round it, running your fingers through the surface, you are intensely aware of the circle of sky framed by the black yews beside you.

BELOW: The foam of fountains among rose-beds and statuary at Rottneros in Sweden turns away from nature in celebration of decor.

Sir George Sitwell studied the Italian use of water and described some of its effects in his great essay 'On the Making of Gardens'. 'Water-reflections,' he wrote, 'are actually more delightful than the views they repeat . . . for the gloss of the water-film is like the coat of old varnish that mellows a picture; it gives breadth, connection and unity.'

Clearly the pool must have something pleasant to reflect. Good architecture makes the best reflections of all. The modern house that is worth reflecting, however, is rare. This

is where small figures, statues, pergolas and the tracery of nearby trees are all-important. Half the point of all the balustrades and nymphs and putti round Italian pools is their doubling in the water. Then suddenly 'that strange power the eye has of clearing away reflections by the change to a longer focus' shows us the fishes and the submerged plants and their shadows on the bottom.

With formal pools the water is the point; not the plants, but there must be plants, and fish, or the water will stagnate. Water-lilies have all the qualities of sculptured formality you could want. But they must not be allowed to get out of hand. At least two-thirds of the surface should be open water. It is possible to use only underwater plants and have a clean and healthy pool, but difficult without some degree of shade: constant sunlight promotes the growth of green plankton or algae. Without competition they can make the water too green.

It is better to avoid waterside or water-related plants at the margin: better to emphasize the architecture of the edge and move smartly to grass or plants of contrasting character. Perhaps a single clump of iris or reed, a sudden vertical, will emphasize the strong horizontal of the water. Perhaps, on the contrary, it will just look bitty and indecisive. Certainly one sees many pools where a small concession to marginal planting has grown inexorably until an unkempt fringe straggles halfway round the water.

If any proof were needed that water is not an inert medium it is the amount of chemicals and filtration we need to keep a swimming pool in the artificial state we are pleased to call clean.

Maintaining swimming pools is scarcely gardening, but swimming pools are important components of modern gardens – now certainly the commonest form of 'formal' pool. If they were full of black reflecting water they could be a valuable part of any garden plan. Unfortunately the relentless blueness of the majority makes them stand out as sports equipment, almost impossible to harmonize with the proper tranquility of a garden.

Except in the Californian idiom of outdoor living, it is generally best to let a swimming pool dominate a compartment of its own and avoid having to seek uneasy compromise in the rest of the garden. Let it be near the house but screened away by a thick hedge or a tall wall; a garden room for bathing – never the centrepiece of the garden. Attempts to disguise them as other than swimming pools by adding fountains, islands and other gimmicks very rarely work.

The fountain is to the pool what the stream is to the pond, yet compared with busily trickling cascades fountains are sadly out of fashion. It is quite in keeping with the philosophy of our times that water going uphill is considered wasteful and ostentatious, while water going downhill is environmentally acceptable – or some such cant – even if it first has to be pumped up behind the scenes.

Yet perhaps we overlook the role of fountains as celebrations of light and water: events rather than processes. There is no need for a fountain to be always playing. Even those at Versailles were only turned on for parties.

Even if a fountain is essential to wake up what would otherwise be a dull or sombre pool it can easily be engineered to have several moods: bubbling perpetually, perhaps; surging on Saturdays and rising to a plume only on still, sunny days when there is something to celebrate.

APPOSITE ASSOCIATIONS APPROACHES TO

PLANNING WITH PLANTS VARY FROM THE METICULOUS TO THE HIT-AND-MISS. SOME GARDENERS

WILL NOT STIR UNTIL THE WHOLE GARDEN IS MAPPED OUT LIKE A MILITARY CAMPAIGN.

There are others (the majority, I strongly suspect) who wander round vaguely with their latest plant acquisition in their hands. They try vainly to visualize it in flower, out of flower; next year, five years hence, and finish by planting it in the only available space – or so they think until they find their fork crunching into a lurking bulb.

The latter are not lost souls. They include excellent gardeners who simply have poor memories and unmethodical minds. Some of the most experienced gardeners never make deliberate plans but go by 'feel', often shifting plants from place to place as they outgrow their positions, or simply to enjoy the effect of a new combination of shapes and colours. Experience brings confidence in moving plants about – some plants even seem to enjoy it.

It is an excellent idea to plan your basic planting in black and white before you even consider colour. It may eventually be the colour that will beguile you and create the mood of the garden, but just because colour is so beguiling it can blind you to weaknesses in composition, and leave boring patches where no shape or texture stands out to give point to the rest.

Everyone can think of associations of two or more plants that have made them pause and look twice; perhaps appreciate some shape or texture for the first time; or perhaps just given them the pleasure that harmonious composition of any kind can give. A good garden is full of these incidents, from its general plan down to touches of minutest detail.

Such associations can take place on one of several planes. They can be contrasts or complements, involving shapes, sizes, tones, textures, modelling or form, bulk and apparent weight. They can take place entirely on an intellectual level: because we know that a group of plants grow together in a certain mountain range, or are all indigenous to a region, or were collected or bred by one man. They could all be roses Josephine grew and Redouté painted. E. A. Bowles had a corner of his garden where he planted all the deformed and contorted plants he could find. Indeed, there are countless reasons for planting this next to that before turning to what is now the overriding consideration: colour.

Importance in the garden picture is related to density as well as to size. Density could be described as the apparent weight of an object. Dense objects have more impact than diffuse ones. Tones as well as masses have their apparent importance – a fact that black and white pictures show much better than pictures in colour. Dark tones recede; light ones advance towards you. There can be a fundamental contrast between two otherwise very similar plants – and hence an apposite association – just because one reflects more light than the other.

ABOVE: *Mingling similar but unrelated foliage makes a minor garden incident – but appeals through its quiet demonstration of harmony.*

BELOW: *Association is not limited to plants. The owner of this thatched cottage had the wit to see that its old box hedge could echo its tumbling contours perfectly.*

ABOVE: *A repetition of shape and colour in two plants which are quite different is a telling form of association; here played out in* Veronicastrum virginica 'Alba' *and* Macleaya cordata.

Contrast for its own sake can easily be (and often is) overdone. A garden that sets out to alternate big with little, light with dark, matt with shiny, relentlessly all around you is fidgety and unrestful. It is essential to establish a dominant theme or scale first; then to look for the right variations on it. A single fern growing by a rock in a wide area of moss is far more effective than a scattering of the same fern here and there throughout the moss. On the other hand scattering different ferns at random would be a greater mistake.

Perhaps the most telling associations of all take the form of a visual pun, when in one sense two plants are the same; in another quite different. An example might be plants of precisely the same shade of green but on a totally different scale. The designer Sylvia Crowe gives as an example box and banana leaves used in the gardens of the Alcazar, Seville. Another example might be bergenias and winter heliotrope in early spring. The leaves of both are big, bold, roundish in outline and low on the ground, but the bergenias are dark and richly glossy, the heliotrope's pale and completely matt. Another is bridal wreath, *Francoa ramosa*, with the wand flower, *Dierama pulcherrima*; two tall, slender waverers to interweave their white clusters and purple bells.

In a wider garden sense, a mixed border for example, there are bound to be contrasts and complements to be picked up and enjoyed if you can detect them in the general jumble (though many border plants, particularly the daisies, are depressingly similar in structure). Here the secret is to choose a particular motif and make it sufficiently obvious. Gertrude Jekyll's famous border was interrupted by a doorway flanked by terrifying great clumps of the prickly *Yucca gloriosa*. Next to it came a great tumble of the big spurge of lighter grey-green colour (*Euphorbia characias* subsp. *wulfenii*), but in long knobs instead of spikes. Then farther along the border the sword-leaves of irises reminded one of the opening chord of yucca.

THE NATURE OF COLOUR

Some of the world's greatest gardens have limited themselves so radically in the use of colour that one can almost say it was omitted from their philosophy entirely. The great Italian Renaissance gardens were compositions in form and mass, light and shade – but not in colour. At Versailles the flower colour in the parterres

RIGHT· *'Shadows are in reality, when the sun is shining, the most conspicuous things in the landscape next to the highest lights' – John Ruskin's remark explains the rich variety of colours provided by only two kinds of flower, a peony and a pansy, both red, with rain bending their petals so that the light is reflected quite differently from either side, giving the effect of completely different tones.*

was entirely coincidental to the great architectural and spatial concept. The English landscape garden was thought of in terms of space, planes, modelling – and, of course, historical and literary associations. The colours were green, stone and water. Organized plant colour seems to have come late into the consciousness of garden designers. Sir William Chambers (1723–96) is said to have been the first to suggest the substantial grouping of flowers of one colour to form a patch.

Today we tend to put more emphasis on colour, both in flowers and leaves, than on any single aspect of gardening; yet with remarkably little knowledge or understanding. Most gardeners are entirely undiscriminating. Many nurseries sell seeds of popular flowers in 'mixed shades'. Their criterion is brightness, regardless of quality, or of what the colours may do to one another. Similarly among trees and shrubs any colour is conceived to be an improvement on 'mere' green: purple- and gold-leaved trees proliferate not because those colours are good in themselves or do anything more than muddle the picture, but because they are, simply, 'colours'.

There are a few gardeners who have a painter's – and it needs to be a painter's – understanding of the relationships between colours and the harmonies that are possible with their careful use. The musical image is apt, for what happens when

ABOVE: *Light has a 'colour temperature', conventionally measured in 'degrees Kelvin' – a measure of the temperature to which a notional black object would have to be heated to emit light of a given colour. The chart above shows the colour temperature of light from various sources, ranging from the low-temperature light of a candle to the very high-temperature light of a bright blue sky. Despite appearances, and the conventional feeling that blue is a 'cool' colour and red a 'warm' one, the photograph (above left), taken at noon, has a much higher colour temperature than the photograph (left), taken in the glow of dusk.*

*The pure hue above is **red**; at half-strength **rose**; as a very light tint it becomes **pale pink**.*

*Red moving towards blue is **magenta** at its most intense; fading to **mallow**, and at its lightest to **orchid pink**.*

*The half-way hue between red and blue is **purple**, fading first to **violet**, then **mauve**, then **lavender**. **Lilac** is another name for a pale purple tint.*

*Blue with red added is **gentian** at its most intense, **delphinium** at about half-strength, becoming **periwinkle** as it grows paler.*

*Pure or **spectrum blue** is extremely rare in flowers. A slightly paler form is **hydrangea blue**. **Forget-me-not** is a washed-out pure blue.*

colours interact can be almost as powerful, and yet remains as mysterious, as the mingling of musical sounds.

What, for a start, is colour? It is reflected light, edited by the pigment of the surface that is reflecting it. Unreflected daylight is more or less white. White light is a combination of all the colours of the spectrum (or rainbow). The function of a pigment is to absorb some parts of the mixture and reflect back the others – which we see as its colour. The more pigments there are the more light is absorbed, and the colour is said to be 'saturated'. Not only the pigments but also the texture of the surface affects the reflection. A piece of satin and a piece of velvet may be dyed precisely the same colour, yet the satin will appear lighter, since its smooth texture reflects more light.

Pigments are coloured molecules, which like all molecules contain electrons that determine which colours are absorbed and which reflected. If the electrons have short, rapid wave movements they absorb the short light waves, which are blue, and by consequence reflect its opposite, which is yellow.

Not only do we find a wide range of pigments in plants, but their ability to absorb or reflect depends on the chemistry of other substances present in the plant. Proteins, tannins, sugars and acids are all able to affect their colour.

Of the two main classes of pigments one is insoluble, existing in the sap as minute solid particles. These are the carotenoid (yellow to orange) pigments, including xanthophyll, which provides the yellow of roses, and carotene, which makes carrots (and shellfish) red. The question 'why did the lobster blush?' has the single answer that a combination of carotene and proteins kept it blue while it was on the sea-bed. But when the water boiled the proteins took their leave.

The second great class of pigments are the anthocyanins, which are soluble in water and hence liable to even more volatile behaviour, readily reacting, for example, to the acidity of cell-sap. Among the anthocyanins are pelargonidin ('geranium red'), delphinidin ('delphinium blue') and cyanidin, the red of roses until a genetic mutation brought pelargonidin into the sap of the startling 'Super Star'.

Between them these three cover the spectrum, with the exception of yellow. Not just acidity but combinations with sugars and tannins make delphinidin, for example, vary between greenish-blue and magenta, and pelargonidin between scarlet and violet-blue. As far as simple acidity is concerned they react like litmus paper, turning red in the presence of acid and blue in an alkaline solution.

It is the anthocyanins that give a reddish tinge to new shoots and leaves; many roses are examples. Again in autumn they form in the sap in reaction to high light intensity and low temperatures – turning the leaves, as their chlorophyll ebbs, to the vivid reds, oranges and purples of autumn.

So these are the 'true' colours of plants; their pigments. But if colour is reflected light, the other important element is the light being reflected. For the intensity and 'temperature' of daylight vary all the time, from dawn to noon to dusk, with the angle of the sun and with the passing of clouds. They vary even more with the latitude and the humidity. In Britain the light is always slightly soft and blue. Mediterranean and sub-tropical light give harsh contrasts and violent shadows.

The more intense the light, the stronger, more absorptive, more 'saturated' the colour needs to be to give a truly 'coloured' impression; the dimmer the light, the more the reflective power of pale colours makes them glow. Pastel colours look feeble at noon in summer even in Britain; far more so in Mediterranean light – but towards dusk they show up more and more. By nightfall red flowers have disappeared altogether, while white ones shine like lamps.

LEFT: *A full-dress double herbaceous border in full cry demonstrates that harmony and contrast both have their place in an ambitious and confident planting scheme.*

BELOW: *The colour wheel is a conventional way of demonstrating the relationship between the colours of the spectrum by dividing them into segments of equal width. It ignores the fact that the wave-bands of different colours as seen, for example, in a rainbow are wider or narrower in order to show the complementary colours directly opposite to one another. This very early colour wheel was painted in 1839 by the French chromatographer Chevreul, who designed the Gobelin tapestries of the period. Since his time the range of colours available in paint pigments and dyes has been enormously enlarged. Turquoise, for example, was very subdued until the 1930s, when ICI produced the brilliant pigment known as monastral blue.*

CONTRAST AND HARMONY

The sort of colour co-ordination taken for granted in decorating and furnishing a room is rare in garden planning. Partly I suspect it is because most of us are very vague about the precise colours of flowers. They come and go leaving an imprecise memory. Hardly anyone goes to the trouble of finding their exact match on a colour chart, or even picking a flower and carrying it over to another plant to see whether the two 'go' together or not. Timing is not so simple either – we may think two plants will complement one another only to find that one has finished flowering before the other has really started.

Time is the enemy in another way as well. We only find that our two rhododendrons look perfectly horrible in flower together after we have spent several years nurturing them. So we live with the swearing colours and comfort ourselves with the untruism that the colours of nature cannot clash.

In a garden colours are never seen singly as they are on a colour card. There is always a context of surrounding colours – with green, of course, normally dominant. Which means there is always an interaction: the colours are always affecting each other for better or for worse, for louder or quieter, for lighter or darker.

The language of colour is concerned with defining and naming particular points on the spectrum or colour wheel and describing the relationship between them. Colours which are neighbours in the spectrum normally harmonize with each other, while those on opposite sides of the wheel contrast. Red and green, for example, are 'complementary': that is, in maximum contrast.

Red, yellow and blue are described as 'primary' colours because all other colours can be produced by mixing them. Side by side they produce violent contrasts, having nothing at all in common. The three mid-points between the primary

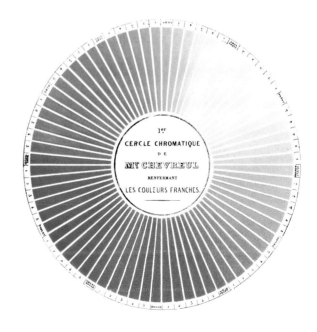

ABOVE: *Harmony is achieved here by
sticking to the blue-mauve segment of the
spectrum analyzed on page 226, lightened
with white and softened with green.*

colours are green, orange and violet. Although they also contrast the effect is less violent; they have certain pigments in
common. Various 'triads' of colours (produced by turning
an imaginary triangle in the colour wheel) are classic examples of successful and satisfying colour-planning.
Sage/plum/buff and citrus/slate/russet bear the same relationship to each other as red/yellow/blue, yet they
emphatically harmonize rather than contrast.

In technical terms each colour is given three 'attributes'
or 'dimensions': its hue (that is where it occurs on the spectrum; if you like the 'pure' colour); its tone or brightness
(which means how much of the pigment is present; therefore how much light it absorbs; therefore how intensely
'coloured' it appears); and its saturation, or purity. In the
spectrum the colours are fully saturated – as pure as possible. Any mixture with grey or white lessens their purity and
hence their degree of saturation.

Contrast and harmony depend not just on the relative
positions of the hues in the spectrum but also on their other
'dimensions'. There can well be a contrast between neighbouring colours if one is very dark in tone and the other very
light, or one is intensely saturated and the other washed out.
Conversely colours that, judging by their place on the spectrum alone should contrast strongly, can appear harmonious
if they share a common dimension in, let us say, a very light tone or a very dark one.

Artists give precise meanings to such dimensions of colour. 'Tone' is a pure
hue darkened by the addition of grey, scaled from 0, the lightest, to 10, the darkest. 'Tint' is a hue lightened by the addition of white, 'shade' a hue darkened by
the addition of black.

It is easy to exaggerate the difficulties in a barrage of jargon. But in practical gardening experience there is an unexpectedly simple rule of thumb at hand,
which is that the spectrum divides more or less evenly along a line drawn between
green and red, into those flowers and leaves containing blue in their make-up and
those containing yellow. Many very effective colour schemes are made by the free
use of one or the other of these two ranges, with only very limited and careful (if
any) interpolation from the other.

A SINGLE COLOUR

The short cut to making a big impact with colour, as with everything else in the
garden, is to be ruthlessly singleminded. If you can bring yourself to devote a part
of your garden to one colour only, with variety limited to heights, shapes and tones,
you will have a picture people will take away with them. It need only be for one
season that you impose the rigid discipline. It is possible – though far from easy
– to have a garden that is yellow in spring and red in the autumn: but for total
conviction the whole setting, including the leaves of the background shrubs, or
hedge, or trees, must be made to join in the scheme.

The monochrome garden seems to have been yet another invention of the
astonishing Gertrude Jekyll in the last quarter of the nineteenth century. As a
painter she studied and understood colour better perhaps than any gardener before

her. In devoting whole self-contained sections of gardens to single colours her idea was to set moods in motion. Like all designers she wanted to manipulate the reactions of her audience. By making them pass through an archway from a cool enclosure of blues and greys to a glowing gold and yellow garden she could be sure of exclamations: 'It's like sunshine after rain!'

Strong doses of one colour undeniably affect the mood of the viewer. If yellow is warming and cheering, soft blues and mauves are soothing, red and orange are exciting, white is at once peaceful and lively, fresh and yet somehow formal.

White is much the easiest single colour to handle. The choice of white flowers is almost infinite. A remarkable number of flowers that we think of as being other colours have a white form as well. There are white agapanthus as well as blue, white campanulas, white phlox, white roses, white (or at least cream) red hot pokers,

ROOTS IN HISTORY

OUR PRESENT SET OF IDEAS OF WHAT CONSTITUTES A GARDEN HAS

LONG ROOTS BACK INTO HISTORY; NOT JUST OF OUR OWN

COUNTRIES BUT OF ALL CIVILIZED LANDS.

AS FAR AS WE KNOW GARDENING FIRST

STARTED, QUITE INDEPENDENTLY, IN TWO

PLACES – EGYPT AND CHINA. EGYPTIAN

GARDENS WERE BASED ON IRRIGATED

SMALLHOLDINGS IN THE DESERT, CHINESE

ON IMPERIAL HUNTING PARKS IN WHAT

WAS THEN THE RICHEST COUNTRY IN

PLANT LIFE THE WORLD HAS KNOWN

SINCE THE ICE AGES.

THESE TWO SOURCES STARTED TRADITIONS THAT WERE

DIAMETRICALLY OPPOSED IN EVERY WAY, AND WHICH CAN BE ➤

ABOVE: *Beth Chatto's new woodland garden in Essex develops one of the great themes of 20th-century gardening, bringing deep understanding of plants to a sublimely simple conclusion.*

summarized as the formal and the informal; the straight-edged and the flowing; the architectural and the naturalistic.

Until the beginning of the eighteenth century the Egyptian tradition, transmitted through the Greeks and Romans, the Persians, the Moors, the Italians and the French, reigned supreme in the West, but had no influence at all in the East – east of India, that is. Then suddenly the English started to garden in what was to all intents and purposes the Chinese way. To what extent Chinese ideas reached and influenced Europe is still unclear. Missionaries in China sent pictures that were certainly known to such connoisseurs as Lord Burlington. Sir William Temple, in 1692, wrote about the 'pleasing irregularity' of the Chinese style.

Whether Chinese or original or both, though, the English style was taken up wholesale in the century that followed and has been, with the exception of occasional classical revivals, the dominant mode of thinking about gardens since. In turn, however, it has borrowed from the vocabulary of the classical style, so that today in most deliberately planned gardens the two idioms are inextricably mixed.

None the less there remains the basic dichotomy of what we now call the 'formal' and the 'informal' – which goes straight back to the diverse roots of our gardening ideas.

The principal development that has overlain this chopping and changing of styles has been the stress laid on plants for their own sakes. The story of modern gardening, from the late eighteenth century on, has been the story of greater and greater interest in plants and more and more variety, with correspondingly less emphasis on the underlying design of the garden.

The limit of the undesigned garden was reached with the concept of the woodland garden, which started in the middle of the nineteenth century and reached its climax in the middle of this. Woodland gardening is closely linked to the cult of the rhododendron. (The first Himalayan kinds need sheltered forest-like conditions.) Some woodland gardens began as collections of specimen trees and surprised their owners by turning into woods as the trees grew. Some of the best have a plan of glades and vistas derived in part from the classical, in part from the naturalistic schools. Many, however, are simply highly coloured woodland with all the thought given to the cultivation and juxtaposition of plants.

Where layout is concerned, if there is a significant modern departure from the twin traditions it is towards abstract shapes echoing ideas in painting and sculpture. Modern patios and small gardens frequently have no straight lines or traditional formality, yet their flowing forms are definitely not of nature's making. Their spiritual ancestors are the works of Mondrian, Picasso or Moore – even if Mondrian's and Moore's was Michelangelo, and Michelangelo's the classic theories of Divine Proportion and the Golden Rectangle.

PREVIOUS SPREAD
(LEFT): *Fragonard's 'Le Petit Parc' has lessons for garden design of all kinds and times . . .;*
(RIGHT): *. . . and so does a lacquer bridge in Japan.*

IN A PERSIAN GARDEN MEDITERRANEAN,

AND HENCE THE WHOLE TRADITION OF WESTERN GARDENING HAD ITS ORIGINS IN EGYPT

BETWEEN THREE AND FOUR THOUSAND YEARS AGO.

Since Egypt is a natural desert, depending for its fertility entirely on irrigation from the Nile, its gardens were planted round reservoirs and along canals of the kind used for irrigation. The canals were straight for practical reasons; trees planted for shade naturally followed them in straight rows. It was logical to have the main water tank for supply, for fish, for the sacred lotus and for general refreshment and repose in the centre.

Hence, the theory goes, the axial designs, the straight lines, the 'formality' of all classical Mediterranean-inspired gardens to our own day – via the Persians, whose style swept eastwards to India and westwards to Spain with the spread of Islam, and the Romans, whose adaptation of Egyptian style was eventually to be repeated by the Renaissance.

The Persians have a special place in the story of gardening. No race has been more captivated by garden pleasures. In the words of the historian Arthur Upham Pope 'the need for a garden is more deeply rooted, more articulate, and more universal in Persia than the Japanese passion for flowers or the English love of country'.

The vast aridity of Persia and its pitiless sky made the high-walled garden, with the shade of its trees and its air cooled by streams and fountains, the simple recipe for paradise. The Koran's promise of paradise, in fact, is precisely that – a steady supply of black-eyed houris 'of resplendent beauty, blooming youth, virgin purity and exquisite sensibility', in a garden pavilion shaded with palms and pomegranates, beside streams not only of water but of wine and honey. The word 'paradise' originally meant a hunting park, and it is still a Persian word for garden.

The Persian garden plan remained resolutely formal; an elaboration of the Egyptian plan, commonly based on the form of a cross. Two main waterways divided the garden in four – representing, it is said, the four quarters of the universe. Often the centre of the cross was a brimming tank, lined with blue tiles to accentuate the freshness of the water. In bigger gardens subsidiary canals divided and subdivided the space again and again. Little tinkling jets and rills made sure that the water was heard as well as seen. Tall chenar trees (oriental planes) shaded the centre, while round the edges cypresses, pines, poplars, date palms, almond, orange and other fruit trees cooled and scented the air. There are no statues, as Islamic law forbids idols in human form.

The season for flowers is brutally short in Persia, which must have intensified their pleasure in them for the brief duration of spring. The canals were sometimes lined with borders of flowers (as they are in the Generalife gardens in Granada, a direct descendant) and flowers were encouraged to grow promiscuously in long grass (or clover, which stayed green for longer) under the trees. Tulips, irises, primulas, narcissi,

BELOW: *Water as the expression of life: the 14th-century Generalife gardens in Granada are the finest still existing in the Persian/Arab tradition.*

RIGHT: *The Mughal Empire of 16th-century India has left us our clearest pictures of the garden art developed in Persia and Arabia. Two distinct traditions appear: the formal and the natural, or naturalistic. In this painting of Prince Babur at the spring of Khawaja Sih Yaran the two are strangely mingled. A mountain stream pours from a lion's mask high in the hills, then cascades down to fill a formal pool where ducks play, then flows on as a wild brook among rocks.*

jonquils, hyacinths, hollyhocks, evening primroses, violets, anemones, pinks and carnations, lilies, lilac and jasmine are all mentioned. Many bulbs are natives of Persia, but the Persians were also the first people to go plant hunting abroad.

Their most treasured flower of all was the rose – partly, it may be, because it went on flowering when other flowers were past. Persia's native roses include the brilliant yellow and red *Rosa foetida*. Almost certainly trade or conquest had introduced the Chinese perpetual-flowering rose.

Lacking flowers in summer the Persians used faience tiles on every surface to provide colour. Some early paintings show wide pavements of green tiles as a substitute for grass, which would inevitably be brown for most of the year. Ornamental fowl were another way of bringing colour into the garden. Peacocks are native forest birds of India, from Assam south to Ceylon.

By the thirteenth century, following the almost incredible campaigns of the Mongol emperor Genghis Khan, the routes to China were well established and the Chinese influence can be seen distinctly in Persian painting. All the surviving paintings of gardens date from this period or later, and many of them show strangely Chinese-looking features; not only details of architecture but naturalistic meandering streams with rocky margins. In fact Chinese gardening. Whether such gardens were ever actually made or not, it is the first meeting of East and West in garden art.

ITALIAN GARDENS IT IS EASY TO GAIN THE IMPRESSION
THAT THE HISTORY OF ITALIAN GARDENS IS WRITTEN IN THE MARGINS OF THE HISTORY OF

ITALIAN ARCHITECTURE.

All the characteristic features seem to be builders' work: staircases, balustrades, cascades, pavilions and pavements – even the cypress avenues are imitations of colonnades. Certainly when we speak of a garden in the Italian style we mean one with more than a modicum of masonry – and thus, alas, one of a kind that will probably never be built again.

The origins of the style are obviously found in Ancient Rome. The rich Romans were as adept as anyone has ever been in the theory and practice of making themselves comfortable. They took the greatest pains to site their villas on hillsides with exceptional views, where cooling breezes would reach them, above the malarial valleys. Within the villas

there were courts and colonnades designed for every phase of wind and weather: a cloister for exercise, for example, would face south-east to catch the low winter sun but escape the summer heat. With outdoor dining-rooms and enclosed swimming pools (heated and unheated) the interpenetration of house and garden was total. Spanish patios give us some idea of the principle – but perhaps California furnishes the best modern examples of such indoor-outdoor living.

When the Renaissance picked up the threads of Roman design the evidence of ancient practice was best preserved in the ruined buildings. Other gardens, beyond the immediate precincts of the villa, had disappeared. We now know that there was scarcely a mode of gardening that the Romans did not practise; from the purely formal, to the woodland, to 'landscape', to the fantastic cave-and-grotto. One of their weaknesses was topiary, which they practised to excess. But when Pliny remarks 'on a sudden in the midst of the elegant regularity you are surprised with an imitation of the negligent beauties of rural nature', it is hard to know what picture we should conjure up.

ABOVE: *San Simeon, W. Randolph Heart's 'castle' in California, is the nearest the modern world provides to the feel of Ancient Rome. The grandiose swimming pool harks back to Hadrian's villa below, even if the scale is puny in comparison with the original.*

LEFT: *The strongly architectural basis of Italian gardens stems directly from Ancient Rome. The Emperor Hadrian's villa at Tivoli rambled over 700 acres, with endless courtyards, pools, gardens and grottoes, all encompassed with columns and enlivened with fountains and statuary.*

RIGHT: *The Villa Borghese at the end of the 16th century was still in transition between the enclosed garden of the Middle Ages and the grand architectural statement, all steps and fountains, of the Renaissance.*

BELOW: *By 1600 the Baroque taste was allowing grottoes and woodland to invade the formal garden. The source for the cascade at the Villa Aldobrandini is a 'natural' piece of rockwork in the woods, although its final destination is strictly architectural and formal.*

The little garden-making that went on in the Mediterranean countries in the Dark Ages was probably confined to the monasteries and the courts of emperors and kings. The royal pleasure-grounds in Palermo and Naples were some sort of hybrid of Islamic hunting-park (inherited from the conquering Saracens) and Roman villa. The great thirteenth-century treatise on agriculture, Crescentius' *Liber Ruralium Commodorum*, describes flowery parks and menageries that seem more Moorish than medieval. But he also describes what was clearly the standard domestic garden of the Middle Ages – the *hortus conclusus*, or walled enclosure, with a fountain, turfed seats, vine-shaded arbours and beds of flowers and herbs.

This was certainly the sort of Tuscan garden Boccaccio described in the *Decameron* in the middle of the fourteenth century. It was Boccaccio's friend Petrarch who first accomplished what William Kent was to repeat, with so much more publicity, three hundred and fifty years later in England: he 'leaped the fence and saw that all Nature was a garden'. Petrarch, who lived at one time in Provence, climbed Mont Ventoux to admire the view – an excursion his contemporaries considered dangerously eccentric. He also delved back into Virgil for instructions on how to proceed with his gardening.

As the Renaissance gathered force in the Florence of the Medicis precepts for gardening were eagerly gleaned from the classics, notably by the architect Alberti. The most revolutionary garden was that of the Villa Medici, of about 1460, at Fiesole. The Tuscans, however, were fond of their old enclosed gardens and inclined rather to adapt them with a grotto here, a statue there, possibly to align them along a central axis in the classical fashion, rather than uproot them and start great building works. There are still gardens around Florence that are more medieval than Renaissance.

It was in Rome that the fully fledged Renaissance garden first emerged, as a prelude to the rebuilding of St Peter's. In 1503 Pope Julius II commissioned Bramante, who was later to draw up the plans for the basilica, to build the Vatican gardens – and build was the word. The Cortile del Belvedere at the Vatican became the prototype for dozens of works of imaginative roofless architecture. The elements are stairs, colonnades, statues in niches, and fountains. Nature was scarcely allowed to breathe.

Bramante's successors, Ligorio and Vignola, brought the Italian garden to its climax with their masterpieces of the middle years of the sixteenth century: the Villa d'Este at Tivoli, the Villa Farnese at Caprarola, and the Villa Lante near Viterbo.

It is hard for us to imagine them as they looked when they were built, 'white from the mason's hand'. As Gertrude Jekyll wrote, 'precious qualities come by age, both of masonry and vegetation. The abrasion of hard edges and the falling out of mortar are a gain, for the lichen laps over the bruised moulding and the mortar is replaced by a cushion of moss.'

But as time went by fashion did begin to shift away from a sense of total control. It may just have been that the trees were growing up and adopting picturesque attitudes in the once strict gardens, but by 1600 Baroque taste was actively encouraging them to do so. By the time the Italian style was eclipsed by the French in the seventeenth century, areas of wild wood and naturalistic grottoes were the height of fashion.

COMPONENTS OF THE ITALIAN STYLE

The garden-architects of the Renaissance coined an idiom so powerful that its freshness is now hard to comprehend. We have all seen so many grand flights of stone stairs, monumental fountains, niches, cascades, double ramps, terraces and balustrades, along so many axes leading to so many porticoes in front of the grand villas, hotels and casinos of the world that it takes a slight mental effort to look at the picture below with fresh eyes.

The Villa Lante, near Viterbo, some 40 miles north of Rome, has been chosen so often by critics as the most perfect garden in Italy, and one of the most beautiful spots on earth, that it is worth looking for its special qualities. What

LEFT: *A fresco in the Villa Lante at Viterbo shows the radical plan of an elaborate architectural conceit wedded to an (admittedly exaggerated) wild landscape. It is right to be reminded, amid the serenity and even solemnity of such gardens in their old age, that they were built for fun as well as philosophy. Even the most sophisticated churchmen were amused by practical jokes. Guests at the Villa Lante were led into an enclosed garden where they were soaked to the skin by concealed water jets.*

ABOVE: *Many Italian gardens have such flourishes of water, spouting and tumbling in joyful wetness. The Villa d'Este at Tivoli, near Rome, has perhaps the finest waterworks of all.*

makes this particular formalized hillside so especially enchanting and satisfying?

First, it is clearly a garden for the garden's own sake. It was begun in 1566 as a country retreat for Cardinal Gambara. He is said to have commissioned Vignola, who had established his reputation in the long-drawn-out construction of Cardinal Farnese's palatial villa and gardens at Caprarola nearby. Gambara wanted something simpler, with more emphasis on garden beauty and little on the house – so little in fact that it is chopped in half and becomes two dignified but modest pavilions that introduce the garden rather than the usual reverse arrangement.

The axial plan – everything along a central straight line – is thus made to refer solely to the garden itself. The stress falls principally on the elaborate water-parterre in the foreground; as polished and humanized an outdoor space as it is possible to imagine. Then the eyes and feet are drawn upwards to find the source of all this sparkling water, and are led inexorably, in a series of detours (enough to make you face in every direction as you go, and glance back repeatedly at the scintillating fountain and the spacious view beyond) into closer and closer acquaintance with the water and, almost imperceptibly, deeper and deeper into the heart of green nature.

On the way the water takes many forms: spouts, jets and runnels; a rippling rectangle in the middle of a dining-table where wine was cooled and perhaps dishes floated from guest to guest; a formal cascade between recumbent river-gods; and then a long foaming channel in imitation of the Cardinal's coat of arms – the claws of the crayfish – repeated to keep the water white and writhing between the encroaching walls of green.

All this leads to an upper terrace where small pavilions flank a shady spring and paths radiate away into deep groves of ilex: a classical reference as fundamental as could be.

What the garden is saying, although to simplify it so is to miss half the point and all the nuances, is that there is an essential link between the utterly humanistic and artificial brilliance of the water parterre and the mysterious primeval source of its life: the woodland spring. Later Baroque gardens were to dally with the wild woods, bringing them by degrees into the picture. Here they are clearly defined as the all-important context for a human *tour de force*.

You are free to choose either end of the garden as the climax or, as the Cardinal probably intended, to regard the tension between the two, played out in garden terms, as the point and purpose of the villa.

The Villa Lante is a relatively small garden, but none of the garden masterpieces of Italy are very big – certainly nothing on a scale approaching the French extravaganzas of the next century. It is partly because of this modest human scale that their message is so clear and convincing. Perhaps, of all the gardens ever made, they have the strongest sense of comprehensive unity. When their style has been revived, as it was with a vengeance in the nineteenth century in countless expensive and usually meretricious examples, it has generally been amid distractions that have robbed it of its single-minded clarity. Italian is a term of honour; Italianate a term of reproach.

FRANCE: THE GRAND MANNER

TO EPITOMIZE FRENCH GARDENING WITH THE WORK OF LE NÔTRE IS NOT TO BELITTLE WHAT WENT

BEFORE HIM. FRENCH MEDIEVAL GARDENS WERE AS FINE AS ANY IN EUROPE.

In the French renaissance of the sixteenth century a fury of building and garden-making swept through the country. Every great château was endowed with a girdle of glorious gardens in what might be called a high-flying medieval manner. Although Renaissance ideas were in full flood it proved impossible to apply logic and symmetry to craggy old castles. Du Cerceau's great volume of surveys of *Les Plus Excellents Bastiments de France* shows every detail of dozens of these gardens. Their flavour can still be tasted at Villandry, or in the painting below.

By the beginning of the seventeenth century, with a Medici as Queen of France, the royal palace gardens in Paris (the Tuileries and the Luxembourg) were largely Italian in plan. Those of St Germain-en-Laye downstream on the steep banks of the Seine, begun for Henri IV in 1594, were directly inspired by the Villa d'Este.

At the same time French gardeners were working out their own versions of Italian models in a style more suitable to France. Most influential among them was Claude Mollet, royal gardener at the Tuileries, who is credited with the creation of *parterres de broderie* of an elegance never seen in Italy, and also with insisting on the importance of the avenue. When Le Nôtre was born in 1613, son of one of Mollet's staff, the milieu for his genius was set, and he was in the midst of it.

Nicolas Fouquet, Chancellor to the young Louis XIV, met Le Nôtre through his fellow-student, the painter Le Brun, and commissioned him to design the gardens of his palace at Vaux le Vicomte, just south of Paris. But the great *fête champêtre* that Fouquet gave to celebrate his creation, on 17 August 1661, was a mistake. The jealous and malicious young king not only ruined and imprisoned him but went on to steal Le Nôtre (and indeed most of Fouquet's garden).

Suddenly the scale of gardening was astonishingly enlarged. Already the French, gardening on the relatively flat land of the Ile de France and the Loire valley in contrast to the Italians' hillsides, disposed their parterres more generously under their castle walls. But now the decimal point was moved. The unit of measure was no longer one human being but a curtsey of courtiers. Le Nôtre declared: 'I cannot abide a limit to a view.' He drove his canals by kilometres, and his avenues and allées were not suffered to stop before the horizon.

Sheer scale alone made his work revolutionary. But his success in handling such sweeps of landscape came from the application of strict principles. He always deliberately pushed back the planting from the building, making it stand proud from flat parterres, or sometimes water; the symbol of its proprietor's dominance over all he surveyed. He took the Italian principle of an axial plan and pushed it to the limits, with a vast clearing as the main axis, walled with trees

ABOVE: *André le Nôtre was as gentle and down-to-earth as his designs were logical and grand.*
BELOW: *Medieval châteaux imposed severe limitations on garden design.*

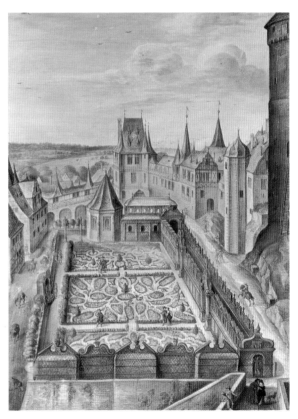

RIGHT: *Le Nôtre designed the gardens of Versailles to stand back from the vast palace. It dominates the central axis, the mile-long Grand Canal, and the innumerable fountains, theatres, temples and statues along the criss-crossing allées in the encircling forest.*

in perfect symmetry. The main cross-axes were always at right angles; between and within them diagonals and clearings and *jeux d'esprits* of every sort might multiply.

He was recreating the criss-crossing rides of the great hunting forests of Chambord and Cheverny on the Loire, but filling them with elegant and spectacular incidents in infinite variety. He used long reflecting waters: the moats of older châteaux, or reminders of them. Above all he used fountains. Louis XIV was a hydromaniac, if there is such a thing. Never were fountains so many, so massive, or so marvellous. There was never enough water for the King's desires, or even enough to operate more than a few of the multitude at one time. Thousands of troops were added to the builders labouring on endless aqueducts to bring more.

Le Nôtre designed gardens for many of the French nobility, but Versailles is the epitome of them all. It manages to be a great work of art, built with overweening pride and callous brutality, yet with extraordinary imagination and love. Needless to say Versailles was envied and imitated by every ruler in Europe. But none ever approached it in artistry or majesty. None had Le Nôtre.

FRANCE SINCE LE NÔTRE

By the end of the seventeenth century more than half the country within fifteen miles of Paris was covered with the gardens of the courtiers of Louis XIV and Louis XV.

BELOW: *Magnificent as the Versailles fountains are, there was never enough water for them. Louis XIV himself wrote the guide-book to the gardens.*

Far from being the exception, Versailles was simply the biggest and best of scores of such gardens, one abutting on another.

The pupils of Le Nôtre continued to pour out such performances until they became the basic garden style of almost every château in France, not to mention all the courts of northern Europe. They continued to draw inspiration from Italy and refine Italian ideas with French sophistication. Their innumerable cascades, for example, were built of finest coursed ashlar in contrast to Italy's often relatively crude masonry. They carried the art of *treillage* to new heights of elaboration and finesse and made grottoes with all the hydraulic automatons and singing birds they could devise.

Yet inevitably the mood changed. Versailles without the personality of the Sun King became oppressive, sad and boring. Even in his lifetime he demanded constant change, for any garden that relies so heavily on architecture, inanimate objects and special effects, without the mystery of developing plants to keep adding interest, will eventually become stale. The court moved on; it fell into disrepair.

About 1750 a number of events fired the move to a new direction. At court Madame de Pompadour rebuilt the modest little palace of the Trianon, made a working dairy, and started cultivating flowers. News came back from England (the two countries were briefly at peace) that gardens there were being remodelled on new and 'natural' lines. And letters from missionaries in Peking gave enthusiastic if imprecise accounts of Chinese gardens, in which nothing was symmetrical, but different parts of the garden, marked by buildings in different styles, signified different moods: '*Scènes enchantés, horribles, riantes.*'

Within another ten years the signs of the times were clear. In 1760 an English poem celebrating nature, James Thomson's 'The Seasons', was translated into French and became a craze. In 1763 Jean-Jacques Rousseau's *La Nouvelle Héloïse* became a best-seller. Rousseau, in the words of the critic Taine, 'made the dawn visible to people who had never risen till noon, the landscape to eyes that had only rested hitherto on drawing-rooms, the natural garden to men who had only walked between tonsured yews and rectilinear borders'.

In the same year the Marquis de Girardin began France's first 'landscape' garden at Ermenonville, north of Paris, where, fifteen years later, Rousseau was to die and be buried, by moonlight, on the Ile des Peupliers. The year Rousseau died Queen Marie-Antoinette set to work with an English gardener to create the Petit Trianon. Le Nôtre's world was dead and the world of romantic fantasy had begun.

By the time the Queen had finished with the Petit Trianon it boasted (or had boasted, for buildings were pulled down almost as soon as they were put up) a pagoda, a Chinese aviary, a theatre, a temple of Diana, Turkish fountains, a dairy and a farm, a hermitage, a *salon hydraulique*, an ancient temple on a large rock, a thatched cottage and a stone bridge. Finally it acquired the little hamlet that still exists, complete with operating peasantry, and furnished by the (English) gardener with masses of flowers. At this point the Revolution interrupted operations.

But as soon as the Revolution was over the *style anglo-chinois* hit France with full fury. Thomas Blaikie, a Scots former undergardener at the Petit Trianon, was employed on all sides to design gardens. The Revolution and the *style anglo-chinois* between them destroyed many of the truly French gardens of the old houses and put in their place '*le jardin anglais*'; at its best a total funfair of kiosks, ruins and assorted follies; at its worst a boring travesty of the English model.

The enlightening feature of this age was the new passion for flowers. The Empress Joséphine at La Malmaison

ABOVE: *The indecision of a Paris garden of 1770. It was divided into French, Italian and English compartments.*

BELOW: *The apotheosis of the potager at Villandry, near Tours, is a reconstruction of the 16th-century style of du Cerceau. The vegetables are changed twice a year.*

ABOVE: *The greatest of French 20th-century gardeners, the Vicomte de Noailles, was eclectic. He blended the old Italian style with consummate plantsmanship at his villa near Grasse.*

collected not only every variety of rose but every new plant of any kind. Redouté and others made matchless paintings of them. The passion for new plants extended to trees, and *bouquets d'arbres exotiques* appeared alongside every château.

The English style has co-existed with the French ever since. There have been various classical revivals, but without much hope, for the distinctive French style is the Grand Manner which, without a genuine megalomaniac at the helm, is all too apt to end in pompous pastiche.

Where French gardening is at its best today is in suitably scaled-down versions of the classic style, with all its swagger and *hauteur*, and above all in the national style that goes straight back to the crowded cultivation of the sixteenth century. *Jardin de curé* – 'parson's garden' – is the expression for the sort of straightforward plot where flowers, vegetables and well-trained fruit-trees grow side by side. The onion lies down with the rose. The soul of France is here; beauty arises from the logic and the discipline.

Where French gardening is at its worst is in the garden-centre style of the suburbs and country villas, which obliterates everything native and necessary and replaces it with blue and yellow conifers, red roses and geraniums.

By the 1990s the time was ripe for another new direction. Once more it came from England – but this time not as a fashion in design but in a new sensibility to plants. It is plantsmanship and a growing awareness of ecology that will shape French gardening in the twenty-first century.

DUTCH GARDENS

The role of the Dutch in the history of gardening has mainly been that of consummate nurserymen – turning the riches of the plant world into comfortable cash. They still dominate Europe's nursery trade today (and not only in bulbs) as they did in 'the Dutch century' – the seventeenth.

But the high Dutch style of that time is almost lost. One magnificent example has been brought back to life: the royal palace of Het Loo. But Het Loo is the Dutch Versailles, and what was distinctively Dutch about the lost gardens of Amsterdam's millionaire merchants was their compact scale and sense of enclosure. As far as the towpath of the canal was all the view they were interested in.

The Japanese, who also garden small, keep it simple. They try to express limitless Nature with a distillation of her attractions: a rock, a tree, a fern. The Dutch took the opposite view, filling their little yards with the most elaborate furnishings they could devise. This was the race and the age that developed the still-life to sublimity.

As florists they loved marbled, frilled, striped, doubled flowers. Apart from tulips, hyacinths, ranunculus, crown imperials, carnations, roses and auriculas were their favourites. Some say their taste for the highly coloured came from their trading contacts with the Orient and the Indies; some from their often cheerless weather. They made fitting beds for their fancy flowers in intricately flowing designs, trimmed with box hedges and punctuated with obelisks, statues and conceits of topiary. Topiary was carried to such lengths that it became identified in foreign minds with Holland, though in fact it goes back to the Romans. Avenues were a Dutch passion. Where the scale ruled out tall trees, clipped hedges (usually of hornbeam) were a common feature – and may well be a Dutch invention.

A watery approach was almost inevitable, as the land reclaimed by drainage from the sea is divided by regular canals. Where canals were absent prosperous houses were provided with moats to create the same effect. The swans that paddled these waters were another important feature. Fountains presented a problem. Tall jets were impossible. The low water pressure of a country without hills would allow no more than a falling arc. Where water would not glitter, therefore, gilt was employed. Fountains, statues and gates were painted and gilded with none of the reticence that decrees that lead should be grey and wrought iron black.

The great concentration of rich burgers' villas lined the banks of the Vecht, a twenty-mile stretch of river between Utrecht and Muiden on the Zuider Zee near Amsterdam. The Vecht was to Amsterdam what the Brenta was to Venice 200 years earlier. Scores of trim houses and their gardens faced the waterway in what seems from engravings of the time to have been an atmosphere of perpetual regatta, with drinking parties and little orchestras and merchants' wives sitting in their gazebos gossiping about the waterborne passers-by.

All this is gone. Holland has swept away its past to take the lead in new ways of using plants. Holland is intensely horticultural, still besotted with flowers, but also radical, finding abstract, unconventional ways of using them.

LEFT: *The Dutch garden of the 17th century was packed with incident: a* jardin clos *full of ornament, topiary and novel flowers. Avenues and water were essential elements of a style more domestic than the French.*

CHINA AND JAPAN

ABOVE: *The mountains of central China with their fantastic peaks have been a main influence in shaping the Chinese idea of natural beauty.*

BELOW: *The gardens of Suzhou, near Shanghai, are intricate compositions of many ornate buildings, courts and walls but few plants.*

Where the flora of Europe had been decimated by the ice ages, and even North America's seriously depleted, eastern Asia had kept its primeval diversity of plants intact. The north China plain, at the time when Chinese gardening began, perhaps about 2000 BC, had a flora of unique richness: trees, shrubs and flowers of almost every genus of the northern hemisphere.

The gardener's contribution in such circumstances was simply to order and emphasize what was already there. Buildings and bridges, terraces, steps and gateways turned wooded lakes into gardens without a tree planted or a seed sown. The hunting parks of the early emperors were simply the landscape enclosed.

Of course the Garden of Eden did not last. The population grew; the forests were cut down; a more sophisticated nobility found a mere house in a wood insipid and looked for more extravagant ideas.

The Han dynasty, contemporary with the ascendancy and greatness of Rome, was the first to unify China. The emperor Wu, like Caesar Augustus not so long after him, was tempted by the notion of immortality. It was Wu who hankered after the legendary Mystic Isles, the home of the Immortals, supposed to lie somewhere in the mists of the North China Sea. The story goes that, failing to find them in reality, he decided to recreate them in fantasy; and so created the lake-and-island garden that has been reproduced, with variations, again and again both in China and Japan.

The myth was an elaborate one. Some of the isles were supported on the backs of giant tortoises. They could be reached only if the traveller was carried by a bird – the giant crane. In Wu's garden these beasts were symbolically represented by suitable rocks. Rocks were also collected to form the islands and give the lake shore something of the feeling of a sea coast. Wu laid the foundations of the garden art of China.

The Han dynasty cracked in about AD 200 and its prosperity gave place to wars and uncertainty. Its bulwark to the north, the Great Wall, was overrun by

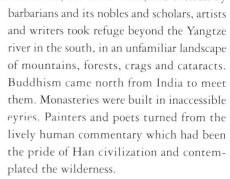

barbarians and its nobles and scholars, artists and writers took refuge beyond the Yangtze river in the south, in an unfamiliar landscape of mountains, forests, crags and cataracts. Buddhism came north from India to meet them. Monasteries were built in inaccessible eyries. Painters and poets turned from the lively human commentary which had been the pride of Han civilization and contemplated the wilderness.

China had already arrived at its Rousseau and Wordsworth. A description of a fourth-century monastery could almost be from *The Prelude*. 'Within the grounds Hui Yuan laid out a grove for meditation. The mist condensed on the trees and dripped on the mossy

LEFT: *The Grand View garden in Peking recalls the ancient original of a great park with lakes and summer houses. The weeping willow originated in northern China.*

paths. Every spot seen by the eye and trodden by the foot was full of spiritual purity and majesty.'

In due course the cult of the wilderness descended to the plain. China's experience of her own mountains, not ancient and rounded by millennia of erosion like
Wordsworth's Lake District but geologically young, sharp-cragged and spectacular, became part of her notion of the beautiful. Garden-making on the old
lake-and-island pattern returned, but with its soft contours changed. Rocks themselves, as reminders of the mountains, became objects of extreme admiration; the
bigger and craggier the better – however confined the space. The intricacy and
architectural bravura of such rock-filled gardens, alive with fearsome dragons, has
to be seen to be believed. The canal city of Suzhou near Shanghai has a concentration of examples.

To think of Chinese gardens merely as picturesque pastiches of nature is to
miss the point. It is not just the forms of nature that the gardener sets out to capture, but its spirit. Gardens were (and still are) sited following the energy-lines of
the earth on the geomantic principles of Feng Shui. By distilling the essence of a
wild landscape the gardener even hopes to absorb its energy himself – to be more
powerful and live longer.

By the end of the sixth century a new emperor was displaying his power and
security by lake-and-island garden-making on a scale worthy of Louis XIV. The
Western Park was seventy miles in circuit, employed a million men to build it,
and contained four huge lakes – one of them thirteen miles round. The architecture that set off this preposterous park was gaudy and grandiose. Endless red palaces
and pavilions with roofs of glittering coloured tiles and upswept eaves lay among
the lotus-covered lakes, the weeping willows, the acres of grotesque rocks.

This was the picture that greeted the first Japanese envoy to China in AD 607.
Japan had already learned something of China's splendour via Korea, which lies
between the two, and had long been a Chinese colony. It seems that the Japanese
genius for assimilation is nothing new: within a few years of the envoy's return
Japan had the first Chinese-style lake-and-island garden of her own.

Giant strides are inevitable in the long history of China, but so conservative
are the Chinese that centuries have gone by without perceptible change. Six hundred years of high civilization lay ahead, at least for parts of the empire: the period

ABOVE: *The moon-gate is a recurring theme in the domestic-scale Chinese garden. High walls enclose a maze of small spaces, allowing glimpses from one to another to suggest that there is always more to see.*

of the T'ang and Sung dynasties. Landscape-painting and gardening advanced hand in hand to reach what is generally considered their highest point of achievement in the twelfth century under the Sung emperor Hui Tsung.

The flowering of Japanese culture took place at the same time, in the three hundred and fifty peaceful years of the Heian period. Fashions and manners we think of as distinctly Japanese were developed from the Chinese by this astonishing court. We know from its literature, including the famous *Tale of Genji*, that it reached as high a point of worldly refinement and sensibility as any civilization before or since.

The Japanese contribution to the Chinese original was an intense love of nature. Japan is one of the loveliest countries on earth. Where China has the stark contrast of mountain and plain and the extremes of a continental climate, Japan is all a chaos of volcanic hills, swathed in forests almost as rich in plants as China but with the gentler weather of islands and an endless wild seacoast. It turns its back on Siberia and looks towards the Pacific. The seasons are pronounced but not extreme: summer is hot; winter snowy but sunny and not intensely cold; spring and autumn are long, slow and glorious. Rain comes and goes all year round, giving the earth a patina of moss, enabling trees to grow on the rocks of the rugged coast, feeding an infinity of springs and rills.

The Heian capital was Kyoto. The site seems to have been chosen for its beauty, more as a resort than a seat of government. Wooded hills cradle it and a thousand streams from the hills murmur and splash in its hundreds of gardens. Boating on the garden lakes, writing poems to the flowers, choosing stones and designing cascades, even sitting all morning to watch the fluttering smoke of a bonfire were the pastimes of the Heian court.

No original Heian garden exists today, but a reconstruction was made in 1894 to celebrate Kyoto's 1,100 years as the capital. The Heian shrine, as it is called, is one of the gayest, most delightfully contrived gardens on earth, with whole orchards of cherries, thickets of azaleas, islands of water lilies and acres of irises. There are plenty of rocks, but they are submerged in flowers. How near to the original it is we shall never know, but to view smoke uncurling in such a place would seem completely right. Genji is believable there.

Gradually, though, the Japanese love for the simple and rustic reasserted itself. The highly coloured Chinese style was transformed into something more in tune with the Japanese mind; a way of gardening in which nature was given all the credit; in which the art was to conceal art and make the garden appear simply a part of a perfectly harmonious natural world. Zen Buddhism, which arrived in Japan about this time, preached canons of art which exactly coincided with the mood: avoidance of the trite, the obvious, the emphatic.

By the year 1200 the art of naturalistic landscape was mature. The famous Moss Garden in the western hills of Kyoto dates from this period. Its dry cascade, composed of flat-topped boulders, is totally convincing as a natural rocky outcrop. Unlike both earlier and later gardens the stones in no way suggest mountains on a different scale.

In due course fine rocks became objects of enormous value and prestige, to be given as favours; even plundered as booty. A successful warrior, in the centuries of upheavals that followed the Heian peace, could carry off his enemy's garden, rocks, trees and all, as the greatest treasure he possessed.

Chinese influence was not dead. The masterpieces of Sung art were prized and imitated in Japan even though it was hard to reconcile their romantic fantasy with Japanese naturalism. The Sung style with rocks was to set them boldly on their ends; horizontal strata pointing skywards in imitation of China's rugged unweathered hills.

Examples of both styles exist in Kyoto. Out of the conflict of ideas came the finest landscape gardens ever built: the estate gardens of the Muromachi period, contemporary with Renaissance Florence, and itself something of a Renaissance. The Gold and Silver Pavilions are the two masterpieces of the period, built in 1394 and 1482, at the beginning and end of this great artistic climax.

DEVELOPMENTS IN JAPAN

The great Muromachi period of the fourteenth and fifteenth centuries that created the Gold and Silver Pavilions was followed by a century of bloodshed, during which castles were the order of the day. The seventeenth century, however, saw another wave of garden-making – the last of great landscape gardens – in which most of the existing lake-and-island gardens were made or remade. All the existing Imperial villa gardens belong to this time.

It is almost impossible to believe, seeing these perfect landscapes, that they had no influence on what was to happen in England less than a century later. Enlarge the scale, substitute classical architecture, and Stourhead lies before you. The curving lakeshore, the soft sweeps of grass, the advancing woods and scattered temples are all familiar. Even the rocks and islands could almost be English. What really gives the game away is the pines: each tree pruned with infinite art into a pastiche of a pine's proper posture. The maintenance of a Japanese garden is mostly pruning the trees. To the Japanese it is the only way that they can be in proportion and harmony with their surroundings. If there is a parallel in Europe it is in the French style of trimming trees into walls of green. As for the English, they let their gardens run wild, by these standards, from the moment they plant them.

It was not just lordly landscapes that grew to perfection in the Muromachi renaissance. Little temple courtyards were arranged as contemplative gardens with transcendent

artistry. The most famous of these strange abstractions in sand and stones, Ryoan-Ji (see the previous page), dates from the same generation as the Silver Pavilion, the climax of Japanese landscape art. It consists simply of fifteen apparently random boulders scattered in groups about a walled yard, emerging from a surface of gravel raked to resemble, one supposes, the waves of the sea. The garden is viewed from the wooden platform that runs along the open side of the house: only the duty-monk with his rake is allowed in. Twenty generations have mused on its meaning . . . if it has one.

The same period invented the tea ceremony, which crystallized the culture of Japan into a ritualistic form – in a garden setting. The object of the ritual is to impress the participants with the virtues of urbanity, courtesy, purity and imperturbability – in a world where their opposites are very much more common. The path to the tea-house became loaded with symbolism as the place of preparation. Guests enter through a simple gate and go to a covered bench to wait. The host sounds a gong and the guests, not more than five, file on stepping stones past a well, first to a stone basin with its laver for ritual cleansing, then to the tea-house. Its low door forces you to enter in a humble posture.

The essence of a tea-house is a mood of rural calm with a patina of mossy age, impeccably swept and sprinkled for dewy freshness. So another style of gardening on a small scale came into being, again employing simple means to reach a definite spiritual, or perhaps moral, end.

ABOVE. The garden of the Silver Pavilion, Ginkaku-Ji, was the last masterpiece of the Muromachi period - contemporary with Renaissance Florence. Its romantic naturalism is interrupted by outcrops of raked white sand.

BELOW: Most Japanese gardens, especially tea gardens, are extremely small – even cramped. The viewer sits on the tatami (right) and loses himself in contemplation of the planting, dreaming of wide landscapes.

Both styles were developed throughout the seventeenth century in countless examples (though very few were as highbrow as Ryoan-Ji). Courtyard gardens tended to become gently suggestive of scenery, using water where it was available, imitating it where it was not with dry cascades of stone and swirling rivers of sand round mossy promontories. In most gardens some particular tree is singled out for attention and shorn and propped into a singular shape. Clipped evergreens are used to suggest more rocks, or perhaps distant hills. Where the real hills can be seen they are 'borrowed' into the garden to form part of the composition.

In complete contrast with Western gardens, which use the widest possible palette of plants, far wider than the natural flora round them, the Japanese sternly

exclude all but a narrow conventional range. The woods around Kyoto hold a far greater variety than its gardens. Flowers are not neglected. They are cultivated in great variety and remarkable perfection, but rarely as part of the garden picture, rather as clusters of pots round the kitchen door.

Today there are so many of the smaller kinds of garden and their derivatives in Japan that it is almost impossible to follow their historical development. Nor perhaps does it matter very much. No doubt it is difficult for Japanese visitors to Europe to distinguish between, for example, Decorated and Perpendicular church windows.

It seems, though, as if the inspiration waned in the eighteenth century. In place of monks and warriors a new middle class took to gardening, and inevitably looked for 'rules'

to follow among the works of pure imagination they inherited. Professional gardeners were happy to supply them, inventing a great deal of mumbo-jumbo, which for a long while stood between their successors and a straightforward appreciation of a great treasury of garden art.

THE WEST LEARNS FROM JAPAN

When Japanese gardening first began to influence the West and whether there is any relationship at all before the end of the nineteenth century remains an unresolved question. Looking at the picture (above), of a piece of gardening that could so easily have been done in England in the eighteenth century (but which was done in Japan a hundred years earlier), it is hard to believe that no plans, or rumours of plans, had ever at that stage passed between the two countries.

BELOW: *Japanese design is so powerful that a single object – this is a Torii, or Shinto gate (minus its lower cross-bar) can bring a Japanese dimension to an English garden.*

Apparently they did not, and the West had to wait until 1893 for its first coherent account of Japanese garden-making – in Josiah Conder's *Landscape Gardening in Japan*. The West was curious, but not very impressed. Conder, unfortunately, was guided by Japanese professional gardeners of an era of mannerism and decadence – in fact, of Japanese Victorianism. His book shows little sign of the brilliant clarity and decisiveness, or the exquisite sense of scale and texture that we have since learned to look for. Early Western imitations of Japanese gardens have been given a bad press. But clearly a great deal of the fault lay in the quality of what they were imitating.

The true quality of earlier Japanese gardens was not revealed until the 1930s, when the scholar and artist Mirei Shigemori

ABOVE. *Confusion can arise when the austerity of a dry landscape is brought into the romantic framework of a western garden. But* BELOW: *this English example is a successful transplant of the style Japan derived from China.*

published his twenty-six-volume study of the classical masterpieces. The Second World War intervened, both in the restoration of the old gardens and in their appreciation by the West. It is only recently, in fact, that we have had a chance to see the perfection of the real thing.

Fifteenth-century Japan sounds a very remote period and place to modern Western gardeners. But hardly any era of any country's history has produced so much of artistic relevance to today. The simple lightweight modular architecture of houses that developed in that period still continues and has deeply influenced the West. The philosophy and method of their gardens have even more to offer.

The Japanese art is one of concentrating the attention on essentials: be they strong shapes or subtle nuances. It is the art of editing – the most necessary part of gardening. In a Japanese garden you become intensely aware of the characters of the plants and objects around you. Some, such as the tonsured trees, because they are so strange; others, such as the pebbles and moss, because they are so appropriate, so well ordered, and so well kept.

Above all Japanese ideas are relevant to small gardens. Many gardens in Japan are mere door-yards. If it is too much to ask the Western eye to see a microcosm of a wild sea coast in two or three rocks, a bamboo and a diminutive reflecting pool, there is another sense in which concentrating on a few well-chosen, well-proportioned natural objects achieves that link with nature which we seek in gardens. Japanese gardeners garden for the permanent picture. They will go to any lengths to perfect a view and then any lengths to keep it precisely so, unaltered year after year, season after season. The bones of the garden are the evergreen plants and, of course, the all-important rocks.

On the stage of this static garden seasonal changes become dramatic happenings. It begins with the great festival of cherry blossom, when the whole country is an operetta orchard, with people in their best clothes picnicking tipsily under the pink-frothy trees; then the massed ranks of azaleas, clipped into rigid forms which seem incongruous as they burst into flower. Then irises by the water, with tame carp in their brilliant motley cruising between them, combine to make a startling picture. And so eventually to the year's climax, when the maples smoulder and blaze in gardens and woods.

The Japanese style is much more readily acceptable in America than in Europe – certainly more than in England. American gardeners already agree with the idea of setting a permanent scene, relying heavily on evergreens, in which the seasons pass as actors. Climate has a great deal to do with it. So has laziness. Not so the English, who, if they love gardening at all, must always be pottering about watching the daily development of their plants. The owner's involvement is a very English thing. Japanese and American gardens have this in common: they are largely maintained by contractors.

Conversely, just as each dish in a Japanese meal is served separately, often exquisitely, in a tiny bowl, so I suspect a Japanese would find riotous English mixed borders – like our meat and two vegetables with plenty of gravy – a gross and inexplicable waste of good things by mixing them together.

ENGLISH REVOLUTIONS IN A SIMPLIFIED,

BUT NOT ABSURD, VERSION OF HISTORY, EUROPE'S THREE GREAT GARDENING STYLES HAVE

FOLLOWED EACH OTHER LIKE A SERIES OF TIMED DETONATIONS, WITH ENGLAND'S COMING LAST.

The Medieval style was nationless, and also curiously timeless. One can argue that it still persists in a million back gardens all over Europe and beyond.

The first explosion was in Italy in about 1500, followed by a century of inspired gardening, with its influence spreading far and wide. France's followed in about 1650 and had a briefer conflagration – chiefly because it centred on one man of genius. England's followed rather less than a century later and had a longer flowering, a greater development, and finally the greatest influence of all.

To complete this pocket sketch we must include the Dutch, not as creators of a revolutionary style but as the industrious nurserymen who, from about 1550 to the present day, have been important improvers and innovators and the main suppliers of many kinds of plants, from bulbs to trees.

The first premise of the medieval garden was that it was enclosed; separated from the various other outdoor areas where people kept pigs or practised fighting. Its enclosure was to protect its fruit, vegetables, herbs and flowers, and to make it a place of beauty and tranquillity. All early representations of pleasure gardens show the same sort of arrangement: a high wall surrounding a grassy plot with a fountain, a few trees (or sometimes no trees but tall flowers in the grass), usually a seat or seats covered with turf and frequently an arbour – a wooden gallery with plants trained over it. The arbour appears less in the earlier pictures but has a long career, reaching its climax in the sixteenth century, and still battling on today in the form of the pergola. A bathing, or at least a paddling, pool was an occasional, more luxurious, feature. Tents, an eastern notion imported by the Crusaders, were set up specially for parties.

One can imagine such gardens remaining largely undesigned. If there were flower beds, they were in simple shapes, sparsely planted. Except in the gardens of monasteries and the parks of palaces, prestige and display were not involved.

The rigid medieval structure of society began slowly to alter in the fifteenth century. The invention of printing, the capture of Constantinople by the Turks, the voyages of the Portuguese and the rediscovery of the classics in Italy brought a fundamental change in men's attitudes. If they fought no less they thought more. In England when the house of Tudor won the Wars of the Roses and went on to close the monasteries, men who would have been otherwise engaged were free to write, draw, observe and plan in secular affairs. The study of plants and the improvement of gardens was soon engaging the best minds in the land.

The Tudor king Henry VIII had famous, if somewhat childish, gardens full of painted wooden beasts, topiary and labyrinths, and 'knots' – the rustic English forerunners of the later parterres. By the middle of Henry's reign came the first sure sign that people were curious about plants and wanted

ABOVE: *All medieval gardens start with the idea of enclosure, with cultivation along only the simplest lines. This is from the 15th-century* Livre des Prouffits Champêtre et Ruraulx..

BELOW: *The Old Palace at Hatfield, near London, has the finest existing example of a 16th-century knot garden for herbs and 'simples'.*

ABOVE: *Scotland, with a wilder landscape and climate than England, was not so tempted to pull down its ancient garden walls. Scots gardeners have tended to be craftsmen in a conservative spirit. The parterre at Pitmedden, based on the 17th-century design, has no surviving equivalent in England.*

BELOW: *One of the famous series of engravings by Knyff and Kip of English country houses towards 1700 shows a typical synthesis of Italian, French and Dutch ideas at Dyrham Park near Bath. The site could hardly be handled in the French way, with radiating allées, so Italian-style terraces and ramps were built on a cross-axis to the Franco-Dutch parterres and canals.*

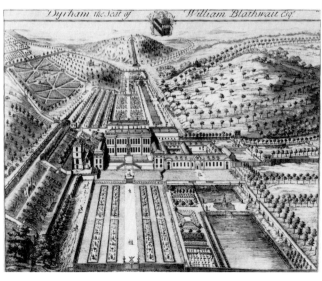

to know more: the first English translation of a herbal. By the year after his death in 1548 there appeared the first original English book on plants, William Turner's *The Names of Herbes*. Twenty years later came the first practical gardening book in English, Thomas Hill's *The proffitable arte of gardening*, written for the gentlefolk in their modest country manors. Unlike the castles of the French these were straightforward houses whose gardens could start at their windows.

These two books started a stream of English garden and plant literature that has never paused since, and which has no equivalent elsewhere. The Elizabethans and Jacobeans were writing at the moment of crystallization of the English language, with a freshness, enthusiasm and accuracy that still makes us humble and grateful. Sir Francis Bacon's famous essay is the best surviving description of an Elizabethan garden – in spirit magical: in design and detail remarkably naive.

There was money to build ambitious gardens in Elizabeth's reign, and vast formal layouts were undertaken, just as they were in contemporary France – though the English would have been out of date by French standards.

England caught up in the reign of James I. In 1607 the Huguenot Salomon de Caus crossed the Channel, followed in 1620 by his brother Isaac. The de Caus brothers were masters of the Renaissance garden arts of perspective, groundworks and hydraulics. They had studied the new gardens of Italy at first hand and found an eager clientele in England. At Ham House, Moor Park, Richmond and many of the royal houses (above all at the Earl of Pembroke's Wilton) England's great Renaissance gardens took shape.

We shall never know how successfully they attempted the Italian form of garden beauty without the climate or the hillside sites of Italy. The Civil War and the Commonwealth destroyed the royal gardens. The rest were swept away in due course by the landscape movement. At any rate their vogue was brief. When Charles II was restored to the throne in 1660 the French style of Le Nôtre was the model every English gentleman was eager to follow.

Just as important as the succession of foreign fashions invading England was the increasing number and knowledge of plants. First Gerard in Elizabeth's reign, then the Tradescants, father and son, both royal gardeners, made botanical collections and eagerly seized on every new plant. The story of the feverish hunt for new plants in the old world and the new is told on pages 76–91. With the growing mania for gardening arose a nursery industry to supply it. In the 1680s the first professional firm of nurserymen, designers and contractors appeared in London: the celebrated Brompton Park nursery to be known as London and Wise.

The accession of the Dutch king William in 1688 provided yet another twist and new direction to what was becoming the principal passion of the English gentry. For two generations, before and especially after 1700, it is possible that in synthesizing all the influences of the previous century the English were making some of the finest gardens the country has ever known. But the wits did not think so.

The essayist Addison and the poet Pope were bored by symmetry and regularity. At the same time, newly rich and confident young Englishmen were making a firsthand acquaintance with Italy. They found it much more romantic and interesting than they expected. They came home in a mood to bulldoze out of existence what they saw as the many derivative formalities descended, however indirectly, from the medieval garden. They wanted to embrace the Italy of the classics, crumbling ruins and all.

ENGLISH LANDSKIP

There is still much learned debate about the exact origins of the English landscape movement. As early as 1685 the diplomat Sir William Temple returned from Holland with a second-hand account of 'irregular' Chinese gardening, or Sharawadgi. Addison, in *The Spectator* in 1712, attacking the excess of topiary, gives favourable mention to Chinese gardens.

ABOVE: *Lancelot 'Capability' Brown (1716–83) came from Northumberland to learn landscaping from William Kent at Stowe (below). His career changed the face of English gardening.*

The notion of an alternative to symmetry was there, yet the rage was still all for the French and/or Dutch style. It seems that the strength of tradition was too strong to be easily shaken off. It had to be prised, little by little, by a variety of critics, painters, gardeners, pattern-makers and poets.

It was in the 1720s that the mood began to change, with published plans by Stephen Switzer and Batty Langley at first merely easing the stiffness of regularity. Charles Bridgeman at Stowe was perhaps the first practising gardener to deliberately adapt the prevailing French model to the English landscape, using 'ha-ha's' to bring parkland flowing into the picture. Sir John Vanbrugh was the eccentric architectural genius who would have ignored rule-books anyway to create the scenes of his fancy. His courage was infectious. Pope, both in his small garden and in his poems, had a wide influence. Claude's and Poussin's paintings are given credit for offering an ideal of classical landscape to follow. From the French themselves the English had learnt not to be afraid of size. Perhaps in the English character there is a residual Celtic longing for the undefined, unregulated, mysterious and suggestive.

Whatever the cause, in about 1730 William Kent, working at Stowe for Lord Cobham, 'leaped the fence'. Suddenly there was no beginning and no end to the garden; it was all 'landskip' (in the spelling of the day) to be idealized as an earthly paradise with strong classical overtones.

BELOW: *Stowe in Buckinghamshire was the crucible of the 'Landskip' movement, developed throughout the 18th century by Bridgeman, Kent and Brown. It defined the naturalistic English style of grass, trees, water and architecture.*

Kent was an architect and painter who succeeded in composing pictures with sweeping lawns, water, trees and architecture. The architecture was as important to the landscape garden as terraces and stairs had been to the earlier formal gardens; but in a different sense. On this occasion each building not only functioned as an accent to beckon the eye but also as some sort of moral, philosophical, or often poetical allegory.

It was Palladio's Venetian neo-Roman style that particularly appealed to the aristocratic English taste. In it they clearly saw much more than mere pleasing proportions: it was a reminder of Roman virtues,

ABOVE: *The essayist Horace Walpole started Stawberry Hill at Twickenham on the Thames in 1747. His 'Gothick' ideas were totally at odds with the prevailing neo-classicism. His garden continued old practices and at the same time foreshadowed the Victorian age.*

RIGHT: *Humphry Repton's 'Red Book' for the Duchess of Devonshire's garden shows (right) the existing garden, with Repton in the chair directing his assistants with their surveyors' poles. Far right is the scene as he intended to improve it, adding a conservatory and a terrace, reshaping the ground towards the river and clearing some of the trees. The biggest change is the cultivation of flowers in the foreground, relegating the landscape to a backdrop. Thus Brown's disciple reinstated the gardening Brown had banished. Repton made scores of such plans for country houses all over England.*

suggesting 'innumerable Subjects for Meditation' and 'giving a great Insight into the Contrivance and Wisdom of Providence'. One might imagine a Chinese scholar or a Japanese monk referring to his garden in this way, but surely not a courtier at Versailles.

To make the plain rolling English countryside a fit setting for such Insights, streams were dammed to form lakes, and trees planted in 'belts' and 'clumps': a belt round the periphery as a screen and windbreak, and clumps on knolls to flank buildings and advance in wings as in the theatre.

Once the formula was devised it became easy to repeat – as Kent's successor, Lancelot Brown, who had also worked at Stowe, found to his infinite profit. He set up in business as a landscape gardener in 1751, found that every potential client's property had distinct 'capabilities' – which gave him his famous nickname – and proceeded to remove as blots on the landscape all those gardens in the old formal style that stood in his way.

That Brown had talent, amounting almost to genius, there is no doubt. But the English have had fits of hating him ever since for obliterating their garden heritage. For within little more than a generation Brown and his imitators had swept away almost all the great formal gardens and replaced them with grass – grass right up to the doors of the mansion. Not even a terrace was suffered to stand in the way. All was to be, as his contemporaries began to complain, 'one uniform, eternal green'.

MUSEUMISM

With Brown the Landskip style of gardening reached its logical zenith, just as the French had with Le Nôtre. Neither style had anywhere to go next, except to compromise and complicate, which the successors of both inevitably did.

It must be stressed that Brown, like Le Nôtre, was dealing with the rich and great. In England, as in France, the smaller manors and rectory gardens went on enjoying their flower beds and fruit trees exactly as before. But garden fashion has never been dictated by modest lovers of flowers.

The element missing in Brown's landscapes, according to a vociferous contemporary school of thought, was the Picturesque. They were looking for more than clumps of trees, temples and serpentine lakes. They objected to 'this flat, insipid, waving plain' and demanded either a return to ancient ways, or higher drama in the landscape – in some cases both.

While Brown was clearing away all but the bare essentials, the expansion of empire was giving the English a taste for the exotic – in architecture, in scenery

and in plants. Kew Gardens was born. Chambers gave it its Pagoda. Horace Walpole built Strawberry Hill in the Gothick style. Curry and chutney from India came onto the national menu. It was all very well having a fashionable park in shades of green, but where were you to put the new trees, shrubs and flowers (let alone the old ones) or build follies in the latest style?

The follies presented little problem. A steady stream of fantastic architecture, from tinsely little Chinese teahouses to sombre mock ruins complete with owls and ivy, joined the noble neo-Romans in the park.

But the cry for flower beds and shrubberies and somewhere to plant 'specimen' trees was bound to mean muddying the pure land-

EXHIBITION EXTRAORDINARY in the HORTICULTURAL ROOM.

skip spring; and it did. Brown's successor was Humphry Repton, the ideal man to introduce the necessary variety without losing the thread. His writings on garden design still read as perfect good sense. He reintroduced terraces and flowers near the house as a foreground to the landscape, allowed walled gardens for privacy and shelter for flowers, planted 'shrubbery walks' and set aside areas for collecting rare trees. He painted his proposals for individual clients in his famous 'Red Books', with before-and-after views. By the time of his death, in 1818, his idea of Variety regulated by Proportion and Unity was accepted as the norm – or more accurately the ideal.

Within a decade of his death there was scarcely a department of what we now consider to be modern gardening that had not been launched. Variety, however, proved very much easier to find than Unity. Nineteenth-century gardeners fell into the same trap as designers in every other medium: they did not know when to stop.

There was a new class of gardener who had made his fortune in the Industrial Revolution and had no liberal or classical education to guide him. There was a new class of garden: the villa garden – no broad acres but enough money to pay for any freak of fancy. The (later Royal) Horticultural Society had been founded in 1804 and gave new impetus and prestige to the cultivation of new plants. Suddenly glass became cheap enough for the middle class to afford greenhouses.

Calm in the midst of this frenzied scene sat the extraordinary John Claudius Loudon, founder and editor of *The Gardener's Magazine*. No writer has worked so hard to absorb and make sense of such a mass of material. His *Encyclopaedia of Gardening*, first published in 1822, makes the previous standard work, Philip

ABOVE: *The Horticultural Society was founded in 1804. Cruikshank's cartoon of a meeting in 1825 describes the members as 'A Pink of Fashion'. 'A Bulb from Holland with offset' (foreground), 'A monstrous Medlar', 'A sprig of Nobility running to seed', and so on. The Society promoted plant exploration in its early years, having correspondents in China and sending David Douglas to North America. At a conference in 1899 it effectively founded the science of genetics. From its foundation it has been the world's premier horticultural organization, promoting experiments and setting standards.*

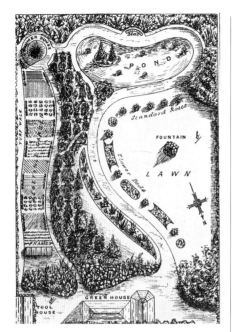

ABOVE: *As the middle class grew and its gardens got smaller, writers like Shirley Hibberd compressed Loudon's 'gardenesque' style, with its landscape roots, into little urban rectangles. Similar designs, without the geometrical beds, are still being published in popular gardening books today.*

Miller's *Gardener's Dictionary* (of 1731, and many later editions) seem almost medieval. Loudon and his wife produced edition after edition of painstaking, detailed history, description, instruction and advice.

'Gardenesque' was the unfortunate title he coined for the style he promulgated, which was intended 'to display the art of the gardener – the individual beauty of trees, shrubs and plants in a state of cultivation'.

It is hard to overestimate the influence of Loudon. He made an honest attempt to synthesize the best of gardening of all times and places. His plans are a development of Repton's, but lay more stress on collecting new plants and on the business end of things; the kitchen garden, nursery, greenhouse and frames. He laid the ground rules for all the new gardens of the Victorian age save the grandest.

There was no end to the books written to urge the collecting of every conceivable class of natural object both indoors and out. Shirley Hibberd's *Rustic Adornments* is the archetype of this eclectic mood. Undoubtedly there was good sense and taste and tradition, and there were certainly lovely flowers in countless gardens unflapped by fashion. But a Cleansing of the Temple was due.

THE CULMINATION: THE VICTORIAN COUNTRY HOUSE

A great English country-house garden in the last quarter of the nineteenth century epitomized the feeling that plants were made for man. Never was so much technology or manpower devoted to horticultural display. The craft of gardening, as distinct from the art, had reached its zenith. The Industrial Revolution, coinciding with the ceaseless import of novelties, made the mastery of their cultivation one of the great status symbols of the time. To employ coal, glass and iron to bring unheard-of exotics into bloom, thousands of miles from their native jungles, gave Victorians every sort of satisfaction.

The gardener-engineer who made the greenhouse a symbol for the Victorian age was Joseph Paxton. A farmer's son from Bedfordshire, he had trained at the Horticultural Society's gardens at Chiswick, and at the age of twenty-three was appointed head gardener at Chatsworth, the Duke of Devonshire's palace in Derbyshire.

Within a few years he had revolutionized this great garden, formed an arboretum with 1,670 species and varieties of trees, given it the tallest fountain in Britain

RIGHT: *The Earl of Shrewsbury's garden at Alton Towers in Staffordshire epitomized the horticultural showmanship of Victorian grandees. J. C. Loudon thought the whole place was 'in excessively bad taste' – which is why thousands still flock to it.*

– a jet 80m (267ft) high – and built the most extensive greenhouses in the country. Paxton became nationally famous in 1850 when he persuaded the giant Amazon water-lily, *Victoria regia* (now *V. amazonica*), to flower for the first time in cultivation. It had been named for the Queen as the most magnificent tribute the plant kingdom could pay her. The water-lily has flowers 30cm (1ft) wide and leaves 1.8m (6ft) across. Paxton built a warm-water tank, with a paddle wheel to simulate the flow of the Amazon, and erected over it an iron glasshouse of entirely novel design.

At the same time, Paxton heard that the Commission, considering designs for the building to house the Great Exhibition in London the following year, had turned down all the 250 plans submitted. His inspiration came at a board meeting of the Midland Railway at Derby. On his blotter he drew a plan for a modular glass and iron building, like the *Victoria regia* house, but 630m (2,100ft) long and 120m (400ft) wide. Its apparently fragile engineering, he said, was based on the leaves of the great water-lily itself. Within a year of its drawing, the great glass-house was built in Hyde Park, opened by the Queen, and popularly christened the Crystal Palace.

This then was the mood, and this the confidence, that created gardens, not only close to the scale of Le Nôtre but with an elaboration of planting that would have made the master blench. A typical great house garden would be divided into as many as ten departments, with up to ten men in each, in charge of the innumerable greenhouses, the rose-gardens, the herbaceous borders, the fruit and vegetable gardens, the rock and water gardens, the lawns and shrubberies, the trees, and above all, the bedding. As John Sales of the National Trust has written, 'No opportunity for display was lost, especially near the house, and the geraniums were relentless.' Rich people, it was said, used to show their wealth by the size of their bedding plant list: 10,000 for a squire, 20,000 for a baronet; 30,000 for an earl; and 50,000 for a duke. On the morning after a storm the gardeners would be out at dawn, replacing battered plants with spares from the greenhouses. One banker is said to have insisted on different climbing roses against the walls of his house each weekend of the summer.

It was not enough that plant-hunters were shipping home unheard-of species every day: the nurseries vied with each other in the new-born art of plant-breeding. Rivalry and jealousy were sometimes intense. The head gardener of one great English mansion was sent out every year on a tour of the nurseries of Germany, France, Holland and Belgium to scour for new varieties to bring home. If he liked them and his employer was pleased with them he would buy every plant to secure a monopoly. It was considered a virtue in plants to be tender and need the shelter of a greenhouse.

Rank upon rank of working greenhouses and frames were needed for the production of bedding plants and the perfecting of vegetables and fruit, particularly out of season. A gardener who could conjure up strawberries at Christmas was a man to reckon with. Many such country house gardens had a skilled staff of fifty or more, besides innumerable 'boys'.

This whole style might best be described as gargantuan gardenesque – following to the letter Loudon's definition of showing off the work of the gardener. Flourishing plants and impeccable maintenance had become their own justification. A pleasing garden picture was a well-kept one, full of masses of brilliant colours and, preferably, strange shapes. The notion of a picture in the painter's sense, as a composition of unity and harmony, dominated the eighteenth century and returned with the twentieth. For almost the whole of the nineteenth it was lost in the excitement of a bottomless hamper of new toys.

ABOVE: *The most faithful restoration of a high Victorian country house garden is at the Rothschild palace of Waddesdon Manor in Buckinghamshire.*

ABOVE: *Gertrude Jekyll and Edwin Lutyens used the Surrey farmhouse style on a manor-house scale at Vann, one of their Surrey gardens. This idealization of the rustic undercurrent of English gardening, stretching back to Elizabethan times, ignored all the garden styles that had come and gone between.*

BELOW: *Also at Vann, Gertrude Jekyll put into practice the precepts of her greatest book,* Wood and Garden, *around the lake with plantings that have influenced the whole of the 20th century.*

THE NOT-SO-GRAND MANNER

'The first purpose of a garden is to give happiness and repose of mind, which is more often enjoyed in the contemplation of the homely border . . . than in any of those great gardens where the flowers lose their identity, and with it their hold of the human heart, and have to take a lower rank as mere masses of colour filling so many square yards of space.' So in 1896 Gertrude Jekyll summed up the argument that changed the direction of gardening yet again.

With the bewildering increase in kinds of plants, technical resources and possible styles throughout the nineteenth century the greatest challenge was that of choice. Writers tended to recommend everything indiscriminately. It was time for a clear-eyed look at what was, and was not, beautiful in the garden and in nature.

Miss Jekyll was a spinster of the cultivated gentry; a painter and a very gifted writer. In the country lanes and cottage gardens round her home in Surrey she found more that was truly worth looking at than in the great centres of horticulture.

At almost the same moment a very different character, a vehement young gardening journalist from Ireland called William Robinson, wrote a book called *The Wild Garden* and, in 1871, started a magazine he called *The Garden*. Miss Jekyll became a contributor in 1875. *The Garden* became the vehicle for revolutionary views, castigating carpet-bedding and all that it stood for, fulminating against formalism, and declaring (at its most moderate) that 'we should not have any definite pattern to weary the eye, but we should have quiet grace, and verdure, and little pictures month by month'.

Love of plants was at the core of it. In *The Garden*, and the many books by its contributors, writing about plants developed a new sensitivity. Robinson's *The English Flower Garden* of 1883 was the bible of the movement. Miss Jekyll's *Wood and Garden*, 1896, was probably its masterpiece. Nobody has written with such clarity and authority before on, for example, the precise use of colour, or why one plant sets off another to perfection.

By great good fortune Miss Jekyll met and formed a partnership with a young architect, Edwin Lutyens. He designed houses and gardens; she planted them. Lutyens was the original genius needed to settle the still-open vexed question of the design of the garden. While others were still reviving Jacobean or Restoration gardens Lutyens coined a new style of his own: a development of farmhouse vernacular into something monumental and full of power.

While the argument raged on about whether gardens should be formal or informal Lutyens designed immensely formal, or at least architectural, gardens and Miss Jekyll planted them. Between them they produced the equation of a maximum of architectural definition – whether symmetrical or not was beside the point – in the planning, and a maximum of informality in the planting.

By dividing up the garden space into definite separate rooms Lutyens gave his partner the opportunity to paint a multitude of distinct pictures with plants. There was space in quite a small area for a woodland glade, cottagey effects, a formal pool, borders of different colours or for different times of year, a bog garden and a rock garden, if they were screened from each other in a carefully articulated plan.

Both Robinson and Jekyll professed to have learned a great deal from cottage gardens. It was certainly not artistic arrangement they learned from the higgledy-piggledy of little plots at the cottage door. It was a sort of humility; the beauty lay in the plants and often their haphazard association. Mostly they were either old garden plants or native flowers.

This attitude has been the key to almost all the English gardens that have been recognized as great in this century. The exceptions are the great woodland gardens, which stride off in a mood of their own into a never-never land somewhere in the Himalayas.

ABOVE: *The true cottage style means infinite devotion to individual plants that together form pictures of great charm. The author Margery Fish practised and preached it in her Somerset garden at East Lambrook.*

Among the most celebrated gardens in the new manner, with enclosures of exuberant but carefully considered planting as their theme, are Hidcote Manor in the Cotswolds, started about 1907; Sissinghurst Castle in Kent, started about 1930; and Crathes Castle near Aberdeen, started about 1929. Of original Lutyens-Jekyll gardens unfortunately very few have survived in a recognizable state. But thousands of others have adapted the principle consciously or unconsciously. Inevitably though it is Miss Jekyll's part, rather than Lutyens's, that modern gardeners play. The planting has to try to make up for lack of architecture or even, often, of a plan.

It is not a revulsion from the bricks and mortar themselves but their cost that has shaped more recent styles. One of the most influential of these was the 'island' beds advocated by the Norfolk nurseryman Alan Bloom, using free-flowing, 'landscape' beds filled with border flowers, or often heathers and dwarf conifers. On a big scale the effect can be very fine, as at Bloom's own garden at Bressingham. Reduced to an urban rectangle it can be much less effective than a wall-to-wall cottage muddle.

Since Bloom the most influential source of ideas has been Beth Chatto, both in her Essex nursery, Unusual Plants, and her books. Beth Chatto faced the problems of gardening on both dry and damp sites and difficult soils in the most positive way: by making a virtue of the natural conditions to give her planting unity

BELOW: *The grand woodland style started with the mid-Victorian introduction of Himalayan rhododendrons. Many splendid examples, such as Wakehurst Place, here, are now in their prime.*

and authority. Her taste for soft-coloured, leafy, ecologically-based planting (*The Green Tapestry* is the title of one of her books) attracted a generation towards this less stressful approach to gardening.

Thoughtful plant-centred gardening has since been encouraged and greatly helped by the computerized consolidation of hundreds of specialist nursery catalogues in the annually published *Plantfinder*, a list of '65,000 plants and where to buy them' now sponsored by the Royal Horticultural Society. The *Plantfinder* was rapidly imitated in France, an indication that interest in plants is overtaking interest in design as the gardener's starting point.

GARDENS ARE FOR PEOPLE

ABOVE: *The emphasis in this design by Oehme and van Sweden on Chesapeake Bay, Maryland, is squarely on the human element. This is a garden for family and social life, not messing about with plants. The ancient Persians would have approved.*

Church's philosophy is summed up in the title of his most influential book. He called it simply *Gardens are for People*.

Americans have made almost every kind of garden. Starting with the English seventeenth-century model (the best example existing anywhere today being the reconstruction of colonial Williamsburg), they have progressed through homely back-yards, opulent imitations of the French and Italian styles and serious and successful versions of the English landscape, to arrive at a style which is uniquely their own: a fusion of influences from almost everywhere, which is now returning what it has borrowed with interest.

In all the gardens of the past there have been the active participants, usually paid gardeners, and the passive ones whose role was to stroll about gossiping, admiring the flowers and the fountains and wondering how much it had all cost. America introduced a new concept, the garden as a play-space, decorated with plants but almost independent of them, where the main activity is not gardening but relaxing, swimming, playing with the children or entertaining friends.

The climate allows many ideas which would be impractical or inappropriate in northern Europe. The swimming pool is often the focal point, with an attendant building of its own as changing-room and perhaps outdoor cookhouse. Garden furniture is scarcely different from indoor furniture. Church devised gardens that needed little gardening for people who had the money and the space but not the inclination to spend their time stooping, nor gardeners to do it for them.

Church compared the first Californian gardens, made by Spanish settlers on a model going back to Moorish patios, with the English landscape style, which had crossed the Rockies from the East. The rich of post-Goldrush California did not stint themselves for lawns, flower beds and exotic trees – all promiscuously watered as the only way of keeping them alive.

But Church saw that the natural way of life in a Mediterranean climate does not divide the house and garden into habitat and setting. The dichotomy of indoor/outdoor, inherited from England, was irrelevant. In this century most houses built in California have been on one level, with the opportunity to step out of the house, at any point, into the garden. Where William Kent leapt the fence, Thomas Church jumped through the window.

The logic is inescapable: fuse house and garden into one. It was the old way of the Spaniards, and across the Pacific Japan provided the same inspiration.

The main components of the garden were no longer the lawns, borders and shrubberies but the features of a private resort: swimming pool, sundeck, barbecue, sand-pit, games area, car-park and perhaps a vegetable plot. Among these functional spaces were interwoven elements of planting, also for practical purposes – trees for shade, bushes for screening, and occasionally, as a purely horticultural treat, a big container of bright flowers or a soft carpet of moss.

Church's genius lay where the genius of great designers always has: in identifying the essential character of the site and interpreting it in his client's terms. The opportunities in the seaside hills of California are magnificent. The views, the

LEFT: *The hallmark of Thomas Church's gardens (this is in San Francisco) was the integration of living spaces indoors and outdoors by the use of decks on different levels, taking advantage of the best existing trees for shade.*

rocks, the shape of the land, the forms of the old live oaks, even the pale layers of the sea-fog were there to be exploited.

Abstract art, Cubism in particular, provided themes in flowing and inter-locking shapes which Church used, where the site allowed, to free the garden from any feeling of boundaries. The hills themselves flowed and interlocked in sympathy. Often the sites were so steep that a third dimension of steps and 'decks' (usually of native redwood planking) gave the garden an even greater feeling of being a house without roof or walls.

Once the style was established the State boundary did not stop it. In other parts of the United States there were other reasons for not wanting a traditional garden. The extreme climate makes most Americans reluctant gardeners, just as England's teasing mildness is constantly bringing us to the garden door to see what bud is bursting. The California garden as Church and his associates conceived it adapts well to un-Californian conditions. It shuts down well in winter and is quick-ly ready for action in summer. Hence the rapid spread of the same sort of hard-edge design to Scandinavia.

LEFT: *In a Napa Valley garden the integration of home life and nature in its near-wild state seems complete.*

WHAT NEXT?

ABOVE: *The film-maker Derek Jarman made a futuristic garden on the beach at Dungeness in Kent, its eye-catcher a nuclear power station and its season limited to summer.*
BELOW: *Integration of garden and farm-landscape is almost total in this Maryland design by Oehme and van Sweden. The farm silos play the role Brown would have given a temple.*

Every factor likely to affect garden-making: resources of knowledge, resources of labour, way of life and artistic inspiration have changed completely in this century.

We have far more species of plant available than our ancestors did; which makes choice harder than ever. We have far more knowledge of the workings of plant life. We have a fraction of the time and practically none of the task force. As for artistic inspiration, not many gardeners even now find themselves inspired by the works of the twentieth century.

In these circumstances our legacy is partly a help, partly a hindrance. The helpful part is the vast body of information on how to grow things which has taken centuries to accumulate. What is less helpful is that so many conventions have accrued to the simple idea of a garden. It is not easy to shake them off or ignore them. They are written and rewritten into every gardening textbook as the received wisdom of the subject. Yet we must shake them off, or at least be extremely selective among them, if we want to make gardens that are a pleasure and not a worry.

The central tension of gardening as we enter the twenty-first century is between the knowledge and love of plants and the lack of time to care for them. It does not matter that lack of time is largely illusory: that labour-saving is a false god. In due course, when there is more leisure than we know what to do with, no doubt labour-intensive crafts will return, gardening among them. For the moment most of us use all the mechanical and chemical aids we are offered to have more time for 'ourselves'. Yet we feel guilty about lavishing fuel and herbicides on gardens as substitutes for precious man-power. At heart we know it is a short-time expedient.

It seems as though the only way to resolve the tension is to discover or invent what sounds like a contradiction of the first principle of gardening: a garden that needs the minimum of control. Under ideal circumstances it would be simply a reversion to a natural eco-system with the lightest of editing. The woodland or 'wild' garden was the first style conceived with this intent, and is still the most workable.

It is more likely, though, especially in a town, to mean creating a new and unnatural one, which is what is usually meant in America by 'landscaping'. The American tradition is to have the garden professionally 'fixed' – to stay fixed, or at least only need a contractor to hose it down once a week. Unfortunately the results are all too often either inert and characterless or bizarre and unnatural; the very opposite of what a self-perpetuating garden could and should be.

The rules for future gardening start with the very fundamentals; take your lead from the climate and soil. To fight is to fight nature.

There will always be plant-collectors who will have none of this. For them the scree

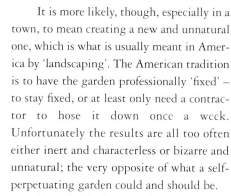

bed and the alpine house were invented. For a keen gardener in a restricted space there is no better way of widening
the horizons than to miniaturize.

Just to collaborate with nature, though, is not gardening. The modern ecological gardener's contribution is
to identify the essence of the site and to dream up an ideal
version of it. If it is a wood or the remains of a wood,
to emphasize the trees for all they are worth. If it is a
marsh, to bring the rustling reeds to the very door. If
it is a desert, to gaze out over sand-dunes and succulents.
If it is an urban yard, to polish it into quintessential urbanity. If it is a soulless suburban house-lot, to mould it round
the house and its occupants which are the reason for its existence.

ABOVE: *The genius of the late Roberto
Burle Marx in Brazil was to use the
forms of tropical plants in gardens and
streets. Here pillars imitating palms
bridge the apparently unbridgeable gap.*

On this page are some examples of what has been done in this spirit, or with
this effect, in widely different settings. They are still very much exceptions. Most
gardeners are hesitant about breaking with horticultural convention. Convention,
in Europe at least, is only just shifting towards the ecological from what you might
call decorative gardening.

In Loudon's time the 'gardenesque' rejoiced in all the artificial things gardeners could do with plants. The 'decorative' style is not so much concerned with
showing off the gardener's skill as in displaying the plants in beautiful associations
with each other.

Perhaps we need not go to the extremes of ecological, no-hands gardening.
Somewhere between emphasis on cultivating plants and composing the idealized
landscapes there is a perfect middle course. The great gardeners, certainly those of
the last hundred years, have performed the balancing act perfectly. What is admirable
about the gardens that have set the pace and influenced the style of modern gardening is that they give as much weight to plants and their cultivation as to pictures
and their composition. It is a tall order. It calls for understanding of the natures
of plants, and observation of their design and behaviour, at the same time as an
artist's eye.

It means mastering the underlying principles of plant life, taking in its variety, and making a well-considered choice. The choice, and the resolution to stick
to it, is the crux of the matter. Nobody can do everything – least of all gardening.

LEFT: *A garden in Arizona that makes a
virtue of desert conditions, using dramatic
cactus as sculpture. Again the designer
has let the site dictate: the one
fundamental rule of gardening.*

INDEX

Page numbers in *italics* refer to picture captions.

A

Aberconway, Lord 130, 131
Absinthe 177
Abutilon 83, 108
Acacia 86, 98, 189
Acaena 167
Acanthus 142, 145
Acer see Maple 98
Achillea 145, *145*, 147, *148*
Actinomycetes 27
Addison, Joseph 257
African violet 67
Agapanthus 84, 148, 229
Agathis 87
Agave 155
Ageratum 155
Alberti, Leon Battista 240
Alcazar 224
Alder 96, 98, 99
Alecost 185
Allium 91, 157, 163, *163*
Almond 237
Aloe 108
Alpines 19, 24, 31, 65, 73, *73*, 78, 94, 165–9, 170
Alstromeria 83, *145*
Alternanthera 155
Altitude 20
Alton Towers *260*
Alyssum 167
Amaryllidaceae 157
Amaryllis 157, 164
Amelanchier 98, 114
American climatic zones 19–20
Amherst, Lady 89
Androsace 169
Anemone 49, 80, 142, *158*, 159, 160, 238
Angelica 184
Anglesey Abbey *150*
Annuals 16–17, 142, 151–5, *151*
Anthemis 147
Antirrhinum 231
Aphids 42
Apical dominance 58
Aponogeton distachyos 173
Apple 57, *58*, 64, 97, 98, 198–9, *198*
Apricot *199*
Aquilegia 142
Arbutus 102
Arcades 213
Architectural features 239, *239*, 240, 241
Archways 213
Arctostaphylos 170
Arenaria balearica 167
Argyranthemum 149, 155
Arnold Arboretum 89, 91
Aronia 114
Artemisia 106, 142, 177
Aruncus 145
Asparagus 187, 195
Asphodel *113*
Aspidistra 214
Aster *149*, 150
Astilbe 145
Aubergine 193
Aubriet, Claude 81, *81*
Aubrieta 81, 167
Aucuba 102

Auricula 143, 247
Aurinia 167
Austin, David 122
Australia 86, 91
Autumn *17*, 18, 113–15, 148–50, 163–4
Auxin 54, 56, 58
Avenues 247
Azalea 33, 65, 81, *81*, 89, 94, 107, 127, 131–3, *131*, *132*, *133*, *142*, *233*, 250

B

Bacon, Sir Francis 215, 256
Bamboo 75, 172, *174*, 175
Banana 155
Banks, Sir Joseph 84, 86, *86*, 87
Banksia 86, *86*
Bark 55
Bark ringing 60
Barnsley House *183*
Baroque style *240*, 242
Bartram, John 82, 83
Basil 185
Bay 185
Beans 64, 187, 188, 189–90
Bedding plants 94, 111, 120–2, *120*, *121*, 152–5, *153*, *155*, 261
Beech 23, 87, 98, 99–100, 106
Beet 155, 194
Beetroot 194
Begonia 154–5, 214
Belon, Pierre 80
Bentham and Hooker 50, 51
Berberis 83, 102, 111, 114
Bergenia 91, 142, 224
Bhutan 91
Biennial plants 151, 152
Bilberry 125, 170
Bindweed 134, 178
Birch 26, 91, 97, *97*, 98, 99, 110
Birds 43, 79
Blackberry 197–8
Black currant 195, 196
Blackspot 42
Blackthorn 106
Blaikie, Thomas 245
Bloom, Alan 263
Bluebell 53, 159
Blueberry 114, 125, 170
Boccaccio, Giovanni 240
Bog gardens 19, 94, 171–3, 176
Bok choy 190
Bonemeal 32, 34
Bonfires 32
Bonpland, Aimé *82*
Boron 33
Boston ivy 134
Botanical descriptions 50–1
Botanical names 51–3, *51*, *53*
Botany 49–53
Bottle-brush 86
Bottom heat 68, 74
Bougainvillea 75, 138, *138*
Bowles, E.A. 158, 223
Bowles's golden grass 174
Box 100, 101, *101*, *102*, 105, *105*, 106, *177*, *182*, 187, *223*, 224, 232, 247
Boysenberry 198
Brachyglottis 177
Bracken 176
Braconid wasp 43

Bradbury 85
Bramante, Donato 241
Bramble 66
Brassicas 187, 190–2, *191*, 193
Breeding, plant 62–3, 188
Bressingham 263
Brickell, Christopher 91
Brick paving and paths 208, *208*, 209
Bridal wreath 112, 224
Bridgeman, Charles 257
Briza maxima 174
Broad bean 189
Broccoli 190, 191
Brompton stock 155
Broom 102, 112–13
Brown, Lancelot 'Capability' 218, 257, 258
Brunnera 142
Brussels sprout 186, 190, 191
Buckeye 114
Budding 68
Buddleja 59, 108, 113, 114, 115
Bugle, creeping *25*, 26
Bulbs 16, 24, 54, 65, 66, 78, 81, *81*, 110, 141, 142, 156–64, *158*, 182, 183, 238
Bullrush 172
Burlington, Lord 236
Burr plant 167
Busbecq, Ghiselin de 80
Buscot Park *218*
Buttercup 171
Butterflies 43, 79

C

Cabbage family 66, 186, 187, 190–2, *191*
Cabbage tree 87
Cactus 16
Calabrese 190, 191
Calceolaria 155
Calcium 31, 33
California poppy 85, *85*, 231
Callistemon 86
Callitriche 173
Calluna 179
Calocephalus 155
Calyx 49, *60*
Cambium layer 55, 56
Cambridge University Botanic Garden 110
Camellia 75, 88, 108, 109–10, *109*
Campanula 119, 145–6, *148*, 167, *228*, 229
Campsis 138, *138*
Candytuft, evergreen *166*, 167
Canna 155
Canterbury bell 152, 155
Cape hyacinth 148, 164
Cape pondweed 173
Carbon dioxide 27, 38, 54
Cardoon *194*, 195
Carex 174
Carnation 66, 148, 238, 247
Carpels *60*, 64
Carpet bedding *153*, 155
Carrot 187, 188, 194
Caryopteris 114
Cassiope 125, 170
Castor-oil plant 155
Catalpa 98
Catch crops 187, 192
Caterpillars 43

Catkins 110
Cauliflower 190, 191
Caus, Salomon and Isaac de 256
Ceanothus 85, 108, *111*, 112, 114, 135
Cedar 85, *95*, 99, 102, 103, 104
Celandine 40
Celeriac 194
Celery 192
Celosia 155
Ceratophyllum demersum 173
Ceratostigma 114
Chadwell, Chris 91
Chaenomeles speciosa 111
Chamaecyparis 102, 103, 104
Chambers, Sir William 225, 259
Chatsworth House *106*, 260–1
Chatto, Beth *236*, 263
Chenar tree 237
Cherry 89, *90*, 98, 110, 111, *141*, 198–9, 250
Chervil 185
Chestnut 67
Chevreul 227
Chicory 192
Childerley Hall *117*
Chile 83
Chimney bell-flower 146
Chimonanthus 110
China 88–91
Chinese cabbage 190
Chinese gardens 88, 236, 238, 245, 248–50, *248*, *249*, *250*, 251, 257
Chives 185
Chlorophyll *17*, 33, 38, 40, 54
Choisya ternata 111
Christmas rose 143
Chromosomes 63
Chrysanthemum 40, 53, 56, *56*, 58–9, *59*, 72–3, 79, *90*, 145, 147, 148, 149, *149*, 155, 231
Church, Thomas 264–5, *265*
Chusquea couleou 175
Cistus 102, 107, 108, 113, *113*
Citrus 75, 237
City microclimates 20
Clark, Lieutenant William 84, *85*
Clarkia 85
Claude Lorraine 257
Clematis 22, 42, 89, *111*, 134, 135, 136–7, *136*, 167, 230
Cleome 152
Clethra 114, 125
Climate 19–20, *19*, 27, 206–7
climatic control 22–4, *22*, *23*, *24*
Climbing plants 123–4, 134–8
Clover 181
Cobaea scandens 138
Cobnut *230*
Colchicum 157, *157*, 163
Cold frames 22, 68, 205
Colenso, William 87
Coleus 155
Colletia armata 110
Colour 94, 223, 224–33, *225*, *226*, *227*, *229*
monochrome designs 228–31, 229
Columbine 142
Comber, Harold 83
Compositae 52, 147
Compost heap 27, 29, 33–4, 205
Compton, Bishop Henry 83

Concrete paving and paths 209
Conder, Josiah 253
Coneflower 47, 148
Conifers 61, 65, 98, 99, 100, 102–4, 263
dwarf *103*, 104, 167
Conservatories 72–5, *72*, *75*, 138
Containers, plants in 29, 34–6, 74–5, 152, 155, 214–15, *214*, *215*
Convolvulus cneorum 178
Cook, Captain James 86, *86*
Copper 33
Coral spot fungus 41–2
Cordyline 87, 155
Coreopsis 147, 153
Coriander 185
Corms 157
Cornflower 145
Corn salad 192
Cornus alternifolia 107
Corydalis flexuosa 91
Cosmos 152
Cotinus 114, 135
Cotoneaster 91, 102, 107, *113*, 114, 167
Cottage gardens *206*, 263, *263*
Cotton lavender 177, 183
Cotyledons 65
Courgette 193
Cox, Peter 91
Crab, ornamental 98, 111
Crambe 145
Cranberry 170
Cranesbill 146–7, *146*, 183
Crataegus × lavallei 98
Crathes Castle 263
Creeping bugle 183
Crescentius 240
Crinum × powellii 164
Crocosmia 84, 148, 157
Crocus 54, 157, 158–9, *158*, 160, 163, 168, 183
Crosses 62–3
Crowe, Sylvia 216, 224
Crown Imperial 80, 160, 247
Cruciferae 52
Cruikshank, George 259
Cryptomeria 103, 104
Crystal Palace 72, 261
Cucumber 193
Cultivars 52–3
Cultural controls 41, *41*
Cunningham, Allan 86, 87
Cunninghame, John 88
Currant 85, 108, 196–7, *196*
flowering 111
Cuttings 67–8, 69, 153–4
Cyclamen *81*, *158*, 163–4, *164*, 168, 230
Cyperus 174–5
Cypress 84, 85, 98, 99, *101*, 102, 103–4, 105, 106, 237, 238
Cytisus 113

D

Daboecia 179
Dacrydium 87
Daffodil 54, 156, *156*, 157, *158*, 159, 160, *160*, 161, 183
Dahlia 40, 83, 145, 147, 149–50, *150*, 157, *158*, *231*
Daisies 66, 145, 147, *180*, 181
Daisy bush 87

Damson 199
Dandelion 192
Daphne 91, 109, 110, 111, 113, 178
Darmera (Peltiphyllum) peltata 172
Darwin, Charles 52, 62, 83
Day lily 41, 141, 146, *147*, 183, 231
Dead-heading 57, 59, 144, 148–9
Dead-nettle 183, *183*
Deciduous plants 16, *17*, 49
Delavay, J.-M. 89
Delbard 122
Delphinium 40, 79, 119, 140, 145, *145*, 146
Dendranthemum 149, *149*
Design 202–5, *202*, *204*
  labour-intensity 204
  style 206–7, *206*, *207*
Deutzia 90, 113
Dew *15*
Dianthus 147–8, 167
Dicentra 142
Dierama 84, 224
Digging 28, 29, 30
Dill 185
Dimorphotheca 84, 153
Disanthus 114
Diseases 41–2
Dividing, propagation by 66
Dog-rose 106
Dog's tooth violet 157
Dogwood 46, 85, 98, *101*, 106, *107*, 110
Dominant and recessive characteristics 63
Dormancy 16, *17*, 18
Douglas, David 84, 85, *85*, 259
Downy mildew 42
Drainage 22, 208
'Drawn' plants 40
Dried flowers 79
Drought 30, 42
Drummond, James 86
Drya 167
Dry landscape gardens *251*, 252
Dryopteris 176
Du Cerceau 243
Dutch gardens 246–7, *247*
Dyrham Park 256

E

Earthworm 27, *27*
East Lambrook 263
Eccremocarpus 138
Echeveria 155
Edinburgh Botanic Garden 133
Eichornia crassipes 173
Elaeagnus 63, 101, *109*
Elm 99, 106
Embothrium 83
Encarsia formosa 43
Endive 187, 192
Endtz nursery 130
English gardens 180, 225, 236, 245, 251, 254, 255–63, *255*, *256*, 257–8, *257*
Enkianthus 125, 170
Epimedium 91, 142
Ericaceae 26, 33, 84, *84*, 125, 170, 178–9, *178*, *179*
Erica 178, 179, *179*
Erigeron 147
Eriobotrya japonica 102
Eryngium 145
Erythronium 157
Escallonia 83, 102, 113
Eucalyptus 86, *86*, 97, *97*, 98, 155
Eucryphia 83, 114
Euonymus 101, 114
Euphorbia 91, *142*, 224

European climatic zones 19–20
Evans, Alfred 169
Evening primrose 85, 238
Evergreens 16, 17, 37, 49, 100–2, *101*
  hedges 105–6, *105*, *106*
  shrubs 107

F

F1 and F2 hybrids 63
False acacia 82
False cypress 102, 103, 104
Farrer, Reginald 90
Fatsia japonica 108
Featherfoil 173
Fences 211, 212–13, *212*
Fennel 184, 192
Ferns 94, 172, 175–6, *176*
Fertilization 54, 60–2, 60, *61*, 64
Fertilizer 32, 34, *34*
Feverfew 155
Ficus 155
Fig 75, 108, 155, *198*
Fir 85, *85*, 98, 99, 102
Fireblight 42
Fish, Margery 263
Flame-flower 138
Fleabane 147
Flowering season 79
Flowers 77–9
  double 61–2
  flower characteristics 47, 49–50
  function 54, 60–2, *60*
  opening mechanism 54
  perfect 60, 61
Foliage 49, 54, *223*, 230, 232
Follies 259
Fontinalis antipyretica 173
Forget me-not 151, 155, *182*
Formal gardens *106*, 206, 210, 221–2, *221*, *222*, 236, 237, 240
Forrest, George 90, 130, *130*
Forsythia 110–11
Fortune, Robert 88, 130
Fothergilla major 114
Fountains 217, 221–2, *221*, *222*, 237, 244, *244*
Fouquet, Nicolas 243
Foxglove 119, *146*, 152
Fragrance 79, 121
Francoa ramosa 224
Fraser, John 83
Freesia 84, 157
French bean 189
French gardens 243–6, *243*, *244*, *245*, *246*
Fritillary 157, *159*
Frost 16, 18–19, 21, 24
  radiation 21, *21*
Fruit 64–6, *64*, 195–9
  cane 197–8, *197*
  forcing early 24
  soft 195–7, *195*, *196*
  top 198–9
Fruit trees 97, 198–9, *198*, *199*, 211–12
  bark ringing 60
  grafting 68
  pruning 57, 58, 199
  tunnel, trained to form 58
Fruticose 177
Fuchsia 72–3, 83, 83, 114, 115, 154, *154*, 155, 177, 214
Fungal diseases 41–2

G

Gages 199
Gaillardia 147, 155
Galanthus 156, 158
Galingale 172, 175

Galtonia 84, 148, 164
Gambara, Cardinal 242
Gardeners' garters 174
Gardenesque style 260, *260*
Garrya 85, 110
Gass, Sergeant 85
Gateways 250, *253*
Gaultheria 85, 114, 125, 170
Gazania 84, *84*
Generalife, Granada 218, 237, *237*
Genetics 62, 63
Genista 113
Gentian 166, 170, *233*
Genus 52, 53
Geology, site 207, 208
Geranium 145, 146–7, *146*, 153–4, 155, *155*
Gerard, John 47, *47*, 51, 80, *82*, 256
Germander 187
Germination 65–6, *65*, 66
Giberellins 56
Girardin, Marquis de 245
Gladiolus 157, *158*
Glass, growing under 24
Gleditsia 97
Globe artichoke *194*, 195
Globe-flower 172
Godetia 85
Golden purslane 192
Golden rod 147
Gold and Silver Pavilions 251, *252*
Gooseberry 195, 197
Gorse 26, 78
Gothick style 258, 259
Grafting 62, 68, *68*
Grape hyacinth 157, *159*
Grape vine 16, 72, 75, 134, *182*
Grasses 78, 141, 172, 174–5, *174*, 180–2
Gravel areas 209
Gravel mulch 31
Gravity 56, 65
Greenhouses 72–5, *72*, *73*, 75, 259, 260–1
Grevillea 155
Grex 130, 131
Grey-Wilson, Chris 91
Grottoes 240, 244
Groundcover 79, 177, 178, 180, 182–3, *182*, *183*
Ground elder 171
Growing points 56, 68
Growing season 20
Growth 78, 78, 79
  controlling 56–60
Guernsey lily 164
Gulf Stream *16*, 17
Gum tree 86
Gunnera manicata 172
Gypsophila 167

H

Habitat and garden design 93–4
Hadrian's Villa *239*
Ha-ha's 257
Hakea 86
Half-hardy plants 16, 151, 152
Hamamelis 91, 109, 114
Ham House 256
Hanbury, Giardino Botanico, La Mortola 20
Hanging baskets 152, 155, *155*, 214
Hardening-off 24, 152
Hardiness, zones of plant 19–20
Hard surfaces 208–11, *208*, *209*, *210*
Hardy plants 16–20, 151
Haricot bean 190
Hart's tongue 176
Hatfield House 96

Hatfield Old Palace *255*
Hawthorn 42, 106, 114, 135
Hazel 110
Hazelbury Manor 231
Heathers 26, 31, 33, 78, 170, 177–9, *178*, *179*, 263
Heaths 84, 170, 177–9, *179*
Hebe 87, 91, 114, 177
Hedges 23, 105–6, *105*, *106*, 247
Hedychium 91
Heian shrine 250
Helenium 147
Helianthemum 167, 177, 178
Helianthus 147
Heliopsis 147
Heliotrope 155, 224
Hellebore *25*, 26, 60, 91, 111, 142–3, *143*
Helxine *183*
Hemerocallis 146, *147*
Hemlock 91
Henry Doubleday Research Institute 188
Herbaceous perennials 94, 139–50, *139*, *140*
Herbaceous plants 5
Herb gardens *183*, 184–5, *184*, *185*
Het Loo 246
Heuchera 142
Hibberd, Shirley 260, *260*
Hibiscus 75, 114, 115
Hicks, David 222
Hidcote Manor 221, 230, 263
Hill, Thomas 256
Himalayan blue poppy 89, 131, 170
Himalayas 91
Hippeastrum 164
Hobbie, Dietrich 131
Hoeing 71
Hoheria 114
Holly 101–2, *105*, 106, 114
Hollyhock 42, 238
Honesty 141, 230
Honey fungus 41, *42*
Honeysuckle 79, 106, 110, 134–5, *136*, 138
Hooker, Sir Joseph 88, *127*, 130
Hordeum jubatum 174
Hormones 54, *54*, 56
Hornbeam 91, 106, *106*, 247
Hornwort 173
Horse chestnut 97, 100
Hortensia 115
Hortus Third 50, 51
Hortus conclusus 240
Hosta 78, 142, *142*, 172
Hottonia palustris 173
Houseleek 167
Hui Tsung, Emperor 250
Humboldt, Alexander von *82*, 83
Humus 27, *27*, 28, 29, 30, 31
Hurst, Dr C.C. 117
Hutchins, Graham 91
Hyacinth 80, 155, 157, *157*, 159, 160, 238, 247
Hybrids 62
Hydrangea 114, 115, 135
Hydrological cycle 14–16, *14*, 15
Hypericum 80, 91, 114, 115

I

Iberis 166, 167
Incarville, Father Pierre d' 88
Incarvillea 91
Informal gardens 236
Insect pollination 61, *61*
Inula 150
Inverewe *16*
Ions 217
Iridaceae 157

Iris 66, 119, 142, *142*, 144, 157, 158, *158*, 168, 172, 224, 237, 250
Iron 33
Irrigation 22
Island beds 263
Italian gardens 224, 239–42, *239*, *240*, *241*, *242*, 257
Ivy 101, 134, *134*, 135, 137, *182*, 183, 214

J

Japan 88–9, 91
Japanese anemone 142, *149*
Japanese bush-clover 114
Japanese gardens 88, 90, 97, *104*, 176, 209, 213, 217–18, 233, 246, 249–54, *251*, *252*, *253*, *254*
Jardin clos 240, *243*, 247
Jardin de curé 246
Jarman, Derek 266
Jasmine 75, 79, 134, 137–8, *138*, 238
Jekyll, Gertrude 139, 224, 228–9, 231, 232, 241, 262–3, *262*
Johns Hopkins Hospital, Baltimore *101*
John Innes compost 35–6
Jonquil *161*, 238
Joséphine, Empress 116, 117, 245–6
Julius II, Pope 241
Juniper 101, *102*, *103*, 104, 183, 232

K

Kaempfer, Engelbert 89
Kaffir lily 84, 148
Kale 190, 191
Kalmia latifolia 101
Kalmiopsis 170
Kashmir 91
Kent, William 240, 257, *257*
Kerr, William 88
Kew Gardens 259
Kingcup 172
Kingdom-Ward, Frank 89, 90
Kinins 56
Kitchen gardens 152, 186–99, 204, 207, 245
  forcing early crops 24
  growing for flavour 79
Knapweed 47
Kniphofia 150
Knot gardens *183*, 255, *255*
Kohlrabi 190, 192
Kolkwitzia 113
Kordes, Wilhelm 118–19, *121*
Korea 91
Kyoto 253

L

Laburnum 189
Ladybird *41*, 43
Lady's mantle 185
Lamb's lettuce 192
Lamium maculatum 183
Lancaster, Roy 91, *91*
Langley, Batty 257
Larch 85, 103
Laurel 100, 101, 102, 125
Lavatera olbia 108
Lavender 79, 85, 106, 114, 178, *182*, 185, *206*
Lawes, John Bennet 31, *34*
Lawns 180–2, *180*, 181
Layering 66, 67, *67*
Leach, David G. 131
Le Brun, Charles 243
Leek 186, 187, 190
Legumes 33, 187, 189–90, *189*

Lemon balm 185
Le Nôtre, André 243–4, *243*, *244*, 256
Lenten rose 143
Lent lily *156*
Lepidotes 127
Leslie, Alan 91
Lettuce 187, 192
Leucojum 158
Leucophyta 155
Leucothoe 101, 170
Lewis, Meriwether 84, 85
Lewisia 168
Light and shade 40, 97, 213
   back-lighting 232, *233*
   tonal contrast in plants 223
Lignin 54
Lilac *112*, 238
Liliaceae 157
Lily 33, *64*, 66, 85, 89, 131, 156, 157, *158*, 160, 161, *161*, 163, 170, 230, 238
Lily-turf 181
Lily of the valley 142, *158*
Lime 26, 33, 91, 99, *206*
Limnanthes 85
Ling 179
Linnaea borealis 52
Linnaeus (Carl von Linné) 51, *51*, 52, *52*, 60, 84, 131
Liquidambar 91
Lloyd, Christopher 57
Lobb, William 83
Lobelia 155
Loder, Sir Edmund 130
Loganberry 197–8
Lomaria 86
London pride 142
London and Wise 256
Long-day plants 40
Lonicera 106, 110, 138
Loquat 102
Lotus 173
Loudenne, Château *186*
Loudon, John Claudius 259–60, *260*
Louis XIV, King 243, 244
Lovage 185
Love-in-a-mist 151
Lupin 33, 85, 142, 144
Lutyens, Edwin 262–3, *262*
Luxembourg Gardens 243
Lysichiton 172
Lyons, Parc Tete d'Or *153*

M

Mache 192
Macleaya 145
Magnesium 31, 33
Magnol, Pierre 52
Magnolia 23, 37, 41, 52, 61, 65, 89, 91, 99, *99*, 101, 135
Mahonia 85, 91, *91*, 101, 109, *109*, 114
Maidenhair fern 176
Maize 188, 193
Male fern 176
Malmaison, La 117, 245–6
Malus 98
Mandevilla 75
Manganese 33
Mangetout 190
Manure 29, 31, 34
Maple 18, 49, 65, 82, 89, 96, 98, *98*, 99, *108*, 114, 230
Marguerite 149, 155
Marie Antoinette 245
Marliac, M. 173
Marrow 188, 193
Marx, Roberto Burle *180*, *267*
Masson, Francis 84
Maximowicz, Carl 131

Meadows 181–2
Medieval gardens 240, 255
Medlar 98
Mehlquist, Gustav A.L. 131
Meilland 122
Mendel, Gregor 62–3
Meristem 68, *69*
Mesembryanthemum 84
Metasequoia 90, 103
Mexico 91
Meyer, Frank 90
Mezereon 109, 110
Michaelmas daisy 79, 82, 83, 145, 147, 148, 149, *149*, 150, 230, 231
Michaux, André 83
Microclimates 20–2, *20*
Miller, Philip 259–60
Mimulus 171
Mind-your-own-business *183*
Mint 79, 185
Miscanthus sacchariflorus 174
Mist propagator 68, *68*
Mock-orange 113
Mollet, Claude 243
Molybdenum 33
Monocots 156
Moor Park 256
Morning glory 138
Mosaic virus 42
Moss campion 168
Mosses 175–6, *176*, 181, *183*, 250
Moss Garden, Kyoto 250
Moths 43
Mottisfont Abbey 118
Mountain betony *165*
Mulching 24, 30–1
Mushroom compost 34
Myosotis scorpioides 182
Myrtle 75

N

Naked lady 163
Names, plant 51–3, *51*, 53
Narcissus 25, 26, 157, 160, *160*, 161, 237
Nasturtium 153, 167, *183*, 231
Nectar 60, *61*
Nectarine 198–9
Nelumbo nucifera 173
Nemesia 155
Nemophila 85, 151
Nepal 91
Nerine 84, 148, 157, 164, *164*, 183
New Zealand 87, 91
New Zealand flax 87, *87*
Nicotiana 152, *153*, *231*
Ninfa *217*
Nitrogen 27, 31, 32, 33–4, *33*, 34, 62
Noailles, Vicomte de *246*
Noble nursery 128
North America 82–3, 84–5
North-facing sites 22
Nothofagus 87, 98
Nothospartium 91
Nurseries 69
Nuttall 85
Nymphaea lotus 173
Nyssa sylvatica 95

O

Oak 33, 54, 65, *65*, 85, 91, 96, 99, 100, 102, 105, 106
Objets trouvés 216
Odora 110
Oehme and van Sweden *264*, *266*
Oenothera missouriensis 85
Offsets 65, 66, 157
Ogisu, Minori 91
Oleander 75, 114, 115, 214

Olearia 87, *87*
Olive 18, 20, 75, 99
Olivers *220*
Onion 187, 188, 190, *190*
Ophiopogon 181
Opium poppy 153
Orchid 61, 69, 73, *74*
Oregon grape 85, 101
Organic gardening movement 43
Oriental poppy 47, 81, 142, 144
Ornamental fowl 238
Osmanthus 107
Ovaries *60*, 64
Ovules 64
Ox-eye chamomile 147

P

Page, Russell 206
Paintwork 233
Palladio, Andrea 257
Palm 155, 237
Pampas grass 174
Pansy 111, 152, 155, *155*
Paper white *161*
Paris daisy 149, 155
Parsley 185
Parsnip 194
Parterres 256
Parterres de broderie 243
Partridge berry 170
Passion flower 75, 135, 138
Paths 208–11, *208*, 209
Paulownia 135
Paving 180, 208–11, *208*, 209
Paxton, Joseph 72, 260–1
Pea 67, 187, 189, 190
Peach 198–9
Peacock 238
Pear 42, 98, 198–9, *199*
Pearl grass 174
Peat gardens 169–70
Pedicularis pectinata 165
Pegging down 59–60
Pelargonium 72–3, 84, 84, 153–4, 155, 214
Pemberton, Rev Joseph 121
Penstemon 85
Penzance, Lord 118
Peony 37, 78, *81*, 91, 112, *141*, 144
Pepper 193
Perennials 139–50, *139*, 140, 194–5, *194*
Pergolas 213
Periwinkle 183
Pernettya 170
Persian/Arab gardens 237–8, *237*, 238
Perspective, use of 95, 97, 213
Pests 41, 43
   biological control 43
Petals 60
Petits pois 190
Petit Trianon 245
Petrarch 240
Petunia 152, 214, *231*
pH 33
Phacelia 85
Philadelphus 79, 107, *112*, 113
Phloem 55, 55, 56
Phlox 146, *147*, 167, 229
Phormium tenax 87, *87*
Phosphorus 31–2, 34
Photinia 102
Photosynthesis 14, 38, 38, 54, 55
Phototropism 40, *40*, 56
Phyllostachys bambusoides 174, 175
Phytoseiulus persimilis 43
Picea omorika 103
Picturesque style 258–60
Pieris 101, 125
Pileostegia viburnoides 138

Pinching-out 56, *57*
Pine 26, 78, 84, 91, 98, 99, 103, *104*, 237, 251
Pinus culminicola 91
Pink 66, 148, 167, 238
Pipings 66
Pitmedden 256
Pittosporum 87
Plane 78
Plant collectors 80–91, 238, 256
Plantfinder, The 69, 263
Plant habit 49
Planting 35–7, 35, 223–33
   late 23
Plantsmanship 47, 49–50
Pleaching *213*
Pleione 90
Pliny 239
Plum 198–9
Plumbago 75
Plumule 65
Pollarding *100*
Pollination 60, *61*, *61*, *62*
Polyanthus 111, 143, 155, *155*
Polygonum tortuosum 91
Ponds and pools 97, 218–22, *220*, 221, *222*
Pope, Alexander 257
Pope, Arthur Upham 237
Poplar 78, 79, *95*, 98, 99, 237
Poppy 47, 79, 81, *81*, 85, 89, 89, 131, 142, 144, 151, 153, 170, 231
Potagers *186*, 187, *245*
Potash 189, 196, 198
Potassium 31, 32, 33, 34
Potato 188, *193*
Potentilla 113, 114
Potting compost 35–6
Poussin, Nicolas 257
Powdery mildew 42
Predators 41
Pride, Orlando S. 131
Primrose 50–1, *50*, 106, 143
Primula 89, 131, 143, *144*, 153, 167, 170, 172, 237
Privet 106, 231
Propagation 66–9
Protea 84, 86, 86
Pruning 55, 55, 57–9
   clematis 137
   fruit trees 199
   late 23
   rose 119, 124
   shrubs 108
   soft fruits 196–7
Prunus 98, 110
Pseudopanax 91
Pseudosasa japonica 175
Purdom, William 90
Pyracantha 102, 114

Q

Quercus robur 91, 99
Quince 98, 111, 199

R

Radicle 65
Radish 187, 192
Ramonda 168
Ranunculus *158*, 160, 247
Raoulia 91, 167
Raspberry 196, 197–8
Receptacles 64
Red cabbage 190, 191
Red currant 196, *196*, 197
Red hot poker 148, 150, 229–30
Red and orange 229, 230, *231*, 232, 233, *233*

Redouté, Pierre-Joseph *49*, *116*, 117, 246
Red spider mite 43
Redwood 84, 103
Reed mace 172
Reeds 171, 172, 174
Renaissance gardens 224, 239–42, 243–4, 256
Repton, Humphry 180, 202, 233, 258, *259*
Rheum 172
Rhizomes 157, *158*
Rhododendron 33, 41, 49, 59, 89, *89*, 91, 94, 101, 107, 111, 125–31, *125*, *126*, *127*, *128*, *129*, 170, 236, *263*
   alpines 127, 131
Rhubarb 186, 187, 195
Ribes sanguineum 85, 108, 111
Richmond 256
Rix, Martyn 91
Robinia 97, 98, 100
Robinson, William 139, 262–3
Rock, Joseph 90
Rocket 192
Rockfoil 167
Rock gardens 90, 94, 165–70, *165*, 248, 249, 251
Rock rose 177
Rodgersia 141, 172
Roman gardens 239, *239*, 247
Root crops 187, 193–5, *193*
Rooting hormones 68
Roots 29–30, 35–7, 55
Rosaceae 52
Rose 63, 65, 78, 89, 94, 113, 114, 116–24, 135, 185, *187*, 211–12, 223, 229, 238, 247
   Alba 116, 119
   bedding 120–2, *120*, *121*
   Bourbon 117–18, *118*, 119, 124
   breeding 116–17, 118
   cabbage 116, *116*
   Chinese 88, 91, 116–17, *117*, *119*, 238
   climbing and rambling *119*, 123–4, *123*, *124*, 136
   Damask 116
   dead-heading 57, 59, 122
   diseases and pests 42, 120, 122
   English 122, *122*
   Floribunda 117, 121–2, *121*, 124
   fragrance 121
   Gallica 116, *116*, 122
   grafting 68
   Grandiflora 121
   hedging 106
   Hybrid China 117
   Hybrid Musk 121, *121*, 122, *124*
   Hybrid Perpetual 118, *118*, 119, 124
   Hybrid Tea 117, 118, 120–1, *120*, 124
   Large- and Cluster-flowered bush 117, *121*
   musk 116, 123, 124
   Noisette 121, *121*, 122, 124
   pegging down 59–60
   Penzance briars 118
   Polypom 120
   Portland 117
   Poulsen 120
   Provence 116
   pruning 119, 124
   repeat-flowering 116, 117, 118
   rootstock suckers 122
   Rose des Peintres 116
   shrub 117–19, *117*
   tea 116, 117, 124
Rosemary 79, 85, 106, 184, 185

Rotation in the kitchen garden 187
Rothschilds *129*, 130, 131, *131*
Rottneros *221*
Rousseau, Jean-Jacques 245
Rowan 100
Royal fern 176
Royal Horticultural Society 79, 259, *259*
Rubus 110, 113
Rudbeckia 82, 148
Rue 185
Runner bean 189
Runners 66
Rushes 171, 172, 174
Rushforth, Keith 91
Russian vine 138
Rust 42
Ryoan-Ji *251*, 252

S

Sackville-West, Victoria 118, 230
Sage *148*, 151, 185
Sage-brush 177
Sagina 155, 167
St Germain-en-Laye *243*
St John's Wort 80, 115
St Petersburg *222*
Salad crops 187, 192–3, *192*
Sales, John 261
Saling Hall 7, *11*, 95
Salpiglossis 153, 155
Salsify 194
Salvia *61*, 85, 91, *145*, 147, *148*, 155
San Simeon *239*
Santolina 106, 177
Sap 55–6, *56*
Saponaria 167
Sarcococca 110
Sasanquas 109
Sasa palmata 175
Saxifrage 78, 167, 169, 172
Scale 78, 97, 206
Scale insects 43
Scarifying 65
Schilling, Tony 91
Schizanthus 153
Scilla 157, 159
Scion 68
Scottish gardens 169–70, *256*
Screens and frames 213–14, *213*
Sea buckthorn 108, 114, *115*
Seakale 195
Seakale beet 194
Seats 216, *216*
Seaweed 34, *34*
Seclusion 96–7
Sedges 172, 174–5
Sedum 67, 91, 167, *231*
Seed heads 79, 145
Seeds 54, 60, 61, 64–6, *64*, 65, 66
    chipping 65
    dispersal mechanisms 65
    dormancy 64–5
    germination 65–6, *65*, 66
    imbibition 65
    scarifying 65
    sowing 65–6
    stratification 65
Sempervivum 167
Senecio 87, 155, 177
Sento Imperial villa *253*
Sepals 60
Shade 40, 97
Shallot 190
Sharawadgi *257*
Shasta daisy *149*
Shield fern 176
Shigemori, Mirei *253*
Shigo, Alex 55–6
Shore-line 78

Short-day plants 40
Shrubberies 107
Shrub roses 117–19, *117*
Shrubs 107–15, 141
    dwarf 167
    sub-shrubs 177–9
Shuttlecock fern 176
Siberian squill 159
Silver leaf disease 42
Sinarundinaria 175
Sissinghurst Castle 230, *263*
Sitwell, Sir George 215, 221
Skimmia 102
Skunk cabbage 172
Skyline 97
Slocock's nursery 131
Sloping sites 20, 210–11
Slugs 43
Smoke bush 135
Snapdragon 42
Sneezeweed 147
Snow 24, 100, 101, *102*
Snowbell 113
Snowdrop 106, *156*, 157, 158, 168
Snowflake 158
Soil 25–34
    acid 26, 108, 125–33, 169–70
    acidity 33
    air content 25, 27–8, *28*, 29
    chalky 26, 26
    chemistry 31–4
    clay *25*, 26, 28–9
    and frost 24
    drainage 28, 29–30, *29*
    humus 27, *27*, 28, 29, 30, 31
    leaching 27, 28
    matching to microclimate 22
    micro-organisms 27
    oxygen content 27–8, 29
    peaty 26, *27*
    pH 33
    potting mixtures 214–15
    as reservoir 28–31
    sandy 26, 28–9
    soil type and garden design 207
    structure 26–8, 34
    sub-soil 25, 27
    texture 26
    top-soil 25, 27
    trace elements 33
    water content 25, 28–31
    waterlogged 27, 29–30, *29*, 42
    water-table 28, 29
Solanum 138, 155
Soleirolia *183*
Solidago 147
Solomon's seal 142
Sophora 65, 91
Sorbus 91, 98, 100
Sorrel tree 125
South Africa 83–4
Southernwood 106, 177
Sparmannia africana 75
Spartium 113
Species 52, 53
Spinach 187, 193, 194
Spinach-beet 194
Spindle 106
Spindle bush 78
Spiraea 112
Sporting 104, 176
Spring 111–12, 136, 141–4, 155, 158–62
Spring greens 190, 191
Spring onion 192
Spring-Smith, Tom 91
Spruce 85, 98, 99, 102–3, *103*, 104
Spry, Constance 118
Spurge 141
Squirrels 43
Squirreltail barley 174

Stachyurus 91, 110
Staking 37
Stamens 60
Standish nursery 128
Statues *182*, 215–16, *215*, *216*, 222
Stepping stones 209, 210
Steps *210*, 211
Sternbergia 157
Stigmas 60
Stipules 49
Stock 153, 155
Stonecrop 167
Stowe 257, *257*
Stratification 65
Stratiotes aloides 173
Strawberry 66, *195*, 198
Strawberry Hill *258*, 259
Strawberry tree 125
Streams *217*, 218–21, *218*, *219*
Streptocarpus 67
Styles 60
Style anglo-chinois 245
Styrax 113
Sub-shrubs 177–9
Subtropical bedding 155
Succulents 16
Suffruticose 177–9
Sugar beet 194
Sumach 98
Summer 113, 136–8, 145–8, 155, 163
Summer hyacinth 164
Summer savoury 185
Sunflower 147, 153
Sunk gardens 210
Sunlight *20*, 21–2, 38, *38*, 40, *40*, 54, 56
Swamp cypress 82, 103, 171
Swede 193
Sweet Cicely 185
Sweet corn 188, 193
Sweet marjoram 185
Sweet pea 65, *137*, 138, 152, *187*
Sweet William 148, 155
Swimming pools 222, *222*
Swiss chard 194
Switzer, Stephen 257
Sycamore 78, 99
Syringa 113

T

Taiwan 91
Tale of Genji 250
Tarragon 185
Tasmania 86
Taxonomy, plant 49–53
Tea 88
Tea gardens 252, *252*
Temperate zones 16–18
Temple, Sir William *236*, 257
Tender plants 16
Terraces 210–11
Thamnocalamus 175
Thistle, giant *213*
Thomas, Graham Stuart 118, 139
Thomson, James 245
Thunberg, Carl Peter 84, 89
Thuya 102, 104
Thyme 85, 167, 185
Tiarella polyphylla 91
Tibet 89–90
Tickseed 147
Tiled surfaces 238
Tomato 188, *192*, 193
Topiary 247, *247*, *255*, 257
Torch lily 150
Tournefort, Joseph Piton de 80–1, *80*, *81*
Town gardens 20, *205*, 208
Tradescant, John, the Elder 80, *80*, 256

Tradescant, John, the Younger 82, 256
Transpiration 14–15, 16, 18, 28, 55
Transplanting 37
Tree fern 87, *175*
Tree peony 112, 144
Trees 46, 96–100
    conifers *see* Conifers
    evergreen 100–2, *101*
    fruit *see* Fruit trees
    grafting 68
    layering 66, 67, 67
    maiden 37
    pleaching *213*
    pruning 55–6, *55*
    seed 65
    transplanting 37, 38–9
Treillage 213, 244
Trianon 245
Trillium 131, 157
Trollius 172
Tropaeolum 83, *135*, 138
Tuberous roots 157, *158*
Tubers 157, *158*
Tuileries *243*
Tulip 54, 78, 80, 155, *155*, 156, 157, *159*, 160, *162*, *162*, 237, 247
Tulip tree 82
Turner, William 256
Turnip 193
Turpin 49
Tusser, Thomas 80
Type specimen 52
Typha laxmannii 172

U

Umbelliferae 52
Umbrella sedge 174–5
Unity, Utility and Proportion 202, *202*

V

Vaccinium 115, 170
Valerian *177*
Vanbrugh, Sir John 257
Vann 262
van Nes & Sons 130
Varieties 52–3
Vascular system 55
Vatican, Cortile del Belvedere 241
Vaux le Vicomte *243*
Veitch's nusery 83, 89
Verbena *231*
Veronica 177, 230
Versailles 218, 222, 224–5, 244–5, *244*
Verticillium wilt 41
Viburnum 102, 110, *111*, 112, 114, 115
Victoria regia (*V. amazonica*) 261
Vignola, Giacomo Barozzi da 241, 242
Vigour 78
Villa Aldobrandini *240*
Villa Borghese *240*
Villa d'Este 218, 241, *242*, 243
Villa Farnese 241, 242
Villa Lante 241–2, *241*
Villa Medici *240*
Villandry *243*, 245
Vilmorin, M. de 188
Viola 155
Violet 238
Viral diseases 42–3, *43*, 68
Virgil 240
Virginia cowslip 142
Virginia creeper 82, 134, 135, *135*

W

Waddesdon Manor *261*

Wakehurst Place *263*
Walled gardens *240*, *243*
Wallflower 151, 152, 155, *155*
Walls 21, 22, 23, 134, 135, 136, 211–12, *211*
Walnut 65
Walpole, Horace *258*, 259
Wand flower 224
Water, soil content 25, 28–31, 38, 54
Waterer's nursery 128, 129, 130
Water in garden design 217–22, 237, *237*, *240*, 242, *242*, 244, 247, *247*
Water gardens 171–3, 174–5
Water hawthorn 173
Water hyacinth 173
Watering 21, 30, *30*, 74, 75, 214
Water iris 172
Water lily 172–3, *250*, 261
Waterlogged soil 27, 29–30, *29*, 42
Water moss 173
Water soldier 173
Water starwort 173
Water-table 28, 29
Water violet 173
Wattle 75, 86
Wayfaring tree 106
Weedkiller 71
Weeds 31, 70–1, 171, 183
Weeping trees 99
Weeping willow 99, 249, *249*
Weigela 41, 113
Western Park 249
Westpark, Munich *140*, 141
Wheler, Sir George 80
White, monochrome designs using 229–30, *229*
White currant 196, *196*, 197
Whitefly 43
Wild flowers 182
Wild gardens 106
Williams, J.C. 109–10, 130
Willmott, Miss 159
Willow 46, *62*, 65, 95, 97, 98, 99, *100*, 108, 110, 167, 168, 249, *249*
Wilson, E.H. 'Chinese' 89, 130, *161*
Wilton House 256
Wind 21, *204*, 207, 212
Windbreaks 23, 96
Window boxes 152, *155*
Windsor Great Park, Valley Gardens *178*, 178
Winter 98, 100–2, 109–10, 178
Wintersweet 110
Wisley *149*
Wisteria 134, 135, *137*, 138, 189
Witch-hazel 109, 110
Wood anemone 142
Wooden board-walks 209
Wooden decking 265
Woodland gardens 106, 134, *207*, 236, *236*, *240*, 263, *263*
Wrought iron 214
Wu, Emperor 248

X

Xylem 55, 56

Y

Yarrow *147*
Yellow 229, *229*, 231
Yellow musk 171
Yew 99, 101, 104, 105, 106
Yucca 155, 224

Z

Zinc 33

ACKNOWLEDGEMENTS

The publishers would like to thank all the photographers, photographic agencies and organizations as listed below. We are particulary grateful to Eric Crichton, John Glover, S & O Mathews, Jerry Harpur Photographic Library, Andrew Lawson Photographic Library, Clive Nichols Photographic Library and the Harry Smith Collection for their hard work in contributing to this book.

AKG 82 bottom right

Ardea 32, 106, /Bob Gibbons 20 top, 58, /P Morris 16 bottom

Bridgeman Art Library /Atkinson Art Gallery, Southport, Lancs 81 top, /Bibliotheque Nationale, Paris 243 bottom, /British Museum 88 bottom, /British Library, London 255 top, /Christie's, London 240 top, /Christies, London 258 top, /Lincolnshire County Council, Usher Gallery, Lincoln 87 top, /Lindley Library, RHS, London 260 bottom, /National Museum of India, New Delhi 238, /Rafael Valls Gallery, London 247, /Royal Botanical Gardens, Kew 77, /The Wallace Collection 234, /Zhang Shui Cheng 248 top

Paul Brierley 60 right

Pat Brindley 176 bottom

Cephas Picture Library /Mick Rock 16 top

Bruce Coleman Ltd /Eric Crichton 179 bottom, /Dr Eckart Pott 42, /Hans Reinhard 74, /Kim Taylor 40

Eric Crichton 67 top, 69, 96, 103 bottom, 108 bottom, 111 bottom, 116 bottom, 119 bottom, 123 bottom, 139, 150 top, 153 bottom, 154, 159 bottom, 166 top, 167, 187, 198 top, 229 bottom, 254 bottom, 255 bottom, 256 top

Ecole Nationale Supérieure des Beaux-Arts 245 top

E.T. Archive /British Museum of Natural History 86 top right, /Linnean Society Library 84 bottom

Mary Evans Picture Library 80 bottom, 85 top right, 88 top, 243 top, 257 top

Valerie Finnis 46, 78, 79 top

Garden Picture Library /Erika Craddock 249, 250, /Marijke Heuff 57 bottom, /Michael Howes 28, /Howard Rice 108 top, /Jerry Pavia 203, 267 bottom, /John Bethell 240 bottom, 263 top, /John Neubauer 215 bottom, 266 bottom, /Lamontagne 23, /Mayer/Le Scanff 30, /Marianne Majerus 211, /Marijke Heuff 105, /Nigel Francis 261

John Glover 45, 72, 94, 113 bottom, 114 top, 115 bottom, 115 top, 122 bottom, 133 bottom, 134, 135 bottom, 142 top, 144, 148 top, 149 top, 151, 156 bottom, 156 top, 157 top, 164 bottom, 166 bottom, 168 bottom, 169 top, 169 bottom, 172 bottom, 174 top, 178, 180 top, 181, 185 bottom, 188, 193, 194, 195, 202, 206 top, 207 top, 216 bottom, 228, 266 top

Robert Harding Picture Library 52, 242, 251 bottom, /G. & P. Corrigan 248 bottom, /Adam Woolfitt 237

Jerry Harpur title, 12, 44, 75, 92, 95 bottom, 98, 99, 118 bottom, 118 top, 123 top, 124 bottom, 129, 137 bottom, 141, 145, 147 bottom, 149 bottom, 150 bottom, 153 top, 176 top, 183 bottom, 184, 185 top, 189, 199 bottom, 205, 206 bottom, 207 top, 208, 209 bottom, 209 top, 212 top, 212 bottom, 214 top, 220, 227, 229 top, 230, 251 bottom, 252 bottom, /Design: Beth Chatto 236, /Design: Julie Toll 192, /Design: Milton Grundy 254 top, /Design: Oehme & Van Sweden 264, /Design: Thomas Church 265 top

John Hedgecoe 14, 70, 71

Hulton Deutsch Collection 47, 80 top, 82 bottom left, 86 bottom

Hunt Institute for Botanical Documentation/Carnegie Mellon University, Pittsburgh, P.A., USA 82 top, 89 top right

Ikona /A. de Luca, Roma 241

Image Select /Ann Ronan Picture Library 67 bottom

Images /Landscape Only 25

Impact /Tadashi Kajiyama 235

Noel Kingsbury 140, 180 bottom, 267 top

Roy Lancaster 91 bottom, 91 top

Andrew Lawson half title, 50, 100, 107, 109 bottom, 110 top, 113 top, 117 top, 119 top, 122 top, 131 bottom, 138 top, 146, 148 top, 155 top, 159 top, 165 bottom, 177 bottom, 183 top, 191, 213 bottom, 215 top, 216 top, 218, 219, 223 bottom, 223 top, 262 top, 262 bottom, /Heligan Manor Gardens, Cornwall 175

Georges Lévêque 13, 152

Lindley Library, Royal Horticultural Society 130 top, /Chris Barker 259 top, /Chris Barker/Humphrey Repton's 'Fragments' 258 bottom, 259 bottom, /Chris Barker/Shirley Hibberd's 'Rustic Adornments', 1895 edition 260 top

MacQuitty International Collection 24, 120 top, 220 bottom

Magnum Photos /Rene Burri 239 top

Mansell Collection 34

S & O Mathews 21, 26, 93, 111 top, 121 top, 124 top, 125 top, 128 top, 128 bottom, 131 top, 133 top, 136 bottom, 136 top, 137 top, 142 bottom, 143, 155 bottom, 168 top, 177 top, 179 top, 182 top, 182 bottom, 190, 196

Mitchell Beazley /Chris Barker 81 bottom left, 81 bottom right, 83 left, 83 centre, 84 top right, 84 top left, 85 top left, 85 top centre, 85 bottom right, 86 top centre, 86 top left, 87 bottom left, 87 bottom right, 89 bottom left, 90 right, 90 centre, /Chris Barker 89 right, /John Garrett 35, 36, 37, /Roy Lancaster 76, /Lindley Library of the Royal Horticultural Society/Chris Barker 48

Tania Midgley 57 top

Paul Miles 101

The Natural History Museum, London 81 bottom centre, 83 right, 116 top

National Trust Photographic Library 256 bottom, /Jerry Harpur 53, /Jerry Harpur 257 bottom, /Neil Campbell-Sharp 197

Peter Newark's American Pictures 85 bottom left

N.H.P.A /John Shaw 17

Clive Nichols 95 top, 97, 109 top, 135 top, 163, 164 top, 171 top, 210, 214 bottom, 220 top, 231, 244 bottom

Oxford Scientific Films /Kathie Atkinson 27 top, /Sean Morris 54 centre, 54 left, 54 right, /Richard Packwood 62 top

Chris Parsons 15

Photos Horticultural 43

Photo Researchers, Inc /A de Menil 22

Reed International Books Ltd /Chris Barker 90 left

Réunion des Musées Nationaux, Paris 244 top

Vivian Russell 200, 201, 217, 246

Saling Hall Press biblio., 7, 11, 59, 102, 103 top, 104, 110 bottom, 117 bottom, 120 bottom, 146 bottom, 147 top, 170 bottom, 171 bottom, 172 top, 173 bottom, 174 bottom, 186, 199 top, 221, 224 top, 224 bottom, 225 bottom, 225 top, 232, 233 bottom, 233 top, 245 bottom, 252 top, 253 bottom, 253 top, 263 bottom, 265 bottom, /Oliver Matthews 213 top,

Scala 239 bottom

Science Photo Library 51, /Dr Jeremy Burgess 33, 56, 62 bottom, 66, /Claude Nuridsany & Marie Perennou 41, 61

Kenneth Scowen 8

Harry Smith Collection 27 bottom, 29, 39, 55, 67 bottom, 73, 79 bottom, 112, 114 bottom, 121 bottom, 125 bottom, 130 bottom, 138 bottom, 165 top, 170 top, 173 top, 198 bottom

Still Pictures /M & C Dents-Huot 18

ARTWORK CREDITS

Brian Delf 20; David Ashby 63; Harry Clow 64; Chris Forsey 65; Chris Forsey 73; Barbara Everard 126–7; Basil Smith 157; John Davis 160–2; Alan Suttie 225; Chris Forsey 226.